The New Politics
of the Old South
3rd edition

The New Politics of the Old South
3rd edition

An Introduction to Southern Politics

Edited by
Charles S. Bullock III
and
Mark J. Rozell

ROWMAN & LITTLEFIELD PUBLISHERS, INC.
Lanham • Boulder • New York • Toronto • Oxford

ROWMAN & LITTLEFIELD PUBLISHERS, INC.

Published in the United States of America
by Rowman & Littlefield Publishers, Inc.
A wholly owned subsidiary of The Rowman & Littlefield Publishing Group, Inc.
4501 Forbes Boulevard, Suite 200, Lanham, Maryland 20706
www.rowmanlittlefield.com

PO Box 317
Oxford
OX2 9RU, UK

British Library Cataloguing in Publication Information Available

Library of Congress Cataloging-in-Publication Data

The new politics of the old South: an introduction to Southern politics /
edited by Charles S. Bullock, III and Mark J. Rozell—3rd ed.
    p.   cm.
Includes bibliographical references and index.
ISBN-13: 978-0-7425-5343-9 (cloth : alk. paper)
ISBN-10: 0-7425-5343-4 (cloth : alk. paper)
ISBN-13: 978-0-7425-5344-6 (pbk. : alk. paper)
ISBN-10: 0-7425-5344-2 (pbk. : alk. paper)
1. Southern States—Politics and government—1951–   I. Bullock, Charles S.,
1942–

F216.2N49   2006
320.975—dc22   2005036626

Printed in the United States of America

∞ ™ The paper used in this publication meets the minimum requirements of
American National Standard for Information Sciences—Permanence of Paper for
Printed Library Materials, ANSI/NISO Z39.48-1992.

Contents

Introduction

Southern Politics in the Twenty-first Century

Charles S. Bullock III and Mark J. Rozell

When V. O. Key (1949) published *Southern Politics*, the region was solidly Democratic. No Republican had been elected U.S. senator or governor in decades, and a generation had passed since a Republican collected a single electoral college vote. For most of a century after Reconstruction, the South provided the foundation on which the national Democratic Party rested. When the party was in eclipse in the rest of the country, little more than the southern foundation could be seen. During periods of Democratic control of the presidency and Congress, as in the New Deal era, the South made a major contribution. After the 2004 election, the Democratic Party in the South had been reduced to its weakest position in more than 130 years. Today Republicans win the bulk of the white vote, dominate the South's presidential and congressional elections and control half the state legislative chambers.

Key's South had an electorate in which Republicans were rare and blacks even scarcer. While he observed that "in its grand outlines the politics of the South revolves around the position of the Negro" (1949, 5), it was not a commentary on black political influence, which was non-existent, but rather an acknowledgment that the region expended much political capital to keep African Americans away from the levers of power. Since implementation of the 1965 Voting Rights Act, black votes have become the mainstay of the Democratic Party—the vote without which few Democrats can win statewide. The votes cast by African Americans have helped elect a black governor (Virginia's Douglas Wilder), eighteen members of Congress and hundreds of legislators and local officials.

Partisan change and black mobilization have not been continuous but have come at different paces in various locales and for different offices. Nonetheless, the changes have been massive. In the chapters that follow, the nature of the changes will be delineated for each of a dozen southern states. This introductory chapter sketches broadly the patterns of the South's politics for which the state chapters will provide rich detail.

PRESIDENCY

For generations southern politicians had no chance to become president because they opposed equal opportunities for African Americans. This prohibition ended when Lyndon Johnson succeeded John Kennedy in 1963. Since the assassination in Dallas, southerners have usually occupied the White House. Ronald Reagan is the only president without southern ties since Jimmy Carter's 1976 victory. The successful Democratic ticket in 1992 marked the first time a major party had two southerners and the first election in which both parties' nominees had been southern office holders. George W. Bush became the fourth southern governor to advance to the presidency within the span of a quarter of a century. This is a reward for the South, which since 1990 has been the region with the most electoral votes.

Even before southerners could reasonably hope to become president, the region's partisan identity began changing. Presidential elections, the first office in which Republicans initially flexed electoral muscles, remain the ones in which southern whites have given the most enthusiastic support to Republicans.

As a bit of history, only twice from 1876 through 1948 did a Republican presidential nominee carry even one southern state. In 1920, Tennessee and Oklahoma responded to Warren Harding's call for a return to normalcy. Eight years later, Tennessee and Oklahoma along with Florida, North Carolina, Texas and Virginia rejected the Democratic nominee— New York, Catholic, anti-prohibition Al Smith. These exceptions from the 1920s had no lasting impact as the South stayed in the Democratic fold throughout the Roosevelt era, although 1944 marked the last hurrah for the Solid Democratic South. In 1948, Alabama, Louisiana, Mississippi and South Carolina broke with the Democratic Party over its anti-discrimination planks and supported the Dixiecrat candidacy of South Carolina governor Strom Thurmond.

In 1952, the Deep South united behind Adlai Stevenson even as all Rim South states except Arkansas rallied to Dwight Eisenhower.[1] Four years later, Louisiana became the first Deep South state to vote for a Republican, making Eisenhower the first GOP nominee to carry the bulk of the South's electoral votes since 1872. The Eisenhower years also saw the first Republicans elected to the U.S. House in decades from Florida, North Carolina, Texas and Virginia.

Partisan change began in the Deep South immediately after the 1964 Civil Rights Act extended federal protections to public accommodations, school desegregation and equal employment opportunities. Sen. Barry Goldwater (R-AZ), one of a few Republicans to break with his party's traditional support for civil rights, rejected the 1964 Act as an unconstitutional invasion of states' rights. His stand, coupled with President Lyndon Johnson's outspoken support for the bill, prompted all five Deep South states to vote Republican for the first time (Carmines and Stimson 1989). Goldwater's popularity also elected the first Deep South Republicans to the U.S. House from Alabama, Georgia and Mississippi.

Since 1972, the South has voted for Republican presidential candidates with the exception of 1976. In the initial post-Watergate election and the first with a Deep South candidate in more than a century, the South almost resurrected its solid Democratic voting pattern as all of the states of the Confederacy except for Virginia rallied behind Jimmy Carter. The reconciliation proved short-lived, and during the three elections of the 1980s, the only Democratic success came in 1980 when Georgia stood by its former governor.

While the South was the most Republican region in the 1990s, Democrats made a comeback when their ticket boasted not one but two southerners. In both presidential elections of the decade, the home states of the presidential and vice-presidential nominees (Arkansas and Tennessee, respectively) voted Democratic. Among Deep South states only Louisiana supported the Clinton-Gore ticket in both elections. Democrats narrowly carried Georgia in 1992, and in 1996, took Florida for only the second time in more than a quarter-century.

The new millennium saw a re-emergence of the solidly Republican South of the 1980s once the Florida recount stopped. Unlike in the Sunshine state where Bush's 2000 victory was measured in hundreds of votes, the GOP decisively carried the rest of the region. In a stinging rebuke,

Al Gore lost his home state of Tennessee 51 to 47 percent. Clinton's Arkansans went for the Republican by a similar margin while Louisiana gave Bush an eight-point advantage.

Despite having North Carolina Sen. John Edwards on the ticket, the 2004 Democratic effort got no traction in the South. Early in the fall some thought that the Kerry-Edwards ticket might be competitive in Arkansas, Louisiana, North Carolina, Tennessee and Virginia in addition to Florida that was universally seen as in play. But as election day drew nigh, Democrats pulled their troops out of all southern states but Florida. Even though midday exit poll results showed Kerry carrying Florida and winning the presidency, the final result held no suspense as Bush beat Kerry by 380,000 votes. Among southern states, only Florida (52.1 percent), Arkansas (54.4 percent) and Virginia (53.7 percent) did not give Bush a landslide victory (i.e., more than 55 percent). North Carolina abandoned its senator, giving him 43.6 percent, which matched Al Gore's 2000 performance.

Both of Bush's elections depended on the South, which provided the bulk of his Electoral College votes. Had he not swept the region in 2000, he would have completed his second term as Texas governor. In 2004, his 286 Electoral College vote total could have withstood the defection of any southern state except Florida or Texas, but various combinations of two defections would also have proven fatal. In terms of the popular vote, Bush carried the South by 5.5 million votes while losing the other thirty-eight states and the District of Columbia by 2.5 million votes. While today's South is not nearly as solidly Republican as Key's solid Democratic South, the region holds the key to success for the party of Lincoln. In good GOP years like the 1980s, the South votes with the rest of the nation; when the nation is less inclined toward the GOP, the South provides decisive support.

CONGRESS

GOP presidential success is now being paralleled in Congress although overcoming the Civil War–induced antipathy toward the GOP took longer in congressional than presidential elections and has been less sweeping. Since 1972, the South has been at least as Republican as the rest of the nation in presidential elections, with the sole exception of 1976 (Bullock 1988, 225). In Congress, however, southern Republicans lagged their northern cousins, due in part to the large numbers of Democratic incumbents (Black and Black 2002), who could often convince voters that they shared the region's ideology and were far more conservative than most northern Democrats (Lublin 2004).

As shown in figure I.1, not until 1993 did the GOP share of southern Senate seats (46 percent) outpace their proportion in the remainder of the nation (42 percent). In the next two elections, the southern advantage increased so that in 1997, Republicans had 71 percent of the seats from the twelve southern states compared with half the remaining seats. In 1998 and 2000, Democrats took back one seat in each election, but Republicans remained stronger in the South with more than 60 percent of the seats.

The 2002 elections did not change the partisan makeup of the South's Senate delegation. Tim Hutchinson, who ended Democratic dominance of Arkansas Senate seats in 1996, fell to Mark Pryor, the son of three-term Senator David Pryor. The handsome, young Pryor would have provided a serious challenge under the best of circumstances. But Hutchinson, a Baptist minister, alienated some of his Christian conservative base when he divorced his wife of twenty-nine years to marry a former staff member.

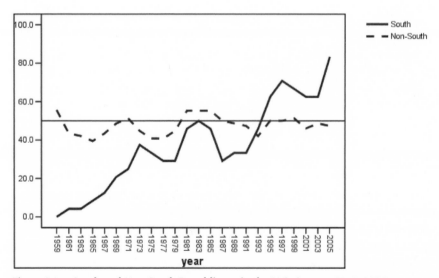

Figure I.1. South and Non-South Republicans in the U.S. Senate, 1958–2004

Republicans offset the Arkansas setback by taking away the Georgia seat of Vietnam War triple amputee Max Cleland. Saxby Chambliss ran a bruising campaign that attacked Cleland for standing with Senate Democrats who demanded unionization rights for workers of the new Department of Homeland Security as the price for approving the new agency. Chambliss characterized Cleland's stand as making national security subordinate to labor unions—not a popular position in a red state that favors right-to-work laws.

The 2004 Senate elections gave Republicans their biggest boost—a 21 percentage point gain that exceeded their 16 point gains in 1980 and 1994. Democrats had to defend open seats in Florida, Georgia, Louisiana, North Carolina and South Carolina. Oklahoma had the only seat in the region from which a Republican retired. All of the open seats proved competitive except for Georgia where Democrats failed to field a quality candidate. While none of the other five winners broke 54 percent, the thrust all went in the same direction as Republicans swept the region's open seats. David Vitter became the first popularly elected Republican ever sent to the Senate from Louisiana. The most competitive race played out in Florida where the presidential opponents spent millions of dollars and they and their surrogates campaigned extensively. Former Bush cabinet member Mel Martinez, who the White House encouraged to run, won a plurality victory with a one-percentage point margin over former university president Betty Castor. The only Democrat to win a Senate election in the South in 2004 was Arkansas incumbent Blanche Lincoln.

Gaining five seats gave Republicans a commanding 83 percent of the region's seats. Nine states had two Republican senators while only Arkansas retained two Democrats. With only four Democratic senators, the party that had dominated the South for generations had collapsed to the size that Republicans had struggled to attain in the late 1960s. Democrats' ranks may become still thinner when Bill Nelson (D-FL) faces reelection in 2006.

In 2005, the GOP majority in the Senate rested on the party's extraordinary success in the South. In the remainder of the nation, Democrats have a 40 to 35 edge, with Jim Jeffords (VT) a Democratically leaning Independent. Unlike in the South where Republicans won five open seats, in the rest of the nation, Democrats picked up seats in Colorado and Illinois while losing in South Dakota. As a consequence of the burgeoning GOP fortunes in the South, the Democratic contingent in the Senate is at its smallest since the 69th Congress, a time when the chamber had only ninety-six senators.

Had Democrats held on to their five open seats in the South, the 109th Senate, like in January 2001, would have had fifty Republicans and needed the vote of Vice President Dick Cheney to organize the chamber and control committee chairs. Had Democrats retained the five southern seats and had Tom Daschle (D) gotten 4,510 more votes in South Dakota, he would have regained the Majority Leader's post.

Broadening GOP House holdings in the South coincides with Republican breakthroughs in presidential voting. GOP House success came initially in urban areas like Charlotte, St. Petersburg, Tulsa and Dallas in the 1950s and 1960s. After 1964, as figure I.2 shows, the GOP share of southern House seats trended upward but with setbacks in the 1974, 1982 and 1986 mid-term elections when Republicans held the White House.

Even in taking control of the House, Newt Gingrich's fellow southerners trailed the northern wing of the GOP. Only after four disaffected Democrats followed Nathan Deal's (GA) lead and shifted partisan allegiance did Republicans have a slightly larger share of the southern House seats

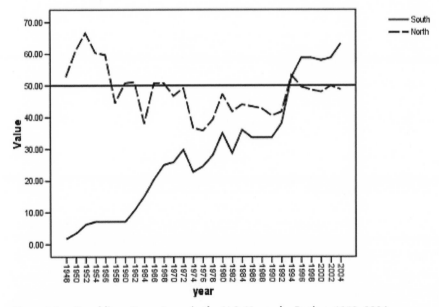

Figure I.2.   Republican Percentages in the U.S. House by Region, 1958–2004.

(56 percent) than the non-southern (53 percent). Since 1997, Republican House control has rested on the South where the GOP currently has 63 percent of the seats. In the remainder of the nation, Democrats have held a narrow majority leaving the 104th Congress as the only time in the last thirty years when Republicans have held most of the non-southern seats in the House.

In the twelve-state South, Republicans registered substantial gains in 1992 (nine seats), 1994 (nineteen seats) and 1996 (eight seats when mid-term partisan changes are included). In the next two elections, the parties held their own as Republicans, who had picked most of the low-hanging fruit, controlled 57 to 58 percent of the House seats.

The reapportioning of congressional seats after the 2000 census beefed up the South, already the nation's most populous region. Florida, Georgia and Texas each received two additional seats while North Carolina gained one seat. Since slow-growing Mississippi lost a seat, the region boasted 136 seats in the first decade of the new millennium.

Once seats had been reapportioned, a number of states resorted to extraordinary levels of gerrymandering. Georgia Democrats sought to wipe out most of the six-seat advantage that Republicans had in the U.S. House in 2001. Democrats prepared a map that national elections expert Stuart Rothenberg described as "an example of partisanship and common sense run amuck" (2005). They hoped to replace the state's 8 to 3 Republican delegation with one in which Democrats would hold a 7 to 6 advantage. In Florida, where Republicans controlled the redistricting process, they sought to enhance their party's influence by designing the two new seats to favor Republicans and endangering a Democratic incumbent. In Texas, partisan stakes were so high that no map got drawn since the Democrats who controlled the House could check the ambitions of Republicans who controlled the Senate and governorship. A federal court drew the Texas map and while the GOP got the two new seats, several sitting Democrats continued to benefit from the gerrymander designed by their party a decade earlier.

Democratic ambitions in Georgia were only partially realized as Republicans retained eight seats while Democrats picked up the two new seats allocated to the state. In Florida, Republicans gained three seats for an 18 to 7 advantage while Democrats lost one. Democrats won a 17 to 15 majority in the Texas delegation even though Republican candidates continued to poll a majority of the congressional votes cast in the state. Republicans came out ahead in Mississippi where the delegation shrank from five to four and a Republican incumbent beat a Democratic incumbent. Democrats won the new seat awarded North Carolina and took a seat away from Republicans in Oklahoma and Tennessee.

With most states using redistricting to eliminate partisan competition, only a handful of seats are marginal. In 2004 a disproportionate share of the fifteen seats that changed partisan hands occurred in the South. The disruptive influence came from Texas. House majority leader Tom DeLay wanted to increase his party's margin in the chamber. Moreover, Texas Republicans continued to chafe under the plan that their state's senior House member, Martin Frost (D), had designed in 1991. To address these concerns, Republicans, who after the 2002 elections controlled both chambers of the Texas legislature and the governorship, redrew the congressional districts in 2003. The GOP gerrymander targeted seven white Democrats. When the 109th Congress convened in 2005 Chet Edwards and Lloyd Doggett were the sole white Democratic survivors. One Democrat changed to the GOP, contributing to a net gain for the party of six seats. The gains in Texas coupled with the loss of a seat in Georgia increased the GOP share of southern seats from 58 to 63 percent. Only Arkansas (three Democrats—one Republican) and Tennessee (five Democrats—four Republicans) had more Democratic than Republican members while the parties evenly divided the four-person Mississippi delegation. Mississippi, Alabama, Louisiana, Oklahoma and South Carolina had two or fewer Democrats each.

GOVERNORSHIPS

As early as 1972, Republican's percentage of southern governorships approximated the share outside the region with about a third of all chief executives being Republicans. After the 1994 election, Republicans led six southern states. This number increased in 1995 when Mike Foster won the Louisiana governorship and grew again in 1996 when Jim Guy Tucker resigned as Arkansas' chief executive after being convicted of a Watergate-related felony and was succeeded by GOP lieutenant governor Mike Huckabee.

Democrats made a comeback in 1998 when their nominees used promises to earmark funds from a Georgia-style lottery for college scholarships to defeat incumbents in Alabama and South Carolina. The GOP effort to win an open governorship failed in Georgia, but in Florida, Jeb Bush, who had lost to the incumbent in 1994, won the open seat. Ronnie Musgrove reclaimed the Mississippi governorship for Democrats in 1999 when that seat came open, and the next year Mike Easley retained North Carolina's governorship for Democrats so that by 2001, the South had five Democratic chief executives—all the Deep South states except Louisiana plus North Carolina.

Republicans enjoyed an extraordinary year in the 2002 gubernatorial elections, which, in retrospect, were a prelude for their Senate successes two years later. The GOP reclaimed the Alabama and South Carolina governorships, but their most unexpected success came in Georgia where Sonny Perdue astonished everyone—including himself and Democratic incumbent Roy Barnes—to become the state's first GOP chief executive since 1872. After former Republican National Committee chief Haley Barbour made Ronnie Musgrove a one-termer in Mississippi, the GOP led seven states that included all Deep South states except Louisiana.

As recently illustrated by Mississippi, Oklahoma, Tennessee and Virginia, Republicans continue to struggle with a problem that has plagued them since their first gubernatorial victories in 1966 (Arkansas and Florida). They have had difficulty retaining the governorship following the retirement of a member of their party. The most extended series of governing came in Virginia where three Republicans held the state's top spot from 1969 to 1981; in South Carolina, which Republicans governed from 1987 to 1999; and Texas, which elected George Bush in 1994 and 1998, and his successor Rick Perry in 2002.[2]

Term-limiting governors—a factor except in Texas—makes it easier for the out party to regain that office than a seat in Congress. Democratic gubernatorial candidates who have had careers in state politics can avoid embracing policies endorsed by their party at the national level that are out of step with southern preferences. By avoiding the national forces that push southern Democrats in Congress to the left, gubernatorial candidates can maintain centrist positions that appeal to many southern voters (Black and Black 2002).

As the GOP matures, it may become more successful at retaining high-profile offices. Although its success has often seemed to percolate downward with the party's initial successes coming in presidential elections and the share of GOP congressional seats exceeding the share of state legislative seats, the idea that a strong party requires grassroots nourishment has merit (Lublin 2004). The growing ranks of Republican legislators and local officials mean both that the GOP will have larger numbers of experienced candidates who may compete for higher offices but also that the ranks of possible Democratic get reduced.

STATE LEGISLATURES

In keeping with the trickle-down theory of partisan realignment, success in state legislatures has proven more elusive to the GOP than have higher offices (Bullock 1988, 235; Bullock et al. 2000). Not until 1984 did Republicans fill more than 20 percent of the seats in lower chambers of the South, a figure only about half as large as their share of U.S. Senate seats at that time. Growth in state senates has come even more slowly than in state lower chambers.

The 1994 elections marked a breakthrough as Republicans gained majorities in several southern legislatures by winning control of the Florida and Tennessee senates and the lower chambers of North and South Carolina. The next year, the two parties split the forty-member Virginia Senate. In 1996 Republicans claimed majorities in the Florida House and Texas Senate, but Democrats retook the Tennessee Senate. The success in Florida marked the first time since Reconstruction that Republicans controlled both chambers of a southern legislature. The 1999 election saw Virginia join Florida with both chambers having Republican majorities, and in 2000, Republicans edged up to half the seats in the South Carolina Senate before party switchers produced a majority. Redistricting that cleared away the gerrymander barricades that Democrats had used to protect their majorities resulted in Republicans consolidating control of the Texas legislature in 2002 and in Georgia in 2004. In 2005, Republicans controlled half the region's legislative chambers with complete control of five states while Democrats also dominated five states. In Oklahoma and Tennessee, each party claimed one house. Republicans have eight of fourteen Rim South chambers while Democrats organized six of ten Deep South states' chambers.

Except for the 1974 Watergate backlash, the regional pattern has been for Republican strength in state legislatures to grow (Bullock et al. 2000). The rate of growth has varied but the arrow has been almost relentlessly upward. In keeping with this pattern, Democrats have infrequently regained majorities in chambers once Republicans win control. Only in the North Carolina House and the Tennessee Senate have Democrats reasserted control. In 2005, Republicans had a one-vote margin in the Tennessee Senate, matching their high water mark achieved briefly in the mid-1990s. In North Carolina, Republicans won narrow majorities in the House in 1994, 1996 and 2002, although a defection resulted in an evenly divided House in 2003–2004. Swings in party fortunes in North Carolina are heightened by the use of multi-member districts that magnify the impact of small shifts in party preferences in a few marginal districts.

Except for the two chambers that slipped out of Republican control, once the GOP has taken over a chamber, the tendency has been for it to increase its seat share up to around 60 percent. In 2005 that figure approximated the GOP percentage in both chambers of Florida, South Carolina, Texas and Virginia and the Georgia Senate. Republicans first took control of the Georgia House in 2004, but if several of the Democratic incumbents who held on that year grow restless as members of the minority and retire, Republicans might well come to hold 60 percent of the seats in that chamber.

PARTISANSHIP IN THE ELECTORATE

Partisan shifts in the ranks of southern officeholders have outpaced changes in reported voter partisanship. As a carryover from the era of one-party politics, most states in the region do not require voters to pledge loyalty to a party when registering to vote. States without party registration allow voters to choose either party's ballot in each primary. In states with partisan registration, like Florida, the GOP has gone far toward eliminating the Democratic advantage, but even that does not capture the Republican gains in congressional and state legislative election.

Where party registration figures are unavailable, surveys help fill the gap. Table I.1 presents exit poll results from the 2000 and 2004 general elections. These figures show that southwide, 43 percent identify with the GOP. Over the four years, the GOP became slightly stronger while Democrats lost support so that the Republican advantage grew to 7 percentage points. Although the size of the shift since 2000 toward the GOP in individual states, like the regional figures, is often modest, Republicans made headway in every state except Oklahoma while the best Democrats could do was to maintain their 2000 percentage in South Carolina and Virginia. In 1996, Democrats still had pluralities in eight states (Bullock and Rozell 1998); in 2004, only Arkansas and Louisiana had more Democrats than

**Table I.1.   Party Identification at the Time of the 2000 and 2004 General Election
(All figures are percentages)**

| | 2000 | | | 2004 | | |
State	Democrat	Republican	Independent	Democrat	Republican	Independent
South	38	41	21	36	43	21
Alabama	41	37	23	32	50	18
Arkansas	42	25	33	41	31	28
Florida	40	38	22	37	41	23
Georgia	41	37	22	34	42	22
Louisiana	48	34	18	42	41	18
Mississippi	40	42	18	38	47	15
North Carolina	41	38	21	39	40	16
Oklahoma	42	44	14	40	43	16
South Carolina	33	39	28	33	44	23
Tennessee	39	37	24	32	40	28
Texas	35	42	23	32	43	24
Virginia	35	37	28	35	39	26

Source: Compiled from exit polls.

Republicans. Republicans have their greatest advantages in Alabama (18 points), Texas (11 points) and South Carolina (11 points).

The most dramatic shifts from 1996 to 2004 came in Alabama where the GOP doubled its support to now boast the largest percentage of Republicans in the South at 50 percent. Over the eight years GOP ranks increased by ten percentage points or more in Louisiana and Mississippi (Bullock and Rozell 1998). In half the states the GOP advantage now exceeds five percentage points.

In 1996, the mean percentage of Republican identifiers in the Deep South states (AL, GA, LA, MS and SC) was 35 while in the Rim South it was 37.9. Eight years later, the average for the Rim South had bumped up to 39.6 percent while in the Deep South it had shot to 44.8 percent. Thus the Deep South, which began the shift toward the GOP roughly a decade later than the Rim South, has become the more Republican subregion. Despite continuing growth of the GOP, in no state does either party command the loyalty of most voters who turned out to choose between Bush and Kerry, although Alabama is 50 percent Republican. To win elections, each party must mobilize its adherents but also attract a share of Independents or voters who weakly identify with the opposition party.

Party loyalties have weakened substantially in the last forty years and the numbers of Independents has grown, although table I.1 shows no increase in Independents early in the twenty-first century. Even many southerners who acknowledge a partisanship leaning nonetheless split their tickets. Changes in voting behavior have come quicker than changes in professed party loyalty so Republican nominees for major offices such as president, governor and senator usually secure larger shares of the vote than would be expected based on party identification data. These gaps have been greatest and were first observed in presidential elections. When Richard Nixon swept the South in 1972, fewer than one southerner in five identified with the GOP (Stanley and Castle 1988, 239). In 1984 when Ronald Reagan repeated the feat, Republican party identifiers stayed well below 25 percent. In 2004, Bush got about 58 percent of the vote in the South, well above the 43 percent of the exit poll voters who identify with the GOP.[3] A disparity, although less dramatic, also exists on the Democratic side where Kerry got 42 percent of the southern vote compared with 36 percent of the electorate that identified as Democrats.

Focusing on the party identification or voting preferences of the southern electorate obscures a growing chasm running along the racial fault line. African Americans support Democratic nominees up and down the ticket at rates of 80 percent and higher. White support for Republicans, while not nearly as uniform as black voting for Democrats, has increased. Figure I.3 shows that across the six most recent presidential elections, Democrats have polled about a third of the white vote in the South. John Kerry slumped to only 29 percent of the white vote. The varied appeal of Democratic nominees in the rest of the nation is not reflected among southern whites who found Bill Clinton no more attractive than Jimmy Carter in 1980 or even Michael Dukakis. Al Gore, who ran as an old-style Democrat proposing numerous new programs that would have expanded the role of the federal government, fared slightly worse among whites than his boss which, along with the absence of Ross Perot who had taken votes from the GOP, explains why the Tennessean lost the entire region.

Until the mid-1990s, Southern Democratic candidates for Congress did relatively well among whites even as their party's presidential nominees struggled. Recently, however, the appeal of southern congressional Democrats has sagged to the level of their party's presidential candidates. Figure 1.3 shows that Democratic House nominees now perform only marginally better among white voters in the region than the party's presidential candidates. The up-and-down off-year-to-presidential-year oscillation that had marked white congressional voting since 1980

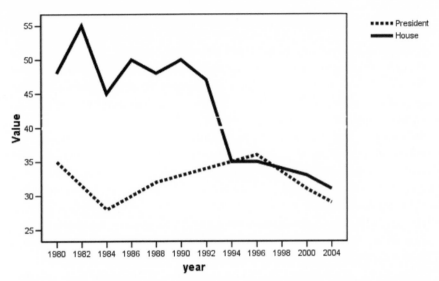

Figure I.3.   Percent White Democratic Votes for President and U.S. House, 1980–2004

ceased in 1994. After seven elections in which between 45 and 55 percent of the whites voted Democratic, support fell to barely a third and has yet to rise (also see Bullock et al. 2005). In 2004, Democratic congressional candidates in the South stumbled along with the support of 31 percent of the white voters but boasted 90 percent support among African Americans.

Republican senatorial candidates have also found success among white voters. Of twenty-five U.S. Senate elections held in the South from 1996 to 2004, only in three did the Democratic nominee poll a majority of the white vote and two of these were incumbents Bob Graham (FL) and John Breaux (LA) who have since left Congress.[4] In less than a third of the contests did the Democrat exceed 40 percent of the white poll, according to exit polls. Exit polls show none of the Democratic nominees in the eight southern states electing senators in 2004 getting a majority of the white vote. Only the one Democrat reelected, Arkansas's Blanche Lincoln, and Betty Castor in Florida managed even 40 percent of the white vote. Four Democrats got 30 percent or less of the white vote with the Democratic nominee in Alabama, attracting only one in seven white voters.

BLACK MOBILIZATION

At about the same time that Republicans began to score their first successes in the region, the Civil Rights Movement began striking off the
shackles of racism. Martin Luther King Jr. and the Montgomery bus boycott, court orders invalidating racially segregated facilities justified in
terms of separate but equal, and innumerable marches and protests
demanding equal access to voting booths, quality education and good-
paying jobs pricked the conscience of the nation and ultimately per-
suaded Congress to change the laws.

The 1965 Voting Rights Act banned the use of literacy tests and good
character tests and provided alternative methods to get registered when
local election officials discriminated against prospective voters because of
their race. Shortly after implementation of the 1965 Voting Rights Act,
black registration jumped. Only 29 percent of the region's voting-age
blacks were registered in 1962; six years later the figure exceeded 60 percent (Rodgers and Bullock 1972, 25). The most pronounced changes came
in states that had been most repressive with the share of age-eligible
blacks registered rising from 19 to 52 percent in Alabama and from 7 to
60 percent in Mississippi. In recent years registration and turnout rates
among blacks have almost equaled those of whites.

In addition to helping elect white Democrats, the black electorate
has also contributed to a growing number of African-American officeholders. Figure 1.4 shows the increase in the number of black legislators
in the South from a scant thirty-five in 1969, of whom fourteen served in
Georgia. In 2001, the most recent enumeration, more than 300 African
Americans sat in southern legislatures. Most of the increase followed a
redistricting that created additional heavily black districts (Handley and
Grofman 1994). Two-thirds of the growth in black representation occurred
within two elections of the 1970, 1980 and 1990 elections.

Creating districts with black concentrations also opened the way for the
first black Democrats in Congress from the South. In 1972, Atlanta and
Houston districts redrawn to be over 40 percent black elected Andy Young
and Barbara Jordan. Two years later Harold Ford won a 47 percent black
Memphis district. The 1980s saw the election of Mike Espy from the Mississippi Delta, and when Lindy Boggs retired, William Jefferson succeeded
to her New Orleans district. The 1992 redistricting sent a dozen new black
members to join the five African Americans representing the South. The
quantum leap in 1992 resulted from demands by the U.S. Department of

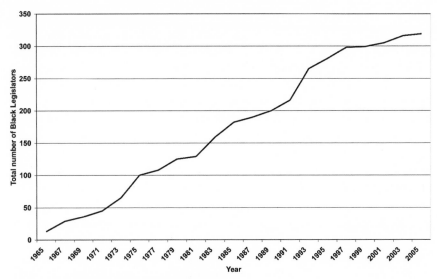

Figure I.4. Numbers of Black State Legislators

Justice that states maximize their numbers of majority-black districts. And while the Supreme Court found many of these districts to be unconstitutional and their black percentages were reduced, all continue to elect African Americans except in Louisiana where Cleo Fields opted to seek the governorship rather than another term in the House.

The post-2000 redistricting had less impact than the previous decades, but it did result in additions to the Congressional Black Caucus. Georgia became the first southern state to be represented by four African Americans when David Scott won a metro Atlanta district barely 40 percent black. After Texas Republicans implemented a mid-decade redistricting in 2003, Al Green defeated the incumbent in the Democratic primary in a 38 percent black district to become the third African American in that state's delegation.

RACE, PARTY, AND POLITICAL CONSEQUENCES

Blacks have succeeded in winning congressional districts that are only about 40 percent black in population because of the cohesiveness of the

African-American vote. Today's South in which nine in ten blacks often vote Democratic and most whites back Republicans gives each party advantages in distinctive types of constituencies. As reported in table I.2, Republicans hold three-fourths of the congressional seats in districts less than 10 percent black and more than 80 percent of the seats in districts 10 to 19.9 percent black. If we exclude the seven heavily Hispanic Texas districts represented by Democrats, then Republicans have 87 percent of the seats less than 10 percent black and 84 percent of the seats having populations 10 to 19.9 percent black. At the other end of the scale, Democrats represent all districts at least 40 percent black and all but one of these legislators is an African American. No Republican represented a district that had a 2001 population more than 34 percent black. The rapidity with which Republicans have come to dominate heavily white districts is apparent since as recently as 1991, Democrats still had most of the seats even in the districts that were less than ten percent black. The kind of districts in which white Democrats most often win—that is, ones with black populations between 20 and 39.9 percent—shrank from 50 in 1991 to 30 in 2005, which helps explain the drop in Southern Democratic members of Congress.

White voters are forsaking the Democratic Party in congressional elections as reported in figure I.3, and the Democrats who remain in heavily minority districts may prefer a candidate of their race. The Congress elected in 2004 reflected that pattern. Of the fifty Southern Democrats in the House almost half are minorities. Eighteen are African American with at least one from each state except Arkansas and Oklahoma, while five Latinos represent districts in Texas's Rio Grande Valley.[5] Georgia and

Table I.2.   District Racial Composition and Percent GOP House Seats, Controlling for Racial Composition of the District, 1991, 2001 and 2005

Percent Black	2005	N	2001	N	1991	N
0–9.9	77.4 percent	51	75.0 percent	52	44.4 percent	36
10–19.9	81.8	33	64.2	28	36.7	30
20–29.9	55.0	20	48.0	25*	21.4	28
30–39.9	60.0	10	63.6	11	36.4	22
40–49.9	0	7	0	5	0	2
More than 50	0	11	0	11	0	4

* Democrats also held 48 percent of the seats in this category in 2001 with the remaining legislator being Virgil Goode (D) who resigned from the Democratic party in 2000 and won reelection as an Independent.

Compiled by author

Texas have more minority- than Anglo-Democrats while four other states have one black and one white Democrat. The five Deep South states sent eight African American and six white Democrats to Congress.

Table I.2 shows that overwhelming shares of the congressional districts at either end of the spectrum are won by a single party. A review of election returns for individual districts reveals that in the South, like the rest of the nation, hotly contested races are rare. In 2004, only five Republicans got between 45 and 55 percent of the vote and one of these faced an incumbent Democrat after redistricting paired two Texas incumbents.

While districting plans that carefully separate Democrats and Republicans have largely eliminated serious contests for the U.S. House, Democrats can still often make U.S. Senate and gubernatorial elections close. Of eleven senators elected in 1996, in only Mississippi, Oklahoma and Tennessee did the winner break 55 percent. In 2002, seven of nine southern senators who faced opposition won less than 55 percent of the vote.[6]

Open seats can be especially competitive; the 1996 Louisiana contest ended in almost a dead heat, and Max Cleland (D) won with a plurality that year. Blanche Lincoln won an Arkansas open seat in 1998 with 55 percent of the vote while Bill Nelson (D) scraped by to win Florida's open seat with 51 percent in 2000. The 2002 election had three open seats in the South while in 2004 there were six; only one winner got more than 55 percent of the vote. While incumbents usually fare better, from 1998 to 2004, Chuck Robb (D-VA), Max Cleland (D-VA) and Tim Hutchinson (R-VA) lost close reelection bids. During this period, Paul Coverdell (R-GA) and Fritz Hollings (D-SC) had close calls but did win new terms.

With the bulk of the white vote going to Republicans, successful Democrats depend on strong showings among minority voters. The bulk of Bill Clinton's 1996 votes in Georgia, Louisiana, Mississippi and South Carolina came from blacks. In 2000, exit polls indicate that blacks provided most of the votes for Al Gore in each Deep South state and, southwide, about 40 percent of Gore's votes came from African Americans. Blacks also accounted for about three of every eight votes won by a Democratic congressional candidate in the region.

Even when black votes are insufficient to elect an African American, successful white Democrats depend heavily on this component of their electorates. This reliance makes Democratic legislators more responsive to black policy concerns and has largely eliminated the traditional southern conservative Democrat from Congress. Both push and pull have been involved in this change. As conservative voters have begun participating in GOP primaries, the Democratic voters have rejected conservative candidates. At the same time, now that the GOP has become competitive, it is a more attractive environment in which a conservative candidate can pursue a political career.

One manifestation of the change has been the demise of the Conservative Coalition on congressional roll calls. Beginning in the late 1930s, the Conservative Coalition of Southern Democrats and Republicans presented the greatest threat to the policy initiatives advanced by liberal Northern Democrats. For years, 20 to 25 percent of all congressional roll calls saw the Conservative Coalition arrayed against most Northern Democrats (Brady and Bullock 1980). By the 1990s the Coalition's activity level had slumped to only one roll call in ten. With the onset of the new century, *Congressional Quarterly*, which had calculated the frequency with which legislators voted for or against the Coalition, ceased to report on this voting pattern because it rarely mobilized since Southern Democrats had become ideologically more like their northern cousins and unlikely to consider Republicans to be ideological soul mates.

The transformation in Congress has been accompanied by a similar change in Democratic primaries. With large numbers of whites participating in GOP primaries, the Democratic primary electorate now has a higher black percentage than the general election turnout. One consequence is the nomination of more African Americans. For example, in 1988 Jesse Jackson led the presidential primaries in the Deep South by capturing almost all of the black votes while many conservative whites voted in the GOP primary (Bullock 1991). Even if a black candidate is not nominated, the likelihood increases of nominating more liberal candidates or of pulling candidates to the left in search of votes. The risk for Democrats is that if their nominees stake out positions further to the left in order to secure support from blacks—the most reliable component of the Democratic party—these stands can drive additional whites to the GOP, rendering the Democratic primary electorate even more liberal.

The importance of Democrats establishing moderate credentials is underscored in the 2004 exit polls showing that only 17 percent of the southern electorate is liberal while the remainder is almost evenly divided between conservatives and moderates. The 2004 exit poll figures indicate an increase in conservatives, up to 43 percent from one-third, while moderates declined from almost 50 percent of the 2000 exit poll participants. The small share of the southern electorate that considers itself to be liberal explains why Republicans so frequently criticize their

Democratic opponents for being too liberal. In statewide southern contests, if the Republican succeeds in attaching the liberal label to the Democratic candidate, that will determine the outcome.

Earl and Merle Black, the leading students of southern politics, observed a few years back that when Democrats offered candidates who were moderate conservatives or conservative moderates, these candidates usually won (1987). In their more recent research, they report that conservatives have forsaken the Democratic Party, and with their exodus near complete, moderates have joined in the move to the GOP (2002). The massive departures from the Democratic Party make it increasingly difficult for Democrats to win—as already documented in this chapter. Inept GOP politicians, some of whom took positions too far to the right, account for recent but short-lived Democratic successes in the late 1990s when they won governorships in Alabama, Georgia, Mississippi and South Carolina. Even more vulnerable than state officials are Democrats originally perceived as moderates who go to Congress and vote too often with the Democratic Party which is dominated by non-southerners. Saxby Chambliss succeeded in convincing Georgians that Sen. Max Cleland (D), a Vietnam triple amputee, had forgotten Georgia values and became too willing to support the initiatives of the national Democratic Party and therefore should be denied a second term.

Republicans run a similar risk in appealing to their core constituency. Their most loyal supporters, both in primaries and general elections, come from the right end of the political spectrum. In general elections, Republicans often win three-fourths of the ballots cast by voters who identify themselves as Christian conservatives while losing the remainder of the vote. To the extent that religious conservatives determine the identity of GOP nominees, they may select candidates too conservative for the bulk of the electorate.

Republicans who are seen as out of the mainstream because they are too conservative struggle to win statewide. Those who would allow abortions *only* to save the life of the mother rarely win statewide offices while those who take less restrictive stands, even though they are to the right of most Democratic candidates, are more successful. And it is not just in the context of abortion that moderation pays a dividend. Republican moderates like Sen. George Allen (VA) have won while hardliner Oliver North, who challenged Chuck Robb six years earlier, was pointed to by some as the one Republican politician who Robb could defeat.

With the demise of southern, conservative Democrats, Congress lost an important counterweight. Democratic Party success in Congress stemmed, in no small part, from its ability to appear liberal in the North but moderate to conservative in the South. Maintaining this Janus-like image required that northerners allow southerners to march to the beat of a different drum and vice versa. In the words of Speaker Sam Rayburn, "You have to go along to get along." This orientation often produced moderately progressive legislation that both northern liberals and southern conservatives could tolerate although neither group saw it as ideal. The Democratic downfall of the mid-1990s results at least in part from the demands that southerners be "good Democrats" (i.e., liberal) if they hoped to achieve influence and status within the party. To secure promotion to exclusive committees like Appropriations or Ways and Means, House Democrats had to support national party goals. Southerners who placed responsiveness to their conservative constituents above adherence to the party line foreclosed the prospects of achieving a seat on a power committee and risked eligibility to lead even subcommittees of lesser committees. In this hostile climate, conservative Democrats Sen. Richard Shelby (AL), Rep. Billy Tauzin (LA) and Rep. Nathan Deal (GA) changed parties, others retired and those who constituents saw as too supportive of Clinton policies lost in 1994 (Black and Black 2002).

The weakness of the South among congressional Democrats is further shown by the inability of a southerner—even a liberal one—to attain a leadership position since Speaker Jim Wright (TX) resigned in 1989. Southerners always had at least one of the top three positions among House Democrats as long as the whip was appointed by the party leader. Beginning in the mid-1980s, the Democratic whip responsible for lining up members of the party behind the party's policy positions has been chosen by the Democratic Caucus. Since the whip has been the stepping-stone for the higher party positions of party leader and, when Democrats are in the majority, the speakership, the inability of southerners to have one of their own as whip has foreclosed party leadership offices to the region. The absence of southerners has meant that no one sat in the senior councils to advocate a more moderate course.

In contrast, southerners have dominated GOP leadership since the 1994 takeover of Congress. Speaker Newt Gingrich, who led the charge that gave Republicans their first House majority since 1954, came from Georgia and Majority Leader Dick Armey (1995–2003) and Majority Whip Tom DeLay (1995–2003) came from Texas. While Midwesterner Dennis Hastert succeeded Gingrich as Speaker in 1999, DeLay moved up to Majority

Leader upon Armey's retirement. In the Senate, Mississippi's Trent Lott served as Majority Leader from 1996–2002, when Bill Frist from Tennessee succeeded him.

While there are southern urban districts, often represented by blacks or Latinos, in which the representative can take stands in line with the policy preferences of the national Democratic Party, it would be suicidal for a Democrat to seek statewide office in the South by embracing the policies articulated by Democratic leaders in Congress. Georgia's former Democratic Senator Zell Miller (2000–2005), who worked for the reelection of President Bush in 2004, castigated his party for taking stands so alien to his fellow partisans in the South that party leaders like Hillary Clinton, Ted Kennedy or Nancy Pelosi would be unwelcome interlopers for most Southern Democratic candidates. Franklin Roosevelt in a Depression era referred to the South observing that "I see one-third of a nation ill-housed, ill-clad, ill nourished." Miller recast this statement charging that today the Democratic Party's attitude toward the South is, "I see one-third of a nation and it can go to hell" (Miller 2003, 9).

If congressional Democrats continue to be well to the left of the GOP, Republican efforts to recruit good candidates and win more offices in the South will be helped since many white southerners equate the Democratic Party with failed liberal reforms as evidenced by their rejection of Al Gore and John Kerry. The last thing that Democrats in the South need is actions and pronouncements from the congressional wing of the party that underscore such perceptions.

The chapters dealing with individual states will more fully explore the themes set out in this chapter. Each state, of course, has it own unique features so that no two have taken the same paths toward greater participation of minority groups and the emergence of two-party competition.

REFERENCES

Black, Earl, and Merle Black. 1987. *Politics and Society in the South*. Cambridge, MA: Harvard University Press.

Black, Earl, and Merle Black. 1992. *The Vital South: How Presidents Are Elected*. Cambridge, MA: Harvard University Press.

Black, Earl, and Merle Black. 2002. *The Rise of Southern Republicans*. Cambridge, MA: Harvard University Press.

Brady, David W., and Charles S. Bullock III. 1980. "Is There a Conservative Coalition in the House?" *Journal of Politics* 42: 549–59.

Bullock, Charles S., III. 1983. "The Effects of Redistricting on Black Representation in Southern State Legislatures." Presented at the annual meeting of the American Political Science Association.

Bullock, Charles S., III. 1984. "Racial Crossover Voting and the Election of Black Officials." *Journal of Politics* 46 (February): 238–51.

Bullock, Charles S., III. 1988. "Creeping Realignment in the South," in Robert H. Swansbrough and David M. Brodsky, eds., *The South's New Politics: Realignment and Dealignment*. Columbia, SC: University of South Carolina Press, 220–37.

Bullock, Charles S., III. 1991. "The Nomination Process and Super Tuesday," in Laurence W. Moreland, Robert P. Steed and Tod A. Baker, eds., *The 1988 Presidential Election in the South*. New York: Praeger, 3–19.

Bullock, Charles S., III. 1995. "The Evolution of Redistricting Plans in Georgia in the 1990s." Presented at the annual meeting of the Association of American Geographers.

Bullock, Charles S., III, and Mark J. Rozell. 1998. "Southern Politics at Century's End," in Charles S. Bullock III, and Mark J. Rozell, eds., *The New Politics of the Old South*. Lanham, MD: Rowman and Littlefield, 3–21.

Bullock, Charles S., III, Ronald Keith Gaddie and Donna R. Hoffman. 2000. "Regional Realignment Revisited." Presented at the annual meeting of the American Political Science Association.

Bullock, Charles S., III, Ronald Keith Gaddie and Donna Hoffman. 2005. "Consolidation of the White Southern Congressional Vote," *Political Research Quarterly* (June).

Carmines, Edward G., and James A. Stimson. 1989. *Issue Evolution: Race and the Transformation of American Politics*. Princeton, NJ: Princeton University.

Handley, Lisa, and Bernard Grofman. 1994. "The Impact of the Voting Rights Act on Minority Representation: Black Officeholding in Southern State Legislatures and Congressional Delegations," in Chandler Davidson and Bernard Grofman, eds., *Quiet Revolution in the South*. Princeton, NJ: Princeton University Press.

Lublin, David. 2004. *The Republican South*. Princeton, NJ: Princeton University Press.

Miller, Zell. 2003. *A National Party No More*. Atlanta: Stroud and Hall.

Rodgers, Harrell R., Jr., and Charles S. Bullock III. 1972. *Law and Social Change*. New York: McGraw-Hill.

Rothenberg, Stuart. 2005. "Mid-Decade Redistricting: What's Appropriate?" *Roll Call* (January 24).

Stanley, Harold W., and David S. Castle. 1988. "Partisan Changes in the South: Making Sense of Scholarly Dissonance," in Robert H. Swansbrough and David M. Brodsky, eds., *The South's New Politics: Realignment and Dealignment*. Columbia, SC: University of South Carolina Press, 238–52.

NOTES

1. The South is often divided into five Deep South states (Alabama, Georgia, Louisiana, Mississippi and South Carolina). The remainder of the region is

referred to as the Rim South or Peripheral South—the term preferred by blacks (1992).

2. Republicans won three consecutive Alabama gubernatorial elections (1986-1994) but did not govern throughout that period since Lieutenant Governor Jim Allen, a Democrat, succeeded Guy Hunt upon the latter's removal and imprisonment.

3. Exit polls underestimate Republicans in the electorate to the extent that Republicans may be more likely than Democrats to cast early or absentee ballots.

4. The sponsors of the surveys did not consider exit data for 2002 to be reliable and those elections are excluded from our analyses.

5. In 2004, two other heavily Latino Texas districts elected Anglo Democrats while the 23rd district, where Latino's constitute a bare majority of the voting age population, elected an Hispanic Republican.

6. No Democrat challenged Trent Lott (R-MS) or John Warner (R-VA).

PART I

THE DEEP
SOUTH STATES

1

South Carolina: Change and Continuity in the Palmetto State

Robert P. Steed and Laurence W. Moreland

In *Politics and Society in the South,* Earl and Merle Black argued that Daniel Elazar's concept of traditionalistic political culture provides a useful context for understanding much of the South's political history (Black and Black 1987, esp. chapter 2). Although variants of individualistic political culture occasionally manifested themselves in populism and entrepreneurial individualism, traditionalism most fully captured the essence of the southern political past.

The Blacks' assessment is certainly consistent with V. O. Key's analysis of South Carolina politics at the middle of the twentieth century (Key 1949, chapter 7). The overriding concern with race and the maintenance of white supremacy in the state suppressed competing tendencies toward a class-based populistic politics and shaped South Carolina politics into patterns congruent with Elazar's traditionalistic political culture with its emphasis on paternalism, elitism, social hierarchy, a limited role for government and conservatism characterized by strong defense of the status quo (Elazar 1972, 99–102). During the first half of the twentieth century and into the post–World War II period, South Carolina's political system was marked by one-party politics, low voter turnout, a large percentage of disenfranchised African Americans in the population, white political leaders willing to use the race issue for their benefit and malapportioned state legislatures (Key 1949, chapter 7; Bass and DeVries 1976, chapter 11).

By the end of the 1950s and into the 1960s, however, changes were underway which would dramatically alter South Carolina politics over the next decades. Increased urbanization (and industrialization), economic development and diversification, the pressures of the civil rights movement and a more heterogeneous population were accompanied by a decline in racist rhetoric on the part of candidates and public officials, an enlarged (and eventually integrated) electorate and a reduction in the political influence of rural areas (Bass and DeVries 1976; Barone and Ujifusa 1995; Kuzenski 2003). In this altered environment, the South Carolina party system began a marked transformation as well.

In this partisan transformation, South Carolina paralleled the larger South. A solidly one-party Democratic state prior to World War II and on into the early 1960s, it began to become more competitive with the slow growth of the Republican Party in the mid-1960s. The key factor in this increasingly competitive partisan battleground was the growth of Republican electoral strength, first at the presidential level and later at the congressional and state/local levels. Closely connected to these electoral developments, both parties developed organizational structures that were sufficiently institutionalized by the 1990s to perform a variety of functions within the state's political system.

PARTY AND ELECTORAL PATTERNS, 1960–2000

Background. From the 1890s to the 1950s the Democratic Party dominated the South Carolina party system. At the presidential level, for example, Democrats won every election from 1900 to 1964 with the single exception of 1948 (when favorite son Strom Thurmond carried the state as the States' Rights Party candidate). Not only did the Democrats consistently win, they won impressively, dropping below 90 percent of the vote only once during this period (at 87 percent in 1944). Similarly, prior to the 1960s there were no Republican successes in senatorial, congressional, gubernatorial or state legislative elections, and Democrats often ran unopposed in the general elections.

One of the earliest and clearest manifestations of the crack in the state's Democratic solidarity came with its support of Strom Thurmond in 1948. Although the state returned to the Democratic fold in the next three presidential elections, it was by razor-thin margins unheard of in the preceding half-century—51 percent of the vote for Adlai Stevenson and John F. Kennedy in 1952 and 1960, respectively, and only a plurality of 45 percent for Stevenson in 1956 (with the remaining 55 percent going to incumbent Dwight Eisenhower or to Independent Harry Byrd). Thus, by 1960 the state was poised for significant change. Already underway at the presidential level, change would soon become evident as well in at least a few other offices.

Electoral Patterns, 1960–2000.[1] In 1964, Senator Thurmond made a dramatic switch from the Democratic Party to the Republican Party, followed roughly two months later by a 59 percent vote in South Carolina for Republican presidential candidate Barry Goldwater. The events surrounding Goldwater's strong showing in the state (and in the Deep South generally) were important to Republican Party development not only because they added Deep South states' electoral votes to the Republican column for the first time in modern history but also because they brought the race issue into the picture. Whereas Republican support in the 1950s had been largely based on conservative economic concerns among a growing white middle class located mainly in developing urban areas, support for Goldwater was rooted mainly in those segments of the southern population—often blue collar and rural—who were most concerned with defending the Jim Crow system of racial segregation (Topping, Lazarek, and Linder 1966; Bartley and Graham 1975, 105–110; Kuzenski 2003). Goldwater had cast a vote in the U.S. Senate against the 1964 Civil Rights Act, and this was widely interpreted as an indicator of his opposition to the civil rights movement. Strom Thurmond's endorsement of Goldwater and his subsequent party switch strengthened this perception.

In a related development, Second District Congressman Albert Watson supported Goldwater, was stripped of his seniority by House Democrats, resigned and switched parties. Watson regained his vacant seat in a special election in 1965, thus becoming the first Republican elected to Congress in the state since Reconstruction. The following year both Watson and Thurmond won reelection to their respective seats. Also, in 1966 the Republican Party nominated Joseph Rogers as their first gubernatorial candidate in decades. Rogers won a highly respectable 42 percent of the vote and carried three counties, an unexpectedly strong showing accompanied by Republican victories in contests for sixteen seats (of 124) in the lower house of the state legislature.

Over the next fifteen years, the Republican Party established itself as a viable electoral party by consistently winning one, and sometimes two, of South Carolina's six seats in the U.S. House of Representatives and Thurmond's seat in the U.S. Senate. Additionally, Republicans constituted a persistent minority in the state legislature, and the party broke through with a close gubernatorial victory in 1974 (although this was largely attributable to a series of internal problems in the Democratic Party relating to the legal disqualification of the primary-winning candidate and the subsequent bitter feelings related thereto). At the presidential level, where the Republicans were most impressive, between 1964 and 1980 the only Democratic victor was fellow southerner Jimmy Carter in 1976.

The last two decades of the twentieth century brought continued slow, but steady, movement toward a competitive two-party system in South Carolina. During this period, the Republican Party won every presidential election in the state, won three of five gubernatorial elections (with the 1990 win being a true landslide), continued to split the state's two U.S. Senate seats and won half or more of the state's seats in the U.S. House of Representatives in eight of eleven elections (see table 1.1). As in many other southern states, the 1994 congressional elections marked an important breakthrough for Republicans in South Carolina as they established control of two-thirds of the House seats, control they have maintained in every election since.

The state legislative elections in 1994 were also important for Republican growth. After steadily pushing their share of state house seats up during the 1980s and early 1990s, a combination of additional victories and party switches in and around the 1994 elections gave Republicans a majority in the lower chamber for the first time in this century (the 1994 elections also saw Republicans winning seven of the state's nine constitutional offices, including the governorship). In the state senate their share of seats rose above 40 percent between 1992 and 1996, as well.

In this changed political environment, the South Carolina Democratic Party found it progressively more difficult to compete with an increasingly vigorous Republican Party. By the mid-1990s, it appeared that Democrats at the statewide level had become an endangered species, and it appeared that Republicans would likely reelect governor David Beasley in 1998 and pick up the U.S. Senate seat held by then seventy-six-year-old Democrat Ernest F. ("Fritz") Hollings. Looking ahead to 2000, Republicans expected to maintain control of the lower chamber of the state legislature and gain control of the state senate.

Despite the Republican momentum of the previous thirty years, however, the 1998 elections did not go as many expected. Indeed, in an election that seemed crucial for the survival of the Democratic Party as a

Table 1.1. Republican Strength in South Carolina, 1980-2000 (in percentages)

Year	Vote for President	Vote for Governor	Vote for U.S. Senator	U.S. House Delegation	State House Delegation	State Senate Delegation
1960	48.8	0.0	0.0	0.0	0.0	
1962		0.0	42.8	0.0	0.0	0.0
1964	58.9	0.0	0.0	0.0		
1966		41.8	62.2/48.7*	16.6	13.7	
1968	38.1**		38.1	16.6	4.0	16.0
1970		45.6		16.6	8.9	
1972	70.8		63.3	33.3	16.9	6.5
1974		50.9	28.6	16.6	13.7	
1976	43.1			16.6	9.7	6.5
1978		37.8	55.6	33.3	12.9	
1980	49.4**		29.6	66.6	13.7	10.9
1982		30.2		50.0	16.1	
1984	63.6		66.8	50.0	21.8	21.8
1986		51.1	35.6	33.3	25.8	
1988	61.5			33.3	29.8	23.9
1990		69.5	64.2	33.3	33.3	
1992	48.0**		46.9	50.0	40.3	34.8
1994		50.4		66.6	48.3***	
1996	49.8**		53.4	66.6	56.5	43.5
1998		45.2	45.7	66.6	53.2	
2000	56.8			66.6	56.4	50.0**

Notes: * Special election to fill unexpired term of office.

** Three-way contests: Republican Richard M. Nixon won with 38.1 percent to American Independent Party candidate George C. Wallace's 32.3 percent and Democrat Hubert H. Humphrey's 29.6 percent in 1968; Republican Ronald Reagan won with 49.8 percent to Democrat Jimmy Carter's 48.1 percent and Independent John Anderson's 1.6 percent in 1980; Republican George H.W. Bush won with 48.0 percent to Democrat Bill Clinton's 40.5 percent and Independent H. Ross Perot's 10.1 percent in 1992; in 1996, Republican Bob Dole won the state with 49.8 percent to Democratic incumbent Bill Clinton's 44.0 percent and Reform Party candidate's H. Ross Perot's 5.6 percent.

*** Party switching by Democrats after the election resulted in increases in the Republican percentage; after the 1994 election the Republican Party held 52 percent of the state house seats and 43.4 percent of the state senate seats; after the 2000 elections, such a switch gave Republicans 52.2 percent of the state senate seats.

Sources: South Carolina State Elections Commission Reports for the listed elections.

competitive party in South Carolina, the Democrats were able to take advantage of short-term forces to stun Republicans in the state.

These short-term forces included, perhaps most important, the Democrats being able to persuade Senator Hollings to run for reelection and, thus, head the Democratic ticket. Democrats, especially Democratic gubernatorial candidate Jim Hodges, were also aided by a series of missteps by Governor Beasley. Foremost among these was his stance on an issue almost unique to South Carolina—whether the Confederate battle flag should continue to fly atop the statehouse, an issue on which Beasley reversed his earlier position and called for its removal, much to the surprise of many fellow Republicans in the state legislature and across the state. Other important short-term factors included the infusion of money into the campaign from the video-poker industry which feared that moralistic Republicans would seek to ban such gambling and a clever move by Democrat Jim Hodges to connect two popular issues—improvements in education and the creation of a state lottery (which he said would provide money for his proposed educational improvements). The result was that about 20 percent of self-professed Republicans crossed party lines and voted for Hodges. The Democrats were thus able to elect Hodges (with 53 percent of the vote) and three other candidates for statewide constitutional offices, and reelect Hollings (also with 53 percent of the vote).

The 1998 elections enthused Democrats and surprised, even demoralized, Republicans. The 2000 state party conventions reflected these reactions as Democrats predicted a party resurgence in the state while Republicans, in a rare show of dissension, pointed fingers and engaged in a struggle over party leadership. An attempt to dump the state party chair, Henry McMaster, who seemed too closely identified with the 1998 losses, eventually failed in a very close vote, but only after a number of emotional convention speeches revealed the depth of Republican concerns.

Whether the 1998 election results were interpreted as a sign of Democratic revitalization or as a fluke grounded in short-term issues and events, few expected much impact on the 2000 election in the state. The strength and consistency of Republican support in presidential elections was so firmly established by 2000 that most considered it a lock to vote for George W. Bush. While some Democratic Party leaders such as Bob Coble, mayor of Columbia, gamely insisted that the state was winnable for Al Gore (Bandy 2000), most did not. Both candidates saw South Carolina as being in the Bush column from the start—Bush's popularity in the state was apparent inasmuch as his nomination effort had received a huge boost in the South Carolina primary earlier in the year—and neither spent any time in the state during the campaign. No member of either candidate's campaign team visited South Carolina during the campaign, nor did either campaign even buy television time in the state.

The results were consistent with the predictions. Bush carried the state handily with just under 57 percent of the vote, improving on his father's 48 percent in 1992 and Dole's 50 percent in 1996. This improvement was expected because Ross Perot's presence in the two previous elections had cut into Republican support; what was not expected was Al Gore's poor showing. Despite Bill Clinton's unpopularity in the state (he regularly took a drubbing in newspaper editorial pages across the state and on local talk radio), Gore failed to improve appreciably on Clinton's vote, winning only 41 percent of the vote, barely better than Clinton's 40 percent in 1992 against an incumbent and less than Clinton's 44 percent in 1996. In short, the 2000 election confirmed the Republican hold on South Carolina's presidential vote. For the eighth time out of the previous nine presidential elections, and for the sixth consecutive time, the Republican ticket took the state's eight electoral votes.

Party Organizational Development, 1960–2000.[2] Prior to the 1960s, party organization in South Carolina was virtually non-existent: There were so few Republicans that there was nothing to organize and, consequently, there was no need for Democratic organization either. (See Moore 1983; Jordan 1962; Key 1949.) With the increased electoral competition in the early 1960s described in the previous section, both parties began to give increased attention to their respective organizations. This was especially the case for the Republicans. Between 1962 and 1965, Republican state chair J. Drake Edens, Jr., built the state's first genuine party organization and is regarded by many as the father of the modern Republican Party in South Carolina (Moore 1983; Bass and DeVries 1976: 24). This, combined with the modest electoral gains of the mid-1960s and the significant financial support of South Carolinian Roger Milliken, president of the third-largest textile corporation in the world, the Republican Party had a small but active nucleus interested in organizational development. By 1966, the Republicans had established a well-structured, multi-divisional headquarters with a cadre of full-time salaried administrators (*Standard Operating Procedures of the South Carolina Republican Party Headquarters*, 1966).

Largely because the Democrats were still dominant, their response to the Republican organizing effort was slow. The focus of the State Executive Committee was less on competing with the Republicans than on administering the electoral system, especially the party's primaries. While the Democrats began to take some notice of the emerging Republican threat and moved to improve fundraising and other candidate support activities, their main concerns related to changes occurring within the Democratic Party itself.

Specifically, the South Carolina Democratic Party found itself wrestling with a tangle of changes in election law (for example, the 1965 Voting Rights Act) and party rules related to the Civil Rights Movement's attack on laws denying African Americans the right to vote and on party rules excluding them from participating in party activities (see, for example, Crotty 1983; Price 1984: chap. 6; Polsby 1983; and Steed and McGlennon 1990). At the same time, and in a related matter, South Carolina Democrats struggled to deal with what many considered to be unwelcome changes in the national party: an increasingly liberal image (and policy positions), often reflected in the nomination of locally unpopular presidential candidates such as George McGovern. The challenge was one of remaining a part of the national organization without alienating South Carolina voters to the detriment of state and local Democratic candidates.

During the 1970s, the Republican Party continued its organizational development at the local level, especially in the state's urban centers, even though its main campaign involvement was still at the presidential level. The election of Republican James B. Edwards to the governorship in 1974 helped to spur further organizational development over the next two decades. Through the 1970s and on into the 1980s, the Republican Party continued to operate a permanent, well-staffed headquarters in Columbia, succeeded in getting a county chair in almost every county, worked to expand local organizations and regularly organized well-attended, efficient state conventions.

By the 1980s, as the turmoil of adjusting to new national party rules and the entry of African Americans into the party organization diminished, the South Carolina Democratic Party began to concentrate more of its organizational effort on meeting the growing Republican threat, particularly as Republican success in presidential elections began to trickle down to state and local elections. It was especially important that the Democrats find a way to hold together a fragile biracial coalition. Black voters were important to the party's electoral chances, and black party activists were becoming more and more important to the party's organizational operations as well. By the late 1980s, African Americans were well represented in state conventions, even constituting a majority of delegates in 1988 (when Jesse Jackson was a candidate for the Democratic presidential nomination), and they were a growing presence in precinct organizations (though still a relatively small minority at this level as late as 1992). Unfortunately for the party, many white Democratic activists were still having problems accepting blacks who did not share their ideological and issue orientations, and the party, therefore, faced a significant

threat to internal cohesion on platforms, candidates and election campaign strategy (see Steed and McGlennon 1990; Steed, Moreland and
Baker 1995a). To their credit, state Democratic leaders worked through
these shoals and steered the organization in the 1990s intact.

By the end of the twentieth century, both parties in South Carolina had
established well-organized party operations. Both maintained and oper-
ated permanent headquarters in Columbia, and both had a full slate of
administrators and staff. Both state parties were primarily concerned with
advancing party interests in the state, providing campaign assistance to
the party's candidates for state and national office and serving as a liaison
between the national and local parties. A related activity concerns the
development and maintenance of local organizations throughout the
state. In this regard, the state party acts as a general service agency assist-
ing local parties in fundraising, candidate recruitment, general communi-
cations and the like. For both parties, the heavy reliance on volunteers and
interns and the frequent turnover of key staff personnel has often posed
problems related to continuity and organizational memory, both of which
hinder organizational efficiency. However, in both parties this has begun
to be addressed with more careful attention to record keeping and staff
retention.

Clearly, then, the development of a competitive electoral system in
South Carolina in the post–World War II period was accompanied by the
development of stronger, more active party organizations. One last indicator of the sweep of party change in the state can be found in data on
delegates to the parties' state conventions and data on local party officials.
These data show that not only do both parties succeed in attracting activists at various organization levels, they also attract activists who differ
on a number of variables in ways that are congruent with the interparty
differences found among activists outside the South. For example, supporters of the Religious Right are primarily found among Republican
Party activists while African Americans are primarily found within the
ranks of the Democratic activists (for fuller discussion of these data see
Steed and Moreland 2000; Steed and Moreland 2001; Steed and Moreland
2003). Similarly, an ideological party sorting has occurred in the state as
Republicans have become strongly conservative and Democrats have
become increasingly less conservative and more liberal over the last two
decades of the century (see Steed and Moreland 1999). These party
changes are illustrated by data on local party officials' ideological and
issue positions collected in 2001 and presented in tables 1.2 and 1.3. At

Table 1.2.   Ideological Orientation of Local Party Activists in South Carolina, by Party, 2001 (in percent)

Self-Described Political Philosophy	Democrats	Republicans
Very liberal	24	0
Somewhat liberal	35	*
Moderate	25	5
Somewhat conservative	12	35
Very conservative	5	60

* less than 1.0 percent

Source: 2001–2002 Southern Grassroots Party Activists Project

Table 1.3.   Positions of Selected Issues for South Carolina Local Party Activists, 2001 (in percentage liberal)

Issue Position	Democrats	Republicans
Social Issues		
Equal role for women	96	83
Abortion as personal choice	83	22
School prayer	43	7
Government aid to minorities	86	27
Death penalty	64	16
Government regulation of managed health care	2	12
Stricter handgun control	87	13
Affirmative action (for blacks)	42	3
Government assistance to women	88	28
Job protection for gays	88	18
Economic Issues		
Fewer services to reduce government spending	90	16
Defense spending	15	2
Environmental spending	66	9
Public education spending	84	13
Crime prevention spending	4	11
Social Security spending	68	17
Flat tax	59	15
School vouchers	90	20
Government job provision	52	4

Source: 2001–2002 Southern Grassroots Party Activists Project

the beginning of the new century, then, South Carolina had developed a highly competitive two-party system that structured politics in the state in ways unheard of a half-century earlier.

CONTEMPORARY SOUTH CAROLINA
ELECTORAL AND PARTISAN POLITICS

The Elections of 2002.[3] Going into the 2002 election season, both parties had reason for optimism. The Democrats were buoyed by success in state elections four years earlier and by their enjoying having the incumbent governor, James Hodges, running for reelection. Republicans, still largely convinced that the 1998 elections were a fluke, saw the results of the 2000 elections as further evidence of their growing strength in the state. Additionally, South Carolina Republicans were optimistic about holding the U.S. Senate seat vacated by Strom Thurmond who had served just under a half-century in that chamber.

The electoral centerpiece was the contest for governor, and a number of high-profile (and not so high-profile) Republicans stepped up to compete for their party's nomination. In something of a surprise, former congressman Mark Sanford made it into, and then won, a run-off primary. The general election contest was also hard fought as both parties poured time and money into the campaign.

A spirited contest for Strom Thurmond's open Senate seat added more spice to a campaign year already heated by the Republican primaries of the summer and the gubernatorial race. Republican Lindsay Graham, a member of Congress who had gained some national name recognition in his role as a House manager in the impeachment of President Bill Clinton and who had won the Republican nomination, ran as the favorite against former South Carolina Supreme Court justice and college president Alex Sanders.

The two major issues which had benefited the Democrats in the 1998 gubernatorial election—the Confederate battle flag placement and the education lottery—were largely settled and, hence, no longer very salient to South Carolina voters in 2002, and in the end the advantages of incumbency were not enough to save Jim Hodges in an increasingly Republican state. In addition, another factor may have been what some Democratic leaders (such as U.S. Representative James Clyburn) complained was an overreliance on high-tech tactics over traditional campaign methods that may have diminished black turnout at the polls (Stroud 2002). In fact, not only did Mark Sanford win, his 53 percent majority was the second highest Republican gubernatorial vote percentage in modern history, surpassed only by Carroll Campbell's landslide 70 percent in 1990. Sanford's vote fit the pattern of Republican voting strength in the state as he ran strongest in the three urban corridors centered around Greenville-Spartanburg in the north, Columbia in the midlands, and Charleston in the coastal lowcountry (see table 1.4). Just over two-thirds of the state's total votes were cast in these three urban corridors, and Sanford won 56 percent of them; Hodges carried only two of the fifteen counties in these urban areas. Even though Hodges won 53 percent of the vote in the remaining counties (mostly rural and small town with only about one-third of the state's electorate), this was clearly insufficient to overcome

Table 1.4.   2002 Urban Corridor Gubernatorial Vote (percent)

Corridor	Hodges	Sanford
Lowcountry (Charleston) Urban Corridor		
Berkeley County	42	58
Charleston County	44	56
Dorchester County	39	61
Horry County	46	54
Totals for Corridor	44	56
Midlands (Columbia) Urban Corridor		
Aiken County	35	65
Edgefield County	49	51
Florence County	48	52
Lexington County	34	66
Richland County	57	43
Sumter County	56	44
Totals for Corridor	47	53
Upstate (Greenville-Spartanburg) Urban Corridor		
Anderson County	46	54
Greenville County	38	62
Pickens County	34	66
Spartanburg County	41	59
York County	49	51
Totals for Corridor	41	59
All Urban Corridors	44	56
All Other Counties	53	47

Percentages are of the total vote cast; totals may not always equal 100 percent because of rounding and votes for minor party candidates.

Sanford's advantage in the urban-suburban Republican strongholds. These geographic patterns also reflected a continuing racial divide within the South Carolina electorate with whites voting strongly Republican and African Americans voting even more strongly Democratic.

In the Senate race, Lindsay Graham defeated Alex Sanders by an even larger margin. While Graham improved on Sanford's vote percentage a bit (gaining 54 percent of the vote), this increased margin was mainly attributable to Sanders's running well behind Hodges with only 44 percent of the vote (to Hodges's 47 percent). The presence of two third-party candidates—Ted Adams (Constitutional Union Party) and Victor Kocher (Libertarian Party)—apparently affected the Democratic candidate disproportionately. As in the gubernatorial election, Graham ran strongest in the urban corridors (with 57 percent of the vote to Sanders's 41 percent), but he also beat Sanders in the remaining counties by 48 percent to 47 percent.

In the elections for other state constitutional offices, the news for the Democrats was not any better as they won only two, State Treasurer and Superintendent of Education. Similarly, Republicans won four of the six congressional races to maintain their two-thirds majority in the state's congressional delegation for the fifth consecutive election, and they maintained control of both chambers of the state legislature. In short, the 2002 elections suggested strongly that the Democratic successes of 1998 were aberrations and that the Republican Party had established itself as the majority party in South Carolina state politics as well as in South Carolina presidential politics.

The Elections of 2004. Although South Carolina Democrats were staggered by the 2002 election results, they were still clearly in a competitive position, at least in state and local elections. As the 2004 election campaigns opened, there was additional hope that a national ticket could be constructed that would aid state Democratic candidates even if it could not carry the state. Inasmuch as South Carolina's Democratic presidential primary was scheduled early in the delegate selection process, there was some hope that it would be able to influence such an outcome. In this vein, then, it was encouraging to state Democrats that Senator John Edwards of neighboring North Carolina (and a native of South Carolina) won the South Carolina primary in a multi-candidate field. In the final analysis, of course, the presidential nomination went to John Kerry, but his selection of John Edwards as his running mate was certainly aimed at strengthening the ticket's appeal in the South—and in South Carolina. In fact, even though Kerry was from Massachusetts, usually enough to condemn a candidate in the Palmetto State, he possessed strong military credentials which state Democrats hoped would blunt such condemnation. While few thought the Kerry–Edwards ticket would carry the state, there was some guarded optimism that it would not overly hurt state and local Democrats.

As the campaign unfolded, it quickly became apparent that Kerry and Edwards themselves had largely written off South Carolina as a potential source of electoral votes. There was no television campaign by either party's ticket, and surrogates largely made what few campaign visits there were to the state (for example, Laura Bush visited in mid-September, but even that visit was primarily to stump for the Republican senatorial candidate, Jim DeMint). Both presidential campaigns expected a Bush–Cheney victory and, consequently, concentrated their time and resources in other states.

The major race thus became the race for the open seat in the U.S. Senate created by the retirement of Democrat Ernest F. Hollings. South Carolina Republicans saw this as an excellent opportunity to gain a seat historically held by the Democrats while the Democrats considered retaining control of the seat to be highly important to their continued viability in the state. As with the gubernatorial nomination, a number of strong candidates emerged to compete for the Republican nomination. A hard-fought contest ended in the run-off nomination of Congressman Jim DeMint.

In sharp contrast to the Republicans who had numerous attractive candidates vying for their nomination, and reflecting the reduced strength of the Democratic Party in the state, the key problem the Democrats faced was finding a viable candidate to run for the seat. The nomination ultimately went to Inez Tenenbaum, the State Superintendent of Education and one of the two remaining Democrats holding statewide office. With 76 percent of the primary vote, Tenenbaum was by far the strongest candidate in the field.

The Tenenbaum–DeMint race quickly became highly heated and contentious. Both candidates crisscrossed the state, flooded the media with ads, engaged in a series of debates in various venues in different parts of the state and collected and spent huge sums of money by South Carolina standards. As had happened in the 1998 gubernatorial race, Tenenbaum appeared to have identified a couple of key issues which resonated with the electorate: She attacked DeMint's proposal for a flat tax as an alternative to the federal income tax as unfair to average (working-class and middle-class) people, and she attacked DeMint's absenteeism in Congress as an abdication of his responsibility to represent the people of the state. She also worked hard to position herself near the moderate center of the political spectrum and on some issues, such as the death penalty and strong support for the military, even slightly to the right of center. This seemed to be a fairly effective counter to DeMint's effort to depict her as a liberal Democrat who would be allied with other liberals such as Ted Kennedy and Hillary Clinton if elected to the Senate. DeMint's major criticisms focused on alleged mistakes Tenenbaum made as Secretary of Education, the continuing poor ranking of the state's education system and her connections to various special interests in the state. DeMint played strongly on his Republican ties, noted that his election would help give President Bush a working majority in the Senate and ran numerous television ads in which President Bush endorsed his candidacy and urged voters to support him at the polls.

Most other campaigns in the state paled in comparison with the white-hot Senate race. The expectations were that the Republicans would win the presidential election in South Carolina, that the congressional seats would remain distributed at 4 to 2 in favor of the Republicans and that the Republicans would retain control of the state legislature. As the campaign unfolded, the only real question concerned the Senate race. Surveys revealed a race close enough to give Democrats real hope of victory.

The election results were a real disappointment for the Democrats. As expected, Bush and Cheney won an easy victory in the presidential election with 58 percent of the vote, Republicans retained their 4 to 2 margin in congressional seats and they retained majorities in both houses of the state legislature. The stunning blow to the Democrats came with Tenenbaum's loss to DeMint in the Senate race. Not only did Tenenbaum lose, she lost by a 54 percent to 44 percent margin. This was only a slight improvement over the Democrats' 2002 showing with a less vigorous campaign and a less active (and less visible) candidate.

In both key races, Republican support again tended to be greatest in the state's urban areas. As shown in table 1.5, Bush again ran strongest in the three urban corridors, a pattern mirrored by DeMint in the Senate race. Perhaps of even greater concern for South Carolina Democrats, Bush also defeated Kerry in the state's remaining counties by a 7 percent margin. While Tenenbaum managed to hold the non-urban counties, the margin was a thin 50 percent to 48 percent of the total vote cast.

Exit polls revealed that Bush led Kerry among most of the standard

Table 1.5.   2004 Urban Corridor Presidential Vote (percent)

Corridor	Kerry	Bush
Lowcountry (Charleston) Urban Corridor		
Berkeley County	38	61
Charleston County	47	52
Dorchester County	36	63
Horry County	36	62
Totals for Corridor	41	57
Midlands (Columbia) Urban Corridor		
Aiken County	33	66
Edgefield County	42	58
Florence County	43	56
Lexington County	27	72
Richland County	57	42
Sumter County	50	49
Totals for Corridor	43	56
Upstate (Greenville-Spartanburg) Urban Corridor		
Anderson County	32	67
Greenville County	33	66
Pickens County	25	73
Spartanburg County	35	64
York County	34	64
Totals for Corridor	41	59
All Urban Corridors	39	60
All Other Counties	46	53

Percentages are of the total vote cast; totals may not always equal 100 percent because of rounding and votes for minor party candidates.

demographic and socioeconomic groups in the state: men (63 percent) *and* women (55 percent), *all* age groups (ranging from 51 percent of those between the ages of 18 and 29 linearly upward to 61 percent of those 60 or older), all income categories from $30,000 per year and up, Protestants (75 percent) *and* Catholics (62 percent), and so on. The only major exceptions to the pattern were Kerry's success among low-income groups and especially among African Americans. Indeed, the racial divide which has characterized South Carolina voting since the late 1960s again was the most prominent dividing line within the electorate; Bush received 78 percent of the white vote in the state while Kerry received 85 percent of the black vote.

CONCLUSION

Party and electoral developments in South Carolina over the past half-century or so have largely paralleled those in the region as a whole. The state has evolved from a one-party Democratic stronghold through an extended period of Republican growth into a competitive two-party system wherein the Republicans have gained the upper hand.

Both the 2002 and 2004 vote totals and vote patterns reveal much about the current state of party competition in South Carolina. The election outcomes once again show the contemporary strength of the Republican Party in presidential and state politics. Republicans routinely carry the state in presidential elections and by consistently substantial margins. This is nothing new in that Bush's 2004 victory marks the seventh consecutive Republican presidential win—and tenth out of the last eleven presidential elections. Similarly, while not for as long a period, Republicans have established firm control of a majority of the South Carolina congressional delegation and a majority of the seats in each house of the state legislature. They have held one seat in the U.S. Senate since Thurmond's party switch in 1964, and in 2004 gained control of the second.

Electoral patterns confirm the extent of Republican growth in the state. Not only have Republicans been winning, they have been winning by substantial proportions. Most telling in this regard is Jim DeMint's victory over Inez Tenenbaum in 2004. An attractive, energetic Democratic candidate running hard and spending large amounts of money, Tenenbaum was able to win only 44 percent of the vote. In fact, recent elections suggest that Democrats running statewide races can now generally expect a normal vote in the 41 to 45 percent range.

A related concern for South Carolina Democrats is their dwindling share of the white vote, a long-term trend that has now become routine. In the last two presidential elections, for example, Gore and Kerry polled just 26 percent and 22 percent, respectively, of the white vote. While Democrats can rely on a consistently heavy black vote (typically 80 percent or more), African Americans are a minority of registered voters in the state (less than 30 percent) and, thus, cannot offset the large Republican advantage among whites (see Kuzenski 2003; Moreland and Steed 2002). Moreover, Democrats have seen their advantage in the non-urban counties of the state reduced, even losing these counties by narrow margins in the 2002 senatorial election and in the 2004 presidential election.

South Carolina has not returned to the one-partyism of fifty years ago, nor is it likely to in the foreseeable future. The contemporary Democratic Party clearly has a stronger position than the Republican Party had in that earlier era: It has a solid voting base, it has a viable organizational structure and it is competing in an electoral context which is vastly different (legally, culturally, economically and demographically) than in the days of the Democratic Solid South. Although the Republican Party has become the dominant force in South Carolina politics, the Democrats are still competitive. Democratic victory increasingly depends on the presence of short-term factors (e.g., issues such as the education lottery or Republican miscues in specific campaigns), but victory is still sufficiently within reach to keep Republicans alert. In short, South Carolina has developed a competitive political system in which both parties must work to maintain effective organizations, attend to voters' concerns, recruit strong candidates (and energetic activists), run serious campaigns and work toward organizing state government effectively. This is in sharp contrast to the state's politics just a few decades ago.

REFERENCES

Bandy, Lee. 2000. "Gore Can Win in South Carolina, Coble Says." *The* (Columbia) *State*. September 9: B1.

Barone, Michael, and Grant Ujifusa. 1995. *The Almanac of American Politics 1996*. Washington: National Journal.

Bartley, Numan V., and Hugh D. Graham. 1975. *Southern Politics and the Second Reconstruction*. Baltimore: The Johns Hopkins University Press.

Bass, Jack, and Walter DeVries. 1976. *The Transformation of Southern Politics*. New York: Basic Books.

Black, Earl, and Merle Black. 1987. *Politics and Society in the South*. Cambridge, MA: Harvard University Press.

Broach, Glen T., and Lee Bandy. 1999. "South Carolina: A Decade of Rapid Republican Ascent," in *Southern Politics in the 1990s*, edited by Alexander P. Lamis. Baton Rouge: Louisiana State University Press.

Crotty, William. 1983. *Party Reform*. New York. Longman.

Elazar, Daniel J. 1972. *American Federalism*. New York: Thomas Y. Crowell.

Fowler, Donald L. 1966. *Presidential Voting in South Carolina, 1948–1964*. Columbia, SC: University of South Carolina Bureau of Governmental Research and Service.

Graham, Cole Blease, Jr. 1988. "Partisan Change in South Carolina," in *The South's New Politics: Realignment and Dealignment*, edited by Robert H. Swansbrough and David M. Brodsky. Columbia, SC: University of South Carolina Press.

Jordan, Frank E., Jr. 1962. *The Primary State: A History of the Democratic Party in South Carolina 1876–1962.* Columbia, SC: South Carolina Democratic Party.

Key, V. O., Jr. 1949. *Southern Politics in State and Nation.* New York: Knopf.

Kuzenski, John C. 2003. "South Carolina: The Heart of GOP Realignment in the South." Pp. 25–47 in *The New Politics of the Old South,* 1st ed., edited by Charles S. Bullock III and Mark J. Rozell. Lanham, MD: Rowman and Littlefield.

Moore, William V. 1983. "Parties and Electoral Politics in South Carolina," in *Politics in the Palmetto State,* edited by Luther F. Carter and David S. Mann. Columbia, SC: University of South Carolina Bureau of Governmental Research and Service.

Moreland, Laurence W., Robert P. Steed and Tod A. Baker. 1986. "South Carolina," in *The 1984 Presidential Election in the South: Patterns of Southern Party Politics,* edited by Robert P. Steed, Laurence W. Moreland and Tod A. Baker. New York: Praeger.

Moreland, Laurence W., Robert P. Steed and Tod A. Baker. 1991. "Different Cast, Same Drama in the Palmetto State," in *The 1988 Presidential Election in the South: Continuity Amidst Change in Southern Party Politics,* edited by Laurence W. Moreland, Robert P. Steed and Tod A. Baker. New York: Praeger.

Moreland, Laurence W., and Robert P. Steed. 2002. "South Carolina: Republican, Primarily," in *The 2000 Presidential Election in the South: Partisanship and Southern Party Systems in the 21st Century,* edited by Robert P. Steed and Laurence W. Moreland. Westport, CT: Praeger.

Moreland, Laurence W., and Robert P. Steed. 2005. "South Carolina: Republicans Consolidate Their Gains." *American Review of Politics* (forthcoming).

Polsby, Nelson W. 1983. *Consequences of Party Reform.* New York: Oxford University Press.

Price, David E. 1984. *Bringing Back the Parties.* Washington, DC: Congressional Quarterly Press.

Standard Operating Procedures of the South Carolina Republican Party State Headquarters. 1966. Howard H. "Bo" Calloway Collection, Richard B. Russell Memorial Library, The University of Georgia.

Steed, Robert P. 1997. "South Carolina," in *State Party Profiles: A 50-State Guide to Development, Organization, and Resources,* edited by Andrew M. Appleton and Daniel S. Ward. Washington, DC: Congressional Quarterly Press.

Steed, Robert P., and John McGlennon. 1990. "A 1988 Postscript: Continuing Coalitional Diversity," in *Political Parties in the Southern States: Party Activists in Partisan Coalitions,* edited by Tod A. Baker, Charles D. Hadley, Robert P. Steed and Laurence W. Moreland. New York: Praeger.

Steed, Robert P., Laurence W. Moreland and Tod A. Baker. 1992. "The South Carolina Party System: Toward a Two-Party System," in *Government in the Palmetto State: Toward the 21st Century,* edited by Luther F. Carter and David S. Mann. Columbia, SC: The University of South Carolina Institute of Public Affairs.

Steed, Robert P., Laurence W. Moreland and Tod A. Baker. 1995a. "Party Sorting at the Local Level in South Carolina." *The National Political Science Review* 5:181–196.

Steed, Robert P., Laurence W. Moreland and Tod A. Baker. 1995b. "South Carolina:

Toward a Two-Party System," in *Southern State Party Organizations and Activists,* edited by Charles D. Hadley and Lewis Bowman. Westport, CT: Praeger.

Steed, Robert P., and Laurence W. Moreland. 1999. "Ideology, Issues, and the South Carolina Party System, 1980–1996." *The American Review of Politics* 20: 49–74.

Steed, Robert P., and Laurence W. Moreland. 2000. "Black Political Activists and the South Carolina Party System, 1986–2000." Paper presented at the 2000 annual meeting of the Southern Political Science Association, Atlanta, GA, November 2000.

Steed, Robert P., and Laurence W. Moreland. 2001. "The Group Bases of Southern Parties, 1984–2000: The Case of South Carolina." Paper presented at the 2001 annual meeting of the Southern Political Science Association, Atlanta, GA, November 2001.

Steed, Robert P., and Laurence W. Moreland. 2003. "South Carolina: Party Development in the Palmetto State." *The American Review of Politics* 24: 91–108.

Stroud, Joseph S. 2002. "High-tech tactics fail Democrats." *The* (Columbia) *State.* November 10: A1.

Topping, John C., John R. Lazarek, and William H. Linder. 1996. *Southern Republicanism and the New South.* Report issued to the National Republican Party and the New Haven Ripon Society, Cambridge, MA.

NOTES

1. The summary overview of this period of South Carolina electoral history is taken from Fowler 1966; Moore 1983; Moreland, Steed and Baker 1986; Graham 1988; Moreland, Steed and Baker 1991; Steed, Moreland and Baker 1992; Steed, Moreland and Baker 1995b; Broach and Bandy 1999; Moreland and Steed 2002; and Steed and Moreland 2003.

2. For a more extensive discussion of party development in South Carolina, see Steed (1997).

3. For more detail on the 2002 and 2004 elections in South Carolina, see Moreland and Steed (2005).

2

Georgia: The GOP Finally Takes Over

Charles S. Bullock III

A s recently as 1991 Georgia might have qualified as the most Democratic state in the South. Republicans held none of the statewide offices, only one congressional seat and less than a fifth of the state legislative seats. Following the 2004 elections, Republicans occupied nine of fifteen statewide posts, including the governorship, and seven of thirteen congressional seats. Georgia had joined Florida, South Carolina, Texas and Virginia as southern states in which the GOP controlled both houses of the legislature and Republicans had more influence in Georgia than in the Old Dominion where a Democrat served as chief executive.

Improving Republican fortunes accompanied dramatic growth. The 2000 census revealed that Georgia's population had soared by more than 26 percent—the largest percentage gain east of the Mississippi River. In the mid-1990s the state passed North Carolina to become the nation's tenth most populous. Less than ten years later, the Peach State had edged New Jersey out to rank ninth in population. At the Atlanta airport, the nation's busiest, a fifth runway was under construction. With half the population living in metro Atlanta where they had to deal with the nation's longest average commutes to work, Georgia had long since shed the "Rule of the Rustics" that V. O. Key (1949) observed.

BACKGROUND

Rural dominance continued unchecked until the early 1960 when the U.S. Supreme Court's one person, one vote decisions increased urban and sub-

urban influence. Prior to the *Baker v. Carr* decision, the Georgia apportion-
ing system allocated at least one House seat to each of the 159 counties. As
a slight genuflection to population differences, the eight most populous
counties received two additional seats while the next thirty largest counties got a second seat for a total of 205 representatives. A rotational system
ensured that even the least populous county got to select a state senator
every third term.

Georgia not only gave rural areas exceptional influence in the legislature, it also allowed rural voters to exert greater control over statewide
offices than occurred in any other state.

In Democratic primaries for statewide offices—and no Republican won
a statewide election until 1980—and often congressional contests, victory
hinged on winning county unit votes rather than popular votes. The anal-
ogy here is the presidential Electoral College. Each county's unit vote
equaled twice its number of seats in the state House so that Fulton
County, which includes most of Atlanta, had six votes. Three tiny counties with a few hundred voters each could easily offset the Atlanta vote,
and in the days of boss-controlled counties, manipulating the rural vote
was far easier than campaigning successfully in large urban counties. A
statewide official from that era observed, "Give me five good men in 100
rural counties and I could run the state under the county unit system"
(Campbell 1983). The rural bias led the foremost practitioner of rustic politics, three-term governor Eugene Talmadge, to assert that he never
wanted to carry a county with a streetcar line. As witnessed in the 2000
presidential election, popular vote outcomes can differ from results based
on winning political subdivisions, and Talmadge won his last gubernatorial contest although another candidate got more popular votes. A judicial
challenge invalidated the county unit system just before the 1962 election.

Close behind the demise of the county unit system came nationally-
applicable court decisions establishing one person, one vote for legislative
districts. These orders produced a more immediate racial impact in Georgia than elsewhere in the South. Atlanta's large black population ensured
the creation of African-American seats in the legislature once districts had
equal populations. In 1962, Leroy Johnson won a Senate seat to become
the first member of his race to serve in a southern state legislature in modern times. When the House was redrawn to eliminate counties as the basis
for representation, African Americans entered that chamber, as shown in
table 2.1.

Redistricting also opened the door for Republicans. A couple of north
Georgia counties had, like the mountain areas of Tennessee and North

Table 2.1. Partisan and Racial Makeup of the General Assembly and Congressional Delegation, 1963–2005

	Percent Republican		Percent Black		U.S. House	
Year	House	Senate	House	Senate	GOP	Black
1963	1.0	5.6	0	1.9	0	0
1965	11.2	16.7	3.4	3.7	10.0	0
1967	10.2	14.8	4.4	3.7	20.0	0
1969	13.8	12.5	5.9	3.7	20.0	0
1971	11.3	10.7	6.3	3.7	20.0	0
1973	16.1	14.3	7.8	3.6	10.0	10.0
1975	13.3	8.9	10.6	3.6	0	10.0
1977	13.3	7.1	11.7	3.6	0	10.0
1979	11.7	8.9	11.7	3.6	10.0	0
1981	13.3	8.9	11.7	3.6	10.0	0
1983	13.3	12.5	11.7	7.1	10.0	0
1985	13.3	16.1	11.7	10.7	20.0	0
1987	15.6	17.9	13.3	10.7	20.0	10.0
1989	20.0	19.6	13.9	12.5	10.0	10.0
1991	19.4	19.6	15.0	14.3	10.0	10.0
1993	28.9	26.9	17.2	16.1	36.4	27.3
1995	36.7	37.5	17.8	17.9	72.7	27.3
1997	41.1	39.3	18.3	19.6	72.7	27.3
1999	43.3	39.3	18.3	19.6	72.7	27.3
2001	42.2	42.9	20.0	19.6	72.7	27.3
2003	40.0	53.6	21.7	17.9	61.5	30.8
2005	55.0	60.7	21.7	19.6	53.8	30.8

Compiled by author

Carolina, sent Republicans to the legislature but the minority party could have caucused in a phone booth. Once urban counties got more than the three-seat maximum awarded by the county unit system, upscale suburban neighborhoods began electing Republicans. In 1964 Barry Goldwater became the first Republican to carry the state's electoral votes, and his coattails contributed to the election of the first GOP member of Congress since Reconstruction and a jump in state legislators.

GOP STRUGGLES

The GOP seed watered by Goldwater seemed destined to produce a bountiful harvest in 1966 when Democrats nominated for governor Lester

Maddox, a restaurateur known for his racist rantings in the *Atlanta Jour-nal-Constitution* and chasing off prospective black customers with an axe handle. Republicans countered with Bo Callaway, heir to a textile fortune who epitomized country club Republicanism. Maddox ran an under-funded campaign, but his attacks on blacks and Communists stirred the same rural passions that had elected the Talmadges (Bartley 1970, 69–72).

Unlike in Arkansas and Florida where Republican gubernatorial candi-dates capitalized on the racial conservativism of their 1966 Democratic opponents, Callaway refused to reach out to African Americans, explain-ing that to do so "would be playing politics." The response of the frus-trated advisor who had urged seeking black support was, "What the hell do you think you're playing, Bo?" An attack on the outgoing governor, several of whose lieutenants were working covertly for Callaway, drove away more potential supporters and contributed to a write-in campaign for progressive former governor Ellis Arnall (1943–1947) who had lost the runoff to Maddox. When the ballots were counted, Callaway had a 3,039-vote lead but, because of the Arnall write-ins, no majority. In the absence of a majority, Georgia law passed the choice to the General Assembly where Democrats stood by their party.

Despite losing the governorship, GOP prospects remained sufficiently promising that in the autumn of 1968 five statewide officials switched parties to support Richard Nixon. This high-profile support proved insuf-ficient as Georgians, still outraged at federal demands that schools be desegregated and barriers to voting eliminated, gave George Wallace a plurality.

As often happens in the South, Georgia Republicans won their first sig-nificant sub-presidential election in the midst of Democratic disarray. In 1980, Sen. Herman Talmadge sought a fifth term following a highly publi-cized divorce, bouts of alcoholism and a Senate reprimand for financial misconduct. Like a bleeding swimmer attracting sharks, Talmadge drew three serious primary challengers but ultimately managed almost 60 per-cent of the vote in a bitter runoff against Lieutenant Governor Zell Miller. Talmadge returned to Washington where Congress was still in session believing the general election to be a mere formality—as it had always been previously.

The GOP nominee, a little-known typewriter salesman, capitalized on the incumbent's absence and a series of misjudgments. Talmadge failed to replenish his campaign treasury which the runoff had depleted, and he refused to debate his opponent despite the challenger's weak speaking skills. By the time Congress adjourned and Talmadge returned home, the momentum had switched to Republican Mack Mattingly. The Talmadge era begun half a century earlier by his father ended as Atlanta suburbs delivered majorities of better than two to one to the GOP upstart. Even majority-black Fulton County (Atlanta) rejected the Democrat, casting 57 percent of its votes for Mattingly. The dynasty founded by the man who never wanted to carry a county with a street car ended in the urban counties he had ignored with the *coup de grace* administered by African Americans in repayment for Eugene Talmadge's race baiting. Herman Talmadge's 27,000-vote defeat came despite President Carter's 236,000 majority in the one southern state to give electoral votes to a Democrat during the 1980s. Georgians had learned to split their ballots.

The Mattingly victory provided a rare down-ticket bright spot for the GOP. Landslide victories by Reagan in 1984 and Bush in 1988 offered little coattail pull in the legislature, and the GOP did not exceed pre-Watergate levels until the latter half of the 1980s. Sandwiched between Reagan's 362,000 majority and Bush's slightly larger margin was Mattingly's 1986 defeat by 22,000 votes. Underscoring the GOP's inability to make down-ticket headway, Aistrup (1989) showed Georgia to have the weakest Republican Party in the region. During the 1980s, Republicans never managed to win more than 20 percent of the congressional delegation, a poorer performance than in any other southern state.

AWAKENING FROM DORMANCY

Rip Van Winkle slept in the Hudson Valley for twenty years, a brief nap compared to the 121 years that elapsed after Republican Rufus Bullock (Duncan 1995) was driven from Georgia's governorship in 1871 and when the GOP again won a state office elected statewide. The breakthrough came via Georgia's majority vote requirement that had saved the Democrats in 1966. The presence of Libertarian candidates captured slivers of the vote which forced general election runoffs in 1992 for a renegade Democrat running for the Public Service Commission (PSC) and Sen. Wyche Fowler who had unseated Mattingly.

Having lost the state to President Bill Clinton by 13,714 votes, Republicans sought revenge in the runoffs. With no other federal elections to be decided, an all-star team of national Republicans campaigned for Paul Coverdell and deluged the state with money. Coverdell who had come up 35,000 votes short in the general election, reversed fortunes and retired Fowler while Republicans captured the PSC seat by an even larger margin (Fenno 1996; Bullock and Furr 1997).

The 1992 election also saw Republicans add three House seats to the one held by Newt Gingrich since 1979, giving the GOP its largest share of the delegation since 1874. The minority party also surged to more than a quarter of the state legislative seats, making its biggest single-election gains since the Goldwater election.

REDISTRICTING 1990S STYLE, OR HOW THE DEMOCRATS GOT MUGGED BY JUSTICE

Republican gains in Congress and the General Assembly could not have been achieved without the assistance of the U.S. Department of Justice (DOJ). Georgia, like all southern states except Arkansas, Oklahoma and Tennessee, must get approval of districting plans from DOJ or the federal district court sitting in the District of Columbia. This requirement of Section 5 of the 1965 Voting Rights Act (VRA) was designed to keep obdurate southern governments from erecting new barriers to black political participation once old ones were knocked down. By 1992, the VRA had been amended to bar statutes or practices that had the effect of diluting minority political influence even if there had been no intention to discriminate. DOJ used this new provision to demand that jurisdictions *maximize* the number of districts in which blacks constituted a majority of the voting age population.

DOJ rejected two districting plans that created a second majority-black congressional district and demanded a third district with a 57 percent black population in southwest Georgia. In putting the finishing touches on the two additional majority black districts, computer technicians went block by block, placing those with an African-American majority in a black district while assigning blocks with white majorities to neighboring white districts.

Bleaching districts provided both a direct and an indirect benefit for Republicans. The direct impact resulted from concentrating black voters, the most loyal Democrats, so that the adjacent bleached districts became more Republican (Lublin 2004). The indirect effect is that after creating districts more favorable to Republicans, stronger candidates come forward to carry the GOP banner. In 1992, GOP state legislators gave up secure seats to win election in two congressional districts. The First District became whiter when 50,000 African Americans in Savannah were excised and put in the Eleventh District. The Third District lost the black population of Columbus to the 57 percent black Second District. In the other district picked up by Republicans, John Linder, who had lost by 9,000 votes in 1990, eked out a 2,676-vote victory. Had DeKalb County not been split along racial lines in order to make the Eleventh District 64 percent black, it would have been easy to put enough blacks in the Fourth District to elect a Democrat but not threaten black ambitions in the Eleventh.

Racial gerrymandering influenced the 1994 results in Districts Eight and Ten as Republicans won another three seats. The percent black in the Eighth dropped from 35 to 21 in 1992 and declined from 25 to 18 in the Tenth. The other GOP pickup, the Seventh, shifted parties as a result of growing suburbanization with new, affluent voters who had little attachment to the senior Democratic incumbent. The GOP tide lapped higher in April 1995 when Nathan Deal of the Ninth district became the first of five southern House Democrats to change parties during the 104th Congress. Deal's defection left no white Democrats in Georgia's delegation. As Lublin (2004) has argued, racial gerrymandering devastated white Democrats' officeholding ambitions in Georgia's congressional delegation.

SHUTTING THE BARN DOOR
AFTER THE HORSE IS OUT

So many members of the Georgia House rejected DOJ demands for a third majority-black district that the Speaker had to cast the decisive vote to approve the plan. In North Carolina, Duke law professor Robinson Everett took the course urged by Georgia dissidents and challenged that state's race-based Twelfth District that snaked 160 miles along I-85 from Durham to Gastonia. In 1993, the Supreme Court found Everett's challenge to be justiciable and ordered a trial. Before the North Carolina challenge could be resolved, a similar suit filed in Georgia became the first racial gerrymander case decided on its merits by the Supreme Court. In *Miller v. Johnson* (1995), the Supreme Court struck down Georgia's Eleventh District that stretched 250 miles from suburban Atlanta to Savannah for violating the Equal Protection Clause since it had been drawn predominantly on the basis of race. A three-judge federal panel subsequently invalidated the 57 percent black Second District on the same grounds.

The 1996 elections occurred under a new plan that adhered to county boundaries except in the Atlanta metro area and did away with land bridges and fingers reaching into urban areas to connect dispersed pockets of African Americans. The plan eliminated black majorities in the Second and Eleventh Districts while restoring the general outlines of the pre-1992 First, Eighth and Tenth Districts, making them more than 30 percent black.

Despite the shifts of populations in the 1996 plan, that year's elections ushered in no changes in the state's congressional delegation. Although civil rights leaders had warned that blacks could not win in districts without an African-American majority, Sanford Bishop won the Second District with 54 percent of the vote while Cynthia McKinney took 58 percent against an aggressive challenger. Both black incumbents easily disposed of white primary challengers.

Democrats who hoped to take advantage of higher black percentages in Districts Eight and Ten were disappointed as the incumbents secured narrow margins. In these districts with GOP incumbents, as well as in the two with black Democratic incumbents, the voting patterns were quite similar as Democrats won almost all African-American votes while approximately two-thirds of the white vote went to Republicans (Bullock and Dunn 1999). This pattern recurred in 1998, a remarkable drop from the 57 percent of the white vote won by Democratic congressional candidates in 1990.[1] White partisan loyalties in districts with racial compositions that Democrats could have probably held in the early 1990s had eroded too much for Democrats to unseat incumbents despite infusions of black voters.

PARTISAN BALANCE

Statewide election results showed a very competitive state during the 1990s. In 1992, Bill Clinton won the state by fewer than 14,000 votes, the closest outcome in the nation. Four years later, Georgia was among the few states to shift parties as Bob Dole got a 27,000-vote plurality.

Narrow victories also characterized several high-profile contests in the mid-1990s. Max Cleland (D) reversed Bob Dole's fortunes to take a 30,000-vote plurality in the 1996 race to fill Sam Nunn's (D) Senate seat. Competitiveness was also the rule in 1994, when the state's constitutional offices were on the ballot, although unlike in the past Republicans now eked out narrow victories. Three Republicans supplanted Democratic incumbents for down-ticket offices with each victor taking 51 percent of the vote or less. Zell Miller (D) won reelection as governor with 51 percent of the vote, saved by the popular HOPE scholarships that enabled him to cut into GOP majorities in suburbia.

HOPE, funded by the state lottery—the creation of which had been the major plank in Miller's 1990 campaign—pays for tuition and books at state-supported colleges and technical schools for all Georgia high school grads with B averages who maintain those grades in college. HOPE has proven very popular with middle-class parents most of whose children go to college since it provides tuition for these students thereby saving their parents tens of thousands of dollars.

DEMOCRATS HANG ON

Republicans had anticipated that in 1998 they would finally win the governorship, pick up additional constitutional offices and perhaps take a majority in at least one chamber of the legislature. They realized none of these hopes. The candidacy of former attorney general Michael Bowers, expected to be the GOP's strongest candidate for governor since Bo Callaway in 1966, imploded after he acknowledged a long affair with a former secretary. Despite a tarnished straight-arrow image, Bowers labored on but lost to Guy Millner, who had carried the party's banner in the 1994 gubernatorial and 1996 senatorial contests.

As in his previous bids, Millner tapped his fortune to fund the campaign and seemed to be headed for victory as he led in the polls right up until the closing days of the campaign. He and other Republicans, however, fell before a record black turnout. African-American voters had multiple motivations. Among these were intemperate statements made by Mitch Skandalakis, the GOP nominee for lieutenant governor, who boasted that if elected, he would kick Atlanta mayor's Bill Campbell's ass—Campbell is an African American. This threat was coupled with Millner's opposition to affirmative action programs and used to stimulate black turnout through a mailing made by the Democratic Party to the household of every black voter.[2] The presence of three African Americans among statewide Democratic nominees—two of whom won—provided an additional impetus. Finally Democrats tapped black support for Bill

Clinton, who faced impeachment and removal from the office, by targeting a recorded telephone call from the embattled president to each black voter's household. These efforts boosted black turnout to a record 23 percent of all voters, up substantially from four years earlier, and African Americans continued casting 90 percent of their votes for Democrats.[3]

As black participation rose, Republicans' core support group shrank. As table 2.2 shows, whites who identified with the religious right constituted a smaller share of the electorate in 1998 than previously. This group regularly gives more than 70 percent of its votes to GOP nominees while the remainder of the electorate casts most of its votes for Democrats. Thus in 1998, Republicans' strongest supporters withdrew from participation while the Democratic base surged.

Democrats, who had historically campaigned as individual candidates, ran as a team in 1998 and it was a balanced team. The set of statewide aspirants included three African Americans, two women and two candidates from south Georgia. Mark Taylor, the nominee for lieutenant governor, mobilized his south Georgia supporters. His massive victory in his home area contributed to the margins of other Democrats.

While the 1998 election can best be characterized as a stand-pat election with incumbents of both parties succeeding and Democrats holding on to positions that came open, Democrats emerged euphoric. The GOP that

Table 2.2. Proportion of Georgia's General Election Voters That Belong to the Parties' Core Constituencies and Their Voting Preferences (All numbers in percentages)

	1992	1994	1996	1998	2000	2004
Blacks						
Exit Polls	20	16	24	29	26	25
Verified by Secretary of State	NA	NA	21	23	23	25
Democratic Support for						
President	87	—	92	—	91	88
Governor	—	90	—	90	—	—
U.S. Senator	86	—	83	89	93	87
White Religious Right/Evangelicals	NA	26	22	19	20	35
Democratic Support for						
President	NA	—	11	—	13	16
Governor	—	23	—	27	—	—
U.S. Senator	NA	—	22	15	36	13

Source: Exit poll data and estimates of support from Voter News Service except as noted.

dominated the congressional delegation and believed itself destined to take over state government had been stopped dead in its tracks. Republicans were stunned by their total lack of new success.

Georgia's 2000 elections resembled those of 1998 in that little changed. Each party retained a seat on the five-person PSC with the successful Democrat being the first African American to serve on this body. In the top-of-the-ticket contests, the parties each scored a victory as George Bush coasted to a 300,000-vote majority while former governor Zell Miller, who had been appointed to the Senate in July when Paul Coverdell died, polled 58 percent of the vote against a special-election field of six.

Only modest changes occurred in the state legislature. Republicans concentrated their efforts in the Senate where they needed to add seven seats in order to block Democratic gerrymanders in the upcoming redistricting battles. The GOP knocked off two incumbents and claimed that they came within 5,500 votes of their goal (Johnson 2000), although Democrats maintained a 32 to 24 advantage. Republican failure to win the Senate allowed Democrats to enact one of the most extreme gerrymanders in the nation, a topic to be discussed later.

While major changes in party control failed to materialize, 2000 displayed significant changes in Georgia's legislative competition. Candidates spent record amounts of money with totals in excess of $100,000 common and twice that amount not rare. The biggest spender was a Republican House member who switched to the Democratic Party just minutes before the end of the candidate filing period. He faced two candidates who qualified by petition and then had to meet one of these—who had strong support from the GOP—in a general election runoff. Reports indicate that the incumbent spent as much as $500,000 in a losing race (Williams 2000). This candidate and several others had so much money that they could buy time on Atlanta network stations.

Beginning in the latter half of the 1990s, state legislative contests illustrated a pro-Democratic bias in the districting scheme. In the 1996 general election, 75,000 more votes were cast for Republican than Democratic state Senate candidates even though the Democrats emerged with a 34 to 22 edge in the chamber (Baxter 1996). The pattern was repeated in 1998 as Republicans secured 52 percent of the statewide vote for the state Senate but only 39 percent of the seats and 53 percent of the state House votes compared with 43 percent of the seats. In 2000, once again, Republicans outpolled Democrats statewide taking 55 percent of the vote for the Senate but winning only 45 percent of the seats. Republicans hoped that this strength would translate into majorities in the state legislature when those chambers emerged from redistricting.

REPUBLICAN COMING OF AGE

The Republican's long march toward majority status that had begun with the Goldwater election of 1964 finally became a reality in 2002. After fifty consecutive gubernatorial elections won by Democrats, former state senator Sonny Perdue pulled off what many believed to have been that year's most startling upset. Although outspent by a factor of more than six to one and struggling to even get on television, Perdue denied the reelection bid of Roy Barnes.

To pull off the upset, Perdue had to add to the Republican base. One basis for attracting disaffected Democrats was the Barnes flag. Barnes pushed the legislature to adopt a new state flag that dramatically shrank the size of the St. Andrews Cross of the Confederate States flag that had dominated most of the Georgia flag since 1957. This action infuriated heritage groups like the Sons of Confederate Veterans. They made their displeasure known by picketing any event at which Barnes appeared. In addition to the "flaggers," the name applied to these protestors, Barnes also alienated teachers. The governor had pushed through a major education reform that called for smaller classrooms. While teachers might have agreed with his objective, he lost their support when it appeared to them that he thought them to be largely incompetent and uncaring. Joining these groups were law enforcement officials and other leaders in many rural counties who were angered by the new districting maps pushed through by Barnes that split counties that had heretofore been maintained wholly within a single district. Elected officials run the risk of alienating some former supporters as they go about governing and making decisions. Most incumbents, however, are able to augment the ranks of their initial supporters by attracting new support. Barnes failed to do so, and his own tracking polls showed him unable to consistently break through the 50 percent support barrier despite dumping of millions of dollars into television advertising.

Barnes's underfunded challenger ran a grassroots campaign that concentrated on seventy counties that in 1998 had split their votes by supporting Barnes for governor but the reelection of Republican Paul Coverdell to the Senate. Perdue reasoned that if he could carry the counties that had demonstrated a willingness to split their votes and add them to counties that consistently voted Republican he could win. If one were to grade the Perdue campaign on success, he would earn an "A" since he carried sixty-five of seventy swing counties he had targeted.

The Republican success did not stop with the governorship but also included the election of Saxby Chambliss who defeated Max Cleland's reelection bid for the Senate. Cleland's defeat also resulted from his alienating of key constituents. Cleland had enjoyed widespread popularity as Georgia's secretary of state. Indeed his popularity was so widespread that when he announced for the Senate, no other Democrat came forward to challenge him. His narrow 1992 general election victory hinged upon support from moderate Democrats who expected their new senator to follow in the footsteps of the retiring Sam Nunn. But when Cleland got to Washington, he became caught up in the fierce partisan battles. With the Senate narrowly divided between the two parties, each put a premium on loyalty. By the time that Cleland got to the Senate, the conservative Southern Democratic contingent that had frequently held the balance of power in the chamber beginning in the 1940s had been decimated. With no senior role models from his region to help guide him, Cleland fell under the spell of national Democrats. The Democratic leadership of Tom Daschle (SD), Ted Kennedy (MA) and others staked out positions far to the left of most Georgia voters.

Cleland's position was further damaged following Zell Miller's appointment to fill the Coverdell vacancy. Miller quickly became the most conservative Democrat in the chamber and, like traditional southern Democrats, frequently voted for programs supported by the GOP. This made Cleland's more liberal positions all the harder for moderates in Georgia to understand. Despite frequently positioning himself to the right of Cleland, Miller proved to be the embattled incumbent's strongest supporter. Miller cut television ads for Cleland and when Republicans attacked Cleland, Miller manned the barricades and fired off salvos in defense of his colleague.

President Bush's proposal for creating a Department of National Security provided the final piece in the GOP campaign to depict Cleland as "too liberal for Georgia." Miller quickly embraced the President's position while Cleland stood by the Daschle alternative which sought to ensure that the employees of the new department could unionize. Republicans attacked Cleland charging that he placed protection of unions above national defense. Georgia is a right-to-work state that has been inhospitable to union activity, thus making the Republican charges all the more damaging.

The relationship between race and voting was striking. Of the 113 counties in which blacks constituted less than 33 percent of the registrants, Perdue won all but three. Chambliss almost matched Perdue's feat by carrying 105 of these counties. The strong showing among white voters enabled the Republicans to score breakthroughs in a number of rural counties in south Georgia that in the past had been part of the Democratic coalition. A huge question mark for the future was whether whites in these counties supported Republicans because of disappointment over the policy decisions made by Governor Barnes and Senator Cleland or that 2002 signaled a permanent conversion to the GOP.

The 2004 state legislative results went a long way toward answering the question about the extent of change in Georgia's white electorate. Republicans won all thirty-three Senate districts in which blacks constituted less than 30 percent of the registrants. Democrats retained all but one of the more heavily black Senate districts. The remarkable success of Republicans in winning districts that were more than a quarter black in registration was less striking in the House where a number of long-time Democratic incumbents managed to hold on. However, the voting patterns in these districts suggested that once the Democratic incumbents step aside, Republicans will be well positioned for gaining these districts too.

The white voters who abandoned Democratic state Senate candidates provided little support for Democrats at the top of the ticket. John Kerry and Democratic Senate nominee Denise Majette got little more than 20 percent of the white vote according to exit polls—only about half the support they would have needed to win.

Republican legislative candidates received help from the top of their party's ticket. George Bush carried Georgia by 548,000 votes as the Kerry campaign never seriously contested the Peach State and lost 133 counties. In the U.S. Senate contest, Johnny Isakson, a member of the U.S. House who had spent a quarter of a century in the state legislature and had two previous statewide runs under his belt, carried 140 counties in easily defeating Denise Majette. The presence of Majette as the Democratic nominee underscored the problems plaguing the once-dominant party that failed to convince either the lieutenant governor or secretary of state—the two most attractive leaders of their party—to contest the Senate seat.

Not only did GOP legislative candidates have coattails to grasp, a referendum stimulated conservative voters to come to the polls. Georgia's ballot contained a constitutional amendment prohibiting gay marriage—a proposal that evoked overwhelming support. The presence of this amendment might also account for the jump in evangelical voters who, as reported in table 2.2, constituted 35 percent of the white electorate. All of these elements combined to make Georgia one of the states with the greatest increase in turnout and the GOP benefited from the heightened voter interest.

Republicans' only disappointment occurred in the Twelfth congressional district where John Barrow defeated the accidental Rep. Max Burns. Democrats would have won this 40 percent black district in 2002 had they not nominated one of the least-electable candidates to have a major party nomination. With Barrow's victory, Republicans had their smallest share of Georgia's congressional delegation (7 of 13) since 1993.

BASES OF PARTISAN SUPPORT

If Democrats retain the overwhelming support of African Americans and get 40 percent of the white vote, they can fashion narrow statewide majorities. The recent past illustrates the impact of these variables. An analysis of Zell Miller's 1994 reelection done by Democratic campaign consultants Alan Secrest and Mike Sanelli's (1995) showed that 41 percent of the white vote provided a sufficient bulwark for Democrats.

Presidential candidates have had the hardest time attracting white support, and in the last four elections the Democrat has failed to exceed a third of the white vote. This is insufficient in a two-person contest but in 1992, when Ross Perot took 13 percent of the state's ballots, Clinton got just enough white votes to squeeze out a plurality. White votes for Democrats below the presidential level have drifted downward. The 1986 Democratic Senate candidate ran relatively poorly for that time among whites but that may have been because he challenged an incumbent. In 1988 and 1990, state-level Democrats got about half the white vote and won by what would now be considered to be comfortable margins. In the next two elections, Democrats who faced stiff competition struggled to get to 40 percent of the white vote and could win only with strong black turnout. While Democrat Max Cleland won a plurality in the 1996 Senate election with 39 percent white support, he slipped by thanks to a Libertarian who siphoned off 4 percent of the vote.

The 1998 elections witnessed two favorable changes for Democrats. Black turnout continued to rebound from its 1994 low, reaching 23 percent, which enabled Democrats to win with slightly less than 40 percent of the white vote.[4] Thurbert Baker won the race for attorney general with 38 percent of the white vote. Lieutenant Governor Mark Taylor made the strongest showing for a Democrat among whites and took almost 46 percent of their votes.

African-American support for Democrats remains lopsided and constant up and down the ticket. Democratic congressional candidates consistently get more than 90 percent of the black vote (Bullock and Dunn 1999). Exit polls sometimes show Republicans doing slightly better among blacks in some up-ticket contests, and in 1996 black support was lower than at any time in the past as Cleland failed to get 85 percent of the black vote. If Republicans' share of the black vote reaches the mid-teens, and if Libertarians stop running for office, Democrats will be hard pressed to win statewide.

Race is not the only divide in the Georgia electorate. Republicans do better in north Georgia. In 1992, Clinton carried only half a dozen counties north of Atlanta, and two years later Governor Zell Miller won only eight counties in that area and that included his home county and one of its neighbors. Miller's inability to win his own corner of the state is in stark contrast to the friends-and-neighbors pattern Key (1949) identified. In 1998, only one county north of Atlanta was classified as solidly Democratic by a GOP pollster (Willson et al. 1999). Most of the counties in north Georgia meet the pollsters' definition for being solidly Republican. Democrats do well in the diagonal swath of the Black Belt cutting across the middle of the state. All but six of the counties carried by Al Gore in 2000 were in the Black Belt, and of the six exceptions, three were at the center of Atlanta's metropolitan area and a fourth is dominated by the University of Georgia. The Gore success pattern emerged again in the 2002 gubernatorial and Senate contests and the 2004 presidential and Senate elections.

Republicans' growing electoral success showed up in the 2004 exit polls that depicted an electorate in which 42 percent claimed to be Republicans while 34 percent identified with the Democratic Party. These figures exactly reversed what the 1992 exit poll had found and are the first time Democrats have been the minority party. These figures demonstrate that neither party can win statewide if it only mobilizes its own members; victory requires attracting voters who identify with neither party. For the first time, if each party has equal success in mobilizing its supporters, Republicans start markedly closer to the 45 percent share of the vote needed for victory in the general election.[5]

As another indicator of the development of two-party competition, participation in the GOP primary has grown. The GOP held its first statewide primary in 1970, but until the 1990s, no more than one in ten voters helped choose Republican nominees. Table 2.3 shows that as recently as 1990, participants in the Democratic primary outnumbered Republicans nine to one. Republicans attracted growing shares of primary participants during the 1990s, reaching 46.2 percent of all voters in 1998.

Most voters continue to ask for the Democratic ballot when they show up at the open primaries, but in both 2002 and 2004, just under half the voters participated in the GOP primary. The most recent off-year primary saw 400,000 more Republican voters than in 1990. Since the total primary participation had changed little since 1990, the 2002 Democratic primary attracted almost 500,000 fewer voters than the 1990 primary. Virtually no African Americans vote in the GOP primary, which means that rising Republican turnout results from whites opting out of the Democratic primary. Because of these defections, blacks cast a larger share of the Democratic votes. Until 1998, blacks accounted for less than a quarter of the Democratic primary vote except in the extremely low-interest 1994 primary. The high share of votes cast by blacks in 1994, an election that elicited little interest among whites, supports the proposition that as whites opt out of the Democratic primary, the African Americans' vote becomes proportionally larger. In the last two elections, just under half the Democrats were African Americans.

In 2004 Democratic participation reached its highest point since 1992

Table 2.3. Participation in Georgia Primaries, 1990–2004

Year	Total Turnout	Democratic	Democratic % Black	GOP	GOP % of Turnout	Turnout of Registrants
1990	1,171,131	1,053,013	24.6	118,118	10.1	43.5
1992	1,151,971	875,149	22.1	276,822	24.0	40.1
1994	761,371	463,049	39.2	298,322	39.2	25.8
1996	1,182,168	717,302	22.5	474,866	40.2	33.7
1998	905,383	486,841	36.4	418,542	46.2	23.7
2000	960,414	613,884	31.3	340,001	35.6	26.7
2002	1,102,611	575,533	45.2	527,078	47.8	28.6
2004	1,418,838	731,111	47.2	671,961	47.4	35.4

and blacks cast 47.2 percent of the votes. The U.S. Senate candidacy of Denise Majette, an African American seeking to move up from the U.S. House, undoubtedly spurred interest among black voters. Majette defeated a self-made millionaire who spent heavily on television while she ignored that expensive medium. Her selection as the Democratic nominee and her subsequent landslide loss point to the problems that accompany the changing makeup of the party primaries. With conservative voters having decamped to the GOP primary, liberals like Majette are better positioned to win Democratic nominations, but liberals cannot win statewide general elections in a state in which fewer than one in five voters think of themselves as liberals while more than 40 percent tell exit pollsters that they are conservatives.

REDISTRICTING 2001: DEMOCRATS TAKE
GERRYMANDERING TO NEW EXTREMES

The Atlanta metro area added almost a million people in the 1990s as Georgia passed North Carolina to become the nation's tenth most-populous state. This exceptional growth continued a trend begun in the 1980s when Georgia picked up an eleventh seat in Congress. Well before the census, communities began angling for one of the two congressional seats gained in 2000. Athens hoped to become the center of a district in the northeastern quadrant. Republicans hoped to place a new district in the Atlanta suburbs and to reduce black concentrations in some of the three districts currently filled by Republicans that were more than 30 percent black. These districts, in the absence of a Republican incumbent, might send a Democrat to the House. Atlanta suburban growth also necessitated relocating state legislative seats from south to north Georgia and from central cities to surrounding areas, which boded well for Republicans who do well in north Georgia and newer suburbs.

The non-retrogression standard applied by federal authorities when assessing the racial fairness of southern districting plans bars proposals that endanger sitting black legislators. The obligation to maintain districts in which African Americans feel comfortable coupled with the often significantly overpopulated districts represented by Republicans raised spirits in the GOP, which expected to see the most loyal Democratic voters soaked up in heavily black districts.

In the redistricting struggles of the early 1980s and 1990s, Republicans joined forces with African Americans (Holmes 1998). The coalition could be easily outvoted and consequently achieved its objectives only when the U.S. attorney general, operating under Section 5 of the Voting Rights Act, refused to preclear the plans. In 2001, unlike in the past, a coalition of African Americans and Republicans would constitute a majority in both legislative chambers and could enact its preferences. While the GOP invited its old partner back, blacks, seeing how much Republicans had gained from past joint efforts, assigned higher priority to maintaining Democratic majorities in the legislature than to maximizing the number of black seats. An ideological coalition of Republicans and conservative white Democrats like the one that emerged in 1995 in the Senate during unsuccessful efforts to redraw congressional districts after *Miller v. Johnson* also failed to materialize, leaving Republicans with no partners.

Since Republicans had been consistently winning most of the votes statewide in House and Senate contests and since the state's growth areas tended to vote Republican, it would be difficult for Democrats to retain control of the legislature. However, if Republicans captured a majority in a legislative chamber, one of the biggest losers might be Gov. Roy Barnes, who could be the first Georgia governor to experience the challenge of divided government. With the stakes so high, Barnes played an unprecedented role during the 2001 special sessions to redraw Georgia's districts.

Under Barnes's watchful eye, Georgia's state legislative districts became less compact as Democrats strung together often far-flung Republican enclaves. One Republican Senate district that consisted of five counties on the north side of Atlanta was overpopulated by 21,000. One might have expected it to become smaller as it shed the additional population in order to meet the one person, one vote requirement. Its redesign, however, sent it sprawling 200 miles, running across more than half the state's northern border (at points less than 2,000 feet wide) as it stretched from Atlanta suburbs to South Carolina after brushing past Tennessee and North Carolina. A six-county Senate district that came within 653 people of being exactly at the state population mean was redone to include five entire counties and parts of another eleven counties. The creative cartography was necessary in order for Democrats, who were consistently outvoted by Republicans in state Senate and House contests statewide, to hold on to their majorities in the two chambers.

Democrats also sought to use their control of the state legislature to gain congressional seats. They designed a congressional plan in which the two new seats earned through population growth had black voting age populations of just under 40 percent. With hundreds of thousands of whites participating in the Republican primary (see table 2.2), these districts would likely have a majority black electorate in the Democratic primary, and given their black concentrations, the winner of the Democratic primary in these districts would almost certainly win in November. When redrawing existing districts, Democrats paired two Republican incumbents in each of two districts, thereby creating two more open districts. Both of these open seats had a voting history that indicated a strong likelihood of electing Democrats. If the 2002 elections played out as past results indicated they should, Georgia's new plan would send to Congress seven Democrats and six Republicans, a gain of four by Democrats, which might tip control of the U.S. House.

Designing districts to help Democrats more than double their ranks in the congressional delegation required creative cartography. In the early 1990s, new extremes in gerrymandering were achieved through the use of geographic information systems that integrated demographic and political data and permitted the rapid creation of plans with instantaneous reports of each district's racial and partisan composition. A decade after using these techniques to meet Department of Justice demands for additional majority-black districts, partisans turned to them to further their goals. In Georgia, Democrats carefully split counties and even precincts along partisan lines; in Virginia, where Republicans controlled the legislature and governorship, similar practices promoted the GOP. These partisan ploys, which gave less deference to the boundaries of counties and cities, produced less compact districts.

Democrats' gerrymandering fell far short of its objectives. They won the two new congressional seats, but Republicans held on to an 8 to 5 majority in the delegation. Republicans managed to retain two seats as a result of poor choices made in the Democratic primaries. In the more blatant case, a 40 percent African-American district became the most heavily black district in the nation to elect a Republican. Max Burns won this district when the Democratic nominee's arrest record turned out to be longer than his political record. The Democrat had been arrested five times but had never held public office. Moreover, the Democrat had a weak grasp of the issues and generally made a bad presentation.

In the state Senate, Democrats believed their plan would increase their membership by five. Instead, Republicans scored a net gain of three. While the 2002 election returned a Democratic majority, this slipped away when four newly elected Democrats succumbed to the appeals of GOP

Governor-elect Perdue and changed parties, giving Republicans a 30 to 26 majority. Only in the state House did Democrats retain a majority, although the House plan designed to add fifteen seats to the Democrats' majority won them only four more seats.

Both the House and Senate plans came apart in 2003 when a federal court ruled that they violated of the Equal Protection Clause requirement of equal populations among districts. Democrats explained that they had drawn the misshapen districts in order to underpopulate districts in South Georgia and the city of Atlanta while overpopulating districts in suburbia and north Georgia. The federal district court found this behavior unconstitutional under the *Baker v. Carr* precedent established in 1962. Thus the careful Democratic effort to soak up Republicans by overpopulating their districts by 4 percent or more while underpopulating Democratic district by like amounts was struck down. When the legislature failed to take corrective action, the court had a plan drawn that brought all districts to within + / − 1 percent of the ideal population.

The elections in 2004 demonstrated the degree to which Democrats had gerrymandered the invalidated plans. Republicans gained four more Senate seats, and in the House their share of the seats increased by 15 percentage points as reported in table 2.1. The gains solidified GOP control of the Senate and for the first time since Reconstruction gave them a majority in the House.

The federal court declined to find the congressional plan unconstitutional. However with Republicans in control of both legislative chambers and the governorship, they took corrective steps in 2005. Following the lead of Texas, which had redrawn its congressional districts in 2003, Georgia Republicans carried out a mid-decade congressional redistricting. The likely consequence of the new map in Georgia is far more modest than in Texas where Republicans scored a net gain of six seats. In Georgia the main objective was to shore up the district of a Republican. Only one district held by a Democrat became significantly more vulnerable in the new Georgia map.

CONCLUSION

GOP success spread slowly in Georgia. Sixteen years elapsed from the initial Republican presidential success to the first statewide victory. Another twelve years passed before Republicans won a state rather than a federal statewide office. By the mid-1990s, the GOP finally dominated Georgia's congressional delegation and held most statewide offices and 40 percent of the state legislative seats. But at that point the GOP stagnated, and by 2001, Democrats had taken back a U.S. Senate seat, a Public Service Commission seat, reclaimed the post of attorney general and picked up several state house seats. Despite these setbacks, Republican candidates for the state House and Senate had polled a majority of the votes cast for the state legislature in recent elections even as they have struggled to win 40 percent of the seats in these chambers. Despite frequent changes in election laws (Bullock 1998) and an extraordinary set of gerrymanders pushed through by Democrats in 2001, their unprecedented run of control of state government finally collapsed early in the new century. Like weary workers stacking sand bags in the face of a flood, Georgia Democrats' efforts proved insufficient to divert the GOP tide. Once the GOP breached the critical bulwark it quickly pushed its share of Senate seats to 60 percent and won a House majority in 2004, taking advantage of fairer electoral districts.

Democrats now find themselves at their weakest in more than 130 years. The maps in place for the state legislature make it unlikely that Democrats can regain majority status in either chamber during the remainder of the decade. While Republicans may have peaked in the Senate, they are likely to score additional gains in the House as senior Democrats—some of whom may find it difficult to adjust to minority status—retire.

The 2006 elections for constitutional offices take on heightened significance for Democrats. Their top two office holders, Lt. Gov. Mark Taylor and Secretary of State Cathy Cox passed on the 2004 Senate election in order to run for governor. If Gov. Perdue wins reelection, the brightest stars of the Democratic Party will have been extinguished. Moreover Republicans may win those two posts being vacated by Democrats.

On the other hand, if a Democrats wins the governorship in 2006, that will provide a base from which to begin rebuilding. A Democratic governor could veto Republican legislation and by using that threat promote enactment of some Democratic policy preferences. A Democratic governor would also be able to raise much-needed money for the party and help in candidate recruitment.

County office holders remain overwhelmingly Democratic (Bullock 1993). While Republicans win additional local offices with each election, Georgia's multitude of counties, most of which remain untouched by urban development, provide refuge for the declining numbers of "yellow-dog Democrats." White electors who eagerly vote Republican for president on down through state legislator retain traditional partisan loyalties when choosing sheriffs and county commissioners. The tradition of Democratic dominance in many communities remains so strong that, like a taboo, it goes unchallenged. The ambitious do not seriously consider running as Republicans in many counties (Lublin 2004). In some counties that regularly go Republican in top-of-the-ticket contests, the local Republican party remains small and inactive. A student, after attending a Republican meeting in a county where the GOP racks up majorities in statewide contests but has yet to score a victory locally, observed, "I was the only one there with any teeth."

The opposite pattern exists in a smaller number of suburban counties. Here Republicans dominate the ranks of local officeholders sometimes to the exclusion of Democrats. While there are relatively few Republican counties, a large share of the state's population lives in these suburban counties (Lublin 2004). As counties around Atlanta and other metropolitan areas develop, Republicans win local offices. A pattern that has frequently been repeated is for a county to elect a few Republicans to the county commission or school board and then, once the newcomers outnumber the natives, the county will have an all-Republican slate of officers in short order. In older Atlanta suburbs, yet another transformation is underway as Democrats have eliminated most Republicans from offices in DeKalb and Clayton Counties, both of which were majority black in 2000, and have even made gains in Cobb and Gwinnett Counties, which had been the most Republican bastions in the state in the early 1990s but are becoming more racially diverse.

Despite a lingering loyalty to Democrats in rural counties, Democratic claims on white voters have shrunk dramatically. Recent polls have shown Democrats constituting only a third of those who turn out while Republicans claimed the loyalty of more than 40 percent in the 2004 exit polls. As voters, especially the younger ones who have no ties to the Democratic Party, bring their local behavior in line with their party preferences up ticket, Republicans will score additional gains in local government.

REFERENCES

Aistrup, Joseph A. 1989. "Top-Down Republican Party Development in the South: A Test of Schlesinger's Theory." Presented at the annual meeting of the Midwest Political Science Association, Chicago, IL.

Bartley, Numan C. 1970. *From Thurmond to Wallace: Political Tendencies in Georgia, 1948–1968.* Baltimore: Johns Hopkins.

Baxter, Tom. 1996. "Rapid Suburban Growth Undercuts 'One Man, One Vote.'" *Atlanta Journal* (December 3): C2.

Bullock, Charles S., III. 1993. "Republican Officeholding at the Local Level in Georgia." *Southeastern Political Review* 21 (Winter): 113–31.

Bullock, Charles S., III. 1995. *Georgia Political Almanac, 1995–1996.* Atlanta: Cornerstone Publishing.

Bullock, Charles S., III, and Richard Dunn. 1996. "Election Roll-Off: A Test of Three Explanations." *Urban Affairs Review* 32 (September): 71–86.

Bullock, Charles S., III. 1998. "Georgia: Election Rules and Partisan Conflict." In *The New Politics of the Old South,* edited by Charles S. Bullock III and Mark J. Rozell. Lanham, MD: Rowman and Littlefield.

Bullock, Charles S., III, and Richard E. Dunn. 1999. "The Demise of Racial Districting and the Future of Black Representation." *Emory Law Review* 48 (Fall): 1209–1252.

Bullock, Charles S., III, and Robert P. Furr. 1997. "Race, Turnout, Runoff and Election Outcomes: The Defeat of Wyche Fowler." *Congress and the Presidency* 24 (Spring): 1–16.

Campbell, J. Phil. 1983. Personal interview, March 1.

Duncan, Russell. 1995. *Entrepreneur for Equality.* Athens: University of Georgia.

Fenno, Richard F., Jr. 1996. *Senators on the Campaign Trail: The Politics of Representation.* Norman: University of Oklahoma.

Holmes, Robert A. 1998. "Reapportionment Strategies in the 1990s: The Case of Georgia." In *Race and Redistricting in the 1990s,* edited by Bernard Grofman. Bronx, NY: Agathon Press.

Key, V. O. 1949. *Southern Politics.* New York: Knopf.

Lublin, David. 2004. *The Republican South.* Princeton, NJ: Princeton University Press.

Johnson, Eric. Election email memo.

Miller v. Johnson, 115 S.Ct. 2475 (1995).

Secrest, Alan, and Mike Sanelli. 1995. "A Precinct-level Analysis of Racial Voting Patterns in Georgia's 1994 General Election for Governor." Alexandria, VA: Cooper & Secrest Associates.

Williams, Clint. 2000. "Contest's Price Tag a Record." *Atlanta Journal* (November 25), p. G1.

Willson, Lauren, Whit Ayres, Cheryl Martin and Jon McHenry. 1999. *Georgia Voting Trends and the 1998 Election.* Atlanta: Ayres, McHenry and Associates.

NOTES

1. Democrats might poll more of the white vote in recent elections if they offered stronger challenges to Republican incumbents.

2. Georgia registration materials indicate the race of the voter, facilitating the development of a mailing list of black registrants.

3. The 1998 exit poll estimated that blacks cast 29 percent of the vote while the 23 percent figures comes from the voter validation study done by Georgia's secretary of state. Exit poll figures may reflect efforts by the GOP to encourage its supporters to vote absentee, which would result in an election-day electorate that was blacker than the full set of participants. The state did not undertake voter validation efforts until 1996 so that we rely on exit polls for earlier years and the 2000 voter validation results were not available when this went to press. Absentee voting was lower in earlier years so that this potential cause of distortion in exit polls should be less severe.

4. This turnout figure comes from the state's voter validation program and is six points lower than the 29 percent estimate produced by exit polls.

5. After Fowler's 1992 general election runoff defeat, Democrats changed the law so that 45 percent of the vote sufficed in a general election. This change enabled Max Cleland to win the 1996 Senate election without a runoff.

3

❦——✦——❦

Alabama: From One Party to Competition, and Maybe Back Again

Patrick R. Cotter

I n the days of the "old" South, relatively few Alabama citizens participated in the state's politics. Those who did were whiter, more male
and better off than the public as a whole. Most notably, African-American
citizens were almost totally excluded from the state's elections, despite
the fact that race was a central concern of Alabama's politics. What did
dominate the state was a disorganized, multi-factional Democratic Party.
Year after year, Democratic candidates from president to the most local of
offices won the support of large majorities of the state's voters. Meanwhile, the Republican Party was largely, but not totally, absent from the
state as a political organization, among officeholders and in the hearts
and minds of Alabama's voters.

Now Alabama's politics are quite different. The state has a much larger
and more representative electorate. African Americans actively participate in all parts of Alabama's politics, including holding public office. In
the last several decades, party competition has emerged, developed and
matured in the state. Both parties now have active organizations throughout the state. Both Democrats and Republicans are found among Alabama
officeholders. Both parties can also claim the allegiance of a significant
number of the state's citizens. Indeed, Republicans now not only are competitive in Alabama but may be on the verge of becoming the state's dominant party.

As the chapters in this volume show, other southern states have experi-

enced similar political changes since the days of the old South. The pace
and process of Alabama's political transformation is, however, unique.
The same may be true for the state's political future.

POLITICAL CHANGE IN ALABAMA

Participation. During the first half of the 1900s, voting turnout in Alabama
was low, even compared to other southern states (Key 1949, 492). Then,
generally less than one in five of the state's voting-age population participated in Alabama elections. One source of this low participation rate (in
addition to the low levels of education and income found among the
state's citizens, and the absence of competitive parties mobilizing voters)
was the structural barriers the state erected, which made it difficult for
many Alabamians to register and then actually cast a ballot. Alabama was
not alone among southern states in using disfranchisement devices such
as the poll tax, literary tests and a white primary. Alabama's suffrage
restrictions, and particularly its cumulative poll tax, were, however, especially effective (Strong 1972).

The region's mid-1900s "Second Reconstruction" slowly removed or
reduced many of the structural barriers to registration and voting found
within the South. Alabama's political leaders mostly resisted efforts to
reduce voting barriers. Ultimately, however, the state's (and region's)
resistance failed. As a consequence, voter turnout in the state's general
elections for president (and other offices) began to increase (table 3.1).[1]
The 1965 Voting Rights Act was especially important in this change. Its
effect is seen in the particularly large jump in voting turnout that
occurred in Alabama between 1964 and 1968.

With the higher rate of turnout in the state's elections, voting participation in Alabama has for the last twenty years or so been quite close to
the national average. Indeed, in the recent 2004 presidential election, the
estimated turnout rate among the voting-age population in Alabama (54.8
percent) was almost exactly that found in the nation as a whole (55.5 percent).

Moreover, not only was voting turnout low in the old South but also
those who did participate were quite unrepresentative of the population
as a whole. With the increase in voting participation since the mid-1900s,
Alabama's electorate has become more representative, especially with
regard to race and gender. Indeed, research shows that racial differences

Table 3.1.   Voter Turnout in Presidential Elections, United States and Alabama, 1920–2004

Year	*Percent of Voting-Age Population Voting*		
	U.S.	*Alabama*	*Difference*
1920	44.2%	20.5%	23.7%
1924	44.5%	13.4%	31.1%
1928	52.4%	19.0%	33.4%
1932	53.2%	17.6%	35.6%
1936	57.7%	18.7%	39.0%
1940	59.8%	18.9%	40.9%
1944	54.0%	15.0%	39.0%
1948	51.8%	12.6%	39.2%
1952	62.2%	24.1%	38.1%
1956	60.1%	27.6%	32.5%
1960	63.8%	31.1%	32.7%
1964	61.9%	36.1%	25.8%
1968	61.1%	52.9%	8.2%
1972	55.2%	43.4%	11.8%
1976	53.7%	46.8%	6.9%
1980	53.1%	49.1%	4.0%
1984	54.0%	50.9%	3.1%
1988	50.7%	47.0%	3.7%
1992	55.2%	55.2%	0.0%
1996	48.9%	47.7%	1.2%
2000	51.3%	50.0%	1.3%
2004	55.5%	54.8%	0.7%

Source: Rusk (2001), Federal Election Commission, U.S. Bureau of the Census, 2004.

in participation have largely disappeared within the state (Cohen, Cotter and Coulter 1983).

An increasing number of African Americans holding elected office within the state is another indictor of how political participation patterns have changed within Alabama. In the days of the old South, Alabama had virtually no elected black officials. Now African Americans fill about 17 percent of the roughly 4,400 elected government positions within the state (Bositis 2003).

African Americans currently hold an even larger proportion, about 25 percent, of the seats in the state legislature. Indeed, Alabama is the only state in which the proportion of African Americans in the state legislature is equal to the percentage of blacks in the population as a whole (Bositis 2003).

An African American has held one of the state's seven congressional seats since 1992. Democrat Artur Davis, the state's current African-American congressional representative, won his seat in 2002 when he defeated incumbent Earl Hilliard. Davis's victory was seen as part of a generational shift in African-American political leadership in the South (Halbfinger 2002).

Party competition. In the days of the old South, Alabama's electoral politics were solidly Democratic. While there was some Republican presence in parts of the state, overall the GOP had little influence (Webb 1997). Instead, as tables 3.2 and 3.3 show, only a small percentage of the Alabama voters typically supported Republican presidential or gubernatorial candidates during the first half of the 1900s.

Republicans did enjoy a temporary increase in support in 1928 when

Table 3.2. Republican Support in Presidential Elections, United States and Alabama, 1920–2004

Year	Percent of Total Vote		
	U.S.	Alabama	Difference
1920	60.3%	31.9%	28.4%
1924	54.0%	26.0%	28.0%
1928	58.2%	48.5%	9.7%
1932	39.6%	14.1%	25.5%
1936	36.5%	12.8%	23.7%
1940	44.8%	14.3%	30.5%
1944	45.9%	18.2%	27.7%
1948	45.1%	19.0%	26.1%
1952	55.1%	35.0%	20.1%
1956	57.4%	39.4%	18.0%
1960	49.6%	41.7%	7.9%
1964	38.5%	69.5%	− 31.0%
1968	43.4%	14.0%	29.4%
1972	60.7%	72.4%	− 11.7%
1976	48.0%	42.6%	5.4%
1980	50.8%	48.8%	2.0%
1984	58.8%	60.5%	− 1.7%
1988	53.4%	59.2%	− 5.8%
1992	37.4%	47.6%	− 10.2%
1996	40.7%	50.1%	− 9.4%
2000	47.9%	56.5%	− 8.6%
2004	50.7%	62.5%	− 11.8%

Source: Rusk (2001), Federal Election Commission, U.S. Bureau of the Census, Alabama Secretary of State.

Table 3.3. **Republican Support in Alabama Gubernatorial Elections, 1922–2002**

	Percent of Total Vote
1922	21.3%
1926	18.8%
1930*	38.2%
1934	12.7%
1938	12.5%
1942	10.5%
1946	11.3%
1950	8.9%
1954	26.6%
1958	11.2%
1962	0.0%
1966	31.0%
1970	0.0%
1974	14.8%
1978	25.9%
1982	39.1%
1986	56.3%
1990	52.1%
1994	50.3%
1998	42.1%
2002	49.2%

* Independent candidate

Source: Rusk (2001); Alabama Secretary of State.

the state's Democrats split over the presidential nomination of Al Smith, the Catholic, anti-Prohibition governor of New York. This split continued into the 1930 Alabama state election. However, unity returned with the Depression, the election of Franklin Roosevelt and the popularity of his New Deal programs among Democrats (Rogers, Ward, Atkins and Flynt 1994). These same factors further weakened the state's Republican party in terms of both organizational strength and voter support (Webb 1997).

In the post–World War II years, Republican strength in Alabama began to grow. In particular Dwight Eisenhower in 1952 and 1956 and then Richard Nixon in 1960 each received about 40 percent of the presidential vote in Alabama—roughly double the support received by any other Republican presidential candidate in the preceding twenty years. This increase in GOP support was aided by the state's growing urban population and economic development, the policy positions taken by the national parties which resulted in some of the state's young business leaders become active within the GOP, and by splits among Alabama Democratic leaders over both civil rights and economic issues (Strong 1972; Barnard 1974).

A major breakthrough occurred for Alabama Republicans in 1964. In that year's presidential contest Barry Goldwater won almost 70 percent of the state's vote. The GOP also won several of the state's congressional seats in 1964, some of which they continue to hold.

Republican support plummeted in 1968, when Alabama's own George Wallace was an Independent Party presidential candidate. However, in the 1972 contest, Richard Nixon won a landslide within the state, receiving more than 70 percent of the vote against George McGovern.

In 1976, Jimmy Carter reclaimed Alabama for Democrats. However, at least as of this date, 1976 was the last time that Democrats won a presidential contest in the state. Instead, beginning with a narrow Ronald Reagan victory against Carter, Republicans have carried Alabama in each of the presidential elections conducted during the last quarter-century. The GOP's margin of victory in some of these contests has been relatively small. Still, in each presidential election since 1984, Alabama has voted more Republican than has the nation as a whole.

Republican strength has also grown in Alabama below the office of president. However, while the direction has been the same, the pace of partisan change at the state level has been slower, even when compared to other parts of the South. The most likely source of this distinctiveness is the political career of George Wallace. (For discussions of Wallace's political career see, for example, Carter 1995 and Permaloff and Grafton 1995).

When Key (1949) wrote about Alabama politics during the days of the old South, he noted the general lack of organization and continuity in the state's electoral politics. In short, Alabama lacked a durable faction such as the Byrd organization in Virginia or the Crump machine in Tennessee. Similarly, Alabama had no spectacular political figure, such as Eugene Talmadge in Georgia, who could personally dominate the state's politics over the course of several elections.

George Wallace's almost thirty-year-long career changed this situation. Indeed, when Wallace finally retired from electoral politics in 1986 it was noted that for Alabamians, "His endurance as a political figure is such that no voter younger than 50 can recall participating in a gubernatorial election in which George Wallace was not a candidate or at least a controlling influence" (Schmidt 1986).

Wallace's longevity (he was elected governor in 1962, 1970, 1974 and 1982, and his wife Lurleen was elected governor in 1966) was based upon his considerable political skills and his ability to be both an economic progressive and a racial (and later a social) conservative. In particular, Wallace won his first election to governor by taking an unqualified position in support of segregation. As he told one 1962 campaign rally, "As governor of your state I will stand strong for segregation. Some people say you are too strong, but how can you be too strong in what you believe? There is no middle ground. You are either for it or against it" (*Anniston Star* 1962).

Wallace later apologized for his segregationist stance. He also claimed that the motivation behind his actions had been misinterpreted. "Our actions in being anti-big government were translated into being racist" (*Anniston Star* 1982).

Throughout his career Wallace also consistently portrayed himself as a spokesperson and a protector of Alabama's interests, particularly against what he argued was an intrusive and unresponsive national government. Explaining his appeal among the state's voters, Wallace explained, "The reason they prefer me is that I have been representative of the average citizen of Alabama. I have not been the voice of the special interests in Birmingham and Montgomery. I didn't let the big-money interests run me" (Barton 1982).

At the same time, Wallace pursued distributative public policies, best remembered in Alabama in the form of free textbooks for public school students and an extensive system of community colleges located throughout the state. For example, when accused in his 1982 campaign of being a big-spending liberal, Wallace replied, "I'm going to be a big spender on education, a big spender on roads, a big spender on county roads, a big spender on the disadvantaged. . . . If that makes me a liberal, then I'm a liberal" (Funk 1982).

Wallace's blend of issue positions made him a difficult candidate to run against. This was particularly true for Alabama Republicans, who found that they could not outflank Wallace on social or racial issues but were themselves easy targets for his populist appeals as a representative of the average Alabamian. As a consequence, as long as Wallace remained active in Alabama's politics, GOP strength in state elections remained relatively weak.

Wallace finally did retire from state politics during the early stages of the 1986 gubernatorial election. This action set off a rancorous conflict over control of the Democrat Party (for a discussion of this campaign, see Cotter and Gordon 1999). Eventually this developed into a contest between Lieutenant Governor Bill Baxley, supported by education, civil rights and labor groups within the Democratic Party, and Attorney General Charlie Graddick, supported by business and conservative interests. Graddick barely defeated Baxley (by a 8,756-vote margin out of more than 900,000 votes cast) in the Democratic runoff. Baxley, however, refused to concede defeat. Instead, Graddick was soon challenged in federal court over whether, as attorney general, he had violated the preclearance provision of the 1965 Voting Rights Act by issuing an order that the existing Democratic Party rule prohibiting Republican primary voters from "crossing-over" and voting in the Democratic runoff election should not be enforced. After a series of hearings, the court supported this challenge. Consequently, Graddick was denied the nomination and, instead, a party committee named Baxley as the Democratic gubernatorial candidate. The uproar this decision caused led many of the state's voters to support, and ultimately elect, the heretofore unknown and ignored Republican candidate, Guy Hunt.

Hunt's victory altered political patterns within Alabama. In the eyes of the state's media and campaign contributors, winning the Democratic primary was no longer "tantamount" to victory in the general election. Nor, for potential candidates, was it any longer necessary to be a Democrat in order to have a reasonable chance of winning elections. Further, by using his appointment power to fill vacancies, Hunt could give some Republican candidates the advantage of incumbency.

In 1990, Hunt won a narrow reelection campaign against Paul Hubbert, the head of the powerful Alabama Education Association. Shortly into his second term, however, Hunt was charged with violating the state's ethic laws regarding his personal use of funds donated to his first inauguration. When he was convicted of these charges, Hunt was removed from office and replaced by the Democratic Lieutenant Governor, Jim Folsom Jr.

In the 1994 gubernatorial election, Folsom, the son of a former two-time Alabama governor, faced Fob James. James had first come onto the state's political scene in 1978. In that year, George Wallace was constitutionally barred from seeking a third consecutive term as governor. In what was then seen as the end of the Wallace era, James, a one-time Republican official, entered the crowded Democratic gubernatorial primary. In his well-financed and effective media campaign, James portrayed himself as a successful businessman not tied to the state's existing political patterns or interests. James won the Democratic nomination and then easily defeated the token Republican gubernatorial candidate (future governor Guy Hunt) in the general election.

For a variety of reasons, some of which were outside his control, James proved to be a very unpopular governor. As a result, fulfilling a campaign promise, James did not seek reelection in 1982. His unpopularity, however, set the stage for Wallace's return to the governorship in 1982.

James tried to regain the Democratic gubernatorial nomination in both 1986 and 1990. Each of these efforts was unsuccessful, with James finishing third in both years' Democratic gubernatorial primaries.

In 1994, James switched back to the Republican Party and won the GOP's nomination for governor. That year's nationwide GOP landslide resulted in a number of Republican victories, some of them unexpected, in Alabama. One of these unexpected winners was Fob James who narrowly (50.3 to 49.4 percent) defeated Folsom in the race for governor.

In office, James once again proved to be a controversial and unpopular governor. As a result of his apparent vulnerability, James faced several serious candidates in the 1998 GOP primary. Ultimately, this led to a runoff election between James, who, as a vocal advocate for issues such as school prayer, had strong support among social conservatives, and Winton Blount, a Montgomery businessman and son of "Red" Blount, one of the pioneering members of the state's post-War Republican Party (Strong 1972). James won this primary contest but apparently had little remaining resources or support to draw upon in the general election. As a result, James was defeated by a convincing margin (57.2 to 42.1 percent) in November by Democratic Lieutenant Governor Don Siegelman. In his campaign, Siegelman had focused on the need for Alabama to have a state lottery. The proceeds of a lottery, he argued, would help address the problems facing the state's public education system.

Siegelman managed to get his lottery proposal (modeled on the plan used in Georgia) through the state legislature, and in 1999, a constitutional referendum was held on the issue. In the referendum campaign, Siegelman and his allies spent considerable resources telling voters of the benefits, such as college scholarship and preschool programs, which would result from adopting the "education lottery." Opponents of the measure raised three general objections to the measure. First, they argued that state-supported gambling was immoral. Second, they raised questions about which students would actually receive the lottery-funded college scholarships. Finally, opponents said that the proposed administrative arrangements for the lottery would lead to corruption (Cason 1999a).

In the end, voters rejected Siegelman's lottery proposal by a 45.8 to 54.2 percent margin. The lottery's failure indicates the political power of religious conservatives in the state. It also indicates the distrust that Alabamians have of the state government. As Jim Cooper, the head of Citizens Against Legalized Lottery, explained, part of his group's message to Alabama voters was that "you can't trust politicians" (Cason 1999b).

CONTEMPORARY POLITICS

Republican success in Alabama's presidential elections continued in the 2000 contest. The national Democratic campaign ignored the state throughout the year, deciding it was better to focus campaign resources on more friendly locations. In response, George W. Bush's campaign, feeling confident of victory, also largely by-passed the state. On Election Day, Bush defeated Al Gore in Alabama by 56.5 to 41.6 percent.

Also in 2000, Republican strength at the state level increased with GOP victories in each of the five positions up for election on Alabama's Supreme Court. The most notable among these winners was the GOP's candidate for Chief Justice, Roy Moore. Moore, a circuit court judge from Etowah County, had attracted much attention prior to the 2000 election as a result of disputes concerning his courtroom display of the Ten Commandments and his practice of starting court sessions with a prayer. In the Republican primary, Moore relatively easily defeated several opponents, including an incumbent member of the court seeking to become the chief justice. In the general election, Moore received about 55 percent of the vote, roughly the same level of support won by each of the Republican candidates facing a Democratic candidate for a seat on the Supreme Court.

Once in office, Moore had a 5,280-pound granite block, inscribed with the Ten Commandments, placed in the rotunda of the state judicial building. Eventually, a federal judged ordered Moore to remove the Ten Commandments monument. When Moore refused to obey the court order, the other justices on the court had the monument taken from the building. Later, because of his refusal to obey the court order, Moore was himself removed from office. (For more information about Moore, see Fisher 2004; Johnson 2004.)

Alabama's pattern of competitive gubernatorial elections continued in 2002. Incumbent Don Siegelman easily won renomination in the Democratic primary. Similarly, Congressman Bob Riley, with the apparent support of much of the state's Republican leadership, easily defeated Lieutenant Governor Steve Windom in the GOP gubernatorial primary.[2]

In his general election campaign, Siegelman pointed to the achievements of his administration. He also revived the idea of a state lottery. Throughout the last part of his administration, however, Siegelman was dogged by allegations of corruption regarding state contracts and programs.[3] Riley's campaign focused on these allegations, arguing to the state's voters that as a new face in state government he represented "honest change" (Cason 2002).

For several days after the polls closed, the actual winner of the 2002 gubernatorial election was uncertain. Eventually, however, Riley was declared the winner, defeating Siegelman by an extremely narrow 49.2 to 48.9 percent margin.

As a member of Congress, Bob Riley had never wandered from the Republican anti-tax orthodoxy. Thus, it was somewhat of a surprise when, shortly after becoming governor, Riley proposed a state constitutional amendment involving a massive $1.2 billion tax reform and government accountability plan.

In the campaign leading to a vote on the amendment, the governor argued that his reform plan was needed to address a looming state budget crisis and to address shortcomings in the state education system. Riley also appealed to voters to support his program on moral grounds, arguing that the plan would correct the inequities and unfairness of the state's current tax system. (For descriptions and analyses of the 2003 referendum campaign, see Cason 2003; Wilson 2003.)

Some of the state's business and religious organizations supported Riley's plan, while others opposed it. Most Democratic officeholders and groups endorsed the proposal. Alabama's Republicans, however, were split, with a narrow majority of the party's state executive committee voting to oppose the governor's proposal. Opponents of Riley's plan argued that reduced spending was a better solution to the state's budget problems. They also pointed out that the taxes raised by the proposal were not earmarked for education and could in fact be used for any purpose by state officeholders.

Alabama voters overwhelmingly rejected Riley proposal, 32.5 to 67.5 percent. Its defeat was attributed to citizens' opposition to higher taxes, the ineffectiveness of the pro-reform campaign and Alabamians' general distrust of state government.

Republican success in Alabama continued in the 2004 election. In particular, the state's 2004 presidential campaign was essentially a replay of the 2000 contest. Again, the national Democratic ticket largely ignored the state. During the general election campaign, John Kerry did no campaigning in the state, while John Edwards made one quick fund-raising visit to Birmingham. Similarly, neither George W. Bush nor Richard Cheney visited the state during the presidential campaign. In November, Bush received about 62.5 percent of the total vote, the highest total for a GOP presidential candidate since 1972.

Also in 2004, several supporters of former Chief Justice Roy Moore entered the GOP primary as candidates for positions on the Alabama Supreme Court. Only one of these, Tom Parker, won the party's nomination and then was elected in November. The GOP did, however, win each of the Supreme Court positions up for election in 2004. Republicans now control every seat on the state's highest court.

The 2004 general election also saw another contested constitutional referendum. This involved a proposal to remove segregationist-era language from the state constitution. Among the specific clauses to be eliminated by the proposed amendment was one that said, "Nothing in this Constitution shall be construed as creating or recognizing any right to education." Governor Riley, and many other state leaders, supported the amendment. Others, including Roy Moore, opposed the proposal, saying that removing the clause regarding the state's obligation regarding education would open the door to court-mandated tax increases to support education. On Election Day, the proposed amendment was narrowly defeated, 49.9 to 50.1 percent. This defeat, in combination with the outcome of the 2003 tax referendum, added to the perception that Governor Riley was politically vulnerable.

The 2004 elections also saw Republicans continue their domination of the state's congressional delegation. Since 1992, the GOP has controlled five of the state's seven House seats. Following the 2000 redistricting, only one of the Republican held seats is seen as competitive. Republican Mike Rogers took over this seat in 2002 when Bob Riley decided to run for governor. Despite the district's potential competitiveness, Rogers has fairly decisively defeated his serious, but underfunded, Democrat opponents in both 2002 and 2004.

Currently both of Alabama's U.S. Senators are Republicans. One of these, Richard Shelby, was initially elected as a Democrat. He switched parties the day after the 1994 election—a contest in which Republicans gained a majority of seats in Congress. Shelby faced no serious opposition in winning reelection in either 1998 or 2004. Alabama's other Senator, Jeff Sessions, was elected (with 52.5 percent of the total vote) to an open seat in 1996. He was reelected in 2002, defeating his serious (but again underfunded) Democratic opponent, Susan Parker, by a 58.6 to 39.8 percent margin.

The number of Republican officeholders has also grown within state governments. Here, however, Democrats remain strong, though at a level of dominance far less than that found during the days of the Solid South. In particular, Democrats continue to hold a majority of the seats in both houses of the state legislature (table 3.4). During the 2004 legislative session, Democrats held about 60 percent of House seats and almost 70 percent of the Senate seats.

Democrats also currently hold several of the state constitutional offices such as lieutenant governor, secretary of state, and commissioner of agriculture. The state treasurer, auditor and attorney general are, however, Republicans.

In terms of organizational strength, the findings of the Southern Grassroots Party Activist Project survey show that the two parties are about evenly matched within Alabama.[4] This organizational parity is illustrated in the responses given to questions that asked Alabama's Democratic and Republican county chairs and committee members if they had participated in different types of campaign activities. Overall, table 3.5 shows about an equal level of campaign activity within each group of party activists. For example, more than 70 percent of both Democratic and Republican activists had been involved in distributing campaign posters, lawn signs and literature. Similarly, while Republicans were more likely to have contributed money to a campaign, Democrats were more active in voter-registration activities.

Finally, measures of party identification show that there has also been a rough parity in the number of Democratic and Republican identifiers in Alabama since the 1980s (table 3.6). Before then, Democrats had a clear advantage in the state. Analysis of the party identification data shows, as is the case elsewhere in the country, that African Americans in Alabama are overwhelmingly Democratic in their party attachments. Conversely, white Alabamians are more likely to identify with the Republican than the Democratic Party. Further, among whites in Alabama, males and

Table 3.4. Partisan Makeup of Alabama State Legislature, 1954–2004.

	Percent Democrats*	
	State House	State Senate
1954	100%	100%
1956	100%	100%
1958	100%	100%
1960	100%	100%
1962	98%	100%
1964	98%	100%
1966	100%	97%
1968	100%	97%
1970	98%	100%
1972	98%	100%
1974	100%	100%
1976	98%	97%
1978	96%	100%
1980	95%	100%
1982	92%	91%
1984	83%	80%
1986	85%	86%
1988	81%	80%
1990	78%	80%
1992	78%	77%
1994	70%	66%
1996	69%	63%
1998	68%	63%
2000	60%	66%
2002	61%	71%
2004	60%	69%

* The State House has 105 members. Before 1974, it had 106 members. The State Senate has 35 members. Percentages are based upon total membership (including vacancies).
Source: Statistical Abstract of the United States, Alabama State Legislature web site (www.legislature.state .al.us).

more educated citizens are more likely than others to be Republicans (Cotter and Stovall 1996, Cotter 2002).

SUMMARY

Again, Alabama's politics today are far different from the low-participation, unequal-involvement, one-party patterns found in the state fifty to one hundred years ago. Political participation in Alabama is now both wide-

Table 3.5. **"Which of the Following Activities Did You Do in Recent Election Campaigns?"**

	% Did in recent campaign	
	Democrats	Republicans
Distributed posters or lawn signs	74%	82%
Distributed campaign literature	73%	78%
Contributed money to campaigns	62%	79%
Organized campaign events	44%	38%
Organized door-to-door canvassing	38%	25%
Sent mailings to voters	39%	44%
Conducted voter-registration drives	28%	20%
Arranged fundraising activities	28%	40%
Organized telephone campaigns	27%	27%
Dealt with campaign media	25%	31%
Utilized public opinion surveys	11%	9%
Purchased billboard space	7%	6%
Helped to construct or maintain a campaign Web site	4%	4%

Source: 2001 Southern Grassroots Party Activists Project.

spread and at a relatively high level. Further, Democratic dominance over the state has ended, while Republican strength has grown. As a result, Alabama's party politics are now more balanced in terms of office holding, organizational strength and party affiliations. In sum, Alabama is now a politically active and competitive state.

It is not difficult to imagine that Alabama will continue to be a politically competitive state. However, given the general direction of political change since the days of the old South, it is also not difficult to see Republicans increasingly becoming the state's dominant party.[5]

Which of these outcomes—continued competitiveness or Republican dominance—occurs in Alabama will undoubtedly be influenced by a variety of factors. One of these is the conduct of partisan politics at the national level. Specifically, the chance of Republican domination in Alabama is probably enhanced if Democratic presidential candidates (and national congressional campaign organizations) continue to ignore the state. In terms of fundraising, organizational development and candidate recruitment, it is difficult to see how the Alabama Democratic Party can maintain itself if it experiences a landslide defeat every four years.

The state's partisan future will also, obviously, be influenced by political activities taking place within Alabama. Particularly important here is the potential for serious conflict within the GOP. Alabama's Republicans

Table 3.6.   Party Identification in Alabama, 1981–2001.

Year	Strong + Weak Republican	Independent Republican	Independent Independent	Independent Democrat	Strong + Weak Democrat	Partisan Balance*
1981	24%	10	9	11	47	23%
1982	18%	9	8	10	55	37%
1983	20%	10	10	11	50	30%
1984	27%	12	9	6	45	18%
1985	29%	10	6	11	44	15%
1986	27%	12	10	9	40	13%
1987	30%	14	6	8	43	13%
1988	30%	16	10	8	36	6%
1989	38%	11	6	9	36	−2%
1990	26%	12	13	10	39	13%
1991	28%	15	10	10	37	9%
1992	30%	16	12	8	34	4%
1993	31%	10	11	10	37	6%
1994	31%	14	8	11	36	5%
1995	38%	12	8	10	33	−5%
1996	35%	12	8	9	36	1%
1997	32%	15	10	12	31	−1%
1998	32%	12	8	10	38	6%
1999	32%	11	10	10	36	4%
2001	37%	10	10	5	38	1%
2003	38%	9	7	6	39	1%

* Partisan balance 1—Strong/Weak Democrats—Strong/Weak Republicans
  Partisan balance 2—All Democrats—All Republicans

Source: University of Alabama/ Southern Opinion Research surveys.

have experienced some internal divisions within recent years, as illustrated by the James-Blount primary fight in 1994, the divisions over Governor Riley's tax reform plan in 2003 and the conflict over the 2004 constitutional amendment concerning the state's obligation for public education. The growth, or even continuation, of these divisions is likely to hurt the GOP and help Alabama's Democrats. Just as the 1986 Democratic conflict between Graddick and Baxley opened the door for Republicans at the state level, a similar split among Republicans (most likely between social conservatives such as Roy Moore and more business-oriented Republicans such as Bob Riley) may work to maintain the current competitiveness of the state's politics.

Finally, another factor that may contribute to continued competition is the lack of trust Alabamians express toward state government. This cynicism/alienation, earlier noted by both Key (1949) and Strong (1972), was recently manifested in the outcome of the 1999 lottery referendum and the 2003 tax reform amendment. Partisan competitiveness, at least in the form of rotation in office, may remain in Alabama if the state's alienated and cynical voters continue their recent pattern of frequently replacing one party's group of "rascals" with another.

REFERENCES

Anniston Star. 1962. "Jefferson voters asked by Wallace." May 16, 1A.

Anniston Star. 1982. "Wallace defends his reputation." October 21, 7.

Barnard, William D. 1974. *Dixiecrats and Democrats: Alabama Politics, 1942–1950.* University, AL: University of Alabama Press.

Barton, Olivia. 1982. "Tammy stands by Wallace at Rainsville political rally." *Birmingham News,* September 1, 3A.

Bositis, David A. 2003. *Black Elected Officials: A Statistical Survey, 2001.* Washington DC: Joint Center for Political and Economic Studies (www.jointcenter.org).

Carter, Dan T. 1995. *The Politics of Rage: George Wallace, the Origins of the New Conservatism, and the Transformation of American Politics.* New York: Simon & Schuster.

Cason, Mike, 1999a. "Lottery battle nears end." *Montgomery Advertiser,* October 10, 1A.

Cason, Mike. 1999b. "Lottery fails." *Montgomery Advertiser,* October 13, 1A.

Cason, Mike. 2002. "Riley awaits final count." *Montgomery Advertiser,* November 6, 1A.

Cason, Mike. 2003 "Alabama Governor Hears message from Voters; Cuts to Come." *Montgomery Advertiser,* September 10, 1A.

Clark, John A., and Charles Prysby. 2003. "Introduction: Studying Southern Political Party Activists." *American Review of Politics* 24: 1–19.

Clark, John A., and Charles L. Prysby (eds.). 2004. *Southern Political Party Activists: Patterns of Conflict and Change, 1991–2001.* Lexington, KY: University Press of Kentucky.

Cohen, Jeffrey E., Patrick R. Cotter and Philip B. Coulter. 1983. "The Changing Structure of Southern Political Participation. Matthews and Prothro 20 Years Later." *Social Science Quarterly* 64: 536–49.

Cotter, Patrick R., and Tom Gordon.1999. "Alabama: The GOP Rises in the Heart of Dixie." In *Southern Politics in the 1990s,* edited by Alexander P. Lamis. Baton Rouge: Louisiana State University Press.

Cotter, Patrick R. 2002. "Alabama: a 'Small Time' Election. In *The 2000 Presidential Election in the South,* eds. Robert P. Steed and Laurence W. Moreland. Westport, CT: Praeger.

Cotter, Patrick R., and James G. Stovall. 1996. "Party Identification and Political Change in Alabama: a mid-1990s update." *The American Review of Politics* 17: 193–211.

Davis, John, and Jannell McGrew. 2004. "Judge guts evidence; Siegelman case over." *Montgomery Advertiser*, October 6, 1A.

Fisher, Samuel H. III. 2004. "Judge Roy Moore: Moore may be Less." Paper presented at the 2004 Southern Political Science Association Meeting, New Orleans.

Funk, Tim. 1982 "Flashes of old Wallace Rouse Huntsville Audience." *Anniston Star*, September 24, 5A.

Halbfinger, David M. 2002. "Generational battle turns nasty in Alabama Primary." *New York Times*, June 3.

Johnson, Bob. 2004. "Judge details display fight in new book *Ten Commandments.*" *Mobile Register*. December 30, 2A.

Key, V.O. 1949. *Southern Politics*. New York: Knopf.

McWhorter, Diane. 2001. *Carry Me Home: The Climatic Battle of the Civil Rights Revolution*. New York: Simon & Schuster.

Permaloff, Anne, and Carl Grafton. 1995. *Political Power in Alabama: The More Things Change. . . .* Athens: University of Georgia Press.

Rogers, William Warren, Robert David Ward, Leah Rawls Atkins and Wayne Flynt. 1994. *Alabama: The History of a Deep South State*. Tuscaloosa: University of Alabama Press.

Rusk, Jerrold G. 2001. *A Statistical History of the American Electorate*. Washington, DC: CQ Press.

Schmidt, William E. 1986 "Ending an Era, Wallace Announces He Will Retire," *New York Times*. April 3, 1A, 16A.

Strong, Donald S. 1972. "Alabama: Transition and Alienation." In *The Changing Politics of the South*, edited by William C. Havard. Baton Rouge: Louisiana State University Press.

Thornton, J. Mills III. 2002. *Dividing Lines: Municipal Politics and the Struggle for Civil Rights in Montgomery, Birmingham, and Selma*. Tuscaloosa: University of Alabama Press.

Valelly, Richard M. 2004. *The Two Reconstructions: The Struggle for Black Enfranchisement*. Chicago: University of Chicago Press.

Walton, Val, and John Archibald. 2004. "Siegelman indicated," *Birmingham News*. May 28, 1A.

Webb, Samuel L. 1997. *Two-Party Politics in the One-Party South: Alabama's Hill country, 1874–1920*. Tuscaloosa: University of Alabama Press.

Wilkerson-Freeman, Sarah. 2002. "The Second Battle for Woman Suffrage: Alabama White Women, the Poll Tax, and V.O. Key's Master Narrative of Southern Politics." *Journal of Southern History* 68: 333–74.

Wilson, Glynn. 2003. "Alabama vote roils alliances and stirs moral quandaries." *Christian Science Monitor*, September 8.

NOTES

1. See Valelly (2004) for a recent examination of disfranchisement issue in the South. Recent books by McWhorter (2001) and Thornton (2002) thoroughly exam-

ine some of the important civil rights activities that took place in Alabama. An interesting account of the successful effort to remove the cumulative component of Alabama's poll tax is presented by Wilkerson-Freeman (2002).

2. One by-product of the development of party competition within Alabama is that turnout in the state's primary election has declined. In 1986, more than 35 percent of Alabama's voting-age population participated in the Democratic primary. Since then, voting turnout in the state's Democratic primary has declined. In 2002, for example, about 13 percent of the state's voting-age population voted in the Democratic primary. In 1998, about 11 percent of Alabama's voting-age population voted in the Democratic primary. Some of this decline in Democratic primary turnout is balanced by an increase in the number of voters participating in the Republican primary. Indeed, in both 1998 (11 percent) and 2002 (11 percent), GOP primary turnout was about equal to that found in the Democratic primary. However, total primary turnout in both 1998 and 2002 was well less than that found in earlier years, including the years before the passage of the Voting Rights Act.

3. In 2004, the corruptions allegations against Siegelman finally turned into a federal indictment charging the former governor and several associates with conspiracy, fraud and theft (Walton and Archibald 2004). However, on the first day of the trial, the federal judge hearing the case dismissed most of the charges against Siegelman, citing a lack of evidence. This ruling in turn led federal prosecutors to drop the remaining charges (Davis and McGrew, 2004).

4. For information about the Grassroots Party Activists project see Clark and Prysby (2003, 2004).

5. Even if the GOP gains dominance over Alabama's electoral politics, the increased size and heterogeneity of the state's electorate make it unlikely that Republicans will gain the same level of uncontested control that Democrats enjoyed during the period of the old South.

4

Mississippi: Emergence of a Modern Two-Party State

David A. Breaux, Stephen D. Shaffer,
and Hilary B. Gresham

The Magnolia state has come a long way from the days depicted by V.O. Key (1949) when the Democratic Party was so dominant that most voters were regarded as "Yellow Dog" Democrats, people so partisan that in the general election they would vote for anyone nominated by Democrats, even a "yellow dog," and when Republicans were so rare that political observers joked that they held their party meetings in a phone booth. Today, Republicans have become so strong in federal elections that not since 1976 has a Democratic presidential candidate carried the state's electoral votes, and not since 1988 has even one of the state's two U.S. senators been a Democrat. Republicans have even become competitive in state elections, winning half of the two top statewide elected offices since 1987 and half of all statewide elected offices in 2003. In recent decades white voters, particularly conservatives, have shifted their partisan identifications dramatically toward the GOP, producing a genuine two-party state. Democrats remain powerful in less visible offices, such as the state legislature, where a biracial coalition of Democratic lawmakers continues to enact progressive legislation that belies the new Republicanism of this Deep South state.

GROWING REPUBLICANISM
IN FEDERAL ELECTIONS

The historic dominance of the Democratic Party in Mississippi, because of resentment over the Civil War and Reconstruction, was evident as late as the Franklin D. Roosevelt elections from 1932–1944, when in four consecutive elections well over 90 percent of Mississippians voted Democratic for president. The Democratic Party's adoption of a civil rights plank at its 1948 national convention prompted a walkout by Mississippi's delegation, which backed the States' Rights Party led by South Carolina governor Strom Thurmond and his vice presidential running mate, Mississippi governor Fielding Wright. The state's electorate, over 90 percent white until the federal Voting Rights Act of 1965, backed this racial protest ticket in 1948 as well as an Independent Democratic slate in 1960 instead of John Kennedy. Though the Magnolia State's electoral votes did go to Democrat Adlai Stevenson in 1952 and 1956, the Democrat's vote totals of 60 percent and 58 percent of the popular vote were relatively modest.

The Republican nomination of Barry Goldwater, an unapologetic conservative who even voted against the 1964 Civil Rights Act because of his ideological convictions that the federal government should respect states' rights, transformed the political landscape of Mississippi. Not only did the state's electoral votes go Republican for the first time since 1872, but the 87 percent popular vote total that Goldwater achieved swept in one GOP congressman, chicken farmer Prentiss Walker (Bass and DeVries 1977). Though Republicans lost this seat two years later, when Walker unsuccessfully sought to unseat U.S. Senator James Eastland, claiming that the Boll Weevil Democrat wasn't a "real" conservative, Mississippi once again rejected the Democratic presidential candidate in 1968 by backing the racially and socially conservative Independent, Alabama governor George Wallace.

The reelection of Richard Nixon in 1972 marked Mississippi's transition from backing candidates of racial protest, particularly non-major party candidates, to a willingness to embrace the more conservative major party nationally. Republican Nixon swept Mississippi's electoral votes with 78 percent of the popular vote, and his coattails helped elect two conservative GOP congressmen in more urban districts, Thad Cochran in the 4th district housing the state capital of Jackson, and Trent Lott in the 5th district encompassing the Gulf Coast cities (table 4.1). In both instances,

Table 4.1.   Two-Party Competition in Federal Elections, 1960–2004

Year	% Dem Vote for President	% Rep Vote for President	% Dem Vote for U.S. Senate	% Rep Vote for U.S. Senate	No. of Dem U.S. House Members	No. of Rep U.S. House Members
1960[a]	36.3%	24.7%	91.8%	8.2%	6	0
1962	—	—	—	—	5	0
1964	12.9	87.1	100.0	0	4	1
1966	—	—	65.6	26.7	5	0
1968[b]	23.0	13.5	—	—	5	0
1970	—	—	88.4	0	5	0
1972	19.6	78.2	58.1	38.7	3	2
1974	—	—	—	—	3	2
1976	49.6	47.7	100.0	0	3	2
1978[c]	—	—	31.8	45.1	3	2
1980	48.1	49.4	—	—	3	2
1982	—	—	64.2	35.8	3	2
1984	37.4	61.9	39.1	60.9	3	2
1986	—	—	—	—	4	1
1988	39.1	59.9	46.1	53.9	4	1
1990	—	—	0	100.0	5	0
1992[d]	40.8	49.7	—	—	5	0
1994	—	—	31.2	68.8	4	1
1996[e]	44.1	49.2	27.4	71.0	2	3
1998	—	—	—	—	3	2
2000	40.7	57.6	31.6	65.9	3	2
2002	—	—	0	84.6	2	2
2004	39.7	59.5	—	0	2	2

Source: America Votes series, Congressional Quarterly Publisher, Washington D.C. Editions 6–25. Edited by Richard M. Scammon, with Alice V. McGillivray starting with edition 12, joined also by Rhodes Cook starting in edition 22. 2004 results are from www.cnn.com.

Note: Percentages do not total 100 percent across rows due to minor candidates, some of whom are listed below.

[a] An unpledged Independent Democratic presidential slate received 39.0 percent of the vote.
[b] Wallace's American Independent Party won 63.5 percent of the presidential vote.
[c] Black Independent Charles Evers won 23.1 percent of the U.S. Senate vote.
[d] Ross Perot received 8.7 percent of the presidential vote in 1992.
[e] The Reform party received 5.8 percent of the presidential vote in 1996.

Republicans capitalized on the retirement of Democratic incumbents, divisive Democratic primaries with 6 or 10 candidates, and Nixon's popularity (76 percent and 87 percent of the vote in the 4th and 5th districts, respectively). Both Republican congressmen were popular, with Lott, for example, being the administrative assistant to retiring conservative Democratic congressman Bill Colmer. In addition, a black Independent's vote of 8 percent in the 4th district race split the normally Democratic vote, making Cochran's 48 percent a winning total. Mississippi voters were so content with replacing conservative Democrats with conservative Republicans that Cochran and Lott easily won reelection in 1974 with over 70 percent of the vote, despite the Watergate scandal that hurt Republicans nationally.

The nomination of "born again" southern Baptist Jimmy Carter, a former Georgia governor, in 1976 and the prevalence of conservative Boll Weevils among the Magnolia State's federal officeholders gave Democrats some electoral victories. Carter narrowly carried Mississippi in 1976, and then just as narrowly lost it to Reagan four years later. U.S. Senator John Stennis was unopposed in his 1976 reelection and then easily defeated state GOP executive director Haley Barbour in the senator's last campaign. Stennis's 1982 race illustrated how this courtly southern gentleman was willing and able to effectively use modern campaign tactics, as the Stennis camp ran a series of visually appealing television ads depicting the eighty-one-year-old as physically vigorous (Shaffer 1992, 101). Conservative Democratic congress members Sonny Montgomery and Jamie Whitten, who were eventually to rise to the positions of chairmen of the Veterans Affairs and Appropriations Committees, repeatedly won easy reelections. Democrats seemed to stumble only when their party was divided by race, as Senator Eastland's retirement in 1978 gave rise to a black Independent candidacy of Charles Evers, which split the normally Democratic vote to help elect Republican Thad Cochran as U.S. Senator (Lamis 1990, 53).

Cochran's shocking reelection in 1984 with 61 percent of the vote over popular former governor William Winter, marking the first Mississippi Republican winning a majority of the popular vote in a non-presidential bid since Reconstruction, showed how the partisan winds were blowing toward the GOP, as did Reagan's landslide reelection. Four years later, Stennis's retirement gave Republicans the opportunity to win the second Senate seat. Trent Lott used his massive campaign war chest to run a series of television ads that defused the claims that he was too conservative by painting him as a supporter of Social Security, college student loans, the environment and federal highway spending (Shaffer 1991). Both Republican U.S. senators have continually won landslide reelections. The GOP has also consistently won the state's presidential electoral votes with Clinton's 44 percent of the vote in his 1996 reelection being the Democratic high water mark after the Carter years (table 4.1).

Democrats remain more competitive in U.S. House contests, where their party's broad tent that today includes all ideologies permits them to select candidates that reflect the views of the local constituency's. The creation of a majority black Mississippi River "Delta" district in the 1980s eventually produced liberal African American congressmen Mike Espy in 1986 and Bennie Thompson in a 1993 special election. The 1989 special election of conservative white Democrat Gene Taylor in Trent Lott's old Gulf Coast district temporarily gave Democrats control of all five of the state's House districts. The retirement of Boll Weevil Democrats Jamie Whitten in 1994 and Sonny Montgomery in 1996 saw them replaced by conservative Republicans Roger Wicker and Chip Pickering in districts that had been voting Republican for president since at least 1984. Republicans temporarily gained a third congressional seat when moderate conservative Democrat Mike Parker switched to the GOP in 1996, but his retirement two years later to unsuccessfully run for governor was followed by the election of moderate Democrat Ronnie Shows.

Mississippi's loss of one House seat after reapportionment set up a titanic struggle in 2002 between two popular incumbents, Democrat Shows and Republican Pickering. In what turned out to be the fifth most-expensive congressional seat in the 2002 midterm election and the most expensive congressional campaign in the state's history, Pickering defeated Shows, 64 to 35 percent. The race initially attracted significant attention from party committees and interest groups; however, Pickering's substantial lead in both fundraising and pre-election polls caused much of the campaign activity to evaporate by Election Day.

After the state legislature could not reach a compromise over redistricting, the courts got involved. In the end, a new Third District map drawn by a panel of three Republican-appointed federal judges, and believed to favor Pickering over Shows, trumped the map drawn by a Hinds County chancery judge believed to favor Shows. The major difference was that the federally drawn map retained a larger percentage of Pickering's former district than Show's, and it reduced the black voting age population from 37 to 30 percent. While the new Third District includes small parts of metropolitan Jackson, the state's capital and largest city, it is a predominately rural district.

The two major party candidates had much in common. Both Chip Pickering and Ronnie Shows were born in Laurel, Mississippi. They are both white, Southern Baptists and claim to have a farming background. They both support pro-life, anti-gun control and pro-veterans' rights issues, and both favor a strong military. Their conservative credentials earned both candidates support from the National Right to Life, the National Rifle Association and the Family Research Council. Although similar in many ways, differences between Pickering and Shows became obvious during the campaign. Pickering voted for the North American Free Trade Agreement (NAFTA), while Shows, claiming that NAFTA would result in a loss of jobs for the state, voted against it. Pickering campaigned in favor of tort reform legislation that would cap the amount of money an individual could receive because of "pain and suffering," while Shows argued against such caps. Although he later modified his position, early in the campaign, Pickering favored privatizing Social Security. When confronted by Shows over changing his position on the issue, Pickering said he switched his position because of hard economic times, the unstable stock market and the possibility of war. Shows favored stashing Social Security funds in a "lock box" to prevent the government from raiding it. The American Conservative Union gave Pickering a lifetime rating of 96 out of 100, the highest conservative rating in the Mississippi delegation, and Shows received 66 out of 100, which ranks him as the second most-liberal member in the Mississippi delegation (Breaux 2003).

The biggest difference between Pickering and Shows that emerged during the campaign was the difference in comfort levels with their respective national parties. Pickering was extremely comfortable running as a Republican. He embraced his party's president, congressional leaders and policies. In August, President Bush visited the state and attended a $1,000-per-person fundraising luncheon in Jackson that was slated to raise $500,000 for Pickering. On the other hand, Shows was extremely uncomfortable running as a Democrat. He never talked about his party's last president or its congressional leaders. Pickering capitalized on this throughout the campaign by constantly reminding voters that the first vote cast by the new representative would be for the leader of the House of Representatives, and that while he would vote for a conservative speaker, Shows would vote for a liberal one (Breaux 2003).

The unique dynamics at work in Mississippi's 2002 Third District race brought about a record amount of campaign activity. The electoral advantages enjoyed by incumbent House members in general, and the popularity of the individual members of its state delegation, make it difficult to imagine that Mississippi will once again experience similar levels of congressional campaign activity in the foreseeable future.

PARTY IDENTIFICATION SHIFTS
IN THE ELECTORATE

Not only did Republicans make great gains in federal elections but the electorate's basic psychological identifications began to shift away from the Democratic Party and toward the GOP. As late as 1975, only 6 percent of voters in one survey regarded themselves as Republicans while 51 percent viewed themselves as Democrats (Bass and DeVries 1977, 216). Though Republicans made some gains among whites, even as late as 1982, when for the last time a Democratic U.S. Senator, John Stennis, was being reelected, a majority of whites remained Democratic in partisanship (table 4.2). In addition to his great name visibility, Stennis was benefited by being a Democrat, as 17 percent of voters mentioned his party as the primary reason they voted for him (Shaffer 1992, 101). Since then, Democrats have suffered steady losses among white Mississippians, though African Americans generally remain over 80 percent Democratic. From 1984 through 1990, as Democratic support among whites dropped into

Table 4.2. Party Identification of Adult Mississippians, Whites and Blacks, 1981–2004

| | Among Whites Only | | | | Among Blacks Only | | | |
Year	Dem	Indep	Rep	N Size	Dem	Indep	Rep	N Size
1981	51.0%	9.0%	40.0%	(420)	87.8%	1.2%	11.0%	(164)
1982	53.0	13.3	33.7	(570)	89.0	2.0	8.9	(246)
1984	46.2	14.3	39.4	(398)	82.6	7.6	9.8	(184)
1986	42.4	9.1	48.5	(396)	82.1	6.6	11.2	(196)
1988	43.9	10.5	45.6	(419)	82.2	5.6	12.2	(180)
1990	45.2	5.6	49.2	(394)	84.8	2.9	12.3	(171)
1992	36.9	7.1	56.0	(352)	84.1	2.4	13.4	(164)
1994	29.0	13.4	57.7	(411)	88.4	4.2	7.4	(189)
1996	31.1	11.9	57.0	(386)	82.7	8.4	8.9	(179)
1998	31.0	11.7	57.3	(393)	79.2	8.7	12.0	(183)
1999	34.5	12.5	53.0	(417)	84.2	7.1	8.7	(196)
2000	35.4	8.4	56.1	(367)	90.4	1.7	7.9	(178)
2002	28.1	6.3	65.7	(367)	77.2	10.4	12.4	(193)
2004	22.2	12.9	65.0	(311)	81.8	6.9	11.3	(159)

Source: The Mississippi Poll project, Social Science Research Center, Mississippi State University.

the 40s and the two parties were equally divided in white support, popular Republicans were able to win both U.S. Senate seats. By 1992 a majority of whites were now calling themselves Republicans, and the party's candidates began making inroads in state elected offices, such as governor, lieutenant governor and the state legislature. Democratic support in the 1990s sank into the 30 percents. The early years of the twenty-first century have seen Republican support among whites rise to about 65 percent as Democratic support has sunk below 30 percent. Only the overwhelmingly Democratic orientations of the 36 percent of the state population that is African American keep the aggregated electorate closely divided in partisanship, as 46.8 percent of all adult Mississippians in the latest 2004 poll called themselves Republicans, 42.3 percent were Democrats, and 10.9 percent were pure Independents.

The primary reason for Republican gains among white Mississippians appears to be their conservative values, evident on a variety of issues, not merely racial considerations. Examining five issues asked throughout the twenty-three-year period of the Mississippi Poll project in a multiple regression equation, ideological self-identification was most related to party identification ties of whites, an economic issue scale (incorporating a health care and a jobs and good living standard items) was second in importance and a racial issues scale (including affirmative action and the federal government improving the conditions of blacks and other minorities items) was only third in importance. Table 4.3 illustrates the dramatic gains that Republicans made among self-identified white conservatives, who in the early 1980s were only 52 percent Republican but who became steadily more Republican as the years passed, reaching an 81 percent mark in the early 2000s. Democrats, whose ranks thirty years earlier had furnished such conservative elected leaders as Senators John Stennis and James Eastland and Congressmen Jamie Whitten and Sonny Montgomery, had by the turn of the century become a more ideologically narrow party. Only 12 percent of conservative white Mississippians now called themselves Democrats.

To make up for the conservative white exodus to the GOP, Mississippi Democrats must assemble a biracial coalition that includes many white liberals and moderates and the great majority of African Americans. Though Republicans have made gains among white moderates, they have not yet reached the 50 percent mark. Though Democrats have lost some support even among self-identified white liberals, they retain an edge over the GOP in this progressive group, though do not quite constitute a

Table 4.3. Party Identification of White Mississippians, by Ideological Self-Identification Groups and by Time Periods

| | Among Self-Identified Liberals | | | |
Years	Democrats	Independents	Republicans	N Size
1981–1982	57.3%	16.0%	26.7%	(75)
1984–1990	51.7	8.3	40.0	(145)
1992–2000	51.8	11.7	36.5	(394)
2002–2004	47.9	8.3	43.8	(96)

| | Among Self-Identified Moderates | | | |
Years	Democrats	Independents	Republicans	N Size
1981–1982	55.6%	11.3%	33.1%	(284)
1984–1990	50.2	9.6	40.2	(759)
1992–2000	41.5	15.5	43.0	(718)
2002–2004	35.8	15.0	49.2	(187)

| | Among Self-Identified Conservatives | | | |
Years	Democrats	Independents	Republicans	N Size
1981–1982	39.1%	8.7%	52.2%	(312)
1984–1990	32.3	7.2	60.5	(517)
1992–2000	19.8	7.3	72.9	(1118)
2002–2004	11.9	6.9	81.2	(361)

Source: The Mississippi Poll project, Social Science Research Center, Mississippi State University.

Note: Years have been combined or pooled to maximize the numbers of people analyzed and minimize the sample error. The years are logically combined based on the changing numbers of the two parties' identifiers in the electorate.

majority (table 4.3). Even with Republican gains among conservative whites, Democrats are still able to assemble a biracial, ideologically diverse coalition to win many state and local elections.

EMERGING TWO-PARTY COMPETITION IN STATEWIDE OFFICES

Prior to the enfranchisement of African Americans under the 1965 Voting Rights Act, the Mississippi Democratic Party had been a white-ruled, segregated party. Ross Barnett, elected governor in 1959, had been elected with a campaign song, "Roll with Ross. He's for segregation one hundred percent. He's not a mod-rate like some other gent" (Bass and Devries 1977, 196). His successors, Paul Johnson and congressman John Bell Williams, the latter stripped of his House Democratic seniority for openly backing Goldwater, were also segregationists (Lamis 1990, 46–47). Republicans also reflected the segregationist environment with 1963 gubernatorial candidate Rubel Phillips blasting the national Democratic party's civil rights effort and promising to, "K.O. the Kennedys." Mississippi African Americans challenged the all-white "regular" Democratic Party by creating a rival Freedom Democratic Party and running some black candidates as Independents. The Freedom Democrats joined with white liberals to form a "loyalist" Mississippi Democratic Party, loyal to the national party. The loyalists then challenged the credentials of the regulars at national Democratic conventions and unseated them at the 1968 and 1972 Democratic conventions (Bass and DeVries 1977). Facing ostracism at the national level and the decreasing salience of the race issue to voters as the state finally found itself desegregating, Mississippi Democrats were finally able to assemble a biracial electoral coalition. They elected racially moderate governors in 1971 and 1975, Bill Waller and Cliff Finch. With moderate southerner Jimmy Carter as the party's presidential candidate, the Mississippi Democratic Party in 1976 unified itself under a biracial co-chairmanship of one leader of the loyalists and one of the regulars.

Mississippi Democrats were also forced to unify to confront the growing Republican threat. Meridian automobile dealer Republican Gil Carmichael blasted the old Democratic machine for keeping Mississippi on the nation's bottom of numerous quality of life indicators and won 39 percent of the vote against Senator Eastland in 1972. The moderate Carmichael, who backed such progressive measures as gun control and the Equal Rights Amendment for women, won a post-Reconstruction historic high for Republicans of 45 percent of the vote in a 1975 gubernatorial race against the "working man's candidate," Democrat Cliff Finch. With Democrats nominating the racially liberal and pro-public education William Winter in 1979, Carmichael's re-run campaign for governor garnered only 39 percent of the vote. The biracial Democratic coalition in the early 1980s was so strong in state politics that supporters of one GOP gubernatorial candidate, Leon Bramlett in 1983, accused the Democratic gubernatorial nominee, Attorney General Bill Allain, of having sex with black transvestite prostitutes. Pledging to withdraw from the race if his Democratic opponent passed three independent lie detector tests proving that he wasn't gay, Bramlett garnered only 39 percent of the vote in his losing effort (Lamis 1990, 60). Republican futility in elections for state offices was also evident in the party failing to even field a candidate for lieutenant governor in four of six elections from 1963 through 1983, and failing to elect any Republican to any of the sixty-one state offices elected on a statewide basis during these years (table 4.4). Republican hopes improved in 1987 with progressive Tupelo businessman and chairman of the state Board of Education Jack Reed, who garnered a post-Reconstruction GOP high of 47 percent of the vote in a losing gubernatorial race to Democratic auditor Ray Mabus.

The Harvard Law School graduate Mabus, who had been an architect of Governor Winter's 1982 Education Reform Act as a gubernatorial staffer, had promised while campaigning for governor "Mississippi will never be last again!" Facing a recession but refusing to compromise with the legislature and to raise taxes, Mabus presided over two years of pain-

Table 4.4. Two-Party Competition in State Offices

Year	Popular Vote for Governor Democrat	Popular Vote for Governor Republican	Popular Vote for Lieutenant Governor Democrat	Popular Vote for Lieutenant Governor Republican	Party Control of Eight Statewide Offices Number of Democrats	Party Control of Eight Statewide Offices Number of Republicans
1963	61.9%	38.1%	74.0%	26.0%	11	0
1967	70.3	29.7	100.0	0	11	0
1971[a]	77.0	0	100.0	0	11	0
1975[b]	52.2	45.2	69.5	30.5	11	0
1979	61.1	38.9	100.0	0	9	0
1983[cd]	55.1	38.9	64.3	0	8	0
1987[e]	53.4	46.6	73.4	17.7	8	0
1991[f]	47.6	50.8	41.5	49.5	6	2
1995	44.4	55.6	52.7	47.3	6	2
1999[g]	49.6	48.5	52.9	47.1	7	1
2003	45.8	52.6	37.1	61.0	4	4

Source: Mississippi Official and Statistical Register, 1964–1968 thru 2000–2004, Secretary of State of Mississippi.

Note: Eight offices that are elected statewide in Mississippi include governor, lieutenant governor, attorney general, secretary of state, treasurer, auditor, insurance commissioner, and agriculture commissioner. (Prior to 1983, the Superintendent of Public Education was also elected statewide. Prior to 1979, the Supreme Court Clerk and State Land Commissioner was also elected.) These elections, as well as elections for all state legislators, occur every four years in the November before the presidential election year. Percentages do not total 100 percent across rows due to minor candidates, some of whom are listed below.

[a] Black Independent Charles Evers won 22.1 percent in the 1971 Governor's race.
[b] Black Independent Henry Kirksey won 2.7 percent in the 1975 Governor's race.
[c] Black Independent Charles Evers won 4.1 percent in the 1983 Governor's race.
[d] Gil Carmichael ran as an Independent for Lieutenant Governor in 1983, winning 35.7 percent.
[e] Black Independent Henry Kirksey won 8.9 percent in Lieutenant Governor's race in 1987.
[f] Black Independent Henry Kirksey won 9.0 percent in Lieutenant Governor's race in 1991.
[g] The Democratic gubernatorial candidate in 1999, lacking a majority, was selected by the state legislature.

ful state budget cuts that included education at all levels. Moderate former Democratic congressman Wayne Dowdy, who had lost the 1988 senate race to Trent Lott, won a respectable 41 percent of the vote in the 1991 gubernatorial primary, mocking the incumbent as "the ruler" and pledging that if the challenger were nominated, "Mississippi will never be lost again" (Shaffer, Sturrock, Breaux and Minor 1999, 253). The bitterness of the Democratic primary and public dissatisfaction with the diminishing quality of life in the state helped elect little-known construction executive Kirk Fordice, who had stressed that he wasn't a "professional politician," as the first GOP governor since Reconstruction. Public dissatisfaction also claimed the political life of three-term lieutenant governor Brad Dye, president of the state senate. He had narrowly fought off reformer state senator Ken Harper in the Democratic primary. Harper had run a devastating television ad accusing Dye of being backed by numerous special interests and using $850 of taxpayer dollars for a nice leather office chair. Dye then lost the general election to Democrat-turned-Republican state senator Eddie Briggs, who had promised a "fresh new face" instead of "the tired, old, worn politics of the past" (Shaffer, Sturrock, Breaux and Minor 1999, 257).

The newly competitive state Republicans now faced their own bitter intraparty conflicts. Some GOP lawmakers joined Democrats to override Governor Fordice's veto of a tax increase, needed to prevent more cuts in education, prompting the outspoken Fordice to angrily declare them "pseudo-Republicans" who should be sent home. Though Fordice was reelected in 1995 because of voter satisfaction during a time of a booming economy, Lieutenant Governor Eddie Briggs, who had been accused by some conservative Republicans of not being pro-life enough, was defeated by Democratic state senator and education committee chair Ronnie Musgrove. Only the subsequent resignation of the state auditor and Fordice's appointment of Republican state representative Phil Bryant kept two of the state's eight statewide elected offices Republican. The last state election of the twentieth century was even worse for Republicans, as Democrat-turned-Republican ex-congressman Mike Parker, sitting on his lead, lost a narrow gubernatorial contest to Musgrove, who had unveiled an effective television ad of his accomplishments as lieutenant governor in improving public elementary and secondary education. Moderate Amy Tuck retained the lieutenant governorship for the Democrats, reducing Republicans to holding only one statewide office, auditor.

The seesaw of which party could hurt itself the most in intraparty infighting in this modern era of competitive two-party politics now swung back to the Democrats. Governor Musgrove delivered on his pledge to enact a six-year plan to raise public elementary and secondary teachers' salaries to the southeast average, but this expensive program coupled with a post 9/11 recession produced four years of cuts in other state programs including higher education. Blasting his GOP opponent in 2003, former RNC chair Haley Barbour, as a "Washington lobbyist" whose firm did business with tobacco companies who "poison our kids," Musgrove lost reelection to Barbour, who had decried the massive state deficit and promised that "We can do better" (Shaffer, Breaux and Patrick 2005).

Meanwhile Lieutenant Governor Amy Tuck, who had taken more liberal positions on backing the massive teacher pay raise and urging early (pre-kindergarten) education, resisted pressure from partisan and liberal Democrats to back a congressional redistricting plan that would maximize Ronnie Shows's chances of beating Chip Pickering. Also reeling from Democratic criticism of her support for tort reform, Tuck switched to the GOP before seeking reelection. Democrats nominated a bright, articulate, African American to oppose her in 2003, liberal state senator Barbara Blackmon. Irritated by the divorced Tuck's claim to be pro-life, Blackmon challenged the lieutenant governor to sign an oath that she had never had an abortion. As newspaper editors denounced Blackmon's getting too personally intrusive in the race and as state Republican leaders and the business community rallied to Tuck, the GOP lieutenant governor won a landslide reelection. Republicans also won an open seat for treasurer, as Tate Reeves's spending advantage over the well-qualified Gary Anderson, another African American Democrat, translated into greater name visibility. Reelecting Phil Bryant as auditor once again, Republicans now held an unprecedented four statewide offices (table 4.4), tying Democrats who won the open attorney general contest and reelected the secretary of state, insurance commissioner and agriculture commissioner (Shaffer, Breaux and Patrick 2005).

The Republican emergence as a competitive force in state elections had been heralded by the party finally providing candidates to contest offices historically dominated by Democrats. From 1963 through 1971, only three Republican candidates opposed thirty-three Democrats in statewide executive offices (table 4.5). Beginning with Gil Carmichael's 1975 gubernatorial bid, Republicans now began to challenge roughly half of statewide races through the 1983 elections. The next four elections saw the GOP

Table 4.5.   First Gubernatorial Primary Turnout and State Offices Contested by the Major Parties

	Votes Cast in First Primary for Governor			No. of Statewide Offices Contested in Gen. Election		
Year	Democrats	Republicans	% of Total Cast in Dem Primary	% of Total Cast in Rep Primary	Dem	Rep
1963	474,414	0	100.0%	0%	11	2
1967	684,005	0	100.0	0	11	1
1971	762,987	0	100.0	0	11	0
1975	789,894	0	100.0	0	11	8
1979	737,131	32,452	95.8	4.2	9	4
1983	828,211	0	100.0	0	8	3
1987	807,990	18,853	97.7	2.3	8	7
1991	726,465	63,561	92.0	8.0	8	3
1995	514,649	126,018	80.3	19.7	8	8
1999	545,555	153,142	78.1	21.9	8	6
2003	517,345	190,046	73.1	26.9	7	8

Source: Mississippi Official and Statistical Register, 1964–1968 thru 2000–2004, Secretary of State of Mississippi. 2003 figures are from the Secretary of State's Website and staff.

challenging most contests, including all eight in 1995 and six of the eight in 1999. The 2003 elections saw a historic reversal of party fortunes, as Republicans ran candidates in all eight offices and Democrats ran only seven, declining to challenge incumbent auditor Phil Bryant.

Despite GOP gains, most voters still vote in the Democratic primary, since the great majority of county and local officials remain Democratic. Yet Republicans have made steady gains from their pre-1991 history of generally refraining from even holding a party primary for the top office of governor (table 4.5). Many Republican party organization leaders had been shocked by the unknown Fordice's upset of Democrat-turned-Republican auditor Pete Johnson in the 1991 GOP gubernatorial primary, but Fordice's unapologetic conservatism benefited him against the more moderate Johnson, who was backed by GOP leaders as the more "electable" candidate. Since only 8 percent of voters on primary day participated in that GOP primary, it is likely that such a low turnout was confined to the most conservative element of the state. The Republican share of voters on primary day has since risen to 20 percent in 1995 and 27 percent in 2003.

THE RISE OF PARTISAN POLITICS
IN THE STATE LEGISLATURE

Prior to the 1965 Voting Rights Act, the state legislature was an all-white and nearly all-Democratic institution. Robert Clark, a Freedom Democrat leader, was elected to the state house as an Independent in 1967, and for eight years he constituted the sole African-American lawmaker in a bicameral legislature of 174 members. As African Americans won lawsuits challenging legislative redistricting proposals as discriminatory, their numbers in the legislature rose. Beginning in 1979, all blacks were elected as Democrats, and the numbers of GOP lawmakers also began a slow rise. The 1987 and 1991 elections contested by popular GOP gubernatorial candidates Jack Reed and Kirk Fordice saw Republican legislative numbers rise from 9 to 16 and then to 32, outnumbering black lawmakers by 1991 for the first time since 1975. White Democrats remained the dominant faction, outnumbering blacks and Republicans combined by a two-to-one margin (table 4.6).

Court-ordered redistricting that promoted the creation of more black majority districts, as well as the rising strength of the GOP in Mississippi, produced dramatic change in the legislature's composition after 1991. The number of African Americans has risen from 21 to 36 in the state house and from 4 to 11 in the state senate. Republican gains have been even more dramatic, doubling in the house from 23 to 46 and more than doubling in the senate from 9 to 23. Indeed, though Democrats continued to control both chambers of the legislature after the 2003 election, Republicans (all of whom were white) had the single largest faction in both chambers. The rising numbers of blacks and Republicans were of course accompanied by a big slide in the numbers of white Democrats. Already sliding from their near monopoly of political power in 1963 with 120 representatives and 51 senators, white Democratic numbers between 1991 and 2003 fell from 77 to 40 in the house, and from 39 to only 18 in the senate. White Democrats, who had remained the single largest faction until the 2003 elections, now fell to second place. Black Democrats, formerly second in size in the house, now fell to third in size in both chambers in the face of the increased numbers of GOP representatives (table 4.6).

The need for Democrats to maintain a racially unified party has produced some real gains for black lawmakers in terms of legislative leader-

Table 4.6.   Race and Party Composition of State Legislature

	State House of Representatives			State Senate		
Year	Black Democrats	White Democrats	White Republicans	Black Democrats	White Democrats	White Republicans
1963	0	120	2	0	51	1
1967	1[a]	121	0	0	52	0
1971	1[a]	119	2	0	50	2
1975	4[b]	115	3	0	50	2
1979	15	102	4	2	46	4
1983	18	98	6	2	47	3
1987	20	93	9	2	43	7
1991	21	77	23	4	39	9
1992	30	63	27	10	29	13
1995	35	50	34	10	24	18
1999	35	51	33	10	24	18
2003	36	40	46	11	18	23

Source: *Politics in the New South: Representation of African Americans in Southern State Legislatures.* Edited by Charles E. Menifield and Stephen D. Shaffer. SUNY Press; 2005.

"Political Parties in Modern Mississippi," by Stephen D. Shaffer in *Politics in Mississippi*, 2nd edition. Edited by Joseph B. Parker. Sheffield Publishing Co., Salem, WI, 2001, p. 297. *Mississippi Official and Statistical Register*, 1964-1968 thru 2000-2004, Secretary of State of Mississippi.

Note: The legislature consists of 122 house members and 52 senators. Rows may fail to reach that total due to white Independents. The special legislative election in 1992 was required by court-ordered redistricting.

[a] Representative Robert Clark, an African American and a leader of the Freedom Democrats, was elected as an Independent.

[b] Representative Douglas Anderson, an African American, was elected as an Independent.

ship positions and even victories on important bills and nominations. After the 1991 elections, veteran Black Caucus Representative Robert Clark was elected to the number two leadership post in the House, speaker pro tempore. Newly elected lieutenant governor Ronnie Musgrove in 1996 elevated blacks to chair such powerful senate committees as Judiciary, Constitution, Elections, and Universities and Colleges. Though two white Democrats were selected to the two top positions in the state house after the 2003 election, for the first time an African American was appointed to chair the powerful Ways and Means Committee. Committee chairmanships also translated into some important legislative victories for the Black Caucus. Republican governor Fordice's effort in 1996 to place four white male businessmen on the state College Board was defeated by one vote in the Senate Judiciary Committee, forcing him to nominate one black and one woman along with only two white males (Menifield and Shaffer 2005). Republican governor Barbour's effort to save money by restricting a bond bill in a 2004 special session solely to promote economic development was stymied when Ways and Means Committee chairman Percy Watson invited university and community college leaders to testify about their "needs," leading to a bond bill of $456 million that included a diverse range of state needs in place of Barbour's mere $108-million bill.

White Democrats up until the 2003 elections tended to be the dominant faction on roll call votes. Generally voting with African American Democrats to enact landmark education measures, even those requiring a tax increase, white Democrats broke party ranks and joined with Republicans to enact tough anti-crime and pro-life measures. Democrats of both races successfully overrode Fordice's vetoes of a 1992 tax hike for education, a 1992 higher education bond bill and the 1997 Adequate Education Act. White Democrats even joined with their African-American colleagues to override Fordice's 1995 veto of a telecommunications bond bill that included racial set asides. Black Democrats lost out to a bipartisan, overwhelmingly white coalition that voted to enact longer prison terms (1995 Truth in Sentencing) and crackdowns on school violence (1994) and street gangs (1996), and to require parental consent for abortions (1986) and a waiting period for abortions (1991). Though a majority of whites of both parties backed a cut in the income tax in the Fordice reelection year of 1995, unified African-American opposition doomed the tax cut to failing to achieve the 60 percent margin constitutionally needed for revenue legislation (Menifield and Shaffer 2005).

Mississippi's history of one-partyism has minimized the type of divisiveness that exists between the parties in Washington. As Republicans gained legislative seats, Democratic house speakers and lieutenant governors appointed a few as committee chairs. Republican lieutenant governors have continued this bipartisan tradition. Many landmark bills have been enacted with majority support by both parties and races, such as the 1982 Education Reform Act, the 1987 highway bill to four-lane one thousand miles of roads, the 2000 multiyear teacher pay raise and the 2002 settlement of the Ayers higher education desegregation lawsuit. The parties do not yet organize as caucuses, the entire chamber membership votes for the house speaker, house speaker pro tempore, and senate president pro tempore, and under senate rules the lieutenant governor makes committee assignments. Despite Republicans lacking numeric control of the state senate, popular Republican lawmaker Travis Little was elected President Pro Tempore after the 2003 elections.

CONCLUSION

V. O. Key would hardly recognize today's Mississippi with a sizable legislative Black Caucus that exerts a decisive impact on some public policies and Republicans holding both of the state's U.S. senate seats. Yet in some respects the state has not changed all that much—it still remains an essentially conservative place. Mississippi's conservatism is reflected in a 2001 statewide election where 64 percent of Mississippians voted to keep their 1894 state flag that included the Confederate battle emblem (Breaux and Menifield 2003). Only today, that conservatism has changed its home from that of the southern Democratic Party to that of the national Republican Party. The conservatism of today's Mississippi Republican Party fits so well with the national party that some state Republicans rise to national leadership positions, such as Haley Barbour's RNC chairmanship, Trent Lott's former Republican senate leadership post and Roger Wicker's chairmanship of the 1995 GOP house freshmen.

Yet V. O. Key in detailing the conflict between the poor whites in the Hills and the conservative Delta planters also pointed out that the Magnolia State has a populist strain. The enfranchisement of African Americans, who constitute 36 percent of the state's population, dramatically increases the size of the state electorate's more progressive element even further. Legislative overrides of Fordice's vetoes reflect the limits of a policy of unbridled conservatism promoted by any GOP leader. Democratic comebacks in the 1999 state elections illustrate how fleeting GOP gains in any one election may be. As Governor Barbour today wrestles with elderly citizens protesting his proposed cuts in Medicaid in order to try to reduce the massive state deficit without raising taxes, it seems unlikely that the state will ever turn 180 degrees about from its Democratic heritage and become a solidly Republican state. Intensely competitive two-party politics is a far more likely scenario (Shaffer, Breaux and Patrick 2005).

REFERENCES

Bass, Jack, and DeVries, Walter. 1977. *The Transformation of Southern Politics: Social Change and Political Consequence Since 1945*. New York: New American Library.

Breaux, David A. 2003. "The Mississippi 3rd Congressional District Race," In David B. Magleby and Quin Monson (eds.), *The Last Hurrah? Soft Money and Issue Advocacy in the 2002 Congressional Elections*. Provo, UT: Brigham Young University, Center for the Study of Elections and Democracy.

Breaux, David A., and Charles E. Menifield. 2003. "Mississippi: A Study in Change and Continuity." In Charles S. Bullock III and Mark J. Rozell (eds), *The New Politics of the Old South, An Introduction to Southern Politics*, 2nd ed. Lanham, MD: Rowman and Littlefield Publishers.

Key, V. O. 1949. *Southern Politics in State and Nation*. New York: Vintage, Division of Random House.

Lamis, Alexander P. 1990. *The Two-Party South*. 2nd expanded edition. New York: Oxford University Press.

Menifield, Charles E., and Stephen D. Shaffer (eds). 2005. *Politics in the New South: Representation of African Americans in Southern State Legislatures*. Albany: SUNY Press.

Shaffer, Stephen D. 1991. "Mississippi: Electoral Conflict in a Nationalized State." In Laurence W. Moreland, Robert P. Steed and Tod A. Baker (eds), *The 1988 Presidential Election in the South: Continuity Amidst Change in Southern Party Politics*. New York: Praeger.

Shaffer, Stephen D. 1992. "Party and Electoral Politics in Mississippi," In Dale Krane and Stephen D. Shaffer (eds), *Mississippi Government and Politics, Modernizers Versus Traditionalists*. Lincoln: University of Nebraska Press.

Shaffer, Stephen D., David E. Sturrock, David A. Breaux and Bill Minor. 1999. "Mississippi: From Pariah to Pacesetter?" In Alexander P. Lamis (ed), *Southern Politics in the 1990s*. Baton Rouge: Louisiana State University Press.

Shaffer, Stephen D., David A. Breaux and Barbara Patrick. 2005. "Mississippi: Republicans Surge Forward in a Two-Party State," *American Review of Politics*, forthcoming.

5

Louisiana: African Americans, Republicans and Party Competition

Wayne Parent and Huey Perry

On paper, Louisiana looks remarkably similar to its sister states in the Deep South. Louisiana politics at the turn of the twenty-first century remain distinct. The fascinating politics of Huey Long, Earl Long and Edwin Edwards were only a colorful prelude to the party-switching, racially polarizing, mean and nasty, nationally conspicuous elections in recent years. In the 1990s, Louisiana was host to an erratic, often unpredictable, certainly uneven evolution from Democratic dominance to Republican parity and from virtually white-only participation to genuine black political power. By 2000 Republicans had consolidated their gains. In 1999 Republicans had reelected a governor for the first time in Louisiana history, and in 2000, in perhaps the most evenly contested presidential race ever, the Republican candidate easily won the state. However, after the turn of the century, Democrats remain very competitive. In 2002 Democrats were able to hold onto Mary Landrieu's U.S. Senate seat and in 2003 Kathleen Blanco recaptured the governorship for the Democrats. In 2004, Republicans roared back with a breakthrough win for the U.S. Senate and a very strong showing by President Bush in 2004. Like the remainder of the South, Louisiana Republicans are gaining strength, but Democrats have managed impressive wins and remain highly competitive.

Mississippi, Alabama and, to a somewhat lesser extent, Georgia and South Carolina mirror Louisiana in politically important demographics like income, poverty and education levels and racial makeup. However, in 1996 when Republican Presidential candidate Bob Dole carried all four of those states, Democrat Bill Clinton carried Louisiana in an incredible 12 percent landslide. In 1998 after Democratic Senator John Breaux defeated his Republican opponent in a landslide, Louisiana remains the only state in the South with two Democratic Senators. Although these Democratic victories involved substantial and usually crucial support from blacks, black candidates still fail to win white support. This chapter will address the unique forces in Louisiana that have tempered, but not stopped, the Republican tidal wave in the Deep South. The chapter will also address the emergence of blacks in power and as key players in power politics.

THE EMERGENCE OF THE REPUBLICAN PARTY

To be sure, Republican gains in Louisiana have been dramatic. In 1995 and 1999, Louisianians elected Republican Mike Foster governor by wide margins, and in 2000, not only did Republicans George W. Bush win the state, five of the seven members of the Louisiana congressional delegation elected were Republicans. In 1996 U.S. Senate candidate Louis "Woody" Jenkins came within six thousand votes of becoming Louisiana's first elected member of that body. Republicans are increasing their numbers in the state legislature (see table 5.1) and winning elections at all levels of government. Republican voter registration has surged from less than 1 percent in 1960 to over 20 percent (see table 5.2). Republicans have clearly established themselves as an equal partner in this obviously two-party state.

The agents of change away from the hundred years of Democratic dominance in Louisiana are similar to those other states in the South. In 1956 Dwight Eisenhower became the first Republican to carry Louisiana (and, in the Deep South, only Louisiana) with a probusiness "establishment" Republican message that attracted middle- to upper-income suburbanites. In 1964 Louisiana joined the pattern that established Republican success in the remainder of the Deep South when Republican Barry Goldwater's message of racial and cultural conservativism attracted enough middle- to lower-income whites to carry the state; Republican Ronald Reagan's similar message of strong defense and social conservativism not only carried the state in 1980 and 1984 but helped George H. W.

Table 5.1. Partisan Makeup of the Louisiana Legislature 1962–2004

	House of Representatives		Senate	
	Democrat	*Republican*	*Democrat*	*Republican*
1962	101	0	39	0
1964	103	2	39	0
1966	103	2	39	0
1968	105	0	39	0
1970	104	1	38	1
1972	101	4	38	1
1976	101	4	38	1
1978	96	9	38	1
1980	95	10	39	0
1982	93	11	38	1
1984	91	14	38	1
1986	87	15	34	5
1988	86	17	34	5
1990	89	16	34	5
1992	88	16	34	5
1996	77	27	25	14
2000	70	33	26	13
2004	67	37	24	15

Bush win, although by his smallest margin in the South, in 1988. Republican congressional candidates began winning in the (mostly white) suburban areas surrounding New Orleans, Shreveport and Baton Rouge, and then eventually in (mostly white) rural areas as well.

An examination of the elections leading up the present party system reveal two fairly distinct aspects of Republican appeal. First, as was evident in the Eisenhower victory, is the probusiness, economic appeal to middle-class white suburbanites. Louisiana's higher proportion of urban centers than Mississippi, Alabama and South Carolina provides a fertile ground for suburban political messages that obviously resonated in some of Louisiania's consistently strongest Republican parishes: Republicans have been quite successful around Louisiana's largest urban areas of Jefferson Parish (County) and St. Tammany Parish in suburban New Orleans and the areas in and around Shreveport (Caddo and Bossier Parishes), Baton Rouge (East Baton Rouge and Livingston Parishes) and Lafayette (Lafayette Parish).

The second aspect of Republican appeal was more evident in the Gold-

Table 5.2.   Louisiana Voter Registration by Party 1960–1996

	Democrat	Republican
1960	98.6%	.9%
1961	98.7	.9
1962	98.7	.9
1963	98.5	1.0
1964	98.1	1.5
1965	97.7	1.6
1966	97.9	1.6
1967	97.8	1.6
1968	97.4	1.9
1969	97.4	1.9
1970	97.2	2.1
1971	96.7	2.2
1972	96.0	2.8
1973	96.0	2.8
1974	95.9	2.8
1975	95.2	3.0
1976	93.3	3.8
1977	92.9	4.0
1978	91.8	4.4
1979	89.5	5.3
1980	86.5	7.5
1981	86.0	8.0
1982	85.0	8.4
1983	83.5	9.1
1984	82.2	10.0
1985	79.3	12.8
1986	78.1	13.6
1987	77.5	14.0
1988	75.4	16.4
1989	74.8	17.2
1990	74.1	17.7
1991	73.5	18.1
1992	71.5	19.0
1993	71.1	19.2
1994	70.6	19.4
1995	68.4	20.0
1996	65.4	21.0

Source: Louisiana Commissioner of Elections

water victory. Republicans carried rural white parishes, especially in Protestant north Louisiana, for the first time. These voters were attracted to Goldwater's opposition to the Civil Rights Act. These conservative policy positions were precursors to the appeal to other socially conservative positions on such issues as gun control and prayer in public schools in that they appealed to a similar voter. This second type of Republican voter is now often categorized by using the all-too-limited term, Christian Right. These social/cultural conservatives have formed the second part of the foundation of the Republican coalition in Louisiana.

When Republicans can combine the two appeals of probusiness conservativism and social/cultural conservativism, they are almost impossible to stop. The combination of suburban parishes and rural parishes is a healthy one. Ronald Reagan was probably most adept at combining these messages. Mike Foster, who became only the second Republican elected governor in Louisiana, was also able to win substantial victories in the suburbs and rural areas. If Republicans field candidates that both groups—the "establishment" probusiness conservatives, and the "populist" cultural conservatives—find attractive, Republicans will win often in Louisiana.

THE TENACITY OF THE DEMOCRATIC PARTY

The continued appeal of the Democrats is quite natural to other groups. When, in 1964, the Republican presidential candidate appealed to conservative whites with opposition to the Civil Rights and Voting Rights Act, black Louisianians of all demographic backgrounds began voting overwhelmingly Democratic. Before the Voting Rights Act, Louisiana's blacks were registered at low rates—due mainly to the restrictions to black voting remedied by that act. Black turnout was higher in South Louisiana than in much of the rest of the Deep South, but still tellingly low. Black votes are concentrated in urban areas (notably Orleans Parish) and many rural parishes along the Mississippi River Delta.

The first significant statewide breakthrough for a black/white Democratic coalition came in the election of Edwin Edwards to the governorship in 1971 after he campaigned hard for black support. He rewarded that support by appointing blacks to visible positions and backing black legislators for leadership positions on reapportionment and important policy positions on education, health and welfare legislation. Many Dem-

ocrats like Senators John Breaux and Bennett Johnston followed this successful strategy. However, in 1995, when the first major black candidate
for governor made the runoff for governor, a friction between black and
white Democrats began to show. In that race, which will be covered
extensively later in this chapter, African-American Congressman Cleo
Fields did not receive the endorsement from many of the same white
Democratic officeholders that he and many black leaders had supported
in previous years.

While black support for the Democratic Party is most noticeable, many
whites continued to support the Democratic Party throughout the Republican realignment beginning in the 1960s. The parishes that straddle the
Mississippi River between Baton Rouge and New Orleans are home to a
vast chemical industry and a shrinking group of Southern white labor
union Democrats. The parishes of Assumption, Ascension, Iberville, St.
John the Baptist and St. Charles are predominately white and core Democratic parishes. The Catholic, French Acadian parishes, especially of
southwest Louisiana, have also recently been a tenuous part of the Democratic base. This area, which is roughly the Seventh Congressional District
through the past several decades of redistricting, was the congressional
home base of four-term Governor Edwin Edwards, recent Senator John
Breaux and current Governor Kathleen Blanco.

THE UNIQUENESS OF THE RULES:
LOUISIANA'S OPEN ELECTION SYSTEM

A brief explanation of Louisiana's unique election system must precede
any discussion of Louisiana's contemporary electoral politics. In 1975 the
Louisiana legislature at the urging of Governor Edwin Edwards adopted
an electoral system that was seen as benefiting both the governor and
incumbent legislators (Hadley 1985). The system is unique but straight-
forward. All candidates for office, regardless of party affiliation, run in
one election, and if any candidate receives a majority of votes cast, that
candidate is elected. If no candidate receives a majority the top two candidates, regardless of party affiliation, compete in a runoff. Unlike the
newly adopted California system and similar systems in other states, the
Louisiana system allows two Democrats or two Republicans to compete
in the final election.

Governor Edwards proposed and legislators supported the new system because under it they would often hold an advantage. Incumbents could win outright in the first election, thereby avoiding the cost and unpredictability of running in a general election against an opponent of the other party that, even if not well known, could depend on party support or coattails in a general election. However, as the following discussions of particular elections indicate, this unique system can have other consequences as well.

RACIAL POLITICS: THE 1991, 1995 AND 1999 RACES FOR GOVERNOR

As the 1996 elections approached, the two parties in Louisiana were in similar positions. Each had a coalition that when united was formidable but that when divided, was highly vulnerable. Perhaps overly simply stated: The Republicans were an uneasy coalition of suburban probusiness conservatives and more rural cultural conservatives; the Democrats were a coalition of most blacks, some labor and a small number of socially liberal urban whites. Even though the forms of the coalitions are similar to those nationally, the proportions and opportunities for disruption are different.

The gubernatorial elections of 1991 and 1995 are particularly instructive. In 1991, in perhaps the most spectacular election in a state with a history of spectacular elections, Louisianians were faced with three major candidates for governor. The first, and early favorite, was incumbent governor Charles "Buddy" Roemer, who was elected in 1987 as a Democrat and had become a Republican while in office after having alienated the conservative wing by not signing a restrictive abortion bill. The second was three-term former Democratic Governor Edwin Edwards. Edwards, as noted earlier, was initially elected with a black/labor/Cajun coalition that was a winning combination for the Democrats in the 1970s. Edwards had enjoyed wildly enthusiastic and high approval ratings until he was tried for racketeering in the middle of his second term; although he was acquitted, the trial tainted his image and his effectiveness and his approval ratings plummeted. Finally, the ballot included Republican David Duke who was internationally known as the former Grand Wizard of the Ku Klux Klan. He had won a seat in the Louisiana House of Representatives and had garnered a striking 40 percent of the vote in his 1990 race for the U.S. Senate against incumbent Bennett Johnston. In the first election Edwards ran first with solid support of black voters and some labor support. Duke ran second with a strong showing, especially in the rural white areas of north Louisiana. Roemer, who had the support of probusiness Republicans and Democrats who had turned against Edwards after his trial, finished out of the running. Since no one got a majority of the votes, Edwards and Duke were in a runoff.

The Duke–Edwards race offered two choices that were widely disdained by a large proportion of the voters. Democrat Edwards had become unpopular because of perceived unethical and even criminal behavior. Republican Duke's association with the KKK and use of racist rhetoric caused him to be despised by much of the electorate. Almost all prominent Republican officials refused to support Duke and even endorsed Democrat Edwards. In the end, a bumper sticker summed up the sentiments of much of the electorate: "Vote for the Crook: It's Important." After an election that created an international media circus, Edwards easily won the runoff. The Republican Party in the state had not only lost an election but had to cope with having David Duke as their most visible politician.

The 1995 governor's race illustrated the fact that Republicans were not alone in confronting potentially fatal splits. In that year, several well-known Democrats faced only two Republicans. The Republicans appeared to be in a state of disarray: The candidate endorsed at the state convention, suburban New Orleans state representative Quentin Dastugue, chose not to run, which left former Governor "Buddy" Roemer and little known Democratic State Senator Mike Foster, who switched his party affiliation the day he filed to run for office. The same ballot featured four well-known and well-funded Democrats who would have been "firsts" as governors of Louisiana: two women, Lieutenant Governor Melinda Schweggman and State Treasurer Mary Landrieu, and African-American Congressmen Cleo Fields and William Jefferson.

Even though Roemer had lost support from the Christian Right he was expected to run well based on name recognition. Among the Democrats, Landrieu, who had announce her candidacy a year earlier in a move that angered incumbent Governor Edwards (who had not yet announced his own intentions), was seen as the most likely to make a runoff. A Roemer–Landrieu runoff, however, was not to be.

Foster eventually emerged as the choice of the Christian Right. In a brilliant campaign move, he ran as a "Christian and a gun owner" in ads that had this millionaire businessman wearing a welder's cap. In the last few weeks of the campaign, Foster surged to the top of the opinion polls. Fields, who benefited from the exit from the race of the other black congressman, moved into second place, edging out Landrieu and leaving Roemer behind in fourth place.

The days and weeks of the Foster–Fields runoff proved to be a nightmare for Democratic cohesion. A feud between Fields and Landrieu erupted as a result of a very heated contest to make the runoff. Fields became upset because Landrieu and others in her campaign allegedly warned African-American voters that Fields could not win in the runoff election and that Landrieu could. In effect, the allegation was that African Americans should not waste their vote to achieve symbolic satisfaction when they could help elect someone who would be just as mindful of their interests as Fields would.

Fields attacked Landrieu for that allegation and Landrieu had to publicly deny that her campaign had made such statements. Fields's public criticism of Landrieu probably mobilized enough African-American support to place second in the election and thus qualify for the runoff. Landrieu blamed her failure to make the runoff on Field's public attack and vented her frustration by not endorsing his candidacy. Fields lost to Mike Foster by a landslide.

In 1999, Republican Governor Foster, who was very popular, drew high-profile Democratic opposition in four-term New Orleans Congressman William Jefferson and some relatively minor candidates. Foster again faced a high-profile African-American candidate in his bid for governor. While many major Democratic officials endorsed Jefferson, the race was never perceived as close and Foster won easily.

DEMOCRATS WIN U.S. SENATE
RACES IN 1996, 1998 AND 2002

As Louisiana entered the 1996 elections for president, an open U.S. Senate seat and all seven seats in the U.S. House of Representatives, both parties had reason for concern with party unity. Democrats had reason for concern after the Fields/Landrieu conflict in the governor's race because now it was Fields's turn to be upset. Landrieu entered the U.S. Senate race less than a year after the gubernatorial election and was immediately anointed by the polls as the front runner. Although she slipped to second place in the first election, Landrieu made it into the runoff against Republican State Senator Woody Jenkins. Public opinion polls throughout the runoff period indicated an evenly contested campaign. Initially, Fields refused to endorse Landrieu. Although several prominent African-American political leaders endorsed Landrieu, including Congressman William Jefferson and New Orleans Mayor Marc Morial, the majority of African Americans appeared to be taking their cue from Fields. Until Fields decided to endorse Landrieu, African Americans were faced with a very uncomfortable choice: either vote for Jenkins or abstain.

The Democratic Party leadership was in no position to attempt to negotiate between Fields and Landrieu. Fields was upset with the party's white leaders for refusing to endorse him in the gubernatorial election but enthusiastically endorsing Landrieu in the senate runoff. Fields believed that this double standard was because of his race. It is difficult to argue that Fields's belief is not meritorious. Ultimately, the National Democratic party, in the person of Vice President Al Gore, had to intervene to settle the dispute between Fields and Landrieu. The Louisiana contest had national implications as President Clinton was attempting to reestablish Democratic control of the U.S. Senate. Gore convinced Fields to endorse Landrieu, but Fields's endorsement was not enthusiastic.

If the Fields/Landrieu conflict was simply a personality clash, it would be difficult to derive any lasting meaning that would facilitate scholarly understanding of Louisiana politics since personality clashes often occur in American politics. We believe that in the Fields/Landrieu struggle there was an underlying basis to the feud that helps to illuminate scholarly understanding of Louisiana politics.

The Fields/Landrieu feud represents a growing tension between African Americans and moderate and liberal whites, currently the two mainstays in the Democratic Party's coalition. This tension is erupting in southern politics faster than elsewhere because the growing Republicanization of political leadership has siphoned away conservative party leaders from the Democratic party. This development has made it possible for African Americans and moderate and liberal whites to vie for leadership positions in the Democratic Party in the South for the first time since African Americans became active players in the South in the middle 1960s.

Republicans had problems of their own. Despite the tension in the Democratic Party, Republicans were unable to win the seat. In the first election, two Democrats were leading the pack and appeared likely to squeeze the Republicans out of the runoff. In the final weeks of the first election, key Republican leaders began endorsing Jenkins, who was consistently polling best among the Republican contenders. By the final days of the first election, the Republican strategy had worked and Jenkins roared into first place, with Landrieu second.

Jenkins, who clearly represented the more rural conservative wing of the party had trouble gaining support that might have gone to more suburban conservatives and barely lost the election to Landrieu. Indeed, in the ABC Exit poll, 66 percent of self-described "moderates" voted for Landrieu. Although Landrieu was widely criticized by the Jenkins campaign for being an extremist primarily because of her pro-choice stance, it was Jenkins who lost the support of the middle. The Republicans, by fielding a candidate who was perceived as too conservative by moderates, missed a golden opportunity to capture an open Senate seat.

Although the Senate race was the most closely watched in Louisiana in 1996, two of Louisiana's seven Congressional seats had no incumbent running. Republican newcomer John Cooksey won in the newly redistricted Fifth District in rural north Louisiana and Democrat Chris John won the seat held by Republican convert Jimmy Hayes in southwest Louisiana (Hayes ran unsuccessfully for the Senate seat). Republicans hold a solid 5–2 advantage in Louisiana's congressional delegation.

At the end of 1996, both parties were in a state of conflict and were also highly competitive. Democrats had successfully brought blacks and whites together for a resounding win for President Clinton but had barely found a way to hold on to the Senate seat, even with probably reluctant but strong black support for Mary Landrieu. The Republicans had almost pulled together behind a candidate with visible ties to the conservative wing of the party but found themselves short of a victory (unless the U.S. Senate gives them another chance). This race illustrates well the splits in both parties and suggests that in years to come, success may well depend on failure of the opposite party to heal its divisions.

In the 1998 midterm election, two-term incumbent Senator John Breaux drew little opposition. Republican State Representative Jim Donelon was the only candidate to actively campaign and receive more than token support. John Breaux seemed unbeatable months before the election; this perception was reaffirmed when Republican Governor Mike Foster tacitly seemed to support Democrat Breaux. Governor Foster did not endorse an opponent and stayed neutral in the race. Breaux's grip on the Louisiana electorate is illustrated by this glowing description of Breaux in a 1997 *Shreveport Times* editorial: "Instead of indulging in the partisan, divisive ideological politics that has characterized recent years, Breaux has sought to build bridges between Democrats and Republicans and is widely respected on both sides of the aisle. Breaux speaks for America and Louisiana, not for an ideology and his constituents know it." Senator Breaux carried 64 percent of the vote, winning every parish in the state except Donelon's home parish, St. Tammany.

In 1998 only two of the seven congressional incumbents were challenged. Five Republicans and one Democrat had no opposition and New Orleans Democrat William Jefferson had only minor opposition, winning with 86 percent of the vote. The only congressional race that received any attention was in the Sixth District where six-term incumbent Republican Richard Baker found himself in a surprisingly tight race with a newcomer Democrat with a last name well-known in Louisiana politics. His challenger, Marjorie McKeithen, is the granddaughter of former Democratic Governor John McKeithen and daughter of sitting Republican Secretary of State Fox McKeithen. Baker had two problems: The district had been redrawn in 1996 and was more friendly to Democrats, and Marjorie McKeithen proved to be a strong, attractive candidate with a classic Democratic economic working-class message. The race was extremely close in the last few days, with Baker pulling it out at the end, beating McKeithen by 2,843 of the 191,245 votes cast. To the dismay of many Democrats, McKeithen decided not to run again in 2000, and no other prominent Democrat was willing to run a race against Baker.

While the 1999 reelection of Republican Governor Foster and the 2000 state win by Republican Presidential candidate Bush gave the GOP considerable reason for satisfaction, Democrats roared back in the 2002 and 2003 elections.

In 2002, incumbent Democrat Mary Landrieu appeared to be one of the most vulnerable incumbents in the U.S. Senate. She had won her seat in a squeaker and had to run for reelection in a state that Republican President Bush had carried handily two years earlier. The president and his party were riding a wave of almost unprecedented popularity and were poised to buck historical trends and pick up seats in an off-year election. Republican Congressman John Cooksey, from northwest Louisiana, made it clear that he planned to challenge Senator Landrieu and was initially seen as a formidable candidate.

The dynamics of the election are detailed in this excerpt from *Inside the Carnival: Unmasking Louisiana Politics*:

The Landrieu vs. Cooksey head-to-head battle was not to be, however.

The year before the election, as Cooksey was taking his first steps toward garnering statewide and national support for his run for the Senate, he made a comment on a statewide radio program that defined him and haunted his campaign throughout the next year. After the tragic events of September 11, 2001, Cooksey told reporter Jeff Palermo, "If I see someone come in and he's got a diaper on his head and a fan belt around that diaper on his head, that guy needs to be pulled over and checked," (Author interview with Jeff Palermo, March 11, 2003). The comment was reported widely and ran counter to the Bush administration's very desire to keep religious and racial slurs out of the response to the attacks. Cooksey's campaign never seemed to recover from the remark. The negative reactions to the remark left Republican outside the state unenthusiastic, and the Cooksey campaign began the race clearly handicapped.

Cooksey's problems left room for other Republican candidates to enter the race. The two most prominent were Baton Rouge State Representative Tony Perkins, who had run "Woody" Jenkins's near-miss 1996 campaign against Landrieu, and Suzanne Haik-Terrell, who had defeated Jenkins in a runoff for State Commissioner of Elections in 1999 to become the first female Republican to be elected to statewide office in Louisiana history. While Governor Foster endorsed Cooksey, the National Republican Campaign Committee began funding the campaign of Terrell.

On November 5, 2002, national Election Day, Landrieu led the nine-person field with 46 percent of the vote. Terrell finished second with 27 percent and met Landrieu in a December 7 runoff. Louisiana's odd election system, which allowed for a runoff one month after all of the other U.S. Senate elections had been decided, shoved Louisiana into the spotlight. The national Republican Party, buoyed by victories across the country, turned its attention to Louisiana. Visits from President Bush, Vice-President Cheney and a laundry list of Republican political headliners coupled with an infusion of money from both parties made Louisiana the national electoral epicenter for the four week runoff period.

Landrieu won the election by over 40,000 votes, a victory widely reported as a setback for President Bush and the Republicans and as a consolation to a national Democratic Party that had been badly bruised by the November elections. Landrieu won by energizing the two fundamental elements of Louisiana Democratic support: African-American voters and economic issues. Terrell lost because she was not able to galvanize the Republican base of social and business conservatives" (Parent 2004 57–59).

TWO "FIRSTS" IN THE 2003
RACE FOR GOVERNOR

With two-term Republican Governor Foster constitutionally barred from running for a third term, Louisiana was again preparing for the free-for-all that characterized most non-incumbent governor's races in the past few decades. The 2003 campaign was perhaps the most surprising of them all.

The Democratic contenders was headed by three-term Attorney General Richard Ieyoub, a major player in Louisiana politics since his early career as district attorney in Calcasieu Parish, a crucial swing parish in Cajun southwest Louisiana. Two-term Lieutenant Governor Kathleen Blanco, former Congressman Claude "Buddy" Leach and State Senate President Randy Ewing were all considered formidable candidates as well. Four major Republican candidates eventually emerged. They were former state House Speaker Hunt Downer, Senate President John Hainkel, Public Service Commissioner Jay Blossman and the surprise candidate, Piyush "Bobby" Jindal, a bureaucrat who had headed key state departments in the Foster administration and had also served in the Bush administration.

As the race began in earnest two major developments, one in each party, set the tone. First, both Democrat Ieyoub and Democrat Leach, each with considerable financial and political resources, decided to target the significant and powerful African-American base of the party. Second, Governor Foster endorsed enthusiastically and often Republican Jindal. This left Democrats Blanco and Ewing with the task of appealing to other parts of the electoral spectrum and Republicans Downer and Blossman having to run against the incumbent Republican governor.

As the election progressed, Jindal began to emerge as the one Republican who had the best chance at the runoff. This thirty-two-year-old Harvard-educated Indian American seemed a very unlikely political juggernaut in the Republican Party in Louisiana, but he and his campaign clearly hit a responsive chord, especially among social conservatives. While the backing from Foster may have made him a legitimate candidate, the campaign's focus on a social conservative message repeated often on talk radio coupled with an upbeat television campaign was what made him a front runner. His notoriety as potentially Louisiana's youngest governor and as the first Indian-American governor in the United States may obscured to outsiders the sheer force of his conservative resonating message. By the last few weeks of his brilliant campaign, his place in the runoff seemed guaranteed and his overall prospects seemed very bright. He had the support of both the social conservatives with his message and the business conservatives because of his background, and indeed captured 32 percent of the vote and a strong first-place finish with considerable momentum going into the runoff.

Among the Democrats, Attorney General Ieyoub and Congressman Leach continued to focus their energy on gaining African-American and labor support, but in the end neither could break through. That left Lieutenant Governor Blanco and State Senate President Ewing with a chance to capture the second spot in the runoff. Ewing seemed to score a real coup with the endorsement of New Orleans Mayor Ray Nagin, but it was Blanco whose persistent, methodical centrist campaign never imploded and allowed her to eke past Ieyoub into the second runoff spot, distanced well behind Jindal with 16 percent of the vote.

The Jindal–Blanco runoff set the stage for an oddity in Louisiana. Louisiana was about to experience an election that received almost universal positive national coverage. Both Blanco and Jindal were "firsts." He would be the first Indian-American governor in the United States and Blanco would be the first woman governor in Louisiana history. Neither candidate was tainted with any hint of political corruption (itself a rarity in Louisiana politics) and both were generally well liked among the Louisiana electorate.

While Jindal led many pre-election polls by over ten points in the few weeks prior to the election and was favored by many to win, it was Blanco who made history. During the last few days of the campaign, she was able to paint Jindal as an uncaring bureaucrat and flew past the stunned Jindal camp in the last days of the campaign, winning with a fairly comfortable margin. The post-election analysis did not receive as favorable national coverage as the campaign itself, however, with several articles pointing to Jindal's ethnicity as a reason for his loss.

REPUBLICANS' BIG BREAKTHROUGH IN 2004

After big statewide wins in 2002 and 2003, Louisiana Democrats had reason to feel confident as the 2004 election season began even though the Democrats' most popular state politician, Senator John Breaux, announced he would retire, leaving an open Senate seat to be defended. Louisiana had never elected a Republican to the U.S. Senate and Democrats had high hopes that the streak would continue with most observers predicting that the winner would be Democratic Congressman Chris John who was like Breaux, a conservative Democrat from Breaux's home district in southwest Louisiana. That was not to be the case, and 2004 proved to be a banner year for Republicans, leaving Democrats looking more like their Republican-trending neighbors Mississippi and Alabama than the more competitive state it had been in the last decade.

The 2004 election cycle began with announcements of three well-known candidates for the open Senate seat. Congressman John was joined by two candidates who had briefly talked of runs for governor in 2003. They were Democratic State Treasurer John Kennedy and Republican Congressman David Vitter from suburban New Orleans. In addition, a lesser-known Democratic candidate, New Orleans State Senator Arthur Morrell, received a fair amount of attention as well. With the Republican field to himself, Vitter was seen as a lock for a runoff spot. Since the presidential election guaranteed high voter turnout, Vitter could assume his base would vote and could run a "general election" campaign from the start. Indeed, in addition to several warm personal-introduction televisions spots, the focus of his campaign was on the one high-profile issue where he differed from the Republican establishment—importation of prescription drugs. This populist message together with a rock-solid Republican voting record and Democrats fighting each other secured Vitter's position at the top of the polls.

What Democrats didn't realize until too late, however, was that Vitter's position was much stronger than they had foreseen. Louisiana's odd election system places the top two vote getters into a runoff, and if one candidate receives more than 50 percent of the vote, the candidate wins outright. To the shock and dismay of Louisiana Democrats, Vitter was so strong on Election Day that he won outright with 51 percent of the vote, becoming the first Republican elected to the U.S. Senate from Louisiana.

Chris John and John Kennedy spent most of the campaign focusing on each other and on making sure that Morrell, an African American, was not able to make too much headway into the African-American Democratic base. In addition the Democratic candidates found themselves in a position of being on the same ticket with a presidential candidate who was increasingly seen as doomed in this once-competitive state. The combination of fighting each other and a weak presidential ticket doomed all of the Democrats. The latter problem cannot be overstated. Louisiana was one of only a handful of states where voter turnout was lower in 2004 than in 2000. The legendary Louisiana Democratic voter mobilization drives in recent years had failed to materialize, and Vitter stunned the political establishment by outpacing all Democrats combined.

Republicans had finally elected a U.S. Senator in Louisiana and there were almost no bright spots for Democrats in 2004. President Bush carried Louisiana in almost the same fashion as most other Southern states. New Democratic Congressman Avery Alexander had switched parties and was easily reelected as a Republican. And, in perhaps the most significant blow, Republicans had taken away Congressman John's open Congressional seat in southwest Louisiana. Democrats could point to a win in southeast Louisiana where state Representative Charles Melancon squeaked out a win over Republican Billy Tauzin III, the son of the Republican incumbent who was retiring and left the seat open. But overall, 2004 was clearly a Republican year in Louisiana.

Whether the dominance of Republicans in the 2004 elections was due to a temporary phenomenon, like the popularity of President Bush and the war in Iraq, or more long-term trends, like the migration of Cajun Catholics into Republican ranks, remains to be seen. It is clear, however, that while Democrats certainly remain very competitive in Louisiana, Republican gains in the 2004 elections showed what the right conditions and the right candidates can do for a Republican Party that was very recently considered one of the weakest in the South.

THE DEVELOPMENT OF BLACK
POLITICS IN LOUISIANA

The Republican Party attainment of parity with the Democrats is only half of the story of Louisiana politics in the last few decades. Equally dramatic is the emergence of African Americans as a potent political force. Blacks in Louisiana, similar to the situation in most southern states, began to re-emerge politically in the immediate post–World War II years. As a result of the well-known and successful efforts by southern states to formally suppress black political participation between 1890 and 1910 (see Kousser 1974), the substantial black political participation which had ensued from the Reconstruction era was eventually reduced to a bare minimum between 1910 and 1945 in most southern states. The nation's participation in World War II unleashed a confluence of political, social and economic forces that opened opportunities for southern blacks to begin redeveloping a political presence. This political reemergence took the form of increased voter registration by blacks. The success of the efforts to suppress blacks politically between 1890 and 1910 and the reemergence of black political participation in the 1940s and 1950s can be seen in table 5.3.

As indicated in the table, black voter registration increased dramatically in 1948 and again in 1954. This increase in black voter registration was principally attributable to the U.S. Supreme Court ruling in *Smith v. Allwright*, which prohibited the use of the white primary for violating the Fourteenth Amendment to the U.S. Constitution. The white primary precluded blacks from voting in the Democratic primary, although the small number of blacks who were registered during this period were allowed to vote in the general election.

The white primary essentially denied blacks effective participation in the political process since the dominance of the Democratic Party meant that the only viable electoral competition occurred in the Democratic primary. The Democratic Party always won the general election because the Republican Party was not strong enough to mount a serious challenge. Realizing their denial of effective political participation by the white primary system, most blacks were not inspired to attempt to overcome other formal as well as informal efforts to suppress their political participation during this period. After the elimination of the white primary by *Smith v.*

Table 5.3.   Black Voter Registration in Louisiana

Year	Black Registration	Estimated Black Adult Population	Percentage of Black Adult Population Registered to Vote
1910	730	174,211	.4
1920	3,533	359,351	.9
1928	2,054	359,251	.5
1932	1,591	415,047	.3
1936	1,981	415,047	.4
1940	886	473,562	.1
1944	1,672	473,562	.3
1948	28,177	481,284	22
1954	112,789	481,284	23
1956	152,578	481,284	31
1960	158,765	514,589	30
1962	150,878	514,589	29
1964	164,717	514,589	32

Source: James Bolner, ed., *Louisiana Politics: Festival in a Labyrinth* (Baton Rouge: Louisiana State University Press, 1982), 299. The data for 1910 is for black males only. Women were not allowed to vote prior to the ratification of the Nineteenth Amendment to the U.S. Constitution in 1920.

Allwright, black voter registration in Louisiana increased considerably in the 1950s and the first half of the 1960s.

The Voting Rights Act of 1965 accelerated the rate of black political participation in the state as it did in the entire South. African Americans in 1997 made up 30 percent of the registered voters in the state. There were two major consequences of the significant increase in black voter registration following the enactment of the 1965 Voting Rights Act. One was an increase in the number of moderate and liberal white Democrats elected to office with the help of black voters. The other consequence has been a significant increase in the number of black elected officials. These two developments occurred chronologically in the order in which they are presented in this discussion. One of us (Perry 1983, 1987, 1990, 1996) has suggested elsewhere that this sequence has occurred with enough regularity in the development of black politics to be considered a pattern of black political participation.

Turning to the first impact, the earliest consequence of significantly increased black political participation usually results in the election of at first moderate and then liberal white candidates (Perry 1983, 1990, 1996). The election of Moon Landrieu, a white liberal and father of Mary Landrieu, as mayor of New Orleans in 1967, occurred precisely in this manner. Similarly, in 1971, black voters exerted a critical impact on the election of Edwin W. Edwards, a U.S. congressman from southwest Louisiana, to the governorship. Edwards defeated state senator J. Bennett Johnston in the Democratic primary principally because of the overwhelming support he received from black voters.

In the general election, Edwards received 202,055 black votes, as compared to only 10,709 for Republican Dave Treen (Prestage and Williams 1982). Since Edwards's margin of victory was about 160,000 votes, black support constituted the critical difference. That black voters were able to cast decisive voter support for Edwards was attributable to the fact that Edwards and Treen split the white vote with Edwards receiving 30,000 fewer white votes than Treen (Prestage and Williams 1982, 307–308).

In 1972, state senator Johnston ran successfully for the U.S. Senate seat, receiving the majority of the black vote. Johnston defeated former governor John J. McKeithen. In the 1967 Landrieu election, the 1971 Edwards/ Johnston gubernatorial election and the 1972 Johnston/McKeithen U.S. Senate election, black voters cast the decisive vote for the more progressive candidates. Edwards's 1971 gubernatorial victory and Johnston's 1972 U.S. Senate victory established these two men as fixtures in Louisi-

Table 5.4.   Black Voter Registration in Louisiana, 1965–1996

	Total Voter Registration	Black Registration (La. Board of Registration)	Black Percentage of Registered Voters (La. Board of Registration)
1965	1,190,122	163,414	13.7
1966	1,281,919	238,356	18.6
1967	1,285,933	245,275	19.1
1968	1,411,071	279,468	19.8
1969	1,422,900	291,547	20.5
1970	1,438,727	298,054	20.7
1971	1,633,181	347,098	21.3
1972	1,704,890	397,158	22.3
1973	1,712,850	380,490	22.2
1974	1,726,693	391,666	22.7
1975	1,798,032	408,696	22.7
1976	1,866,117	420,697	22.5
1977	1,787,031	413,178	23.2
1978	1,821,026	429,231	23.6
1979	1,831,507	431,196	23.5
1980	2,015,402	465,005	23.0
1981	1,942,941	454,988	23.4
1982	1,965,422	474,238	24.1
1983	1,968,898	476,618	24.2
1984	2,133,363	533,526	25.0
1985	2,175,264	550,225	25.3
1986	2,141,263	549,916	25.7
1987	2,139,861	551,263	25.8
1988	2,190,634	572,133	26.1
1989	2,113,867	552,781	26.2
1990	2,121,302	561,379	26.5
1991	2,103,334	569,603	27.1
1992	2,241,949	626,678	27.9
1993	2,294,043	636,018	27.7
1994	2,257,080	628,578	27.8
1995	2,400,086	689,046	28.7
1996	2,518,896	724,831	28.8

Sources: Data for 1965 to 1979 were taken from James Bolner, ed., *Louisiana Politics: Festival in a Labyrinth* (Baton Rouge: Louisiana State University Press, 1982), 305. Data for 1980 to 1996 were provided by the Office of the Louisiana Commissioner of Elections, Baton Rouge.

ana politics for the next twenty-five years. Edwards and Johnston won easy reelection to office in 1976 and 1978, respectively, both receiving substantial support from black voters.

The influence of black Louisianians in the 1980 state election was mixed. In the gubernatorial race that year, Edwards could not run for a third term because the state's constitution prohibits a governor from serving more than two consecutive terms. This election was the year that Louisiana's new open elections system went into effect. Republican Treen defeated the Democratic candidate, Louis Lambert, despite strong African-Americans support for Treen.

African Americans had a more positive influence on the 1986 U.S. Senate race. Russell Long, the senior U.S. Senator, had earlier announced that he was going to retire from the Senate at the end of the term. John Breaux, a young U.S. Democratic Congressman, won this race with substantial support from African Americans.

In 1983, Edwards ran for governor against the incumbent Republican governor Treen. This was an evenly contested campaign from start to finish, and in the end Edwards won a narrow victory over Treen with overwhelming support from African-American voters. This was a disappointing defeat for Treen because he had appointed three African Americans to major positions in his administration and had openly sought the African-American vote in the 1983 campaign.

The 1986 U.S. Senate race took place against the national backdrop of the popular Republican president Ronald Reagan having been reelected in 1984. John Breaux, a popular Democratic Congressman, ran against Henson Moore, a popular Republican Congressman. Polls conducted deep into the campaign showed Moore leading Breaux by a considerable margin. Just about at the time that it was widely believed Breaux was not going to win reelection to a second term, a news story broke that the state's Republican Party leadership had plans to conduct a statewide effort to remove African-American voters from the roll of registered voters. This news energized African-American voters to turn out to vote at a very high level in support of Breaux. It also caused a fair number of white voters, who probably were going to vote for Moore but who were repulsed by this effort, to vote for Breaux. There is no doubt that the overwhelming support that Breaux received from an energized African-American electorate was responsible for his election.

In the 1990 U.S. Senate election, the incumbent Democrat Johnston received a very strong challenge from former Klansman David Duke.

Although Duke received 60 percent of the white vote, Johnston won the election with overwhelming support from an energized African-American electorate.

In the 1987 gubernatorial race, Edwards placed second in the open primary election behind Buddy Roemer, a U.S. Congressman from north Louisiana. Edwards decided to drop out of the race and Roemer became governor. In 1991, Edwards ran for governor for the fifth time. This time he placed first in the open primary and entered into a runoff against David Duke. Edwards won the election with strong support from African-American voters. In 1995, in a historic gubernatorial election, former U.S. Congressman Cleo Fields from Baton Rouge made the runoff against Republican state senator Mike Foster. Fields was the first African American to run in a runoff election in Louisiana history. Although Fields received substantial support from African-American voters, he lost the election by a landslide margin.

The substantial increase in black voter registration also resulted in increased numbers of black elected officials. In 1968, there were thirty-six black elected officials in Louisiana. Ten years later, in 1978, the number of black elected officials in Louisiana had increased to 333. As Jewel L. Prestage and Carolyn Sue Williams indicate (1982, 306), practically all of these were local officials, most of whom were elected from predominately black constituencies.

It is a trend in American politics that the higher-level, more prestigious elected offices are the most difficult for blacks to win. Louisiana was no exception in this regard. The first black elected to the state legislature, Ernest "Dutch" Morial, was elected to the Louisiana House of Representatives in 1967. After Morial resigned to accept a judgeship, he was replaced in 1971 by Dorothy Mae Taylor, the first black woman ever to serve in the Louisiana legislature. In 1972, seven other blacks were elected to the state senate. In 1974, Sidney Barthelemy became the first black ever elected to the state senate. By 1980, the number of blacks elected to the state legislature had increased to twelve—ten in the house and two in the senate (Prestage and Williams 1982, 306–307). Additionally, in 1977, Morial made history for a second time when he was elected the first black mayor of New Orleans.

The 1970s represented a watershed period for black officeholding in Louisiana. During this decade, blacks were able to win elections to both houses of the Louisiana legislature and to the mayorship of the largest city in the state. In the 1980s, the number of blacks elected to the state legislature more than tripled. The city of New Orleans has had a continuous history of black mayoral leadership since Dutch Morial's historic mayoral election in 1977. Morial served two terms as mayor and was prohibited by the city's charter from serving beyond two terms. Morial unsuccessfully attempted to have the voters amend the city's charter so that he could run for a third term.

Morial was succeeded by Sidney Barthelemy, who was former president of the New Orleans City Council and Morial's chief nemesis on the city council. Barthelemy, New Orleans's second black mayor, also served two mayoral terms. Barthelemy was succeeded by Dutch Morial's son, Marc Morial, who was a Louisiana state senator prior to his election as mayor. All three of these African-American mayors, except Barthelemy in his election to his first term, won because of overwhelming support from African-American voters. In his election to his first term as mayor, Barthelemy ran a deracialized campaign in which he received a majority of the white and a minority of the African-American vote (see Perry 1996). In 2002 Barthelemy was succeeded by Ray Nagin, a Democratic African American who also received a majority of support in the white community. Nagin caused some political waves when he endorsed Republican Bobby Jindal for governor over Democrat Kathleen Blanco.

In his first win, Barthelemy defeated a strong African-American candidate, William Jefferson, who was a U.S. congressman representing the Second Congressional District which includes most of New Orleans. Jefferson was the first African American elected to the U.S. Congress from Louisiana since Reconstruction.

In 2004, African-American Democratic state Senator Melvin "Kip" Holden defeated incumbent Republican Mayor Bobby Simpson to become Baton Rouge's first black mayor. The mayor of Baton Rouge is also president of the Parish Council; the election requires winning a majority of votes in East Baton Rouge Parish, which has a substantial white majority. Therefore, the election was widely hailed as a major breakthrough for African Americans in Louisiana.

CONCLUSIONS

In the last half-century Louisiana politics has been revolutionized in two ways. First, the Republican Party, which was virtually noncompetitive in Louisiana elections, has emerged to almost parity with the once-dominant Democratic Party. Second, African Americans, who make up almost one-third of the population, have risen from suppression to positions of power. This chapter provides a context and a current snapshot of these ongoing revolutions. In sum, Republicans have won several statewide offices including the governorship, control the state congressional delegation and have made dramatic gains in the legislature. And in 2004, for the first time, a Republican was elected to the U.S. Senate from Louisiana. African Americans have gained tremendous ground in breaking registration barriers, winning local offices and congressional seats but have yet to overcome the patterns of the past by winning a statewide office.

REFERENCES

Bolner, James, ed. 1982. *Louisiana Politics: Festival in a Labyrinth*. Baton Rouge: Louisiana State University Press.

Hadley, Charles. 1985. "Dual Partisan Identification in the South," *The Journal of Politics* 47 (February): 254–68.

Kousser, Morgan J. 1974. *The Shaping of Southern Politics: Suffrage Restriction and the Establishment of the One Party South, 1880–1910*. New Haven, CT: Yale University Press.

Parent, Wayne. 2004. *Inside the Carnival: Unmasking Louisiana Politics*. Baton Rouge: Louisiana State University Press.

Perry, Huey L. 1983. "The Impact of Black Political Participation on Public Sector Employment and Representation on Municipal Boards and Commissions." Review of *Black Political Economy* 12 (Winter): 203–217.

Perry, Huey L. 1990a. "Black Politics and Mayoral Leadership in Birmingham and New Orleans." *National Political Science Review* 2: 154–160.

———. 1990b. "The Evolution and Impact of Biracial Coalitions and Black Mayors in Birmingham and New Orleans." In Rufus P. Browning, Dale Rogers Marshall and David H. Tabb, eds., *Racial Politics in American Cities*. White Plains, NY: Longman.

———. 1990c. "The Reelection of Sidney Barthelmy as Mayor of New Orleans." In Rufus P. Browning, Dale Rogers Marshall and David H. Tabb, eds., *Racial Politics in American Cities*, Second Edition (New York: Longman, 1996).

Perry, Huey L. 1996. "The Evolution and Impact of Biracial Coalitions and Black Mayors in Birmingham and New Orleans." In Rufus Browning, Dale Rogers Marshall, and David Tabb, eds., *Racial Politics in American Cities*, 2d ed. New York: Longman.

Prestage, Jewel L., and Carolyn Sue Williams. 1982. "Blacks in Louisiana Politics." In James Bolner, ed., *Louisiana Politics: Festival in a Labyrinth*. Baton Rouge: Louisiana State University Press.

PART II

THE RIM SOUTH STATES

6

Virginia: The New Politics of the Old Dominion

Mark J. Rozell

Virginia offers an ideal environment in which to study the changing politics of the South. Once the capital of the confederacy, it is the first state in the nation to have elected a black governor. Infamous for its support of massive resistance to public school integration in the 1950s and still subject to Justice Department approval of its legislative redistricting because of a poor history of protecting minority voting rights, the state is undergoing a profound demographic transformation that is changing the nature of racial politics and partisan competition. Once a part of the "solid [Democratic] South," in the 1990s Virginia became a Republican-dominated state. At one point, the GOP controlled the state legislature and the three top statewide offices (governor, lieutenant governor, attorney general). Both U.S. senators elected from the state are Republicans. In 2001, the Democrats broke a string of Republican gubernatorial victories, though the GOP achieved a remarkable twelve-seat gain in the lower House of the state legislature.

For many years a Democratic political machine stymied constructive change and kept the party distant from its national organization and leaders. By the 1980s, Virginia Democratic leaders were pointing the way toward a more centrist philosophy that would better promote the party's chances of winning the presidency in the 1990s. The 1990s witnessed a dramatic realignment of party fortunes with the GOP, ultimately becoming the dominant party in the state. Early in the new century, the Demo-

141

crats control the executive branch and the GOP dominates the state legislature.

More than in most states, many residents of Virginia are strongly aware of their political heritage, both good and bad. Citizens and leaders wage heated political fights over proposals to build homes or retail establishments on undeveloped lands that were once sites of Civil War battles. Although demographic changes have altered the electoral landscape, much of the political culture of Virginia is conservative in the old sense: enamored of tradition, resistant to change, oftentimes even obviously needed change.

At times the cultural resistance to accept change has opened the state to ridicule. When Congress approved a national holiday to honor Martin Luther King, the state legislature responded by declaring that date Jackson-Lee-King Day to also honor Confederate heroes Stonewall Jackson and Robert E. Lee. Black members of the state legislature responded on that celebrated date by carrying posters of their preferred honorees: Jesse Jackson, Spike Lee and Martin Luther King. In 2001, after seventeen years, the combined holiday practice was discontinued and Virginia celebrated Martin Luther King Day. Lee-Jackson Day became a separate date of observance in the Old Dominion.

The capital city of Richmond was mired for several years in a bitter debate over where to place a statue to a black hometown hero, former tennis star Arthur Ashe, who had died from AIDS. The city council and residents initially could not agree to place the statue on historic Monument Avenue, which honors Confederate heroes with imposing statues. The city first agreed to place the statue at a public park and then in light of heavy criticism ultimately honored Ashe with the Monument Avenue location.

The historically all-male, state-supported Virginia Military Institute attracted national attention when it fought a seven-year-long legal battle with the U.S. Department of Justice to maintain the school's single-sex status. In June 1996, the Supreme Court mandated that VMI admit women. Emotions ran deep regarding the Court's decision. In January 1997, GOP state Senator Warren Barry addressed the legislative chamber and declared that women had no place at VMI because they are "physiologically different" from men, their presence in the military causes sexual harassment and "aggressive warrior" men shouldn't be forced "to live in a social slumber party." Most Republican members and some Democrats applauded the speech (Hsu 1997).

For decades the state legislature resisted calls to retire the official state song "Carry Me Back to Old Virginny." Although the lyrics had long been justifiably criticized for being racist, lawmakers defended its standing in a bow to tradition. Finally, in 1997 the state legislature struck a compromise in which it approved a measure to designate the song to "emeritus" status and to commission a new official state song.

Most recently, former GOP Governor Jim Gilmore opened wounds with his declaration of a Confederate History Month. NAACP leaders strongly protested and some threatened to encourage an economic boycott of the state. Gilmore earned some praise from black leaders when he championed separate official celebrations for Lee-Jackson and for King. Yet others weren't satisfied because they would have preferred dropping an official day for recognizing the southern Civil War heroes.

These controversies are illustrative of the modern contradictions of Virginia politics resulting from the reverence to tradition and the need for change. Virginia has progressed enormously in the modern era yet in many ways it remains a bastion of old style southern politics.

THE CHANGING POLITICS OF RACE
AND PARTY COMPETITION

In his seminal work *Southern Politics in State and Nation*, written over one-half century ago, V. O. Key Jr., described Virginia as a "political museum piece." He added that, "of all the American states, Virginia can lay claim to the most thorough control by an oligarchy" (Key 1949, 19). At that time, the Democratic political machine of Harry F. Byrd dominated state politics. Byrd served as governor of Virginia from 1926 to 1930 and as U.S. Senator from 1933 until he retired in 1965. He assembled his machine from the county courthouse organizations of the landed gentry, who preferred stability over economic growth and were fiercely committed to racial segregation.[1]

The machine succeeded in part by restricting participation: In 1945, just 6 percent of the eligible adult population voted in the gubernatorial primary—in a one-party state, the only election that mattered (Sabato 1977, 110). Frank Atkinson described how the state literacy requirement restricted participation by whites as well as blacks. He noted that prospective registrants had to answer extraordinarily difficult questions: for example, to state how many people signed the Declaration of Independence, or to name the counties in the Twenty-seventh Judicial District. One college graduate who failed the test received a postcard saying "Yo hav fald to rechister" (Atkinson 1992, 15).

Although the Democratic Party had a minority faction of "antiorganization" members, Key described them as "extraordinarily weak, [having] few leaders of ability, and [being] more of a hope than a reality" (Key 1949, 21). Republicans were few and far between, and their candidates had no hope of winning a general election. In this way, Virginia resembled many other southern states—overwhelmingly conservative, overwhelmingly Democratic. During the 1950s, Virginia's Democratic machine led a massive resistance to school desegregation, choosing to actually close the public schools rather than obey a federal court order.

Like other southern states, Virginia supported Democratic presidential nominees throughout the early part of the twentieth century. The state's electorate defected to the Republicans only in 1928, when the Democrats nominated a Roman Catholic, Al Smith, who opposed Prohibition. But Byrd himself feuded with Franklin Roosevelt and Harry Truman and dissented from the growing Democratic support of greater civil rights for blacks. Byrd openly expressed his contempt for "Trumanism" and signaled to state Democrats that it was acceptable to vote Republican at the presidential level.

In the 1944 presidential election and thereafter, Virginia supported Republican presidential candidates in every election except the Lyndon Johnson landslide of 1964. In their classic study of southern politics, Earl and Merle Black show that in the period between 1952 and 1964, Virginia was more supportive of Republican presidential candidates than any other southern state (Black and Black 1987, 266). Many of the conservative Democrats of the Byrd machine were more comfortable with Republican presidential candidates than with their more liberal Democratic opponents. In the post-Byrd era, Virginia remained solidly Republican at the presidential level. In 1976 Virginia was the only southern state to back GOP nominee Gerald Ford over Jimmy Carter. When many other southern states were backing Democrats Bill Clinton and Albert Gore in 1992, 1996 and 2000,Virginia backed George Bush, Bob Dole and George W. Bush.

After World War II, the population growth in the southwestern coal mining counties, the naval activity around Norfolk and Newport News and the growing number of government workers in the northern Virginia suburbs of Washington, D.C., changed the demographic makeup of the state and weakened the Byrd machine. The influx of black voters and the elimination of the poll tax after passage of the Voting Rights Act further weakened the machine. Byrd machine candidates faced intraparty challenges, most notably incumbent Democratic Senator A. Willis Robertson, father of Rev. Marion G. "Pat" Robertson, lost a primary election in 1966.

As the national Democratic Party moved to the left, many of the more conservative members of the Byrd machine turned to the Republican Party. Moreover, the influx of relatively affluent professionals in northern Virginia and of pro-military citizens in the Norfolk region provided growing numbers of Republican voters. In 1969, with the Byrd machine in disarray, Virginia elected as its first Republican governor a progressive on race issues who drew attention by enrolling his daughter in the predominantly black Richmond public schools. The Republicans won again in 1973, with a candidate who took a less progressive stance on race issues, and in 1977, with a moderate candidate.

By the late 1970s, Republicans held both the U.S. Senate seats and nine of Virginia's ten seats in the U.S. House of Representatives. Virginia moved toward the Republican ranks more rapidly than did other southern states. Between 1951 and 1980 Virginia elected more Republican governors than any other southern state (Sabato 1983, table 4-7).

THE 1980S ERA OF DEMOCRATIC DOMINANCE

The period of Republican control ended in 1981, when Democrat Lt. Governor Charles S. "Chuck" Robb defeated Attorney General J. Marshall Coleman for the governorship. A former marine married to former president Lyndon Johnson's daughter and the lone Democrat elected to statewide office in 1977, Robb won the governorship as a fiscal conservative with progressive views on race and social issues. Robb's philosophical positioning proved to be an ideal combination for the evolving Virginia electorate.

Robb's victory and gubernatorial leadership had a profound impact on state politics. He presided over a booming state economy and used revenues from the economic upturn to increase spending for education. Robb could have easily won a second term, but the state constitution prohibits gubernatorial succession.

Nonetheless, Robb had established for the state Democratic Party a winning strategy: to court the Byrd Democrats and some Republicans with strong appeals to fiscal conservatism, and to energize the moderate and liberal wings of the Democratic Party with progressive appeals on race, education and social issues.

The 1980s, the Reagan-Bush era, were the heyday of success for the Virginia Democratic Party at the state level. In the 1981, 1985 and 1989 elections Democrats swept all three statewide offices (governor, lieutenant governor, attorney general).

In 1985 the incumbent attorney general Gerald Baliles, like Robb before him, ran as a fiscal conservative with progressive views on race and social issues. He easily defeated a more conservative opponent. Most significantly, Virginia attracted national attention for electing a black and a woman to the other state offices. State senator L. Douglas Wilder, a grandson of slaves, confounded analysts by handily winning the lieutenant governor race, making him the first black elected to statewide office in Virginia. State delegate Mary Sue Terry won the office of attorney general with 61 percent of the vote, making her the first woman elected to state office in Virginia.

The significance of Wilder's victory in 1985 to racial politics in Virginia cannot be understated. At the time Wilder was substantially more liberal than the leadership of the state Democratic Party. It was no secret that such figures as Governor Robb had serious reservations about Wilder's electability and some even tried to recruit other leading Democrats to challenge him for the nomination. But when Wilder won the nomination Robb and other Democrats solidly backed his candidacy, despite predictions that a black candidate would sink the entire statewide ticket. Political scientist Larry Sabato was widely quoted in statewide media when he boldly stated that Wilder's odds of winning were worse than 100 to 1 and when he declared the statewide ticket with a black and a woman "too clever by half." The comments exacerbated an already overheated climate regarding the impact of Wilder's race on the elections, and at the candidate's urging, campaign manager Paul Goldman turned up the heat again when he angrily denounced the political scientist as "in danger of becoming the Dr. Schockley of Virginia."[2]

Wilder's victory permanently put to rest the question of whether a black could win statewide office in Virginia. When others went out of their way to draw attention to Wilder's race, he campaigned throughout the state as a traditional southern politician and even ran televised ads in rural communities featuring a rotund white sheriff with a thick accent offering his strong support for the Democrat.

What made many Democrats and analysts uncomfortable about Wilder was his unabashed liberalism and preference to play by his own rules and not be guided by the leadership of other public figures. Wilder openly criticized the national Democratic Leadership Council, a group of prominent party moderates then led by Robb, as a pseudo-Republican organization. He was openly critical at times of Governor Baliles's leadership and policy priorities. Wilder and Robb openly feuded with each other with a testy exchange of letters in which Robb characterized the lieutenant governor as not a good team player, and Wilder vented his anger at Robb for allegedly taking too much credit for the lieutenant governor's victory.

Although Wilder was at times openly disdainful, Robb left office in January 1986 with enormous popularity—so much so that in 1988 incumbent GOP Senator Paul Tribble chose to step aside rather than be challenged by Robb. The Republicans, resigned to their fate, nominated a weak candidate who had never held elected office.

The GOP did nonetheless make a bold move by nominating a black minister, Rev. Maurice Dawkins, to challenge Robb. Dawkins claimed that he could put together an electoral majority by appealing to both Republicans and Democratic-leaning blacks with his philosophy of inclusive conservatism. At a post-nominating convention press conference, reporters asked him how he could seriously believe that a conservative Republican would attract the support of blacks. He responded that the black community is not monolithic and quipped "we're a lot like white folks in that regard."[3]

Dawkins campaigned vigorously in black churches throughout Virginia trying to promote a message of self-reliance and an anti-welfare state. Ultimately his conservative message was a difficult sell in the black community. He attracted only 16 percent of the black vote (and just over 30 percent of the white vote) and 29 percent overall against the popular former governor.[4]

In 1989 Wilder led the statewide Democratic ticket as the gubernatorial nominee. Although many party leaders continued to harbor reservations about his electability, they uniformly backed his candidacy. Despite his clear victory in 1985, many critics speculated that his race would prohibit him from winning the governorship of a former confederate state.

Wilder's candidacy attracted substantial national and international attention because he stood to become the nation's first elected black governor.[5] That a grandson of former slaves stood to accomplish this goal in the state that was the capital of the confederacy made his possible election all the more intriguing.

What became clear during the campaign was that despite all of the attention paid to Wilder's race and—a year after the odious George H.W. Bush presidential campaign ads featuring a menacing-looking black criminal Willie Horton—the possible temptation for the GOP candidate Marshall Coleman to subtly inject racial appeals, neither candidate drew strong attention to that factor. Indeed, during the campaign and especially during his term as governor, Wilder was more likely to endure criticism from prominent black leaders for downplaying race or for not having been a leader in the civil rights movement than from opponents for exploiting race for political gain.

Wilder's victory was by the slimmest margin for a statewide race in Virginia history. With a record turnout of nearly 1.8 million voters (66.5 percent of registered voters), Wilder won by only 6,741 votes.[6] On election night, exit polls projected that Wilder would win by a margin of at least 5 percent and some news stations early on stated that he had won comfortably, only to backtrack later on as the precincts reported a too-close-to-call election throughout the night. Journalists and pollsters later on said that many of the voters had lied in exit polls in order to appear racially progressive. That explanation, although credible, angered many citizens who felt that by injecting racial motivations to voting patterns, the state's accomplishment in electing a black governor had been tainted. The state's flagship newspaper, *The Richmond Times-Dispatch*, ran a political cartoon featuring a cigar-chomping white man with a Ku Klux Klan outfit telling the exit pollster that he just voted for Wilder.

Despite the closeness of victory and speculation that racially motivated voting nearly cost him the election, the national media celebrated Wilder's win as a historic achievement. The three national news weeklies prominently featured stories on Wilder's victory with the titles: "The End of the Civil War" (*U.S. News and World Report*), "The New Black Politics" (*Newsweek*) and "Breakthrough in Virginia" (*Time*).[7]

The state Democratic Party surely had much to celebrate from its sweep of statewide offices in the three 1980s elections. In large part this success could be attributed to the party's use of convention nominations, which led to the selection of electable centrist candidates. That stood in contrast to the party's poor showing in the 1970s, when such candidates as liberal populist Henry Howell prevailed in primary nominations. A string of statewide defeats convinced the party that it could nominate better candidates in conventions than in primaries—a judgment that proved correct.

Yet there was evidence of a Republican resurgence at the grassroots as the party worked vigorously to recruit good candidates for local offices. The Republicans in the 1980s had continued their steady, incremental gains in membership in the Virginia General Assembly, enough so that by 1989 party members could discuss with credibility the possibility of someday taking control of one or even both legislative chambers. In 1967 the Democrats controlled 34 of 40 Senate seats and 85 of 100 seats in the House of Delegates. By the end of the 1980s the GOP had picked up four seats in the Senate and 25 in the House, giving them 10 of 40 and 39 of 100 seats, respectively. It appeared that a few good election cycles could give the GOP control of at least one legislative chamber for the first time since Reconstruction.

Aiding the GOP cause, Wilder had a troubled governorship during a period of economic recession. The era of state budget surpluses and economic growth had ended, and Wilder had to govern during a period of government retrenchment. State agencies and employees had become accustomed to better than usual government support from the Democratic administrations of Robb and Baliles and expected more of the same

Table 6.1. Party Composition of Virginia General Assembly, 1971–2005

	House			Senate		
Year	Dem.	GOP	Ind.	Dem.	GOP	Ind.
1971	73	24	3	33	7	0
1973	65	20	15	34	6	0
1975	78	17	5	35	5	0
1977	76	21	3	34	6	0
1979	74	25	1	31	9	0
1981	66	33	1	31	9	0
1983	65	34	1	32	8	0
1985	65	33	2	32	8	0
1987	64	35	1	30	10	0
1989	59	39	2	30	10	0
1991	58	41	1	22	18	0
1993	52	47	1	22	18	0
1995	52	47	1	20	20	0
1997	51	48	1	20	20	0
1999	47	52	1	19	21	0
2003	38	60	2	16	24	0
2005	40	57	3	17	23	0

treatment from Wilder. With entirely premature thoughts of national office, Wilder committed his administration to a no tax increase pledge and vowed to cut government spending to keep the state budget balanced, as required by Virginia law. He consequently angered traditional Democratic constituency groups, especially in education and social services, as he promoted program cuts and state salary freezes.

As Wilder championed his fiscal conservatism and basked in the praises of such unlikely supporters of the former liberal as the *National Review* editorial board and the libertarian CATO Institute, he planned an ill-fated run for the presidency in 1992. The governor's frequent travels out of state to promote his national profile resulted in an angry Virginia electorate and a popular mocking bumper sticker that read "Wilder for Resident." Wilder further angered Virginians with an ongoing, very public feud with Senator Robb and with state legislators from the northern Virginia region who believed that his policies were slighting the area of the state that had delivered his election.

Indeed, the geographic base for statewide Democratic candidates is in the northern Virginia communities of Alexandria, Fairfax City, Falls Church City and Arlington, and along what is known as the "urban corridor"—a densely populated stretch of land from these northern Virginia communities, south to Richmond and east along the coast in the Hampton Roads–Tidewater region. Excepting the far southwest coal mining communities with a strong labor union presence, the modern Republican base begins west of the urban corridor and covers many of the state's rural areas. On election night in 1989, television maps of voting showed a thin stretch of land along the urban corridor that voted for Wilder while the vast geographic portion of the state chose Coleman. Yet Wilder won with heavy urban support and Coleman later quipped that he wished that Virginia had a statewide version of the electoral college.

Although Wilder left office with ebbing popularity, he could credibly claim some important accomplishments. He indeed kept the state budget balanced for four years and never raised the state income tax. He took the leadership in successfully promoting adoption by the General Assembly of a one-gun-per-month limit bill. That he did so in a state with a strong pro-gun rights tradition was no small feat (Wilson and Rozell 1998).

During Wilder's term the Democratic-controlled state legislature and the state GOP feuded over redistricting proposals that ultimately resulted in the creation of a black majority district. Consequently, in 1992 Democrat Robert C. Scott of Newport News became the first black elected to

Congress from Virginia in over a century. Yet by early 1997 a panel of U.S. District Court judges ruled that the district was unconstitutional because it had been drawn specifically to suit racial considerations (Nakashima 1997).

THE 1990S GOP RESURGENCE

Wilder's governorship nonetheless proved a liability to state Democrats as they sought to extend their string of electoral victories in 1993. The Democrats nominated their two-term attorney general Mary Sue Terry for governor. The GOP nominated former state delegate and one-term congressman George Allen. The GOP campaign quickly seized on public disgust with the feud between Robb and Wilder, as well as the anger toward Wilder for how he conducted his governorship and more anger toward Robb for a series of scandalous allegations about his personal behavior while governor. In his nomination acceptance speech Allen introduced his theme of asking voters to send a message to the "Robb-Wilder-Terry" Democrats, a refrain repeated throughout the election season.[8] The refrain caught on so well that Terry actually ran television commercials reminding voters that her name was "Mary Sue, not 'Robb-Wilder.'"

Terry ran a spectacularly inept campaign, as she alienated her base by denouncing President Clinton's economic policies, refused to accept help from labor union groups and waited until the final days of the campaign to seek Wilder's support. She lacked presence and performed poorly in the media campaign and in debates. Terry lost in a GOP landslide that gave Allen 58 percent of the vote. In an extraordinary case of ticket splitting in a statewide election in Virginia, voters rejected the GOP lieutenant governor nominee Michael Farris, a former Moral Majority leader. Farris ran 12 percentage points behind the top of the ticket while the attorney general candidate, James Gilmore, easily won with 56 percent.[9] Perhaps more significantly to the GOP, for the first time in the twentieth century the party's candidates for the House of Delegates won a majority of the votes statewide, although the Democrats retained control of a majority of the seats.

In the 1994 Virginia U.S. Senate campaign the GOP nominated Iran-Contra figure Oliver North to challenge incumbent Chuck Robb. Due to widespread reporting of personal scandals, Robb appeared the most vulnerable incumbent Democrat in the nation at the beginning of the year. But because the GOP had nominated probably the only party figure who was even more tainted by scandal, Robb won reelection. What made the race particularly noteworthy was that because the two major parties had nominated controversial candidates, two major figures, Marshall Coleman and Doug Wilder, ran as independents. Ultimately Wilder assured Robb's reelection by dropping out of the race. Coleman stayed in the race as the moderate GOP alternative and pulled 11 percent of the vote.

Also key to Robb's victory was Senator John Warner's opposition to North's candidacy. Warner acted as Coleman's benefactor and convinced the former attorney general to enter and stay in the race. Movement conservatives who backed North fumed that Coleman and Warner were "traitors" to the party and vowed to take revenge on the senator when he ran for reelection in 1996.

Exit polling data by Mitovsky International found that North's base included white born-again Christians and gun enthusiasts. He received about 60 percent of the vote from both of those groups and 81 percent among churchgoing gun enthusiasts. Among the 57 percent who fell into neither category, Robb took 65 percent of the vote. Blacks were key to Robb's victory, giving him over 96 percent of their votes.[10]

Although most of the rest of the nation underwent significant change with the 1994 "Republican Revolution," Virginia opted for the status quo, reelecting its senator and ten of its eleven members of the House. But in 1995 the Virginia GOP determined that the previous year's Republican strategy to nationalize congressional elections offered lessons for state legislative campaigns. Under the leadership of Governor Allen, all but two of the GOP candidates for state legislative offices in 1995 met on the state Capitol steps to unveil their ten-point "Pledge for Honest Change," modeled after the "Contract with America."

The goal of the Pledge was to have the GOP candidates statewide adopt a unified message that included not only their policy commitments contained in the Pledge but also their plea to the voters to give the governor legislative majorities in the General Assembly. Governor Allen characterized the elections as a referendum on his leadership and staked his future conservative agenda on winning party control of the legislature (Rozell and Wilcox 1995). His effort failed in large part, polls revealed, because the public perceived Allen as pushing too far to the ideological right and believed that legislative majorities would enable him to push such initiatives as easing gun ownership restrictions and limiting abortion rights. Yet the GOP did pick up two state senate seats to give them twenty of forty seats in the upper chamber, the GOP's best showing since Reconstruction.

In 1990 Republican Senator John Warner was such a strong candidate for reelection that the Democratic Party chose to let him run unopposed. His reelection made him the first Republican in Virginia history to win statewide three times. He did not get a free ride in 1996. He faced a serious intraparty challenge from a candidate backed by the Christian Right and then a historically well-financed Democrat in the general election. Warner survived both challenges and earned a fourth term in the U.S. Senate.

That Warner faced a serious challenge for renomination is telling of the divisive nature of the modern Virginia GOP. The Christian Right currently dominates the leadership and activist base of the state GOP. Warner is very popular in the state, but most of the Christian Right despises him largely because he refused to back Michael Farris's campaign for lieutenant governor in 1993 and he openly opposed Oliver North in 1994 (Rozell and Wilcox 1996).

In the 1990s the Republican Party in Virginia mostly relied on convention nominations to choose its statewide candidates. The GOP occasionally held open primaries for statewide offices: in 1949 and 1989 for governor, and for attorney general in 1997. More recently the trend has favored primaries: for governor in 2001, and for all three statewide offices in 2005.

Unlike the Democratic conventions that were tightly controlled affairs, the GOP conventions of the 1990s were open to almost all party activists who wanted to become delegates. The dedicated party activists who tended to be more conservative than rank-and-file GOP voters, therefore, dominated the party conventions. The conventions enabled a committed group of social movement activists to take control of nominations away from the establishment Republicans who were more moderate and liked John Warner.

The most important event to Warner's 1996 reelection probably was an April 16 federal court decision to uphold an obscure provision of a Virginia law that enables an incumbent to choose his preferred method of renomination. It was clear that Warner could not win renomination in a party convention dominated by the Christian Right. In fact, given the state party's loyalty rule—that only those who pledge to support the party's nominees and faithfully did so in the most recent elections—it was questionable whether Warner would even be credentialed at his own party's nominating convention. When Warner invoked his right to choose a primary, the state party led by the chair challenged the constitutionality of the law that gave the senator that power. When the federal judge upheld Warner's right to an open primary, his renomination was nearly assured.

Former Reagan Office of Management and Budget (OMB) director James Miller challenged Warner in the primary. Miller had unsuccessfully but credibly challenged North in the 1994 GOP convention. Because of strong Christian Right antipathy toward him, Warner had to take the primary race seriously. The state GOP lacked a tradition of primary nominations and no one could predict turnout. But most believed that Christian Right activists would mobilize against Warner.

Perhaps the best evidence of the divide between GOP activists and rank-and-file party voters was the dramatically different results between a state party convention preference poll and the open primary vote. In the former, held just a little over a week before the primary, Miller bettered Warner by a 3 to 1 margin among the more than 2,000 party delegates. But Warner won the primary nomination by a 2 to 1 margin.

In the general election Senator Warner faced Democrat Mark Warner, a former state party chair with a personal fortune of over $100 million. The Democratic nominee spent over $10 million of his own fortune to wage a credible campaign against a very popular incumbent. Virginians reelected the senator with 53 percent of the vote. Senator Warner achieved 19 percent of the black vote—a better than usual showing for a Republican. That blacks constituted only 15 percent of the voters in this election and Mark Warner received a significantly lower percentage of black votes than other Democrats who have won statewide proved important to the senator's reelection. The Democrat Warner was unable to overcome the senator's 58 percent showing among whites.[11]

The 1997 elections continued the move toward GOP dominance in the state. The GOP nominated Attorney General Gilmore and the Democrats nominated two-term lieutenant governor Donald Beyer. What should have been a competitive race turned yet again into a GOP landslide, as Gilmore proved the much more adept campaigner. The GOP nominee rode to victory mostly on the strength of a single-issue appeal: a promise to phase out a very unpopular annual tax on the value of personal property items such as automobiles and boats. With a booming economy and growing state revenues, Gilmore proposed that it was time to eliminate what was commonly called the "car tax." Perhaps most ironically, Beyer, a Volvo dealership owner, miscalculated the populist appeal of the Gilmore proposal, first opposing elimination of the tax and then supporting a modified version of the idea later on.

The GOP swept the two other statewide races as well in 1997. Retired tobacco company executive John Hager, widely considered the weakest candidate that year, won a close election to lieutenant governor. State Senator Mark Earley handily won the attorney general campaign.

Perhaps most significantly, in 1997 the GOP picked up two additional seats in the House of Delegates, giving the party a 50 to 49 advantage (with one independent). With a 20 to 20 tie in the senate and a GOP lieutenant governor to break votes, the party had effective control of the state legislature and complete control of the executive branch for the first time in the modern era. Additional gains by the GOP in the 1999 legislative elections gave the party clear majorities in both houses. Most important, the GOP earned control of redistricting in the state.

In 2000 former GOP governor George Allen defeated incumbent Democratic Senator Charles Robb. The GOP therefore controlled all three statewide elective offices, both houses of the state legislature and had a majority of the U.S. House delegation and both U.S. Senate seats. The GOP realignment in Virginia appeared to be complete.

VIRGINIA POLITICS IN THE NEW CENTURY

In 2001, the GOP looked to sustain its dominance of state politics. That effort ran into the heavy-spending successful gubernatorial campaign of former U.S. Senate candidate Mark Warner. The multimillionaire Warner spent a substantial sum from his personal fortune to finance the most expensive statewide campaign in Virginia history. But money alone was not the story of his victory. Warner looked back to the 1980s model of Chuck Robb and other Virginia Democrats who won statewide by running right-of-center campaigns. Indeed, Warner ran as a pro-Second Amendment, anti-tax candidate, leading many Republicans to argue that the only reason the Democratic Party had won was because its nominee effectively ran as a Republican.

That explanation of the election result was not altogether wrong. The election also was characterized by huge ticket-splitting, as the GOP handily won the race for attorney general and picked up a remarkable twelve seats in House of Delegates races. Hence, the GOP had some basis for claiming that the 2001 elections were not at all a repudiation of the party or of its principles. Warner's stature grew when Lt. Governor Tim Kaine (D) won the 2005 gubernatorial election. Yet, from the standpoint of the political parties, the election was a mixed result. The Republicans won the other two statewide races (Lt. Governor and Attorney General). The Democrats only picked up two seats in the House of Delegates.

Warner became a very popular governor, and as his successes became better known, by the end of his term many in the party were touting him for future national office. Such talk of a Warner national campaign began seriously after Democratic presidential nominee John Kerry lost the 2004 campaign and many analysts said that the party needed to look in the future toward more moderate candidates, preferably from the South.

CONCLUSION: PROSPECTS AHEAD

The Virginia political landscape has undergone profound changes in the modern era. As recently as the heyday of the Reagan era in the mid-1980s it was almost unimaginable to discuss the possibility of Republican control of the General Assembly and the executive branch. Virginia has emerged as a truly competitive two-party state. Demographic changes, especially the phenomenal population growth of the Washington, D.C., suburbs of northern Virginia, have altered state politics forever. Whereas rural legislators for years chaired crucial committees in the General Assembly and routinely blocked legislation favorable to northern Virginia, today a bipartisan alliance of members representing the "urban corridor" exercises substantial influence over state policy and spending priorities. Much of this change is attributable to population shifts that have given a larger percentage of legislative seats to urban and highly populated suburban areas.

These changes have also meant a political environment more conducive to minority group interests than ever before, although most analysts of state politics would agree that much remains to be done. The black community now makes up 17 percent of the state's population, and no Democrat is able to win statewide office without a very substantial percentage and turnout of black voters.

Black candidates have seen their fortunes improve dramatically in the state. The first black elected to the House of Delegates since Reconstruction was William Ferguson Reid in 1968. The following year Douglas Wilder was elected to the state senate in a special election. Today there are five black state senators and ten delegates (table 6.2). Of course Douglas Wilder's statewide elections in the 1980s were historic, and Rep. Robert Scott is the one black Virginia member of the U.S. House of Representatives.

The modern GOP is making an increased effort in the state to reach the black community. When the state party chair in 1994 said that he didn't favor spending a lot of time cultivating black support for the GOP campaign because it was not "cost-effective," many party members openly criticized the comment and made it clear that they did not share this view. Although success has been minimal, the Christian Right movement in the state GOP has actively reached out to the black community to try to forge alliances on social issues where conservative white evangelicals and many blacks share similar views. In one successful endeavor, Christian Right and black church leaders throughout the state formed a coalition to fight a proposal for the legalization of riverboat gambling.

As in the rest of the South and the nation, black voters remain loyal to the Democratic Party. The increasingly progressive new state population and efforts by both parties to reach out to blacks are signs of the political evolution and maturation of a state with a poor historical record on racial issues. The civil rights era brought profound changes for blacks in Virginia in protecting their basic rights under the law in voting, education, employment and housing.

Today much of the politically active black community is pursuing state policies that will help to alleviate vast disparities in spending in school districts and promote better educational opportunities at all levels and stronger social services. Despite much change, Virginia remains a state

Table 6.2.   Percentage of Blacks in VA General Assembly, 1965–2005

Year	House	Senate
1965	0	0
1970	2.0	2.5
1975	1.0	2.5
1980	4.0	2.5
1985	7.0	7.5
1990	7.0	7.5
1995	8.0	12.5
2000	10.0	12.5
2005	11.0	12.5

strongly committed to a view of fiscal conservatism that favors limits on spending programs. For now, leaders of both parties generally agree that, despite cutbacks in some federal domestic programs and more of the burden for services being placed on the states, Virginia should not adopt big-government approaches to solving public problems.

REFERENCES

Atkinson, Frank. 1992. *The Dynamic Dominion: Realignment and the Rise of Virginia's Republican Party Since 1945*. Fairfax, VA: George Mason University Press.
Black, Earl, and Merle Black. 1987. *Politics and Society in the South*. Cambridge, MA: Harvard University Press.
Heinemann, Ronald L. 1996. *Harry Byrd of Virginia*. Charlottesville, VA: University Press of Virginia.
Hsu, Spencer S. 1997. "Fairfax Senator Decries Coeducation at VMI," *Washington Post*, January 10, pp. B1, 4.
Key, V. O. Jr. 1949. *Southern Politics in State and Nation*. New York: Knopf.
Nakashima, Ellen. 1997. "House District in Va. Ordered Redrawn," *Washington Post*, February 8, pp. A1, 10.
Rozell, Mark J., and Clyde Wilcox. 1995. "Governor Allen's Big Chance," *Washington Post*, October 29, p. C8.
———. 1996. *Second Coming: The New Christian Right in Virginia Politics*. Baltimore: The Johns Hopkins University Press.
Sabato, Larry. 1977. *The Democratic Party Primary in Virginia: Tantamount to Election No Longer*. Charlottesville, VA: University Press of Virginia.
———. 1983. *Goodbye to Goodtime Charlie: The American Governorship Transformed*, 2d ed. Washington, D.C.: Congressional Quarterly Press.
Wilson, Harry, and Mark J. Rozell. 1998. "Virginia: The Politics of Concealed Weapons," in John Bruce and Clyde Wilcox, eds., *The New Politics of Gun Control*. Lanham, MD: Rowman & Littlefield.
Yancey, Dwayne. 1988. *When Hell Froze Over*. Dallas: Taylor Publishing.

NOTES

1. For an excellent biography of Byrd and analysis of his lasting impact on Virginia politics see Ronald L. Heinemann, *Harry Byrd of Virginia*.

2. For a detailed description of these events and of Wilder's campaign see Dwayne Yancey, *When Hell Froze Over*.

3. Press conference attended by author, June 11, 1988, Roanoke, Va.

4. Results provided by the State Board of Elections.

5. The nation's only previous black governor had been appointed to the office. Lt. Governor P. B. S. Pinchback of Louisiana, a Republican, held the office of gover-

nor for about four weeks while the elected governor underwent an impeachment trial.

6. Results provided by the State Board of Elections.

7. All three issues were November 20, 1989.

8. Republican nominating convention attended by author, June 5, 1993, Richmond, Va.

9. Results provided by the State Board of Elections. For a detailed analysis of the 1993 statewide elections see Mark J. Rozell and Clyde Wilcox, *Second Coming: The New Christian Right in Virginia Politics*, chapter 4.

10. Mitovsky International 1994 exit poll data.

11. "Virginia Senate Exit Poll Results," (allpolitics.com), November 6, 1996.

7

North Carolina: Two-Party Competition Continues into the Twenty-first Century

Charles Prysby

In 1960, North Carolina Republicans found little to cheer about in the fall election results. The Democratic presidential candidate, John F. Kennedy, carried the state by about four percentage points even though he barely won the national popular vote. Congressional elections were even more favorable to the Democrats, who won a landslide victory in the U.S. Senate race and captured eleven of the twelve U.S. House seats. State elections were no kinder to the Republicans. Democrats swept the statewide races for the ten Council of State offices (governor, lieutenant governor, and eight other executive offices) by comfortable margins, and the vast majority of the state legislative seats were won by Democrats. North Carolina at that time remained a solidly Democratic state, as it had been throughout the century, albeit one in which Republicans were beginning to show some signs of life.

Forty-four years later, the political landscape was quite different. Elections to the national offices in 2004 were especially favorable to the Republicans. The GOP presidential candidate, George W. Bush, won the state with over 56 percent of the two-party vote. In the U.S. Senate election, Republican Richard Burr captured the seat held by Senator John Edwards, who did not run for reelection but was on the ballot as the Democratic vice-presidential candidate. Burr's victory gave Republicans control of both U.S. Senate seats, as Elizabeth Dole won the other seat in 2002. Republicans also won seven of the thirteen U.S. House seats in 2004. Democrats did better in elections for state government. They maintained control of the governorship, won six of the other nine Council of State offices, and retained their majority status in both houses of the state legislature. In 2004, North Carolina was a competitive two-party state.

THE DEVELOPMENT OF
PARTISAN COMPETITION

The movement from a one-party state to a competitive two-party state was not a pattern of smooth and even Republican growth. Table 7.1 summarizes election results for a variety of offices from 1960 to 2004. As we can see, Republican electoral success occurred earlier for some offices than for others. For example, Republicans first won the presidential election in 1968 and thereafter lost it only once, in 1976. However, it was not until 1994 that the GOP was able to capture a majority of the seats in one house of the state legislature, and the party was only able to hold that majority through the 1996 election. Moreover, Republican advances were sometimes followed by reversals. Great gains were made by the GOP in 1972, but the 1974 election, coming in the wake of the Watergate scandal, produced substantial loses. Also, Republicans were able to win the gubernatorial election three out of five times in the 1970s and 1980s, but Democrats have been victorious in the four most recent gubernatorial elections, beginning in 1992.

The 1972 election was an early milestone in the development of two-party competition in the state. Richard Nixon won the presidential election by an enormous margin. Led by a popular candidate at the top of the ballot, Republicans captured other key offices. Jesse Helms won the U.S. Senate seat up for election, and James Holshouser won the gubernatorial election, which marked the first time in the twentieth century that the Republicans won either of these offices. Republicans also increased their presence in the state legislature to 30 percent, a great improvement over what they had just a decade earlier. But, as mentioned earlier, the 1972 gains were followed by significant loses in 1974. Furthermore, Lieutenant Governor Jim Hunt recaptured the governorship for the Democrats in 1976. By the end of the 1970s, Republicans were about where they were

Table 7.1.   Republican Strength in North Carolina, 1960–2004

Year	Percent of Presidential Vote	Percent of Gubernatorial Vote	Percent of U.S. Senate Vote	Percent of U.S. House Delegation	Percent of State House Delegation	Percent of State Senate Delegation
1960	47.9	45.5	38.6	8.3	12.5	4.0
1962			39.6	18.2	17.5	4.0
1964	43.8	43.4		18.2	11.7	2.0
1966			44.4	27.3	21.7	14.0
1968	57.5*	47.3	39.4	36.4	24.2	24.0
1970				36.4	20.0	14.0
1972	70.6	51.3	54.0	36.4	29.2	30.0
1974			37.3	18.2	7.5	2.0
1976	44.4	34.3		18.2	5.0	6.0
1978			54.5	18.2	11.7	12.0
1980	51.1	37.7	50.3	36.4	20.0	20.0
1982				18.2	15.0	12.0
1984	62.0	54.4	51.9	45.5	31.7	24.0
1986			48.2	27.3	30.0	20.0
1988	58.2	56.1		27.3	38.3	26.0
1990			52.6	36.4	30.8	28.0
1992	50.5**	45.1	52.2	33.3	34.4	22.0
1994				66.7	55.8	48.0
1996	52.5***	43.3	53.4	50.0	50.8	42.0
1998			47.9	58.3	45.0	30.0
2000	56.5	47.1		58.3	48.3	30.0
2002			54.4	53.8	50.0	44.0
2004	56.2	43.5	52.3	53.8	47.5	42.0

Notes: The vote is calculated as a percentage of the two-party vote. *In 1968, Republican Richard M. Nixon won the state with 40 percent of the vote; Democrat Hubert H. Humphrey and American Independent George C. Wallace received 29 and 31 percent, respectively. **In 1992, Republican George H. W. Bush won the state with 43 percent of the vote; Democrat Bill Clinton and independent Ross Perot received 43 and 14 percent, respectively. ***In 1996, Republican Robert Dole won the state with 49 percent of the vote; Democrat Bill Clinton and Reform Party candidate Ross Perot won 44 and 7 percent, respectively. The last three columns give the percent Republican following the specified election (e.g., after the 2004 election, Republicans held 42 percent of the state senate seats).

Sources: America Votes (Washington, DC: Congressional Quarterly, 1960–1990) and Statistical Abstract of the United States (Washington, DC: Government Printing Office, 1960–1992), various editions. The 1992–2004 figures were obtained from the North Carolina Board of Elections.

in the early 1960s, except for the fact that Helms held the U.S. Senate seat, which he won again in 1978.

Other key elections occurred in 1980 and 1984. With Ronald Reagan heading the ticket in 1980, Republican John East captured the other U.S. Senate seat, and Republicans increased their strength in both the congressional delegation and the state legislature, although Democrats remained in the majority in both cases. Hunt was reelected governor in 1980, and

Democrats won all of the other Council of State races, keeping the Democrats firmly in control of state government. Republicans advanced further in 1984, when Republican James Martin won the gubernatorial election. Hunt, who was ineligible to run again for governor, challenged Helms in a well-publicized U.S. Senate election that year, which Helms narrowly won after an expensive, bitter, and highly negative campaign. Republicans again increased their presence in both the congressional delegation and the state legislature, although still remaining the minority party in both bodies.

Following the 1984 elections, some observers expected the Republicans to become the majority party in the state, but in the next few elections the GOP was unable to consolidate and expand the gains it made in the early 1980s. In 1986, former Democratic governor Terry Sanford recaptured the U.S. Senate seat won by East in 1980, and Democrats won back two U.S. House seats that year. Republicans also failed to make significant gains in the state legislature in the late 1980s. The major Republican victory during the late 1980s was Martin's reelection as governor in 1988. In 1992, Hunt again ran for governor and recaptured that office for the Democrats. Democrats also did well in U.S. House and state legislative races that year, but in the U.S. Senate election, Republican Lauch Faircloth defeated incumbent Senator Sanford.

The next major Republican breakthrough came in 1994, when the Republicans, for the first time in modern history, won a majority of the U.S. House seats in the state, gaining four seats that year. They also became the majority party in the lower house of the state legislature, also for the first time in modern history. However, in subsequent elections the Democrats were able to reverse some of these gains, despite the fact that the Republican presidential nominee easily carried the state in 1996, 2000, and 2004. Republicans had only a slight edge in the congressional delegation in elections held after 1994, even in the presidential election years. Newcomer John Edwards defeated Senator Faircloth in the 1998 midterm election to retake this seat for the Democrats. Democrats retained a clear edge in state government into the twenty-first century. The governor, most of the other Council of State officers and the majority of state legislators in both state houses were Democrats.

Much of what has happened in North Carolina politics reflects developments throughout the South. While the details and timing of Republican growth vary from state to state, throughout the region Republicans have gained considerably in congressional and state elections in recent decades

(Aistrup 1996; Black and Black 1987, 1992, 2002; Lamis 1984; Lublin 2004; Scher 1997). Years of notable Republican gains in North Carolina, such as 1980 or 1994, were years in which Republicans made substantial gains in many other southern states. Moreover, national as well as regional trends have affected the state. For example, 1994, a year in which Republicans won a majority of the congressional seats in the state, not coincidentally was also a year in which Republicans captured a majority of congressional seats in the region and the country. Most of the change that has taken place in the state would not have occurred absent the forces and changes occurring outside the state. This is perhaps even truer for North Carolina than for other southern states, as North Carolina is the only southern state that schedules its major state elections to coincide with presidential elections. As discussed previously, some of the years in which Republicans made major gains, such as 1972 or 1984, were years in which the Republican presidential candidate was carrying the state by a wide margin.

In the last few elections, North Carolina has been very competitive. Either party appears quite capable of winning major statewide races. For example, even though the Republicans have won five of the last six U.S. Senate elections, in every case the winner captured less than 55 percent of the vote. This suggests that a Democrat has a reasonable chance in future senatorial elections. Similarly, while Democrats have won the gubernatorial elections from 1992 on, the instances where the election did not involve an incumbent governor (the 1992 and 2000 elections) were fairly competitive races, indicating that a Republican gubernatorial candidate can win under the right circumstances. Incumbent governors have a very strong reelection record in the state, which accounts for the more lopsided Democratic victories in the 1996 and 2004 gubernatorial elections.

The one exception to this assessment of statewide partisan competition is the presidential election, as the state has moved in a Republican direction to the point that in the last three presidential elections North Carolina has been significantly more Republican than the country as a whole. In 1996 and 2000, North Carolina was about seven percentage points more Republican than the nation in the two-party vote division. Even in 2004, when John Edwards was on the ticket as the Democratic vice-presidential candidate, the state was five percentage points more Republican than the nation. Thus, the Republican presidential candidate should carry the state in 2008 unless that candidate loses the national popular vote by a wide margin. Even a narrow national loss by the Republican presidential candidate should be accompanied by a comfortable victory in North Carolina. Perhaps if John Edwards were the Democratic presidential nominee in 2008, the state would be considered a toss-up in a close election, but even this is not certain. Nevertheless, as the 2000 and 2004 election results demonstrate, a strong victory by the presidential candidate does not guarantee that Republicans will be highly successful lower down on the ballot.

North Carolina Republicans clearly have made great gains over the past several decades, as the data in table 7.1 show. But from 1996 on, the picture is one of overall stability and fairly intense competition between the two parties, at least for sub-presidential elections. It may be that the Republican advancement within the state has reached its zenith and the party system is now at an equilibrium level. However, we can see that in the past there were periods of Republican growth that were followed by periods of stagnation and then by more growth. Most statewide elections in the state in recent years have been won with less than 55 percent of the vote, so a modest shift of voters toward the Republicans could yield substantial gains in victories. Similarly, Republicans need to pick up only a small number of seats in the state legislature to gain the majority there. Thus, we cannot be sure whether the state will remain in its current highly competitive state or whether it will drift more toward the Republicans in the near future, a development that already has occurred in some other southern states. While it may be difficult to predict future election outcomes in the state, we can gain some appreciation of the likely nature of future partisan conflict by examining conflict in the recent past. The remainder of this chapter attempts to do exactly that.

PARTISAN CLEAVAGES AND COALITIONS

The two parties appeal to different groups of voters. Partisan cleavages in North Carolina are similar to those in the rest of the South and in the nation. Race, religion, social class, and gender are demographic factors that consistently differentiate Democratic voters from Republican ones. The relationship that these variables have to voting behavior can be analyzed by examining data from recent exit polls in the state. Exit poll data for three U.S. Senate elections and three gubernatorial elections from 1996 to 2004 are presented in tables 7.2 and 7.3. Given that these elections involved different offices, years, and candidates, the similarities that we find across these elections in the base of support for each party are likely to reflect relatively solid differences in voter alignments.

Table 7.2 shows the results of the exit polls for the 1996, 1998, and 2004 U.S. Senate elections. In 1996, Senator Jesse Helms defeated former Charlotte mayor Harvey Gantt. Helms previously defeated Gantt in 1990, a race that attracted considerable national attention because polls during the campaign indicated that Gantt might win. Had Gantt won, he would have been the first African-American senator from the South elected in the twentieth century. The 1996 rematch between these two candidates

Table 7.2. Exit Poll Results for North Carolina U.S. Senate Elections 1996–2004

Variable	% Voting for Gantt (1996)	% Voting for Edwards (1998)	% Voting for Bowles (2004)
All Voters	47	52	46
Race			
White (80/79/71)	37	41	30
Black (18/20/26)	90	91	87
Gender			
Male (49/49/41)	42	43	41
Female (51/51/59)	51	59	50
Income			
Under $50,000 (62/51/50)	50	56	59
$50,000 and over (38/49/50)	42	46	35
Education			
No college degree (63/50/55)	45	54	49
College degree (37/50/45)	49	50	46
Identify with Christian Right? (whites only)			
Yes (34/22)	22	25	NA
No (62/74)	58	61	NA
Ideology			
Liberal (16/16/17)	83	84	84
Moderate 47/46/44)	56	65	55
Conservative (38/38/40)	19	18	21

Note: Entries are the percentage of voters in the specified category who voted for the Democratic senatorial candidate (Gantt in 1996, Edwards in 1998 and Bowles in 2004). The figures in parentheses indicate the percentage of all respondents in that category for 1996, 1998 and 2004, respectively. For example, the data for race indicate: (a) that whites were 80% of the electorate in 1996, 79% in 1998, and 71% in 2004; and (b) that 37% of whites voted for Gantt in 1996, 41% of whites voted for Edwards in 1998 and 30% of whites voted for Bowles in 2004. Only the percentages for the Democratic candidates are shown; these were essentially two-candidate races, so the proportion of the vote not going to the Democrat went almost entirely to the Republican.

Source: Voter News Service 1996 and 1998 North Carolina Exit Polls; National Election Pool 2004 North Carolina Exit Poll. No exit poll data are available for the 2002 U.S. Senate election.

did not attract as much national attention, but it still represented a contest between a fairly liberal black Democrat and the very conservative Senator Helms. In the 1998 Senate race, newcomer John Edwards defeated incumbent Republican Lauch Faircloth to retake this seat for the Democrats. Finally, in 2004, Republican congressman Richard Burr defeated Democrat Erskine Bowles, who had been in the Clinton administration, for the seat held by Edwards, who chose not to run for reelection. Bowles also lost in 2002 to Dole, whose victory kept the Senate seat previously occupied by Helms under Republican control; unfortunately, exit poll data for that race are unavailable.

Table 7.3 contains exit poll data for gubernatorial elections from 1996 to 2004. In 1996, incumbent Democrat Hunt was unsuccessfully challenged by state legislator Robin Hayes, who was regarded as part of the more conservative wing of the Republican Party, especially on moral and religious issues. In 2000, the Democratic attorney general, Mike Easely, defeated Republican Richard Vinroot, former mayor of Charlotte, who was considered more moderate than Hayes and who was the candidate whom Hayes defeated for the Republican nomination in 1996. Easley then defeated state legislator Patrick Ballentine in 2004 to win a second term as governor.

RACE

The data in these two tables show that race is the most prominent social or demographic division between the parties. North Carolina blacks vote overwhelming for Democrats, a pattern that exists outside the state as well. Republicans receive their votes almost entirely from whites. Blacks normally constitute about one-fifth of the electorate, so for a Democrat to win a statewide election, he or she normally must win about 40 percent of the white vote and about 90 percent of the black vote, a challenging but achievable goal.[1] Sometimes Democrats have been able to fashion a winning biracial coalition. Other times they have not. For example, in 2004, Easley and Bowles both attracted nearly 90 percent of the black vote, but Easley also won 43 percent of the white vote, while Bowles could capture only 30 percent of this group. That difference in support among whites resulted in Easley being reelected governor while Bowles again failed in an attempt to be a U.S. Senator.

Blacks have been strongly aligned with the Democratic Party since the

Table 7.3. Exit Poll Results for North Carolina Gubernatorial Elections 1996–2004

Variable	% Voting for Hunt (1996)	% Voting for Easley (2000)	% Voting for Easley (2004)
All Voters	56	52	55
Race			
White (80/79/71)	50	43	43
Black (18/19/26)	87	89	87
Gender			
Male (49/47/41)	50	46	51
Female (51/53/59)	61	57	57
Income			
Under $50,000 (62/53/50)	56	55	64
$50,000 and over (38/47/50)	52	47	45
Education			
No college degree (63/58/55)	55	48	57
College degree (37/42/45)	58	55	53
Identify with Christian Right? (whites only)			
Yes (34/24)	38	29	NA
No (62/73)	56	60	NA
Ideology			
Liberal (16/16/17)	83	87	83
Moderate 47/46/44)	67	60	65
Conservative (38/38/40)	30	38	31

Note: Entries are the percentage of voters in the specified category who voted for the Democratic gubernatorial candidate (Hunt in 1996, Easley in 2000 and 2004). The figures in parentheses indicate the percentage of all respondents in that category for 1996, 2000 and 2004, respectively. For example, the data for race indicate: (a) that whites were 80% of the electorate in 1996, 79% in 2000 and 71% in 2004; and (b) that 50% of whites voted for Hunt in 1996 and 43% of whites voted for Easley in 2000 and 2004. Only the percentages for the Democratic candidate are shown; these were essentially two-candidate races, so the proportion of the vote not going to the Democrat went almost entirely to the Republican.

Source: Voter News Service 1996 and 2000 North Carolina Exit Polls; National Election Pool 2004 North Carolina Exit Poll.

civil rights movement of the 1960s. Democrats became clearly identified at the national level as the party that supported civil rights legislation, such as the 1964 Civil Rights Act and the 1965 Voting Rights Act. Some southern Democrats opposed these measures, but these conservative voices within the party quickly diminished over time, and differences between Democrats and Republicans on civil rights and other race-related issues were quite clear by the 1980s. Blacks have responded to these party differences with strong support for the party that they perceive as more committed to racial equality. Moreover, blacks are more likely to be in blue-collar jobs and to have lower incomes, so the appeal of Democrats to working-class and lower-income voters, discussed later, reinforces the tendency for blacks to support Democratic candidates.

Civil rights or other clearly racial issues have not played a central role in all elections in North Carolina, but there are examples when they have been critical. Probably the best example is the 1990 U.S. Senate race between Helms and Gantt, when a controversial televised political ad was run by the Helms campaign just days before the election. This ad, often referred to as the "hands" ad, showed the hands of a white man holding a letter, which he crumpled up. The voice-over indicated that the man had received a rejection letter for a job that he needed and was the most qualified for and that his rejection was due to the fact that the employer had to hire a minority applicant because of a racial quota. The ad ended with the statement that Helms opposed racial quotas and Gantt did not (Jamieson 1992, 97–100).

Race also played a key role in the congressional redistricting controversies of the 1990s. Prior to the 1990s, congressional redistricting conflicts were not particularly divisive in North Carolina. Districts were drawn in a more compact shape, and counties were rarely split across congressional districts. All this changed with the redistricting for 1992. The state added one congressional district for 1992, thereby requiring that there would be substantial revision of district lines. Moreover, the U.S. Justice Department, whose approval was required under the Voting Rights Act preclearance provisions, specified that the state create two "majority-minority" districts—i.e., districts in which blacks would form a majority of the electorate (Sellers, Cannon and Schousen 1998). The state legislature constructed a plan that contained two majority-minority districts, the First and the Twelfth. Both were extremely irregular in shape and cut across numerous county lines. The Twelfth District was particularly singled out for criticism. A long, narrow and in some places barely contiguous district that snaked from Charlotte to Durham, the Twelfth was widely cited for its bizarre shape. The irregular shapes of these two districts affected the other districts, as all but one of the other districts bordered either or both the First or the Twelfth Districts. No district in the state was composed of whole counties. The majority of counties were now split between two or more congressional districts. In some cases, even precincts were split. This complicated cartography was a result of the legal requirements outlined earlier, the desire of members of the state legislature to protect incumbents and the advancements in computer mapping technology that made such constructions feasible.

Within the state, there was conflict over the plan between and within the parties. Many blacks favored creating two districts that would have a high likelihood of electing minority congressmen, but some white Democrats were concerned that the packing of large numbers of reliably Democratic voters into the First and Twelfth Districts would make other districts more difficult for the party to win, thereby threatening the majority hold the Democrats had on the congressional delegation. Some Republicans opposed the plan on principle, arguing that race should not be a basis for drawing district lines. Other Republicans viewed creating majority-minority districts as something that would increase the number of seats held by their party (Sellers, Cannon, and Schousen 1998). The redistricting plan was immediately challenged in the courts on the basis that it was an unconstitutional racial classification of voters. The case (*Shaw v. Reno*, 1993) quickly made its way to the Supreme Court, which remanded the case back to the district court, claiming that there was a right to participate in a color-blind election process, a right that the state might have violated with its district plan (Sellers, Cannon, and Schousen 1998). The case returned to the Court in 1996 as *Shaw v. Hunt*, and the Court ruled that the Twelfth District lines were unconstitutional. Court controversies continued, including two more cases heard by the Supreme Court (*Hunt v. Cromartie*, 1999; *Smallwood v. Cromartie*, 2001). In the end, the Twelfth District remainder an oddly shaped district but to a lesser extent than in its first form.

SOCIAL CLASS

Differences along social class or socioeconomic status lines are present but generally not that strong. Democrats draw somewhat more from lower-income groups, but the pattern for education is less clear, as we can see from the data in tables 7.2 and 7.3. In some cases, the Democratic candidate did slightly better among those with college degrees than among those without, a pattern of support that fails to fit the expectation that Democrats do better among lower-SES voters. Moreover, if we isolate those who have an advanced degree, these voters often were even more Democratic than others with a college degree. Despite the prevailing images of the Democrats as the party of the working class and lower-income groups and the Republicans as the party of business groups and the rich, the reality is that the parties have been less defined by class differences than by other social and demographic cleavages (Fleer, Lowery, and Prysby 1988). However, class differences were more pronounced in 2004. In both the senatorial and gubernatorial elections, there was about a 20 percentage-point difference between upper- and lower-income voters in their vote choice, a much larger difference than can be found in the earlier elections. If the 2004 patterns are repeated in subsequent elections, then class cleavages will be more significant than they have been in the past.

Socioeconomic status is tied to a number of political issues. Democrats are widely perceived as the party that is more likely to pursue policies that benefit those who are less well off, and Republicans generally are thought of as the party that is more favorable to business and upper-income groups. These perceptions match party positions on a number of issues. For example, in the 2004 U.S. Senate election, Democratic candidate Erskine Bowles proposed a significant expansion of government health care programs to cover uninsured children and adults, favored a substantial increase in spending on education and pre-school programs, and opposed any privatization of social security (Prysby 2005). His Republican opponent, Richard Burr, disagreed with Bowles on all of these issues. In the 2002 Bowles-Dole Senate race, Bowles was in favor of increasing the minimum wage and was opposed to the tax cuts proposed by President Bush on the grounds that they were too favorable to the wealthy; Dole disagreed with Bowles on both issues (Prysby 2004). Similarly, in the 2000 gubernatorial election, Republican candidate Richard Vinroot proposed limiting increases in state spending to increases in population and in the cost of living, something that Democrat Mike Easley opposed (Prysby 2002). Easley supported a medical patient bill of rights and government subsidies for prescription drugs for the elderly. Vinroot opposed these items (Prysby 2002).

RELIGION

Religious orientations clearly divide Democrats and Republicans. The difference between Protestants and non-Protestants, important in many northern states, is not crucial in North Carolina, as the vast majority of voters are Protestants. The important differences, at least among whites, are between more fundamentalist and more mainline Protestant groups and between those who are more religious and those who are less so. The Christian Right has emerged as a force in North Carolina politics, particularly within the Republican Party, which appeals disproportionately to whites who are more fundamentalist in orientation and more strongly religious (Luebke 1998, 213-215). The data in tables 7.2 and 7.3 show that Democrats did poorly among those whites who identified with the Christian Right. The question about identification with the Christian Right was not asked in the 2004 exit poll; instead, an item asked respondents whether they considered themselves to be a born-again or evangelical Christian. Whites who classified themselves in that way (a group that represented slightly over one-third of the electorate) were considerably more likely to vote Republican. For example, about two-thirds of white evangelicals voted for the Republican gubernatorial candidate, Ballantine, who won only 44 percent of the overall vote.

Republicans appeal to white voters who are more religious and more fundamentalist in their beliefs primarily because of their stands on social issues. Questions of abortion, gay rights, and separation of church and state have been salient in recent elections. Republican candidates almost always take conservative positions on these issues, and some have placed considerable emphasis on them. Helms in particular focused on social issues, often talking about abortion, homosexuality, pornography, and a general breakdown of morals in society. However, Democrats are not consistently liberal on social issues. For example, in the 2004 gubernatorial election, Easley opposed legalizing gay marriage, supported the death penalty, and avoided taking a position on abortion. North Carolina voters tend to be fairly conservative on most social issues, so it is not surprising that Democratic candidates often are moderate or even conservative on these issues.

OTHER DEMOGRAPHIC FACTORS

Gender differences have become significant in the state, just as they have nationally, with women usually about ten points more Democratic than men. This gender gap is less pronounced among married voters; it is among those who are not currently married that women are substantially more Democratic in their voting behavior. Many people believe that gender differences in voting are primarily the result of so-called women's issues, such as abortion or childcare. However, gender differences seem to be a result of a more general liberalism among women on a variety of issues, including defense and economic issues.

Age differences frequently have been present in voting behavior in North Carolina. However, there do not seem to be consistent patterns on this dimension. For example, Democrats did much better among young voters in 2004. Governor Easley won 63 percent of the vote of those under thirty years of age, compared to 56 percent overall. In the U.S. Senate race, 57 percent of young voters supported Bowles, compared to 47 percent overall. In 1996 a different pattern existed. Democratic governor Hunt did worse among young voters than he did among others, and senatorial candidate Gantt did only slightly better among young voters, even though he was running against Helms, who might have been expected to appeal much more to older voters. Young voters appear to be more volatile, perhaps being particularly affected by short-term forces because they have not developed more stable partisan attachments. Therefore, we should not conclude that because young voters were strongly Democratic in 2004, they will continue to be strongly Democratic as they age.

REGION

In addition to individual demographic factors, region helps to define sources of partisan support. These regional differences are not included in the exit poll results, but they can be identified simply by analyzing the vote totals for different regions or localities. The traditional regional divisions have been between the east (the tidewater and coastal plain areas), the center or Piedmont, and the west or mountains (Fleer 1994, 29–32; Fleer, Lowery, and Prysby 1988; Luebke 1998, 77–80). The west is the traditional source of Republican strength, and it remains an area in which the party still does well. The east is the traditional base of Democratic strength, and it remains disproportionately Democratic, although Republicans have been making gains in the region. The Piedmont falls between these two regions in party strength. However, there is also an important difference between the major urban areas, most of which are in the Piedmont, and the rest of the Piedmont. The non-metropolitan Piedmont has been very favorable to Republicans in recent elections. Democrats have done better in the major cities. For example, in the 2000 gubernatorial election, the Democratic candidate, Easley, matched or exceeded his statewide percentage of the vote in four of the five major urban Piedmont counties, representing the cities of Raleigh, Durham, Greensboro, and Winston-Salem. Only in Mecklenburg County, where Charlotte is located, did Easley do worse than his statewide mark, and this was partially attributable to the fact that his opponent, Vinroot, was a former mayor of Charlotte. In the 2004 senatorial election, Bowles carried four of these five major urban counties, even though he lost the election; he failed to carry Forsyth county (Winston-Salem), but this was largely because his opponent, Burr, represented that area in Congress for ten years.

Of course, one should realize that regional differences are in part attributable to race. Blacks are disproportionately located in the east, giving Democrats a strong base of support there. The west, by contrast, has relatively few blacks, partially accounting for why Democrats do less well there. Still, regional differences reflect more than just race. Republican strength in the west can be traced back to the Civil War era, when sympathy for the Confederate cause was much lower in the mountain areas, where slaveholding was limited (Key 1949, 219–21). Democratic strength among eastern whites has similarly deep roots. The Democratic Party, as the party of white supremacy, dominated this area of the state during the "Solid South" era of the first half of the twentieth century (Key 1949, 219–21).

IDEOLOGY

Most important, ideological orientations clearly distinguish Democratic and Republican voters. Liberals, who are about one-sixth of the electorate, strongly support Democrats. Self-identified conservatives, who are around 40 percent of the electorate, support Republicans, although perhaps not as strongly as liberals support Democrats. This leaves moderate voters as the determining force. In both of the last two gubernatorial elections, the Democratic candidate has been able to win the moderate vote handily. In other cases, Democratic candidates have failed to do so well with the moderate vote, which in turn usually results in their losing the election.

The ideological cleavages among voters reflect differences between the parties and their candidates. In almost every recent major election in the state, the Republican candidate has been more conservative than the Democrat. Sometimes the differences are smaller, with a moderate Democrat facing a moderately conservative Republican; other times the differences are much larger. But the differences almost always exist. For example, in the 108th Congress (2003–2004), the Republican representatives from North Carolina all had high voting scores from the American Conservative Union, each scoring 84 percent or higher (American Conservative Union 2005). In contrast, the most conservative Democratic member of the U.S. House, Seventh District representative Mike McIntyre, had a 2003–2004 ACU score of 56 percent. The other Democrats were all below 25 percent, and three were below 10 percent. Similarly, the two U.S. Senators, Dole and Edwards, were poles apart in their voting records. Dole received an ACU score of 86 percent, compared to less than 10 percent for Edwards (American Conservative Union 2005).

The 2000 gubernatorial election also illustrates the ideological and issue differences between the parties. Information collected by the "Your Voice, Your Vote" project, a partnership effort involving major newspapers and broadcasters in the state, showed that the Republican candidate, Vinroot, differed considerably from the Democratic candidate, Easley, on most issues (Your Voice, Your Vote 2000). Vinroot called for limiting the increase in state spending to the increase in population and in the cost of living, a proposal that Easley opposed. Vinroot also proposed a system of school vouchers, a plan that Easley repeatedly attacked. Easley favored a patient's bill of rights and proposed using state money to subsidize prescription drugs for the elderly, policies that were opposed by Vinroot. Easley supported legalized abortion, which Vinroot opposed, with some very limited exceptions. The two candidates also differed greatly on environmental issues. Easley argued for stronger environmental regulations and penalties for polluters, measures that Vinroot opposed. On some issues, such as the death penalty, the two candidates did not differ, however. In 2004, ideological differences between the gubernatorial candidates were less clear. Running as the incumbent, Governor Easley conducted a different campaign, emphasizing his accomplishments in office and downplaying specific policy issues.

INTRAPARTY DIFFERENCES

Important differences exist within the parties as well. Among Republicans, there have been differences between those who are conservative on economic issues but more moderate on social issues, such as abortion, and those who are very conservative on these social issues. The increased strength of the Christian Coalition in the 1980s increased this tension within the party (Christensen and Fleer 1999; Luebke 1998, 213–215; Prysby 1997a). In 1996, for example, the Republican gubernatorial primary election was a contest between Vinroot, who was identified as a more moderate Republican, and Robin Hayes, who clearly enjoyed the support of the religious and social conservatives within the party. Hayes attacked Vinroot as insufficiently conservative. In particular, Hayes singled out Vinroot's past support for Planned Parenthood, an organization that favored legalized abortion (Luebke 1998, 215). Hayes won the primary, but his strongly conservative message did not play as well in the general election, which he lost to incumbent governor Hunt. Four years later, Vinroot again ran for the Republican gubernatorial nomination, and this time he took pains to emphasize from the beginning that he opposed legalized abortion.

Perhaps the most important tension within the Democratic Party involves the biracial coalition that is necessary for the party's success. Black and white Democrats often disagree over issues that have, directly or indirectly, a racial aspect. Questions of government spending, such as for education or social welfare programs, often fall in this category. Support for educational programs that would benefit lower-income and/or minority children, such as pre-school programs for disadvantaged children, is stronger among blacks. The same would be true for many social welfare programs. In the 1990s, Democratic Governor Hunt pushed for his version of welfare reform, a proposal that a number of black (and other) Democrats criticized as being too harsh. Election laws also have stimulated racial conflict. In the 1980s, the use of the runoff primary was attacked by many blacks as an unreasonable barrier to the nomination and election of black candidates, and the runoff provision was modified in 1989 to apply only in cases where the primary winner failed to capture at least 40 percent of the vote (Prysby 1997a). Redistricting of congressional seats, discussed earlier, also has been a source of conflict within as well as between parties.

Although both parties have their ideological divisions, developments over the past few decades have created more cohesive parties than existed in the past. Many of the conservative Democrats, who once constituted a large block within the party, have left. For example, Faircloth, who was elected as a Republican to the U.S. Senate in 1992, was a prominent Democrat in the 1980s. He was a member of Governor Hunt's cabinet in the early 1980s and a candidate for the Democratic gubernatorial nomination in 1984. The result of this ideological exodus is that the Democrats are now a party of moderate to liberal individuals. Similarly, the Republicans are more clearly conservative now than in the past. The moderate, western Republican tradition, once a very substantial force, is now a smaller faction within the party. In 1972, the victorious Republican gubernatorial candidate James Holshouser was part of the moderate wing of the party. More recently, however, the Republican gubernatorial candidates have been more clearly conservative, although some more so than others. Of course, among voters, one still finds conservative Democrats and moderately liberal Republicans, but even here this is less true than in the past.

Ideological differences between and within parties also are evident in the attitudes of party activists. Surveys of county-level party activists in North Carolina were conducted in 1991 and 2001. The ideological identification of Democratic and Republican activists for both years are presented in table 7.4. The growth of ideological cohesion in both parties is clear. This is particularly true for Democratic activists. In 1991, only 40 percent of Democratic grassroots activists called themselves liberal and nearly one-quarter said that they were conservative. As we can see from the data in table 7.4, these percentages had shifted greatly in a liberal direction by 2001. Republican activists were already fairly clearly conservative in 1991, but they became even more so by 2001, with a majority calling themselves very conservative. These ideological identifications reflect substantial differences on specific issues. These activists differed greatly along party lines on a wide range of economic, social, and civil

Table 7.4.   Ideological Identification of North Carolina Political Party Activists 1991 and 2001

	Democrats		Republicans	
	1991	*2001*	*1991*	*2001*
Very liberal	10	18	1	1
Somewhat liberal	30	39	2	1
Middle of the road/moderate	37	31	12	6
Somewhat conservative	21	10	44	40
Very conservative	2	3	42	53
	100%	100%	100%	100%
	(634)	(398)	(296)	(407)

Source: Southern Grassroots Party Activists data, 1991 and 2001.

rights issues, and these differences were substantially larger in 2001 than in 1991 (Prysby 1995, 2003).

HUNT AND HELMS

For three decades, two individuals, Jim Hunt and Jesse Helms, were particularly important in defining party politics in North Carolina. Both were first elected to public office in 1972, Helms to the U.S. Senate and Hunt as lieutenant governor. Both continued to be highly successful in their own campaigns, each winning election to statewide office four times after 1972. Beyond their individual success, both built organizations that influenced their respective political party organizations.

Hunt achieved political prominence at an early age. He was elected lieutenant governor in 1972, when he was just thirty-five years old, then elected governor in 1976, and reelected in 1980. In 1984, ineligible to run for a third term as governor, Hunt challenged Senator Helms, who was up for reelection that year. It was the only time that the two directly faced each other in an election. The campaign was the most costly and negative one that the state had seen to that point. Helms won a narrow victory, perhaps helped in part by the fact that 1984 generally was a good year for Republicans. Following this defeat, Hunt did not run again for office until 1992, when he successfully ran again for governor. He was reelected in 1996, making him the highest-ranking elected Democrat in state government for twenty of the twenty-eight years between 1972 and 2000.

Helms was the state's most prominent Republican from 1972 to 2002. He was a strong conservative voice within the party, one that helped to pull the party to the right. The realignment of partisan forces that has characterized North Carolina and southern politics over the past few decades is embodied in Helm's career. He won election five times in part by emphasizing divisive issues, including racially related ones, and by portraying his opponent as a liberal who did not reflect North Carolina values (Christensen and Fleer 1999). In doing so, he attracted a substantial number of voters who were not consistent and reliable Republican voters. These "Jessecrats" were disproportionately eastern, lower-socioeconomic status, white voters (Fleer, Lowery and Prysby 1988). Their support, combined with that from reliably Republican groups, provided Helms with a majority coalition.

Helm's two most publicized election victories were his 1984 victory over Hunt and his 1990 victory over Gantt. In 1984, Helms spent heavily, running a series of negative televised political commercials portraying Hunt as both too liberal and lacking in political principles (Luebke 1990, 137–55). Hunt responded with equally negative advertisements, also spending heavily. In the end, Hunt spent $10 million and Helms $17 million, unheard of amounts at the time. Most observers agreed that Helms won more by raising negative opinions of Hunt than by increasing his own positive image among voters (Luebke 1990, 137–55). But while Hunt lost the ideologically charged 1984 election, his victory in his four gubernatorial elections revealed a different candidate, one who was able to emphasize issues with broad appeal, such as improving education, the issue that Hunt was most associated with, and attracting new industries to the state.

The 1990 Helms-Gantt race also received considerable national attention. Gantt proved to be a surprisingly strong candidate, one who also was able to raise considerable amounts of campaign money, partly because he appeared to be running a competitive campaign against Helms. As in 1984, both candidates were able to draw financial support from outside the state. Liberal Democrats from around the country were anxious to retire Helms from Congress, while conservative Republicans were equally anxious to keep one of their heroes on the Senate floor. Helms, who repeatedly criticized Gantt for having "extremely liberal" values, ran a series of negative commercials, attacking Gantt for being closely tied to homosexual groups, approving of late-term abortions done on the basis of the gender of the fetus, favoring tax increases and supporting sizable defense cuts (Prysby 1996). Helms also attacked Gantt personally. One televised commercial argued that Gantt used his minority status to acquire a television broadcast license, which he quickly sold at a substantial profit, the implication being that Gantt had unfairly used his race to benefit financially (Prysby 1996). The most controversial Helms television advertisement was the infamous "hands" ad, discussed earlier. The ad was widely criticized as playing to racial fears, but it also was widely regarded as effective. Helms won the election with 52 percent of the vote. Helms and Gantt faced each other again in 1996, in a similar but somewhat less-intense campaign, which Helms again won (Christensen and Fleer 1999; Prysby 1997b).

Both Hunt and Helms built organizations that both helped their own election efforts and influenced their respective political parties. Hunt concentrated on building a network of key individuals in counties throughout the state, a personal organization that provided both fundraising and grassroots support. Hunt also did much to improve the state party organization. During his first eight years as governor, the state party acquired a new and more spacious headquarters and expanded its staff and budget considerably (Prysby 1997a). Prior to the rise of Republicanism in the state, the Democrats possessed a minimal state party organization, as little more was needed. But as the Republicans put forth more competitive candidates and developed their own state party organization, the Democrats felt compelled to respond, and Hunt helped shape this response.

Helms's organizational efforts were quite different. After his 1972 election, the Congressional Club, later renamed the National Conservative Club, was formed to help retire his campaign debts (Luebke 1998, 162–63). This organization became a highly effective fundraising body, using in particular direct mass-mailing methods. Besides directly aiding Helms in his reelection efforts, the Club played a crucial role in the victory of other Helms-supported candidates, including the successful U.S. Senate campaigns of John East in 1980 and Faircloth in 1992. Helms's organizational effort, unlike Hunt's, lacked a substantial grassroots component. Moreover, Helms and his Club sometimes were in direct conflict with other factions in the Republican Party. For example, in the 1986 U.S. Senate race, the Club supported a primary challenger to incumbent Republican Senator James Broyhill, who had recently been appointed to the Senate by Governor Martin to fill the unexpired term of Senator East. The divisive nature of the primary may have contributed to Broyhill's loss to Sanford in the general election. Helms and the Club parted company in the mid-1990s over some personal matters, and the Club ceased to exist shortly afterwards (Christensen and Fleer 1999; Luebke 1998, 163).

Both Hunt and Helms illustrate the basis for the success of Democrats and Republicans in the post-civil rights South. Hunt represents the way in which southern Democrats have been able to retain a majority of the voters by putting together a biracial coalition that includes, most important, moderate whites. Hunt essentially provided a model that other southern Democrats, such as David Breaux in Lousianna, Bob Graham in Florida, Fritz Hollings in South Carolina, Zell Miller in Georgia and even Bill Clinton in Arkansas, used to win statewide office even as Republicans were repeatedly winning presidential elections in the region.

If Hunt illustrates how contemporary southern Democrats have been able to retain majority support through a biracial coalition, Helms epitomizes how Republicans have been able to attract former Democratic voters through conservative appeals on divisive issues. Especially in his victories over Hunt in 1984 and Gantt in 1990 and 1996, Helms used racial and social issues to attack his opponent as a liberal who was out of touch with North Carolina values. His aggressive ideological campaigns may be seen as a model that some southern Republicans subsequently adopted. However, other southern Republicans have adopted less aggressive campaigns. In the two most recent U.S. Senate elections in North Carolina, the Republican candidates (Dole in 2002 and Burr in 2004) ran more moderate campaigns that did not emphasize divisive social issues.

FUTURE PROSPECTS

North Carolina continues to be a highly competitive two-party state. Whether it will remain intensely competitive is unclear. Republicans hope that they can extend the support that their presidential candidates have received further down the ballot. Clearly, if nearly all the voters who cast a Republican ballot for president in the last two elections had continued to vote Republican for other offices, Republicans would have won many more offices. But there are good reasons why a significant number of Republican presidential voters have voted for Democrats for other offices. North Carolina Democrats generally are more ideologically moderate than their national counterparts, and North Carolina Republicans are often more conservative than northern Republicans, so for some voters there is no ideological inconsistency in voting for a Republican presidential candidate and a Democratic gubernatorial candidate, for example. Also, state government elections often revolve around less ideologically divisive issues, such as improving education, building roads, and attracting new industry, which may help to explain why Republicans have done better in elections for national office than for state office.

Regardless of the level of competitive balance between the two parties, it does seem likely that partisan conflict will continue to involve many of the issues that have been important during the past two decades. Race most certainly will continue to be important, directly and indirectly, in future elections, both dividing the two parties and also creating tensions within the Democratic Party. Religiously related issues are likely to be salient in future elections. Republicans probably will continue to be internally divided between those who are more sympathetic to the Christian Right and those who are more moderate on social issues. Social class and the economic issues that are related to class have been significant in the past and seemed particularly strong in 2004, suggesting that they are likely to be important in the future.

Of course, exactly how these conflicts play out in future elections will depend on the behavior of specific party leaders and candidates. Democrats are likely to emphasize economic issues and downplay social issues, as this strategy seems to have been most successful in the past, but it is not clear exactly how Democrats will position themselves on these issues. One strategy would be to adopt very moderate positions, even on economic issues, hoping to appeal to moderate and conservative swing voters. Another possibility would be to take stronger and more clearly liberal positions, at least on economic issues. Sometimes the same person has adopted both strategies, depending on the year. Easley was more clearly liberal in his 2000 campaign than he was in 2004, for example. Similar questions of strategy exist for Republicans. Will future Republican candidates present themselves as strong conservative voices (e.g., Helms) or as moderate consensus builders (e.g., Dole)? The manner in which Democratic and Republican candidates choose to conduct their campaigns and present themselves to the voters will influence the nature of partisan conflict.

Finally, it is worth remembering that the future of North Carolina politics cannot be considered apart from national politics. If the next decade is one in which Republicans dominate nationally, retaining the presidency and expanding their currently narrow control over Congress, Republicans in North Carolina are likely to prosper. But if instead we see a Democratic resurgence nationally, Republicans are not likely in advance in the state. Given the highly unpredictable nature of national politics over the past ten years, it would be foolish to predict which of these scenarios will actually occur in the next decade.

REFERENCES

Aistrup, Joseph A. 1996. *The Southern Strategy Revisited: Republican Top-Down Advancement in the South.* Lexington, KY: The University Press of Kentucky.

American Conservative Union. 2005. "2003–2004 Ratings of Congress: North Carolina." ACU Web Site. www.acuratings.org/statedelegation.asp?state = nc (accessed April 20).

Black, Earl, and Merle Black. 1987. *Politics and Society in the South.* Cambridge, MA: Harvard University Press.

————. 1992. *The Vital South*. Cambridge, MA: Harvard University Press.

————. 2002. *The Rise of Southern Republicans*. Cambridge, MA: Harvard University Press.

Christensen, Rob, and Jack D. Fleer. 1999. "North Carolina: Between Helms and Hunt No Majority Emerges." In *Southern Politics in the 1990s*, edited by Alexander P. Lamis. Baton Rouge, LA: Louisiana State University Press.

Fleer, Jack D. 1994. *North Carolina Government and Politics*. Lincoln, NE: University of Nebraska Press.

Fleer, Jack D., Roger C. Lowery, and Charles L. Prysby. 1988. "Political Change in North Carolina." In *The South's New Politics*, edited by Robert Swansbrough and David Brodsky. Columbia, SC: University of South Carolina Press.

Jamieson, Kathleen Hall. 1992. *Dirty Politics*. New York: Oxford University Press.

Key, V. O., Jr. 1949. *Southern Politics in State and Nation*. Knoxville, TN: University of Tennessee Press.

Lamis, Alexander P. 1984. *The Two Party South*. New York: Oxford University Press.

Lublin, David. 2004. *The Republican South*. Princeton, NJ: Princeton University Press.

Luebke, Paul. 1990. *Tar Heel Politics*. Chapel Hill, NC: University of North Carolina Press.

————. 1998. *Tar Heel Politics 2000*. Chapel Hill, NC: University of North Carolina Press.

Prysby, Charles. 1995. "North Carolina: Emerging Two-Party Politics." In *Southern State Party Organizations and Activists*, edited by Charles D. Hadley and Lewis Bowman. Westport, CT: Praeger.

————. 1996. "The 1990 U.S. Senate Election in North Carolina." In *Race, Politics, and Governance in the United States*, edited by Huey L. Perry. Gainsville, FL: University Press of Florida.

————. 1997a. "North Carolina." In *State Party Profiles*, edited by Andrew A. Appleton and Daniel S. Ward. Washington, DC: CQ Press.

————. 1997b. "North Carolina: Republican Consolidation or Democratic Resurgence?" In *The 1996 Presidential Election in the South*, edited by Laurence W. Moreland and Robert P. Steed. Westport, CT: Praeger.

————. 2002. "North Carolina: Continued Two-Party Competition." In *The 2000 Presidential Election in the South*, edited by Robert P. Steed and Laurence W. Moreland. Westport, CT: Praeger.

————. 2004. "A Civil Campaign in a Competitive State: The 2002 North Carolina U.S. Senate Election." In *Running on Empty? Political Discourse in Congressional Elections*, edited by L. Sandy Maisel and Darrell M. West. Lanham, MD: Rowman and Littlefield.

————. 2005. "North Carolina: Color the Tar Heels Federal Red and State Blue." *American Review of Politics* (forthcoming in a special double issue, spring/summer, on "Perspectives on the 2004 Presidential Election in the South," edited by Larry Moreland and Robert Steed).

Scher, Richard. 1997. *Politics in the New South*, 2nd edition. Armonk, NY: M. E. Sharpe.

Sellers, Patrick J., David T. Cannon, and Matthew M. Schousen. 1998. "Congressional Redistricting in North Carolina." In *Race and Redistricting in the 1990s*, edited by Bernard Grofman. New York: Agathon Press.
Your Voice, Your Vote. 2000. Web site of the Your Voice, Your Vote Partnership. www.yvyv.com (accessed December 28, 2000).

NOTES

Author's Note: I appreciate the research assistance of Benjamin Anderson, an undergraduate political science student at UNCG, on this chapter.

1. The 2004 North Carolina exit poll had blacks as about one-fourth of the electorate, a much higher proportion than the one-fifth that was typical for previous elections. The reasons for this large increase in the black proportion of the vote are unclear. It might represent a much greater turnout among blacks, relative to the turnout among whites. However, most reports about the campaign indicated that both parties made strong efforts to mobilize their supporters and that turnout was up in the state overall. If this is the case, it seems unlikely that the black turnout could have increased enough to make black voters go from one-fifth to one-fourth of the electorate. It may be the case that this exit poll overrepresented black voters. Thus, we should be cautious in interpreting the 2004 figures for the racial composition of the electorate.

8

Tennessee: Once a Bluish State, Now a Reddish One

Michael Nelson

The history of chapter titles in the scholarly literature on Tennessee politics is in some ways a history in microcosm of Tennessee politics itself. In 1949 V.O. Key invoked the state's southern and Democratic heritage by calling his chapter about Tennessee "The Civil War and Mr. Crump." A quarter-century later, Lee S. Greene and Jack E. Holmes (1972) celebrated the state's transition to racial integration and legislative reapportionment with "A Politics of Peaceful Change." More than a quarter-century after that, John Lyman Mason (2003) marked another feature of Tennessee politics, its consistent contributions to the roster of prominent national political leaders. He called his chapter "Politics and Politicians Who Matter Beyond State Borders."

Most chapter titles have weighed in, as this one does, on the question of party competition in Tennessee. "Genuine Two-Party Politics" was the title of both Jack Bass and Walter DeVries's chapter on Tennessee in 1976 and David Brodsky's in 1998. Alexander Lamis joined the chorus, labeling Tennessee a "Composite of All the South" in a 1984 book called *The Two-Party South*. Taking a different tack, Robert Swansbrough and Brodsky used "Weakening Party Loyalties and Growing Independence" in their 1998 chapter on Tennessee politics. A year later, Philip Ashford and Richard Locker identified the Republican sweep of all three statewide offices in the 1994 elections as "A Partisan Big Bang Among Quiet Accommodation."

Anyone who presumes to join this long and distinguished scholarly procession is well advised to choose his or her own words with care. The title of this chapter toys with the red state–blue state distinction in the election-night maps that the television networks have used in recent years to display which states the Republicans have won (the red ones) and which (blue) states have gone Democratic. In truth, although Tennessee has never been purely red or blue, it has nonetheless evolved from being a bluish state to a reddish one. One-and-a-half party competition, with the Republicans gradually replacing the Democrats in the dominant position, has typified most of Tennessee's post–World War II political history.

Two features of Tennessee geography help to explain why the state has not been solidly Democratic or solidly Republican, even though it has tended one way or the other in different eras. One is the state's location. The labels that scholars have variously used to place Tennessee within the South—"Peripheral," "Rim," "Outer" and so on—all serve to remind that Tennessee is on the northern edge of the South, not embedded within it. Unlike, say, Alabama or North Carolina, Tennessee shares borders with two states that are not generally reckoned as southern, Kentucky and Missouri.

The other geographical feature of Tennessee that bears on its politics is the state's extraordinary length. Tennessee is more than 500 miles long from east to west. A voter in Mountain City, in the state's northeastern corner, lives closer to Canada than to Memphis, which is as far south and west as one can go and still be in Tennessee. With this length comes variety, so much so that the state officially recognizes three "grand divisions" in various ways (including a three-star flag): mountainous East Tennessee, the rolling hills of Middle Tennessee, and the flat fertile lands of West Tennessee.

The rest of this chapter consists of a series of seven prose "snapshots" of Tennessee politics in the postwar era, the first one taken in 1946 and the rest at ten-year intervals through (prospectively) 2006. Although these snapshots unfold page by page within the covers of this book, they might better be imagined side by side in a row, like a spectrum of colors. Pure blue and pure red do not appear on this spectrum. But looked at in sequence, the flow from bluish on the left to reddish on the right is hard to miss.

SNAPSHOT 1: 1946

Tennessee was never a solidly Democratic state, at least not after Andrew Jackson, a Tennessean, left the White House in 1837. In 1844 Tennessee voted for the Whig candidate for president, Henry Clay, even as the rest of the country was electing Tennessee's former Democratic governor, James K. Polk, by nearly a two-to-one electoral vote majority. In the early twentieth century, Tennessee occasionally (1910, 1912, 1928) elected Republican governors. Since 1867, the Second Congressional District has always elected a Republican to the House of Representatives, and since 1880, the First District always has. Indeed, in several elections from the end of Reconstruction until the 1950s, these East Tennessee districts were the only two in the South whose voters sent Republican members to Congress.[1] East Tennesseans also reliably elected Republicans to the state legislature. In 1939, for example, the 17 percent of state House members who were Republicans, and the 12 percent of Republican state senators, were nearly three times as many as in any other southern state (calculated from data in Scher 1992, 166). In presidential elections, Tennessee was the only state in the South to support Republican candidate Warren G. Harding against Democrat James M. Cox in 1920; in 1928 it supported Herbert Hoover against his Democratic opponent, New York Governor Al Smith. Indeed, in presidential elections from 1900 to 1944, Tennesseans gave a larger share of their votes to the Republican nominee for president than the people of any other southern state in all but two elections, and in those two they were a close second.[2]

One could say, then, that in 1946, at the time of this chapter's first political snapshot, Tennessee was the most Republican state in the South. But a more accurate way of putting it would be that Tennessee was the least Democratic of all the southern Democratic states—bluish in a sea of blue. In the twentieth century through 1946, for example, the GOP's three victories for governor paled in comparison to the Democrats' twenty-one, and all three depended on deep but temporary divisions within the Democratic Party. The same could be said of the two (out of twelve) presidential elections in which Tennessee voted Republican. And never were Democratic divisions so serious as to affect Senate elections, which Democratic candidates won without exception. To be sure, GOP strength was unflagging in the Smokies of East Tennessee, which had stoutly resisted secession and supported the Union during the Civil War. But these "Mountain Republicans" nearly marked the extent of Republican influence in the state.[3] To call them the GOP's base would be a misnomer because little was built on it. As V. O. Key (1949, 75) wrote at the time, "Tennessee in a sense has not one one-party system but two one-party systems," with the one-party Republican East considerably smaller than the one-party Democratic Middle and West.

Indeed, Key found that one of the firmest props of the statewide Democratic majority in Tennessee in this era was the reluctance of East Tennessee Republicans to see their party grow. The "Tennessee Republican high command contemplates victory in state races with a shudder," Key wrote (1949, 78), with only mild hyperbole. As the established Republican leadership saw it, growth might mean losing control of the party apparatus to new members. Even worse, it might mean losing the political patronage that Middle and West Tennessee Democratic leaders allocated to their East Tennessee Republican peers in exchange for mild acquiescence to statewide Democratic control. Tennessee politics, Key (1949, 79) observed, was akin to "monopolistic competition" between two firms, each of which preserves its position by allowing the other to dominate a portion of the market without fear of challenge.

As for the state's Democratic Party, it was controlled in large measure by E. H. Crump, the conservative, pro-business Democratic boss of Memphis and surrounding Shelby County. From the 1910s to the early 1950s (the longest period of control by any urban machine politician in the twentieth century), Crump dominated his city with patronage, contracts, "efficient government, a clean city, and other blessings, but all without freedom or liberty" (Key 1949, 63).

In 1932 Crump extended his span of control to include the state government. His approach was simple: He would personally choose candidates for statewide office and, by persuading Memphians to cast their votes for them almost unanimously, give his slate a virtually insurmountable lead in the Democratic primary that, in the absence of serious Republican competition, was tantamount to election. In 1936, for example, the Crump-endorsed candidate for governor, Gordon Browning, won the Democratic primary on the basis of the 59,874 votes he received in Shelby County. Two years later, having fallen out with Crump, Browning's Shelby County vote shrunk to 9,315, costing the governor his bid for reelection. Crump's most reliable allies during his long period of statewide control were Kenneth McKellar, a Memphis Democrat who served in the Senate from 1917 to 1953, and B. Carroll Reece, the first district's Republican House member from 1920 to 1946.[4] McKellar saw to it that Crump controlled most of the federal patronage in the state, and Reece distributed the Republican jobs that Crump allotted to East Tennessee in return for keeping the GOP quiescent in statewide elections.

SNAPSHOT 2: 1956

The first decade after World War II was marked by significant changes in Tennessee politics. Crump died in 1954, but by then his control of the state had already predeceased him by several years. With the end of the Crump regime, several Tennesseans emerged as nationally influential political leaders, an unprecedented development since the Jackson-Polk era of a century before but one that has persisted ever since. And the state went Republican in two presidential elections, this time in ways that, unlike Harding and Hoover's flukish victories in the 1920s, augured a new era of competition for Tennessee's eleven electoral votes.

Lots of fingerprints were on the weapons that slew the Crump machine. Returning veterans eager for change, northern migrants unaccustomed to boss rule, rising labor unions impatient with pro-business conservatism, the gradual waning of organizational vitality that comes with the passage of time and his own bad choices were among the causes of Crump's rapid decline in statewide influence. In 1948, matters came to a head. Crump opposed President Harry S. Truman's bid for reelection in favor of South Carolina governor J. Strom Thurmond, the anti-civil rights States' Rights Party nominee. Thurmond ran well in Memphis and nearby counties in West Tennessee, which in climate, economy and history resembled the four Deep South states that he carried on Election Day. But Thurmond won only 14 percent of the statewide vote in Tennessee. Crump's abandonment of his party in the presidential election helped sour the voters on his candidates for governor and senator, both of whom were soundly defeated in the Democratic primary. The Crump era in state politics, if not in Memphis, was over.

The anti-Crump candidate who won the Senate election in 1948, Estes Kefauver, was the first of three Democrats to enter the national political spotlight. Albert Gore, elected to the Senate in 1952 after beating longtime Crump stalwart McKellar in the Democratic primary, and Frank Clement, who was elected governor in 1952 and reelected in 1954, were the others. All three were more liberal than was the norm in Tennessee or the rest of the South, which earned them the attention of Democrats around the country.

Kefauver parlayed a long series of nationally televised Senate hearings on organized crime into a candidacy for the Democratic presidential nomination in 1952. He lost to Truman's anointed successor, Governor Adlai E. Stevenson of Illinois, but not before winning fourteen of seventeen state primaries, making him the century's first southerner to mount a national campaign for his party's nomination (Black and Black 1992, 100). In 1956 Kefauver lost to Stevenson again, then defeated Gore and Sen. John F. Kennedy of Massachusetts to win the vice presidential nomination when Stevenson threw the choice open to the convention. Clement was featured at the convention as the keynote speaker, but his florid oratorical style, well suited to courthouse squares in rural Tennessee, did not translate well into the national idiom. ("Bombastic cornpone" was one of the kinder descriptions of Clement's long, loud, and melodramatic effort.)

The national Democratic Party's interest in Kefauver, Gore, and Clement in 1956 was not coincidental. Two years earlier, when the Supreme Court ruled in *Brown v. Board of Education* that public school segregation was unconstitutional, all three Tennessee Democrats had responded in ways that set them apart from most other southern political leaders. Clement made clear that the ruling would be enforced in his state, then called out the National Guard when segregationist thugs burned down the high school in Clinton; he was the first southern governor to take such forceful action. Kefauver and Gore were two of only three southern Democratic senators (Senate Majority Leader Lyndon B. Johnson of Texas was the third) who denied their signatures to the Southern Manifesto, a defiant defense of racial segregation signed by nineteen southern senators and ninety-six southern representatives, all of them Democrats.

Because of Tennessee's northern location within the South, the ability of Kefauver, Gore, and Clement to disdain the region's rampant racial conservatism in the 1950s (each survived to win more statewide elections) was not altogether surprising. African Americans in the South tended to be treated worst in the states where their numbers were greatest. In Tennessee, blacks made up 16 percent of the population, second lowest to Texas among the southern states. "In the cities there has long been no serious obstacle to Negro voting" in Tennessee, Key noted (1949, 75). In Memphis, especially, where the state's African-American population was concentrated, black voters had been a mainstay of Crump's power, and he had acknowledged their support by paying their poll taxes and giving them "a fairer break than usual in public services" (Key 1949, 74).

As for the state's Republicans in the first postwar decade, they consistently maintained their two East Tennessee seats in Congress but did not add to them. (The same was true of their representation in the state legislature.) The GOP also continued to lose every election for governor and senator. Sometimes Republican candidates waged strenuous campaigns for statewide office (Reece ran hard for senator and Grand Ole Opry star Roy Acuff for governor in 1948, and each won around one-third of the vote), but sometimes the party ran no candidate at all.

The bright spot for Republicans—and it was bright indeed—was that Tennessee was one of four southern states (Virginia, Florida and Texas were the others) to support the Republican candidate for president, Dwight D. Eisenhower, not just in 1952 but also, despite native son Kefauver's presence on the Democratic ticket, in 1956. Although Eisenhower ran best in traditionally Republican East Tennessee, his margin of victory came from the inroads he made among well-educated, middle-class voters in the state's metropolitan areas—the very group that had been growing most rapidly since the war.

Excitement about Eisenhower drew some of his supporters into local and state Republican politics, as did the presence in Washington, for the first time since 1932, of a patronage-rich Republican administration. The long era of monopolistic competition was about to end. The revitalized GOP extended its sights to the Middle and Western two-thirds of the state, where Democrats had seldom been challenged. Tennessee remained a bluish state in 1956, but Republicans were readying their brushes with red paint.

SNAPSHOT 3: 1966

Richard Nixon extended the Tennessee GOP's winning streak in presidential elections to three in 1960, demonstrating that Republican chances for success in the state did not depend on having a national hero like Eisenhower on the ballot. Yet it was the losing Republican presidential candidate in 1964, the strongly conservative Sen. Barry M. Goldwater of Arizona, whose candidacy raised the state's Republican Party to a greater level of vitality than it had ever enjoyed.

To be sure, some Republican progress was achieved in this period independent of Goldwater's influence. Bill Brock, a Chattanooga businessman who had been drawn into grassroots Republican politics by the Eisenhower and Nixon campaigns, secured the GOP's third East Tennessee House seat by winning the Third Congressional District in 1962. More important, the Supreme Court ruled in *Baker v. Carr*, a landmark 1962 case that originated in Tennessee, and in related decisions that legislative districts must be reapportioned immediately, then after every census on the principle of "one man, one vote." In Tennessee, which had not changed the boundaries of its state House and Senate districts since 1901, this meant transferring many seats from the state's declining rural counties to its growing metropolitan areas, where the GOP was strongest. Republican representation in the state legislature essentially doubled in subsequent elections, rising quickly to around two-fifths of both houses by the late 1960s.[5]

Goldwater's contribution to Republican progress in Tennessee was both organizational and electoral. Organizationally, he inspired and energized legions of economic conservatives and fervent anticommunists, many of them in the Memphis and Nashville suburbs, to become "New Guard" Republican activists committed to winning elections up and down the ballot (Parks 1966). "For the first time," write William Lyons, John Scheb and Billy Stair (2001, 200), "many Middle and West Tennesseans began to think of themselves as Republicans, rather than as Democrats who sometimes voted Republican in presidential elections." In electoral terms, Goldwater established a beachhead for the GOP among socially conservative white working-class voters, previously a mainstay of the Democratic Party (Lamis 1984, 164–65).

In congressional elections as well as in the presidential contest, 1964 was a year of Republican defeats that set the stage for subsequent Republican victories. Senator Gore was up for reelection in 1964, and Kefauver's death in 1963 meant that an election to fill the remaining two years of his term was also on the ballot. Dan Kuykendall, a Goldwater Republican from Memphis, challenged Gore. Howard Baker, an East Tennessee Republican whose father had held the Second District House seat, ran against Rep. Ross Bass, a Kefauver Democrat, to finish Kefauver's term. Both Republicans lost, but Kuykendall's 46 percent and Baker's 47 percent were by far the strongest showings by any Republican senatorial candidates in the state's history.

Two years later, in 1966, Kuykendall ran for Congress in the Ninth District (Memphis and Shelby County) and unseated the Democratic incumbent, making him the fourth Republican in the state's nine-member House delegation and the only one from outside East Tennessee. Baker ran against former governor Clement (who had beaten Senator Bass in the Democratic primary) for a full Senate term in 1966. He won handily (56 percent to 44 percent) to become the first elected Republican senator in the history of the state.

SNAPSHOT 4: 1976

For a time during the decade portrayed in this fourth snapshot, Tennessee politics flashed redder than it ever had, and for a time it flashed bluer than at any time since the 1940s. Underlying this apparent volatility, however, the trend toward a more Republican Tennessee continued. To be sure, both parties usually were successful when a strong national or regional tide was running strongly in its favor, or when an even moderately popular incumbent was running for reelection. But as the country and, especially, the South grew more Republican during the latter third of the twentieth century and the early 2000s (Nelson 2005), Tennessee Republicans were more likely to benefit from outside tides than the state's Democrats. What's more, the state GOP tended to do well in elections when no national or regional trend was at work or when no acceptable incumbent was running.

None of this was apparent yet in 1968, when the only statewide election was for Tennessee's electoral votes for president. Although the Republican candidate, Richard Nixon, defeated Democratic Vice President Hubert H. Humphrey by nearly 10 percentage points, he won only 38 percent of the vote in doing so. The most popular third-party candidate in Tennessee in more than a century,[6] former Democratic governor George C. Wallace of Alabama, won 34 percent to finish second, running best among the same socially conservative working-class whites whom Goldwater had drawn to the Republican ticket in 1964. Clearly, if the Republicans could win back these voters, they could prevail in future statewide elections.

Two years later they did. Nixon's chief political goal as president was to bring Wallace supporters into the Republican fold. The first application of his "southern strategy" came in the midterm elections of 1970. The strategy was moderately successful in most of the South, but spectacularly so in Tennessee. In the Senate election, the conservative Republican challenger, Representative Brock, pounded the liberal incumbent Gore on gun control, school prayer, liberal judges, school bussing, and a host of other social issues. In the open-seat gubernatorial election, a dentist and local Republican leader from Memphis, Winfield Dunn, opposed liberal Democratic lawyer-businessman John J. Hooker. Both Republican candidates were able to add several West Tennessee cities and counties to their party's East Tennessee base, and both were elected, Brock by 51 percent to 47 percent and Dunn by 52 percent to 46 percent. The GOP now controlled all three major statewide offices.

Republican progress continued in 1972. Nixon carried Tennessee with 67.7 percent, accomplishing his goal of winning over early every Wallace voter. (Liberal South Dakota Senator George S. McGovern won 30 percent, barely more in the two-candidate 1972 election than the 28 percent Humphrey had received in three-candidate 1968.) Baker won an easy reelection to the Senate, proving that his first-ever Republican victory in 1966 had not been a fluke. And even though Tennessee lost one seat in the House of Representatives after the 1970 census, Robin L. Beard's victory in a district that straddled Middle and West Tennessee grew the Republican delegation from four to five, outnumbering the Democrats for the first time since Reconstruction.

Tennessee's new pattern of Democratic success when regional or national political trends were running strongly in the party's favor was never more apparent than in the next two elections, 1974 and 1976. The Watergate scandal and Nixon's resignation in disgrace made the 1974 midterm elections a Democratic triumph nearly everywhere in the country. Former representative Ray Blanton, a conservative West Tennessee Democrat, built on the statewide recognition he had secured in his 1972 Senate campaign against Baker and was easily elected as governor. (He beat Nixon White House staff member Lamar Alexander by 55 percent to 44 percent.) In the state legislative elections, the Democrats regained much of the ground they had lost since the mid-1960s, winning a 63 to 35 majority in the House and a 20 to 12 majority in the Senate. Tennessee's House delegation swung from 5 to 3 Republican to 5 to 3 Democratic when Marilyn Lloyd unseated the Republican incumbent in the Chattanooga-based Third District and Harold Ford, a state legislator, defeated Kuykendall in Memphis's Ninth District. Ford became Tennessee's first African-American member of Congress.

In 1976, the tide that propelled Tennessee Democrats was less national than regional. With strong southern support, the party nominated former Georgia governor Jimmy Carter for president. In a very close election against Nixon's successor, President Gerald R. Ford, Carter carried Tennessee and every other southern state except Virginia, the best showing by far of any Democratic presidential candidate since Franklin Roosevelt in the 1930s and 1940s. Carter's 56 percent majority in Tennessee brought Senator Brock's Democratic opponent, state party chair James Sasser, in on his coattails with 53 percent of the vote.[7]

Harold Ford's 1974 election to a term in the House (and to ten subsequent terms) was the most visible success by an African-American political leader in Tennessee during this decade but it was hardly the only one. The Voting Rights Act of 1965 had enfranchised fewer new black voters in Tennessee than in most other southern states because the racial barriers to voting had always been lower. But the act also required states to abandon practices that made it difficult for African-American voters to elect African-American candidates. When Tennessee complied by changing from countywide to district-based elections for state legislature, the number of black state representatives rose from one in 1964 (A.W. Willis Jr., of Memphis) to thirteen by 1977, and the number of black senators rose from none to two.[8] Ford's election to Congress was facilitated by the state's redrawing of the Ninth District's boundaries to maximize the number of African-American voters.

These victories aside, the underlying trend toward a more Republican Tennessee was also a trend away from the party that African-Americans voters overwhelmingly supported. A few Republican politicians actively sought to build biracial coalitions—Baker, for example, ran 6 percentage points behind Nixon statewide in 1972, but 5 points ahead of him in heavily African-American Memphis. But most Republican officeseekers saw little hope of peeling black voters away from their Democratic loyalties and more to be gained by continuing to cultivate white working-class Wallace voters. Not surprisingly, perhaps, every African American elected to state or federal office in Tennessee has been a Democrat.

SNAPSHOT 5: 1986

During the nineteenth and, more recently, the mid-twentieth century, the Tennessee political leaders who strode onto the national stage were all Democrats.[9] Tennessee Republicans made their first appearance in 1977, when Howard Baker was elected Senate Minority Leader by his Republicans colleagues (the first southerner ever to hold this position) and Bill Brock became chair of the Republican National Committee. Brock is widely credited with reviving the GOP's dispirited fundraising, candidate recruitment, and organizational apparatus, both in Washington and at the grassroots. In doing so, he forged the model that successful chairs of both national parties have tried to emulate ever since. Baker united the divided and demoralized Senate GOP into an effective political force during the Carter years.

Reelected to the Senate by a fifteen-point majority in 1978 against Jane

Eskind, a wealthy Democratic businesswoman, Baker emerged as one of the early favorites for the Republican presidential nomination in 1980. Unfortunately, Baker was bucking two strong national trends: His party was becoming more conservative than he was, and, disillusioned by the Vietnam War, Watergate, and a bloated federal bureaucracy, the country had begun looking to the states rather than to Washington for its presidents. (Governors won seven of the eight presidential elections from 1976 to 2004; senators won none.) Both trends worked strongly in favor of Ronald Reagan, the GOP's leading conservative and a two-term governor of California. Baker dropped out of the race after finishing fourth in the New Hampshire primary.

Reagan was elected president in a landslide. In a mirror image of 1976, when Carter carried every southern state but one, Reagan carried all but one in 1980, Carter's home state of Georgia. Although Reagan had long coattails in the South, Tennessee Republicans were unable to take advantage of them because no statewide offices were on the ballot and every incumbent House member ran for reelection against a weak challenger. Still, the addition of twelve new Republican senators transformed Baker from Minority Leader to Majority Leader, increasing his power and prominence.

Baker's reelection to the Senate in 1978 had been accompanied by Republican Lamar Alexander's election as governor. A recent Supreme Court decision, *Buckley v. Valeo*, had authorized candidates to spend as much of their own money as they wanted on their own campaigns. The main effect in Tennessee was to enable wealthy, self-financed candidates to buy nominations but not elections. Alexander, like Baker, faced an opponent with a bottomless checkbook, Democratic banker Jake Butcher. In losing to Blanton in 1974, Alexander had been widely perceived as a preppy country club Republican. In 1978 he shed that image by donning a red-and-black flannel shirt and walking 1,022 miles through the state to visit with voters in their homes, churches and workplaces (Langsdon 2000, 388). Alexander benefited from widespread revulsion with the scandal-plagued Blanton administration. (Among other things, the governor had been selling pardons to violent criminals.) Alexander won an easy 56 percent to 44 percent victory.

Focusing on public education and economic development in ways that earned him national as well as statewide acclaim, Alexander was a popular governor—not the first in Tennessee history, but the first to be constitutionally eligible to seek a second four-year term. Until the state constitution was amended in 1953, governors were elected for two years and, as long as they sat out a term every eight years, could be reelected without limit. The 1953 amendment provided for a single four-year gubernatorial term. Just before Alexander took office, the constitution was amended again to allow the governor to seek a second four-year term.[10] In 1982 he was handily reelected with 60 percent of the vote against the Democratic mayor of Knoxville, Randy Tyree.

Governor Alexander bucked a strong national Democratic tide to win in 1982. Senator Sasser rode it. Sasser, who had worked the grassroots hard during his first term, was reelected against an aggressive challenger, five-term Republican representative Robin Beard, by 62 percent to 38 percent. Democrats also won the House seat that was restored to Tennessee after the 1980 census, expanding their ranks in the nine-member congressional delegation to six.

Like Sasser's reelection in 1982, Democratic victories in the next two elections confirmed the rule that Tennessee Democrats do well when a reasonably popular Democratic incumbent is on the ballot or a strong national or regional tide runs in their favor. Nationally, Reagan won a landslide without coattails in 1984; indeed, the GOP lost two Senate seats in the election. One of them was in Tennessee, where Baker retired, having interpreted his failure to win the presidency in 1980 to mean that he could seek it successfully only if unencumbered by the responsibilities of office. (In any event, he decided not to try again in 1988.) The Democrats united behind Al Gore Jr., a four-term representative from the rural Fourth Congressional District. Gore had distinguished himself in Washington by mastering important but relatively non-ideological issues like organ transplants, infant formula and single-warhead nuclear missiles. When no prominent Republican stepped forward to challenge Gore, the nomination went to Victor Ashe, a state legislator from Knoxville.

Why was Gore spared a strong opponent for an open Senate seat? His own stature (he was already being talked about as a future president) is part of the answer, but only part. Two other, more deeply rooted aspects of Tennessee politics are also relevant. One is constitutional: In Tennessee, unlike other southern states, hardly any statewide offices are filled through popular election. Tennessee's lieutenant governor is elected by the state senate; its comptroller, treasurer, and secretary of state by the entire legislature; and its attorney general by the state supreme court; other executive officials are appointed by the governor. These positions provide springboards for serious gubernatorial and senatorial candidacies elsewhere in the South, but in Tennessee membership in the House performs most of that function by default. If, as in 1984, none of a party's House incumbents are willing to risk their seat in pursuit of higher office, the party usually is left with a weak pool from which to choose its nominee for governor or senator. Ashe campaigned hard in 1984, but his lack of a statewide reputation lost him the election to Gore by 61 percent to 34 percent.

A second deeply rooted feature of Tennessee politics that helps to explain Gore's rise to prominence in 1984 is cultural. Tennessee is one of five states (all of them southern) with a dominant "traditionalistic" political culture (Elazar 1966, 92–94, 110).[11] One of the ways that Tennessee's traditionalism manifests itself is in a deferential attitude toward "an established elite which often inherits their 'right' to govern through family ties" (Elazar 1966, 93; see also Nelson 1998). Gore, the son of a former senator, obviously benefited from this attitude. So, two years earlier, had both candidates for the Fourth District House seat: Republican Cissy Baker, the daughter of Howard Baker (himself the son of a Tennessee congressman), and the winner, Jim Cooper, the son of former Democratic governor Prentice Cooper. Subsequent elections witnessed John Duncan Jr.'s succession to John Sr.'s Second District seat in 1988 and Harold Ford, Jr.'s, succession to Harold Sr.'s Ninth District seat in 1996, not to mention the 1988 election of Bob Clement (his father was Gov. Frank Clement) to the House from the Fifth District.[12] With few exceptions, these candidates were treated as heirs apparent and faced no serious competition for their party's usually coveted nominations for open House seats.

In 1986, Tennessee Democrats did not need to rely on tradition. Instead, they rode the national and regional tides that ran strongly in their party's favor. In the South, Democrats defeated four one-term Republican senators and, nationally, the party regained control of the Senate. In Tennessee, Ned WcWherter, a conservative Democrat from the rural western part of the state and the longtime speaker of the state House of Representatives, won the gubernatorial election against former Republican governor Winfield Dunn by 54 percent to 46 percent. In the early 1970s, Governor Dunn had alienated traditionally Republican East Tennessee by vetoing a bill to establish a medical school in the region. The legislature passed the bill over Dunn's veto, but the bad feeling toward him never ebbed. James Quillen, who had represented the First Congressional District since 1962 (and after whom the new medical school was named) bore an especially long grudge. Dunn lost Quillen's district to McWherter (while Quillen was winning it by more than two-to-one), and he nearly lost the rest of East Tennessee, something no reasonably strong Republican candidate for statewide office had ever done.

The end of 1986 marks the modern apex of the Democratic Party in Tennessee. The governor and both senators were Democrats, as were six of nine members of the state's House delegation, twenty-three of its thirty-three state senators, and sixty-one of its ninety-nine state representatives. But looked at as part of the entire decade, these Democratic victories appear less like a blue landscape than as blue highlights against a reddish backdrop. Not only did Reagan carry the state in 1980 and 1984—the sixth and seventh times the Republican presidential nominee had won Tennessee in the last nine elections—but the excitement he generated in the state allowed the GOP to close the gap in voters' party identification. In 1981, when Reagan took office, 42 percent of Tennesseans identified themselves as Democrats, compared with only 25 percent Republicans. Four years later, the gap had nearly vanished, shrinking from 17 percentage points to 3 percentage points (Lyons, Scheb, and Stair 2001, 194). Throughout the decade, Republicans constituted a larger proportion of the state legislature in Tennessee than in any other southern state (calculated from data in Scher 1992, 166–167). An index of state partisanship devised by Earl Black and Merle Black (1987, 311) for the period 1965–1985 showed that in Tennessee (but nowhere else in the South), the GOP had won a majority of recent presidential, gubernatorial, and senatorial elections. In what seemed their darkest moment, Republicans were poised for the breakthrough that was soon to come.

SNAPSHOT 6: 1996

The decade portrayed in this sixth snapshot was the most eventful in the modern political history of Tennessee, starting with Gore's first quest for the Democratic presidential nomination and ending with the full flowering of the state's growing Republican majority.

Gore's presidential candidacy was an effort to cast himself in a role that others had created and that no one else was stepping forward to perform. In the aftermath of Reagan's crushing defeat of former vice president Walter F. Mondale of Minnesota in 1984, Democratic leaders across the South had decided that they wanted "southern moderate" to replace "northern liberal" as the shorthand description of the party's next nominee for president. They agreed to cluster virtually all of their states' 1988 presidential primaries on the second Tuesday in March, just two weeks after the New Hampshire primary. By creating "Super Tuesday," southern Democrats hoped to attract a popular southern moderate into the race, then anoint him as the nominee (Black and Black 1992, 260–71).

Super Tuesday fulfilled one of its intended purposes—Gore declared his candidacy—but not the other. To be sure, Gore won the primaries in Tennessee and three neighboring states: Arkansas, Kentucky, and North Carolina. But Jesse Jackson, an African-American minister and liberal activist, won Virginia and the four Deep South primaries, and Massachusetts governor Michael S. Dukakis, a liberal and a northerner, swept the two biggest states, Texas and Florida. Gore's candidacy foundered—no surprise, considering that he was a thirty-nine-year-old, first-term senator—and Dukakis's flourished. Election Day in November brought the very outcome that southern Democratic leaders had tried to avert by creating Super Tuesday. The northern liberal Dukakis lost every southern state to Vice President George Bush, a Texan, by a landslide. In Tennessee, Bush ran just as strongly as Reagan had in 1984, winning 58 percent of the vote.

Bush's victorious candidacy for president did not prevent Sasser from winning an easy reelection to a third Senate term in 1988; nor did Gore's defeat hurt him when he ran for a second term in 1990. Both senators executed to perfection the textbook strategy for an incumbent seeking reelection: tend assiduously to constituents' interests and raise so much money that no serious opponent will emerge as a challenger. Neither Bill Anderson, the young East Tennessee lawyer who ran against Sasser, nor William Hawkins, the former economics instructor who challenged Gore, brought anything like a statewide reputation to their races. Nor did either GOP candidate raise more than a tiny fraction of the funds needed to run an effective campaign. Sasser was reelected with 65 percent of the vote in 1988, and Gore with 68 percent in 1990.

Governor McWherter also was reelected without serious opposition in 1990; Republican Dwight Henry, a first-term state representative, campaigned hard but with few resources and secured only 37 percent of the vote to McWherter's 61 percent. Indeed, since the change in the state constitution that allows governors to serve two four-year terms, every governor has been reelected without serious challenge: the Republican Alexander in 1982, the Democrat McWherter in 1990, and Republican Don Sundquist in 1998, with Democrat Phil Bredesen regarded as certain to win reelection in 2006. Tennessee's governors have every incentive to move toward the center of the political spectrum, in part because, as in other states, the challenges a governor faces are less ideological than managerial, and in part for a reason peculiar to Tennessee, the so-called "Wilderbeast."

The Wilderbeast is a bipartisan, centrist coalition in the state senate that takes its name from John Wilder. Since 1971 (longer by far than any other state political leader in the country), Wilder has been elected by his colleagues as speaker of the Senate and thus, under Tennessee's unusual constitution, as lieutenant governor. Wilder is a Democrat who prides himself on working well with governors of both parties. In advance of the 1987 legislative session, when a majority of Democratic senators declared their intention to replace Wilder with a more partisan leader, he forged a coalition consisting of every Senate Republican and enough Democrats to secure reelection. In return, Wilder has consistently appointed both Republican and Democratic supporters to chair all the Senate's committees. The long existence of the bipartisan Wilderbeast has encouraged Tennessee's governors to operate in a similarly centrist—and popular—way.

Although Gore chose not to run for president again in 1992, he ended up on the ticket anyway as Arkansas Governor Bill Clinton's vice presidential running mate. Clinton's choice of Gore defied the canons of traditional ticket balancing: Like Clinton, Gore was a politically moderate, Southern Baptist, baby boomer from an adjacent southern state. But, as a senator, an environmentalist, a Vietnam veteran, and a staunch family man, Gore balanced the pro-development, skirt-chasing, draft-avoiding governor in more subtle and, it turned out, more politically meaningful ways (Nelson 1993).

Tennessee was one of four southern states that Clinton and Gore carried against President Bush in 1992. Clinton received 47 percent of Tennessee's popular vote to Bush's 42 percent, with 10 percent going to independent candidate H. Ross Perot. It is far from certain that Clinton would have won Tennessee without Gore: A Mason-Dixon poll showed Gore adding 7 percentage points to Clinton's own support in the state, well above the margin by which he carried it (calculated from data in Brodsky and Swansbrough 1994, 160).

No statewide elections were on the Tennessee ballot in 1992. Every House member ran and was reelected, enabling Democrats to maintain their 6 to 3 majority in the state's delegation. Part of Tennessee's traditionalistic political culture is expressed in its deference to incumbents. Just as no incumbent governor of Tennessee has been seriously challenged for reelection since the two-term limit replaced the single gubernatorial term, so has no incumbent House member been defeated since 1974, when Ford unseated Kuykendall. Carter in 1980 is the only reelection-seeking president not to carry Tennessee in the past seventy-five years. Even in 1994, when a Republican governor replaced a Democrat, two Republican senators replaced two Democrats, and the state's House delegation went from 6 to 3 Democratic to 5 to 4 Republican, only one incumbent, Senator Sasser, was defeated. All the other changes in party control came through open-seat elections.

Nationally and throughout the South, the 1994 elections were a triumph for the GOP, which took control of Congress for the first time in forty years and, for the first time ever, won a strong majority of southern House and Senate seats. Tennessee, with its complete turnover from Democratic to Republican control of statewide offices, led the way. Sasser ran exactly the wrong sort of campaign, offering himself to the voters for a fourth term by boasting of his Washington connections and declaring that he was his party's consensus choice to be the new Senate Majority Leader. But 1994 was not the year for candidates to stress their clout as Washington politicians, and Sasser lost by 56 percent to 42 percent to Republican Bill Frist, a prominent heart surgeon and political newcomer who branded Sasser the "personification of an arrogant, imperial Congress" and led audiences in chants of "Eighteen years is long enough!" (Black and Black 2002, 268).

Gore's elevation to the vice presidency placed the remaining two years of his term on the 1994 ballot as well. The Democrats nominated Rep. Jim Cooper to oppose Republican Fred Thompson. Thompson was a curious figure; although he had spent most of his career as a backstage Washington lawyer and lobbyist, he was best known as an actor in popular movies like *Marie* and *The Hunt for Red October*. Thompson saved his best performance for his Senate campaign, when he "parked his Lincoln, shucked his lawyer attire, donned blue jeans, cowboy boots, and a western-style khaki shirt, and rolled out what would become the symbol of his campaign, a red extended pickup truck. . . . The transformation to 'Ol' Fred' was one of the most remarkable political makeovers in years" (Ashford and Locker 1999, 211). Thompson carved up the reserved, intellectual Cooper, winning by 60 percent to 39 percent. In the House elections, two young conservative Republicans, Zach Wamp and Van Hilleary, won the open Democratic seats vacated by Cooper and the retiring Marilyn Lloyd, respectively.

The Tennessee GOP also fared well in elections for state office. Republican representative Don Sundquist, who represented the long congressional district that connects the Nashville and Memphis suburbs, defeated the largely self-financed Phil Bredesen, the mayor of Nashville, by 54 percent to 45 percent. In the state legislative elections, the Republicans won a narrow 17 to 16 majority in the Senate (they left the Wilderbeast intact, however) and, despite a Democratic redistricting plan that jammed twelve Republican incumbents into six districts after the 1990 census, won forty of ninety-nine seats in the House of Representatives.

Ironically, one casualty of the Republican sweep in 1994 was the presidential candidacy of former governor Lamar Alexander. Alexander had been striking grassroots chords around the country by promising to shake up Washington with reforms like mandatory term limits for members of Congress. Clinton's political advisers regarded him as the president's most formidable rival in 1996 (Morris 1997, 266). But the GOP sweep in the 1994 congressional elections took the wind out of Alexander's sails. Clearly, the elections showed, Washington could be shaken up without imposing term limits; besides, now that the Republicans were in charge, their interest in changing the rules of the game had flagged considerably. Alexander ran third in the 1996 New Hampshire primary, then dropped out of the race soon afterward in favor of the eventual nominee, former Senate Majority Leader Robert Dole of Kansas.

Clinton and Gore carried Tennessee in 1996, but this time just barely. Nationally, Clinton's popular vote margin rose from 6 percentage points against Bush in 1992 to 9 percentage points against Dole in 1996. But in Tennessee, Clinton's victory margin fell by half, from 5 points to 2 points. In the Senate election for a full six-year term, Thompson put the tires back on his red pickup and easily defeated Democratic lawyer Houston Gordon by 61 percent to 37 percent. Foolishly, Gordon attacked Thompson for being "an accomplished actor" (Swansbrough and Brodsky 1997, 189), making the same mistake that all of Reagan's opponents had made with equal lack of success. Hilleary and Wamp added to the majorities they had received in capturing their House seats from the Democrats in 1994, each of them winning reelection by more than 10 percentage points.

SNAPSHOT 7: 2006

The 1998 elections in Tennessee were relatively uneventful. Like all of his recent predecessors, Sundquist was easily reelected as governor, winning 69 percent against token opposition. No current Democratic leader sought the party's nomination, forfeiting it to a cantankerous figure from the 1960s, John J. Hooker, who won 30 percent. All nine House members ran again and, in keeping with state tradition, all were reelected. In 2000, a similar pattern prevailed. The same nine House incumbents ran and won the same easy victories. Senator Frist, with 65 percent, won a landslide reelection against a token Democratic opponent, former state party treasurer Jeff Clark, who received 32.2 percent.

Only in the 2000 presidential election was politics in Tennessee anything but usual, but in this case the exception was far more significant than the rule. With Clinton barred from running again by the Constitution's two-term limit, the Democratic Party nominated Gore to succeed him. As vice president, however, Gore had neglected Tennessee and, although he located his national campaign headquarters in Nashville, he seldom campaigned there until just before Election Day. Personal and political history apparently reassured Gore that he could take Tennessee for granted: He had never come close to losing an election there and, during the past seventy-five years, the only presidential candidates not to carry their home states were the most severe landslide losers: Republican Alfred M. Landon of Kansas, who won only two states, in 1936, and McGovern of South Dakota, who carried only one, in 1972. Even Goldwater in 1964, Carter in 1980, Mondale in 1984, and Dukakis in 1988, all of them far weaker candidates than Gore, had won their own states.

The Republican nominee for president in 2000, Gov. George W. Bush of Texas, conceded nothing to Gore. Bush campaigned ardently throughout Tennessee, advertised extensively on the state's radio and television stations, and brought in surrogates like actor and National Rifle Association president Charlton Heston to remind Tennesseans of Gore's unpopular support for gun control. Bush carried Tennessee handily, by 51 percent to 47 percent. For more than a month after the election, the eyes of the nation were riveted on Florida, where Gore hoped that recounts would turn the state in his favor and win him the presidency. But if Gore had carried his own state, the outcome in Florida would have been irrelevant: Tennessee's eleven electoral votes would raised Gore's national tally to 277, more than enough to win the election.

While Bush was taking advantage of Tennessee's ever more reddish political coloration, Sundquist was squandering it. As a candidate for governor in 1994, Sundquist had opposed enacting a new state income tax and, when strolling toward reelection in 1998 in a one-sided race, he had said nothing to suggest a change of mind. Voters were therefore astonished (and Republicans apoplectic) when, in 1999 and afterward, Sundquist made an income tax the centerpiece of his second term. After Representative Hilleary's Fourth Congressional District was redistricted to favor the Democrats in 2002, Hilleary sought and won the GOP nomination for governor on an anti-tax platform. Sundquist said that his fellow Republican would be "a horrible governor" (Barone and Cohen 2003, 1476). Despite these deep divisions within the party, Hilleary ran a close second against former Nashville mayor Phil Bredesen, a Democrat and another income tax opponent. Raising money from a broad base of donors this time, Bredesen won the election by 51 percent to 48 percent, and conservative Democrat Lincoln Davis won Hilleary's redistricted House seat.

Another open-seat election, this one for senator, provided Tennessee Republicans with their major victory in 2002. When Senator Thompson decided to retire, former governor Alexander declared his candidacy for the Republican nomination. The state GOP had moved steadily rightward since the early 1980s, when Alexander was governor, and Rep. Ed Bryant, the conservative Republican who had filled Sundquist's seat in Congress when Sundquist ran for governor, challenged him for the nomination. But President Bush, who took a much more active role in recruiting Republican candidates in 2002 than presidents usually do, made clear that he preferred Alexander (Nelson 2004). Alexander did his part by centering his campaign on a host of conservative issues. He defeated Bryant in the primary by 54 percent to 43 percent, then polished off another political veteran, Democratic representative Bob Clement of Nashville, in the general election by an almost identical margin: 54 percent to 44 percent.

Alexander's victory was one of several that helped the Republicans regain control of the Senate in 2002. Shortly after the results were in, Senator Trent Lott of Mississippi, who was slated to become majority leader, remarked offhandedly that the country might have been better off if segregationist third-party candidate Strom Thurmond had won the 1948 presidential election. In the media firestorm that followed, Bush quietly made clear to Senate Republicans that he would rather they choose someone else as majority leader. With White House encouragement, Senator

Frist entered the race and was unanimously elected. Frist was a relatively junior senator, but he had earned his partisan spurs by successfully chairing the National Republican Senate Committee during the 2002 elections.

Although no statewide offices were on Tennessee's ballot in 2004, the presidency was. The Democrats nominated a northern liberal, Sen. John F. Kerry of Massachusetts, to challenge Bush. Kerry chose a southerner, North Carolina Senator John Edwards, for vice president, but, strangely, he made no effort to win North Carolina, much less Tennessee or any other southern state except Florida. Bush carried Tennessee handily, by 57 percent to 43 percent. The GOP also drew within four seats of a majority in the ninety-nine member state House of Representatives and won a 17 to 16 majority in the Senate. When the legislature gathered in January 2005, most Republicans were ready to replace Wilder as speaker with one of their own, but the votes of two defecting Republican senators enabled Wilder to win reelection by 18 to 15.

Looking ahead to 2006, three Tennessee political leaders seem poised to step into the national spotlight. Bredesen, like other recent governors, seems all but certain of reelection to a second term as governor without serious opposition. As one of four southern governors in a party that since the 1960s has only won the presidency when a southern governor headed the ticket, Bredesen is on every political pundit's watch list for 2008.[13] He is joined there by Frist, who pledged the first time he ran for senator that he would step down in 2006 after completing his second term. In retiring from the Senate, however, Frist will be clearing the decks to seek the presidency without distraction in 2008. One of the candidates who probably will vie to fill his open Senate seat is Rep. Harold Ford Jr., of Memphis. Since entering the House as the twenty-six-year-old successor to his father in 1996, Ford has made no secret of his ambition to rise as high as he can in national politics. In recent years, Ford has made hundreds of national cable talk show appearances and speeches around the state in hopes of persuading voters that, as a political moderate, he is the sort of African-American Democrat whom moderate voters of both parties could happily support.

CONCLUSION

As these seven prose snapshots of Tennessee politics since the 1940s show, Tennessee has been transformed from a bluish state to a reddish one—that is, from being basically but not entirely Democratic to being basically but not entirely Republican. The Republicans have held onto East Tennessee while broadening their base to include the Memphis and Nashville suburbs and, increasingly, rural West Tennessee as well. But although the GOP has become the stronger party, the Democrats usually can prevail when a national (1974, 1982, 1986) or regional (1976) tide runs in their favor. In addition, the state's traditionalistic political culture fosters an attitude of deference to incumbents and to established political families, sometimes to the advantage of Democrats.

Although Tennessee has grown steadily more Republican in recent decades, however, it has done so at a slower pace than most other states in the South. Once the least blue state in the solidly blue South, it has become one of the least red states in an increasingly red South. Until the 1960s, for example, Tennessee was one of the few southern states that elected Republican members to the House of Representatives. In 2002 and 2004, it was one of the few that sent more Democrats than Republicans. Until the 1960s, too, Tennessee gave Republican candidates for president their highest level of support in the South. It still tends to support Republicans—even rejecting native son Al Gore in 2000—but some other southern states do so by greater margins. In 2004, for example, Bush won Tennessee by a landslide, but not by as big a landslide as in Alabama, Georgia, Mississippi, South Carolina, and Texas.

One aspect of Tennessee politics that has survived the transition from bluish to reddish is its steady production of national political leaders. The simple explanation may be that anyone who can compete successfully in as regionally and politically diverse a state as Tennessee has been battle-tested in the skills and suppleness required of a presidential candidate in a diverse and far-flung nation. Nothing guarantees that a Tennessean will be elected or even nominated for president in 2008. But any short list of Democratic contenders that leaves off Bredesen, or any comparable list of Republicans that does not include Frist, is probably off the mark.

REFERENCES

Ashford, Philip, and Richard Locker. 1999. "Tennessee: A Partisan Big Bang Among Quiet Accommodation." In *Southern Politics in the 1990s*, edited by Alexander P. Lamis. Baton Rouge: Louisiana State University Press, 193–226.

Barone, Michael, and Richard E. Cohen. 2003. *The Almanac of American Politics, 2004*. Washington, D.C.: National Journal.

Barone, Michael, and Grant Ujifusa. 1981. *The Almanac of Americans Politics, 1982.* Washington, D.C.: Barone and Company.

———. 1991. *The Almanac of American Politics, 1992.* Washington, D.C.: National Journal.

Bass, Jack, and Walter DeVries. 1976. *The Transformation of Southern Politics.* New York: Basic Books.

Black, Earl, and Merle Black. 1987. *Politics and Society in the South.* Cambridge, MA: Harvard University Press.

———. 1992. *The Vital South: How Presidents Are Elected.* Cambridge, MA: Harvard University Press.

———. 2002. *The Rise of Southern Republicans.* Cambridge, MA: Harvard University Press.

Brodsky, David. M. 1998. "Tennessee: Genuine Two-Party Politics." In *The New Politics of the Old South: An Introduction to Southern Politics,* edited by Charles S. Bullock III and Mark J. Rozell. Lanham, MD: Rowman and Littlefield, 167–84.

Brodsky, David M., and Robert H. Swansbrough. 1994. "Tennessee: Favorite Son Brings Home the Bacon." In *The 1992 Presidential Election in the South,* edited by Robert P. Steed, Laurence W. Moreland and Tod A. Baker. Westport, CT: Praeger, 157–68.

Elazar, Daniel J. 1966. *American Federalism: A View from the States.* New York: Thomas Y. Crowell.

Greene, Lee S., and Jack E. Holmes. 1972. "Tennessee: A Politics of Peaceful Change." In *The Changing Politics of the South,* edited by William C. Havard. Baton Rouge: Louisiana State University Press, 165–200.

Key, V. O., with Alexander Heard. 1949. *Southern Politics in State and Nation.* New York: Alfred A. Knopf.

Lamis, Alexander P. 1984. *The Two-Party South.* New York: Oxford University Press.

Langsdon, Phillip. 2000. *Tennessee: A Political History.* Franklin, TN: Hillsboro Press.

Lyons, William, John Scheb II and Billy Stair. 2001. *Government and Politics in Tennessee.* Knoxville, TN: University of Tennessee Press.

Mason, John Lyman. 2003. "Tennessee: Politics and Politicians Who Matter Beyond State Borders." In *The New Politics of the Old South: An Introduction to Southern Politics,* 2nd edition, edited by Charles S. Bullock III and Mark J. Rozell. Lanham, MD: Rowman and Littlefield, 177–94.

Morris, Dick. 1997. *Behind the Oval Office.* New York: Random House.

Nelson, Michael. 1998. "Foreword." In *Tennessee Governments and Politics: Democracy in the Volunteer State,* edited by John R. Vile and Mark Byrnes. Nashville, TN: Vanderbilt University Press, ix–xi.

———. 1993. "The Presidency: Clinton and the Cycle of Politics and Policy." In *The Elections of 1992,* edited by Michael Nelson. Washington, D.C.: CQ Press, 125–52.

———. 2004. "George W. Bush and Congress: The Electoral Connection." In *Considering the Bush Presidency,* edited by Gary L. Gregg II and Mark J. Rozell. New York: Oxford University Press, 141–59.

———. 2005. "The Setting: George W. Bush, Majority President." In *The Elections of 2004*, edited by Michael Nelson. Washington, D.C.: CQ Press, 1–17.

Parks, Norman L. 1966. "Tennessee Politics Since Kefauver and Reece: A 'Generalist' View." *Journal of Politics* 28 (February): 141–68.

Risen, Clay. 2005. "Southern Man." *New Republic* 232 (January 31): 18–21.

Scher, Richard K. 1992. *Politics in the New South: Republicanism, Race, and Leadership in the Twentieth Century.* New York: Paragon House.

Swansbrough, Robert H., and David M. Brodsky. 1998. "Tennessee: Weakening Party Loyalties and Growing Independence." In *The South's New Politics: Realignment and Dealignment*, edited by Robert H. Swansbrough and David M. Brodsky. Columbia, SC: University of South Carolina Press, 76–93.

———. 1997. "Tennessee: Belle of the Presidential Ball." In *The 1996 Presidential Election in the South*, edited by Laurence W. Moreland and Robert P. Steed. Westport, CT: Praeger, 183–96.

NOTES

1. Of the eighty victories Republicans won in Southern House elections during the first half of the twentieth century, fifty (twenty-five apiece) were in the Tennessee's First and Second Congressional Districts. (Black and Black 2002, 59).

2. In 1900 Tennessee was second to North Carolina by 1 percentage point, and in 1928 it was second to Florida by 1 percentage point.

3. For reasons grounded in local politics during the antebellum period, the Highland Rim, a thin line of counties running north to south along the eastern edge of West Tennessee, also opposed secession and later supported Republicans.

4. Reece resumed his first district seat in 1950 after serving as chair of the Republican National Committee and running for senator.

5. Under circumstances akin to the freakish victories of Republican gubernatorial candidates in 1910, 1912, and 1928, the GOP controlled the state House of Representatives by a one-vote margin from 1969 to 1971.

6. In the four-way election of 860, John Bell, a prominent Tennessee political leader, won the state handily as the Constitutional Union Party nominee.

7. As evidence of Carter's coattails, Sasser was one of only four congressional Democrats in the country to run behind Carter (Barone and Ujifusa 1981, 1028).

8. Only modest gains have been made since then. African Americans have occupied three state Senate seats since 1982 and did not win a fourteenth seat in the state House of Representatives until 2000.

9. Andrew Johnson, who succeeded to the presidency when Abraham Lincoln was assassinated in 1865, was a Jacksonian Democrat placed on the ticket when the GOP rebranded itself the National Union Party for the wartime election of 1864.

10. The state constitution bars only third consecutive terms. Although it has yet to happen, a governor could serve two terms, sit out for one or more terms, and be elected again.

11. Respect for family and tradition is part of the reason Governor Alexander's economic development policy was able to attract more tradition-valuing Japanese corporations to Tennessee than to any other state east of California (Barone and Ujifusa 1991, 1143).

12. When Clement left the seat to run for senator in 2002, Cooper, who had moved the Nashville after losing a Senate race in 1994, won it.

13. For example, in a glowing January 31, 2005, cover story on Bredesen in the *New Republic*, Clay Risen (2005) wrote, "Now some Democrats are beginning to think Bredesen is exactly the sort of person they want to see leading the party in 2008."

9

Arkansas: The Post-2000 Elections—
Continued GOP Growth or a Party
That Has Peaked?

Andrew Dowdle
Gary D. Wekkin

In the first edition of *The New Politics of the Old South*, the chapter on Arkansas politics noted that the Republican Party, which had had little successes in state electoral contests since Reconstruction, began steadily growing in strength since 1990. As regression analyses of the Republican vote shares in races for statewide offices and for the state House of Representatives indicated, a "top-down" pattern of Republican growth was responsible for this trend. The best predictor of the percentage of each county voting Republican in statewide and in legislative contests during the 1990s was the percentage voting Republican for president in each county, rather than the percentage of African Americans, evangelicals or any of several measures of "development" (Wekkin 1998, 198–99).

In contrast, the chapter on Arkansas electoral politics in the second edition of this volume took a much more anecdotal approach to the candidates and campaigns of 1998 and 2000, respectively. With the data of the 1990 census increasingly outdated, and with so many zesty stories to tell—such as the weekend voting in 2000 that prompted Governor Mike Huckabee to call his state a "banana republic," and the Republicans' failure in 1998 to recruit quality candidates for open-seat races not only for the U.S. Senate but for state constitutional officers who also sit on the state Board of Apportionment (Wekkin 2003a, 196–200, 211)—this change of direction provided a new approach that helped explain recent political developments in Arkansas.

Now, however, with fresh data from the 2000 census, it is once again the election data, not the political actors, that are the headline stories of Arkansas's 2002 and 2004 elections. As before, "top-down" Republican growth, in which down-ticket Republican success follows success at the top of the ticket more than it reflects the presence of "white flight" or of evangelical worshippers or of homophobia or of economic growth and development, continues to be the most apt description of the slow gains Republicans have made in Arkansas since 2000.

STATEWIDE CONTESTS, 2002–2004

2002 Contests

The 2002 election cycle saw Arkansas Republicans lose some of their recent gains in the contests for statewide offices. Although Republicans Mike Huckabee and Winthrop Paul Rockefeller both won reelection in 2002 as governor and lieutenant governor, respectively, the GOP made no gains in the contests for other constitutional offices (attorney general, secretary of state, treasurer, state auditor, and commissioner of lands), and lost incumbent Tim Hutchinson's seat in the U.S. Senate to Attorney General Mark Pryor, the Democratic nominee and the son of former Arkansas governor and U.S. Senator David Pryor.

Governor Mike Huckabee's putative aspirations to move onto the national political scene received a serious setback in 2002. In 1998, Huckabee had defeated attorney Bill Bristow by a margin of twenty-one points while managing to win sixty-nine of the state's seventy-five counties. Huckabee's preeminent standing in state politics up until the primary elections that spring was such that formidable Democratic opponents either opted to stay out of the race (e.g., state Senator Mike Beebe) or, like Attorney General Pryor, challenge incumbent Senator Hutchinson. Surprisingly the governor was reelected by only a relatively narrow six-point margin (see table 9.1) over Democratic nominee Jimmy Lou Fisher, a party stalwart who had never held an office more substantive than that of state treasurer. As maps 9.1 and 9.2 and their distinctly different legends indicate, the difference between Hutchinson's defeat and Huckabee's victory was the

Arkansas   215

Table 9.1. Percentage of Arkansans Voting Democratic in Contested Races for
President, Governor and U.S. Senator 1976–2004

| | Democratic Percentage of Total Vote for: | | |
Year	President	Governor[a]	U.S. Senator
1976	65.0	83.2	—
1978	—	63.4	76.6
1980	47.5	48.1	59.1
1982	—	54.7	—
1984	39.6	57.3	57.3
1986	—	63.9	62.2
1988	42.2	—	—
1990	—	57.5	—[b]
1992	53.2	—	60.1
1994	—	59.8	—
1996	53.7	47.2	—
1998	—	38.1	54.9
2000	45.5	—	—
2002	—	47.0	53.9
2004	44.6	—	55.9

[a] Arkansas shifted from two-year to four-year gubernatorial terms, beginning with the 1986 election.
[b] Incumbent David Pryor did not have a Republican opponent in 1990, and won 99.7 percent of the vote versus an independent.

latter's greater electoral appeal in a few traditionally Democratic "delta" counties where the White and Arkansas Rivers meet before flowing into the Mississippi, along with slightly greater margins in the Republican base counties of the Ozark Mountains, in the northwest corner of the state.

Hutchinson, a Bob Jones University–bred darling of the Christian Right, squandered his chosen political currency and exposed his flanks by divorcing his wife to marry a member of his staff, while also not raising enough real currency during the preceding two election cycles to discourage a challenge by a quality candidate such as Attorney General Pryor. Raising only $170,443 during the 1997–1998 election cycle and $338,437 during 1999–2000, Hutchinson's cash available at the start of the 2001–2002 cycle was only $232,198—hardly enough to pre-empt a run by Attorney General Pryor, whose office, proven political name and two preceding statewide races made him a quality challenger.[1] Pryor's victory over Hutchinson, although barely larger than Huckabee's at a margin of only 6.8 percent (see table 9.1), seemed a certain thing to most campaign-watchers. Pryor did an excellent job of taking advantage of Hutchinson's self-inflicted problem with religious conservatives in his party's base by de-emphasizing partisan conflict—"Arkansas comes first" was a principle theme of his campaign—and by featuring his own family, including his father, the former senator, in his campaign advertisements. Reflecting the centrist, apartisan approach taken by Pryor's campaign, the Democratic party itself took a much lower profile in this race, providing him with only $51,573 in contributions and $60,727 in coordinated expenditures, compared to the $91,932 and $286,385, respectively, that Hutchinson received from Republican committees. Instead, the Democrats concentrated on amassing a larger sum ($292,983) to be spent on "independent" expenditures for Pryor, compared to only $156,176 in "independent" expenditures for the Republican incumbent.[2]

One of Governor Huckabee's electoral hurdles in 2002 was that his Republican ticket once again was unable to field a viable candidate for the attorney general's office, which was forfeit by default to a powerful and respected Democratic state senator, Mike Beebe. Another electoral liability attributable to the Arkansas GOP's shortage of presentable candidates was that Huckabee's wife, Janet, was tabbed as the Republican nominee for secretary of state, enabling Democrats and the media to characterize her candidacy as an unethical grab for more power and pay by the First Family. Her candidacy not only was unsuccessful, but, according to Republican legislators pressing the flesh daily for their own reelection, was to blame for her husband's severe drop in the polls, as well (Blomeley 2002; Brummett 2002a, 2002b). Mrs. Huckabee was thumped, 62.1 to 37.9 percent of the vote, by incumbent statewide Commissioner of Lands Charlie Daniels, a "well-named" veteran of several statewide election campaigns. In contrast to the Huckabees, fellow Republican Win Rockefeller, whose own well-recognized name in Arkansas politics was offset by his often colorless, low-key demeanor, was able to win reelection as lieutenant governor by the substantial margin of 60 to 40 percent over the little-known but very politically astute Ron Sheffield, an African-American attorney who had staffed the state's reapportionment in 1990 and in 2000, and felt that Rockefeller should have a challenger. The rest of the Arkansas GOP's 2002 ticket for statewide offices (treasurer, auditor, and commissioner of lands, respectively) lost by substantial margins, which nonetheless were 8 to 9 percent smaller than Mrs. Huckabee's margin of defeat.

2004 Contests

The 2004 race for the state's other U.S. Senate seat served to underscore one of the sources of Senator Hutchinson's undoing in 2002. Senator Blanche Lincoln, whose unimpressive victory in 1998 and low approval ratings thereafter were chronicled in the previous edition of this chapter (Wekkin 2003, 199), gathered momentum by raising $306,150 during the 1999–2000 cycle—almost twice as much as Hutchinson had raised during the first two-year cycle following his election in 1996—and $992,297 during the 2001–2002 cycle, leaving her a cash balance of $667,041 going into the 2003–2004 election cycle that helped discourage potential quality challengers such as Governor Huckabee from trying for her seat (Wekkin 2003a).[3] Further discouraging such challengers was the excellent job she did of positioning herself, as Mark Pryor had done in 2002, as a moderate centrist to whom partisan labels did not mean much.[4] As a result, Lincoln drew as an opponent state Senator Jim Holt, a Christian Right Republican who was familiar to political cognoscenti and in state Republican circles, but quite unfamiliar to ordinary voters outside the Republican-tending northwestern corner of the state. The national Republican party decided early that Lincoln's seat could not be won and provided Holt only $15,800 in contributions and no coordinated expenditures at all. Democratic strategists concurred, providing Lincoln no coordinated expenditures but $60,000 in contributions.

The national debate of gay marriage that erupted during the summer of 2004, then, proved worrisome to Senator Lincoln's staff, who fielded literally several hundred telephone calls per day from conservative Christian parishioners as the issue was debated on the floor of the U.S. Senate for several days in early July. Their fears seemed well founded when, following the Christian Right's successful petition campaign to place on the Arkansas general election ballot an initiative defining marriage as a heterosexual union only (Amendment Three), Holt's campaign signage around the state sprouted nested signs urging voters to "Protect Marriage." Given Holt's campaign expenditures of only $148,682 and overall lack of statewide recognition, his receipt of 44.1 percent of the general election vote against Senator Lincoln, who had spent more than $5.8 million during the 2003–2004 election cycle, inspired widespread speculation that Holt's surprisingly strong showing had been boosted considerably by homophobes (Blomeley and Kellams 2004). The similarity between the counties voting most heavily for Holt in 2004 (see map 9.3) and those traditionally voting most heavily for Republican candidates (see maps 9.1 and 9.2 as well those in Wekkin 2003) certainly suggests that Holt's electoral performance, although surprisingly strong overall, derived mainly from the GOP's traditional northwestern Arkansas base.

It therefore seemed reasonable to infer that President Bush, who carried Arkansas in 2004 with 54.5 percent of the vote even though a number of polls had suggested the state could be a toss-up, also had benefited from the turnout for Amendment Three in Arkansas, as he seemingly had in most of the eleven states that had put anti-gay marriage initiatives on the ballot. After all, as map 9.4 indicates, the regional bases of Republican and Democratic strength, respectively, in the 2004 presidential vote bore marked similarity to those evident in maps 9.1 through 9.3 regarding the other statewide contests of 2002 and 2004, respectively, as well as those evident in the preceding two electoral cycles (see Wekkin 2003). Bush's improvement upon his winning margin of only 51 percent in 2000 stemmed from his ability to hold onto much of his 2000 base vote, his ability to win additional support from the high-growth areas outside of Little Rock and in Northwest Arkansas, and somewhat on his receipt of

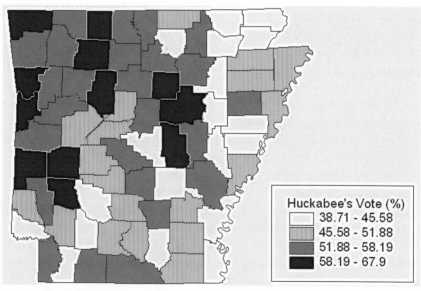

Map 1   Republican Gubernatorial Vote in 2002

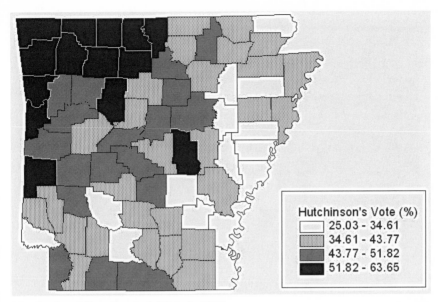

Map 2   Republican Senatorial Vote in 2002

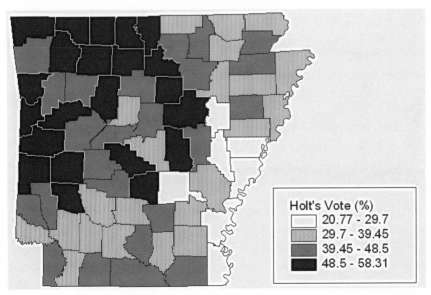

Map 3   Republican Senatorial Vote in 2004

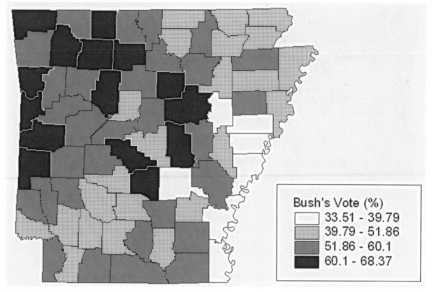

Map 4   Republican Presidential Vote in 2004

more votes in areas in which support for Amendment Three was strong-est. The Kerry presidential campaign's pulling of most of its advertising from the air in Arkansas the last five weeks of the campaign (*USA Today* 2004) also is a factor worthy of consideration; however, it is difficult to know whether this decision contributed to Bush's lead or occurred because of his lead, although the Bush campaign's subsequent reassign-ment of its Arkansas staff to Colorado suggests the latter rather than the former.

In fact, however, as map 9.5 indicates, the statewide distribution of the vote in favor of Amendment Three, which passed by the overwhelming margin of 75.0 to 25.1 percent, was not at all consistent with the distribu-tion of Republican votes for Huckabee, Hutchinson, Holt, or Bush in maps 9.1 through 9.4, or with the distribution of Republican votes during the 1997–1998 or 1999–2000 election cycles (Wekkin 2003), either. In fact, eight counties in the heart of the Republican stronghold in the northwest corner of the state—Boone, Carroll, Madison, Newton, Franklin, Johnson, Logan and Pope—provided among the lowest rates of voting support for Amendment Three. Conversely, a comparable number of counties in the deltas of the Mississippi, Arkansas, and White Rivers—including some of the most Democratic-tending ones in the 2002 and 2004 elections (e.g., Desha and St. Francis counties, with 46.3 and 49.0 percent African-American populations respectively)—provided support for Amendment Three that was 5 to 10 percent higher than the statewide average. This, of course, suggests that homophobia may not have been responsible for Bush's victory margin or for Holt's surprisingly strong showing. Amendment Three, which defined marriage as a heterosexual union, seems to have had as much, if not more, support in the black belts of the Democratic-tending First and Fourth Congressional Districts as it had in the Ozark Mountains of the Republican-tending Third District.

The hypothesis that Republican vote totals in 2004 were helped by Amendment Three was tested by using a multiple regression model consisting of demographic factors, county support for candidates of the winning party in preceding statewide elections and county vote totals for Amendment Three in 2004. As table 9.2 shows, significant, positive relationships between support for the Amendment, on the one hand, and support for President Bush and for GOP Senate candidate Jim Holt, on the other, were obtained. However, county support for Bush in 2000 also was significant at .000, and had a much greater beta weight than did

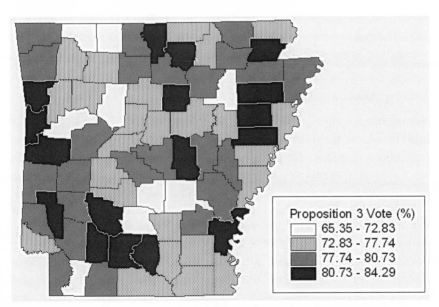

Map 5   Votes For Proposed Constitutional Amendment Three in 2004

county support for the ballot measure, when regressed against the dependent variable of county support for Bush in 2004. Moreover, as the bottom half of table 9.2 shows, adding President Bush's 2004 county vote totals as a control variable to the equation for the 2004 U.S. Senate race made the significant relationship between county support for Amendment Three and the county vote share for Holt disappear. Holt did not run particularly better or worse in areas that overwhelmingly backed Amendment Three. What did significantly improve Holt's 2004 county vote share was presidential coattails—the vote-pulling presence of President Bush at the top of the Republican ticket.

Moreover, Bush's county vote share in the 2000 presidential election also correlated significantly (and more strongly than Senator Hutchinson's own winning vote share in 1996) with the Republican vote share in the 2002 Senate contest, whereas the vote counties would cast for Amendment Three in 2004 did not. In fact, the beta weight of Bush's 2000 vote share in the equation for the 2002 Senate race is virtually identical to that of Bush's 2004 vote share in the equation for the 2004 Senate race. Since none of the equations reported in table 9.2 found either county population density or percentage of African Americans significantly correlated with Republican voter share, and county growth rate achieved significance in only one of the four equations—and extremely weakly at that (B = .041, Beta = .067, sig T = .048)—the evidence from the 2002 and 2004 statewide contests continues to suggest that Republican voting strength in Arkansas grows from the top down.

Looking Ahead to 2006

Arkansas Republicans have had limited success in major statewide races, most of which, however, has occurred during the past twenty-five years. Republican nominees for president have carried the state only five times since Reconstruction, but all five of those victories occurred during the past six presidential elections (1972, 1980, 1984, 1988, 2000, and 2004), amounting to a 62.5 percent rate of electoral success since 1972. Arkansas Republican nominees for governor also have won five times since Reconstruction (1966, 1968, 1990, 1998, and 2002), but these victories account for only 33 percent of the fifteen gubernatorial elections that have taken place since 1966. In contrast, Tim Hutchinson's victory in the 1996 U.S. Senate contest is the only instance since Reconstruction of a Republican having won an Arkansas seat in the U. S. Senate.

Table 9.2. Multiple Regression Correlates of Republican Vote Share in Statewide Contests 2002–2004

Contest	Variable	B^a	SE B^b	Beta^c	Sig T^d
President—2004	Bush 2000	.926	.036	.892	.000
	Growth rate	.041	.020	.067	.048
	Pop. density	.001	.004	.008	.770
	African Amer.	−1.663	1.153	−.034	.154
	Amendment 3	.256	.058	.124	.000
	Constant	−13.138	4.172		.002
	(adj. R2 = .960, sig. F = .000, N = 75)				
Senate—2002	Bush 2000	.451	.072	.437	.000
	Growth rate	.017	.025	.029	.482
	Pop. density	.001	.004	.010	.745
	African Amer.	.035	1.273	.001	.978
	Amendment 3	.031	.068	.015	.653
	Senate 96	.313	.007	.339	.000
	Pryor 98	−.265	.006	−.227	.000
	Constant	19.378	6.817		.006
	(adj. R2 = .951, sig. F = .000, N = 75)				
Senate—2004	Growth rate	.099	.055	.151	.078
w/o Bush coattails	Pop. density	−.009	.009	−.060	.326
	African Amer.	3.645	2.841	.070	.204
	Amendment 3	.581	.130	.261	.000
	Senate 98	.686	.079	.339	.000
	Constant	19.378	6.817		.006
	(adj. R2 = .794, sig. F = .000, N = 75)				
Senate—2004	Bush 2004	.510	.139	.473	.000
w/Bush coattails	Growth rate	.085	.051	.130	.101
	Pop. density	−.007	.008	−.048	.400
	African Amer.	3.440	2.617	.066	.193
	Amendment 3	.216	.155	.097	.169
	Senate 98	.327	.122	.352	.009
	Constant	14.578	10.281		.161
	(adj. R2 = .825, sig. F = .000, N = 75)				
Governor—2002	Bush 2000	.494	.095	.609	.063
	Growth rate	.036	.036	.076	.313
	Pop. density	−.003	.006	.010	.648
	African Amer.	1.230	2.018	.032	.544
	Amendment 3	−.046	.107	−.029	.665
	Govern 98	.247	.083	.288	.004
	Constant	15.784	8.356		.063
	(adj. R2 = .816, sig. F = .000, N = 75)				

(continues)

Table 9.2.   Continued

Contest	Variable	B^a	$SE\ B^b$	$Beta^c$	$Sig\ T^d$
Lt. Governor—2002	Bush 2000	.476	.079	.462	.000
	Growth rate	.078	.037	.130	.035
	Pop. density	−.005	.006	−.036	.458
	African Amer.	1.720	2.075	.829	.410
	Amendment 3	−.197	.106	−.096	.067
	Lt. Gov. 98	.541	.075	.470	.000
	Constant	12.985	8.612		.136
	(adj. R2 = .881, sig. F = .000, N = 75)				

Notes: Correlates are obtained by regressing GOP candidates' vote share in the seventy-five counties against county demographics and county returns for other statewide races. *Bush—2000* = George W. Bush's percent of the 2000 presidential; *Bush—2004* = George W. Bush's percent of the 2000 presidential vote; *Growth rate* = population growth rate from 1990 to 2000; *Pop. density* = population density per square mile in 2000; *African Amer.* = percentage of the 2000 population that is African American; *Amendment Three* = percent of voters supporting Amendment 3; *Pryor 98* = percent of vote received by Mark Pryor in 1998 state attorney general's race; and *Senate 96, Senate 98, Govern. 98* and *Lt. Gov. 98* = totals received by Republican nominees in those respective races.

[a] Slope coefficient
[b] Standard error of slope coefficient
[c] Standardized regression coefficient
[d] Statistical significance of slope coefficient

In 2002, Hutchinson lost reelection to that Senate seat while Huckabee and incumbent GOP Lieutenant Governor Win Paul Rockefeller were re-elected to their offices by margins that were disparate in size (6 percent for Huckabee; 20 percent for Rockefeller) and in geographical distribution. As map 9.6 shows, Rockefeller fared less well in the Ozarks in 2002 than did either Huckabee (map 9.1) or Hutchinson (map 9.2) but much better than the latter two in the southwestern corner of the state and in Pulaski County. The same is true when compared to the 2004 distributions of the vote for President Bush (map 9.3) and for Jim Holt (map 9.4), respectively. Rockefeller's family name and his father's career as governor of Arkansas seem to enable him to draw more votes outside the northwest mountain bastion of the Arkansas Republican party and thus rely much less upon Christian conservatives compared to more traditional Republicans and swing voters. As the equation modeling the 2002 lieutenant governor's race in table 9.2 reveals, Rockefeller had lower levels of support in the counties that most strongly backed Amendment Three but did better in some of the faster growing suburban counties, such as Faulkner and Pulaski.

This split had set up a major struggle in 2006 for the heart and soul of the Arkansas Republican Party, insofar as Rockefeller already has declared his intention to run for governor, as has former GOP Congressman Asa Hutchinson, who in 1996 succeeded his brother, Tim, as the representative from Arkansas's mountainous Third Congressional District until surrendering the seat to accept appointment as director of the Drug Enforcement Administration in 2001 (and then undersecretary of Homeland Security in 2003). However Rockefeller dropped out of the race in the summer of 2005 because of health concerns. Past experience had shown that statewide Republican primaries in Arkansas—when they occur at all—are won and lost in the Third District, where map 9.6 showed Rockefeller to be weaker and the Hutchinson name would have been very difficult to beat.

To offset this weakness, Rockefeller spent money on mailings designed to shore up his credentials as a pro-life social conservative (Wickline 2005). Given the identity of both Hutchinsons with the Christian Right, and Rockefeller's new efforts directed toward that element, the 2006 Republican primary could have propelled the Arkansas GOP firmly into that camp at the expense of the party's pre-evangelical business base and of rapidly growing suburban counties such as Saline as well. On the other hand, northwest Arkansas has replaced Little Rock to such an extent as

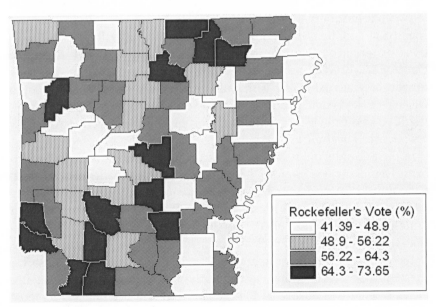

Map 6   Republican Lieutenant Gubernatorial Vote in 2002

the state's economic center of gravity, and the Rockefeller family's interests remain sufficiently identified with Little Rock and Conway County[5]
that Lieutenant Governor Rockefeller's efforts to cut into the Hutchinsons's social conservative base in the northwest may prove futile. In that
case, the 2006 Republican gubernatorial primary could have been so divisive that the party's electoral fortunes thereafter were crippled by fault
lines in which the evangelical-secular divide is reinforced by regional economic rivalry.

CONGRESSIONAL CONTESTS, 2002–2004

Arkansas Republicans did not field an impressive set of candidates for the
state's four seats in the U.S. House in either 2002 or 2004. The closest race
in 2002 was the rematch in the Fourth Congressional District (southwest
Arkansas) between Democratic Congressman Mike Ross and Jay Dickey,
the four-term Republican incumbent from whom Ross had wrested the
seat in 2000. Dickey ran an aggressive campaign, pointing out that his
defeat in 2000 had cost district voters millions of dollars in federal highway funds, and that Speaker of the House Dennis Hastert (R-Illinois) had
promised to return him to his former seat on the Appropriations Committee, with seniority intact.[6] However, despite Dickey's ability to raise and
spend $2.03 million, matching almost dollar for dollar Ross's $2.05 million,[7] experienced Republican strategists such as state GOP Executive
Director Marty Ryall privately admitted that they did not expect Dickey
to win the seat again. Ross won handily, with 60.6 percent of the vote to
Dickey's 39.4 percent, and no Republican challenger came forward to contest Ross's Fourth District seat in 2004, prompting him briefly to consider
running for governor in 2006.

In the Second Congressional District centering on Little Rock, incumbent Democrat Vic Snyder had no Republican challenger in 2002,
although Ed Garner, who had some name recognition from his days as
attorney for the National Football League Players' Association, ran as a
write-in candidate and pulled 7 percent of the vote to Snyder's 92.9 percent. In 2004, Snyder beat back a more determined, but flawed, challenger
in the person of state Representative Marvin Parks, a Christian conservative who had been minority leader in the 100-member Arkansas House
of Representatives during its 2003 session and had been named its most
effective legislator because he had tied up the session with only thirty

Republican colleagues. When the 2003 session of the General Assembly adjourned, Parks, who could not run for reelection due to term limits, tested the congressional waters by trying to raise $200,000 before summer's end, in which case he would run. He met and exceeded his goal, ultimately raising $577,000 and spending all but $3,000.[7]

However, in a classic illustration of the cultural canyon between modern secular America and the Christian Right, Parks, a father of seven who home-schooled his children and gave up his job as a public school teacher when elected to the Arkansas General Assembly, drew for himself a monthly salary of $4,000 from his campaign receipts in order to be able to run for Congress without economic hardship for his family (Robinson 2004). This precipitated a minor firestorm of media commentary and Democratic press releases about the ethics of the now legally permissible practice of using campaign contributions for living expenses. However, the issue never became as large a factor as it probably could have been had the race been closer. Congressman Snyder, despite having voted in 2004 against the proposed federal marriage amendment and having spoken out against Arkansas' Amendment Three (Wickline 2004), hardly broke a sweat running for reelection, spending $880,496 and winning reelection by 58.2 to 41.8 percent of the vote.[8]

No other congressional district contest in 2002 or 2004 came as close as this, or even as close as Ross's 21-point margin over Dickey. Democratic incumbent Congressman Marion Berry, representing the First Congressional District (east Arkansas delta), defeated another former Congressman, the Democrat-turned-Republican Tommy Robinson, by outspending Robinson almost ten-to-one ($1,315,408 to $142,244) and out-polling him by more than two-to-one (66.8 to 33.2 percent) in 2002. Berry then virtually duplicated the feat by beating Republican Vernon Humphrey by 66.6 to 33.4 percent in 2004, spending $947,839 to Humphrey's $23,836.[9] Clearly, Rep. Berry would have all potential challengers know that they can expect to receive the full brunt of his reelection efforts; political retirement could be the only option left after the beating he would try to inflict.

In Arkansas' Third Congressional District (northwest Arkansas), controlled by Republicans without interruption for thirty-eight years, freshman Republican Congressman John Boozman was unopposed and reelected in 2002 with 98.9 percent of the vote. Boozman was elected in a hard-fought special election in 2001 to replace Rep. Asa Hutchinson, who resigned to accept nomination by President George W. Bush as head of the Drug Enforcement Administration. In 2004, he was challenged by state Rep. Jan Judy, who could push him into spending only $543,000 of the $697,000 he had raised while en route to reelection by a comfortable 59.3 to 38.1 percent margin.

STATE LEGISLATIVE COMPETITION

As in statewide contests, Republican strength in contested races for the Arkansas General Assembly has grown since 1990 at an impressive rate, albeit from a low base. Lately, however, this expansion has shown signs of flattening out, or even subsiding a bit. Although the 2002 election cycle witnessed an increase in the number of contested races in both chambers, and the achievement of virtual parity in party vote share in contested races for the House of Representatives, the competitiveness of Republican candidates in contested races for the state Senate fell back by almost 4 percent (see table 9.3). In 2004, the vote share earned by Republican candidates in contested races for the state Senate fell back another 6 percent while that earned by Republicans in contested races for the House fell by almost 2 percent, and the number of contested races for both chambers fell back considerably, as well. The leveling off of the number of contested races for the legislature that seems to be occurring could be a function of

Table 9.3.   Average Republican Vote Share in Contested Races for the Arkansas General Assembly 1992–2004[a]

	Number of Contested Races		Percentage Voting GOP	
Year	House	Senate	House	Senate
1990	22	6	35.7	37.2
1992	25	7	42.8	52.7
1994	33	9	42.7	38.3
1996	34	6	44.3	42.5
1998	45	8	41.5	47.3
2000	28	5	48.2	49.0
2002	33	12	49.4	45.1
2004	28	3	47.7	38.9

[a] The averages shown in the House and Senate columns under the heading "Pct. Voting GOP" are not calculated by adding up the total Republican vote in all legislative races. Rather, they are calculated as the average of the vote shares won by the respective GOP candidates contesting seats. The latter is a better measure of the progress of Republican competitiveness in races all across the state than the former average, which can be influenced by the larger turnouts in some of the state's higher-growth areas, as well as the larger GOP margins in the state's northwest Republican stronghold.

the state's recently enacted terms limits law, which is one of the harshest in the country in that it restricts senators to two four-year terms and representatives to three two-year terms. Why challenge an incumbent of either party, when an open-seat opportunity for the same legislative seat is at most four years away?

Whatever the cause, the limited number of contested races for the Arkansas General Assembly in 2002 and 2004, together with the volume of seat turnover attributable primarily to term limits rather than to electoral competition as such, makes the party's performance in such races a very questionable indicator of the Arkansas Republican Party's overall statewide strength. This, plus the fact that post-2000 redistricting prevents the use of 1998 or 2000 voting data as baseline measures of previous support, makes it still as yet infeasible to replicate the study of the correlates for Republican vote share in 1994 and 1996 legislative races that was reported in table 10.5 of Wekkin (1998, 119).

Table 9.4. Multiple Regression Correlates of Republican Vote Shares in Contested Races for State House of Representatives 2002–2004

Contest	Variable	B^a	$SE\ B^b$	$Beta^c$	$Sig\ T^d$
2002	Bush-2000	.016	.005	.821	.003
	Growth rate	−.003	.002	−.329	.221
	Pop. density	.001	.000	.039	.844
	African Amer.	−.018	.153	−.025	.877
	Amendment 3	−.010	.006	−.351	.115
	Constant	.397	.439		.375
	(Adj. $R^2 = .297$, sig. F = .023, N = 28)				
2004	Bush-2004	.012	.003	.806	.000
	Growth rate	−.001	.002	−.016	.684
	Pop. density	.001	.001	.203	.179
	African Amer.	−.037	.086	−.055	.668
	Amendment 3	−.002	.004	−.065	.684
	Constant	−.094	.288		.748
	(Adj. $R^2 = .564$, sig. F = .000, N = 33)				

Notes: Correlates are obtained by regressing GOP candidates' vote share in contested state house races against county demographics and county returns for other statewide races. *Bush-2000* = George W. Bush's percent of the 2000 presidential; *Bush-2004* = George W. Bush's percent of the 2000 presidential vote; *Growth rate* = population growth rate from 1990 to 2000; *Pop. density* = population density per square mile in 2000; *African Amer.* = percentage of the 2000 population that is African American; *Amendment 3* = percent of voters supporting Amendment Three.

[a] Slope coefficient
[b] Standard error of slope coefficient
[c] Standardized regression coefficient
[d] Statistical significance of slope coefficient

Table 9.5.   Partisan Division of the Arkansas General Assembly 1991–2005

	House[a]		Senate[a]	
Session	GOP	Dem	GOP	Dem
1991–1992	9	91	4	31
1993–1994	10	90	5	30
1995–1996	12	88	7	28
1997–1998	14	86	7	28
1999–2000	25	75	6	29
2001–2002	30	70	8	27
2003–2004	31	69	8	27
2005–2006	28	72	8	27

[a] The total seats in the Arkansas House and Senate are 100 and 35, respectively.

Still, the findings for 2002 and 2004 appear to confirm the earlier finding of "top-down" growth. The Arkansas Republican Party has not benefited at the state legislative level from recent grassroots demographic trends such as in-migration or white flight, or from sociopolitical trends such as the spread of evangelicalism. Rather, any success had at this level seems again to have been due primarily to top-down factors: Once overall party strength, in the form of President Bush's 2000 and 2004 results, was controlled for in the models measuring contested legislative races in 2002 and 2004, respectively, neither election model revealed Republican growth at the legislative level in the faster growing counties (see table 9.4). However, the stalled growth of contested legislative races and of Republican vote shares during and since those races, together with the stalled growth of Republican seats in the General Assembly indicated by table 9.5, also suggests that the coattail effects of those at the top of the Republican ticket may have reached their limits as far as state legislative contests are concerned.

INCREASED PARTISAN IDENTIFICATION
WITH THE GOP

Since 1990, it usually has been the case that the Arkansas Republican Party's steady but slow gains in the number of legislative races contested, the size of the Republican vote share in such races and the number of Republicans elected in such races has not been matched by commensurate gains in partisan affinity among Arkansas voters. During the first four years of the twenty-first century, however, these conflicting patterns have reversed themselves 180 degrees. In 2002 and 2004, despite the slowing or slippage of Republican gains in state legislative races, the percentage of Arkansans willing to identify themselves as Republicans has grown, from 23 percent in 2000 to as high as 30 percent in 2004 (see table 9.6). This increase should not be attributable to any measurement error or to changes of methodology, since the polls documenting this year-by-year increase since 1999 are the annual *Arkansas Polls* done for the University of Arkansas' Diane D. Blair Center of Southern Politics and Society.

Given the increased share of Republican identifiers in the electorate since 2000 and the continuing evidence that Republican voting in Arkansas spreads from the top down, one could infer from the Republicans' recent loss of momentum in legislative races (see table 9.3) and in the growth of their caucuses in the Arkansas General Assembly (see table 9.5) that a critical obstacle holding the Arkansas Republican Party back at this point is the party's shortage of quality candidates for public office. This is an inference with which most observers of recent Arkansas politics would concur.

CONCLUSION

In many ways, it is easy to glance briefly at the 2002 and 2004 elections in Arkansas and simply note that these elections are consistent with Arkansas's comparatively glacial progress away from a southern Democratic stronghold and toward a two-party competitive state. Although the Republicans again won the presidential, gubernatorial and lieutenant governor contests, the state's congressional delegation and state legislature remain strongly Democratic. While George W. Bush's 2004 victory margin was an improvement over that of 2000, a 9 percent margin of victory over a liberal senator from Massachusetts is just not impressive in the context of contemporary Southern political tides. Senator Kerry's 44.4 percent of the vote in Arkansas was his third-best showing in the South, trailing only the rim states of Florida (47 percent) and Virginia (45.6 percent), respectively.

On the other hand, the ceiling in Arkansas has proven to be rather low lately for successful Democratic candidates for statewide office as well. Attorney General Mark Pryor, the son of a popular former U.S. Senator, defeated scandal-plagued Senator Tim Hutchinson only by 9 percent in

Table 9.6.   Partisan Breakdown in Arkansas During the 1990s According to Various Tracking Polls[a]

Date	Variable	% Dem	% Rep	% Ind[b]
__ Nov 91	Mktg Resrch Inst	29	18	53
24 Apr 94	Arthur Finkelstein & Assocs	53	18	27
13 Dec 95	Kieran Mahoney	49	20	29
22 Mar 96	Kieran Mahoney	48	23	27
21 May 96	NRSC (Natl Repub Sen Comm)	44	22	24
28 Aug 96	Kieran Mahoney	51	22	25
19 Feb 97	UCA Citizen Poll	40	19	35
27 Jun 98	Dresner, Wickers & Assocs	48	25	27
22 Sep 98	Dresner, Wickers & Assocs	42	25	34
14 Oct 98	Dresner, Wickers & Assocs	42	25	28
21 Oct 98	Dresner, Wickers & Assocs	42	25	26
29 Oct 98	Olympia, Inc.	36[c]	28[c]	33[c]
27 Oct 99	University of Arkansas SRC[d]	35	23	31
25 Oct 00	University of Arkansas SRC[e]	36	23	35
17 Oct 01	University of Arkansas SRC[f]	33	27	32
20 Oct 02	University of Arkansas SRC[g]	33	28	33
13 Oct 03	University of Arkansas SRC[h]	38	24	31
20 Oct 04	University of Arkansas SRC[i]	35	30	28

[a] All commercial house (consultant) tracking polls results herein are based on a sample size of approximately N = 400, with the exception of the 29 October 1998 Olympia, Inc. results, which are the cumulative results of at least 14 October 1998 tracking polls with a cumulative N of 40,872 (see note below). The reports from which these data are extracted are archived, along with perhaps thirty other poll reports commissioned by the Arkansas Republican Party during the 1990s, in the Archives of the Torreyson Library at the University of Central Arkansas, in Conway, AR.
[b] Combines independent and other identifier categories, but does not include "Don't Know" responses and nonrespondents.
[c] Cumulative results of tracking polls between 12 and 29 October 1998. Significant numbers of "No Party" respondents are lumped with independents and other.
[d] Annual "Arkansas Poll," with an N of 885.
[e] Annual "Arkansas Poll," with an N of 775.
[f] Annual "Arkansas Poll," with an N of 767.
[g] Annual "Arkansas Poll," with an N of 768.
[h] Annual "Arkansas Poll," with an N of 762.
[i] Annual "Arkansas Poll," with an N of 758.

2002. Senator Blanche Lincoln, who had no scandals to her name and had spent much of her term reaching out to a number of important constituencies in the state, could do no better in 2004 than the 55 percent of the vote she had received in 1988, despite outspending her little-known challenger by nearly forty to one.

However, closer inspection of the Republicans' vote totals reveals some important caveats about future Republican competitiveness in Arkansas. These caveats derive from the contrasting fates of various Republican candidates in the state's fastest-growing suburban counties. The 2004 Bush vote totals and the 2002 Rockefeller vote totals in these counties demonstrate that there is a pool of support in these fast-growing areas that can be tapped by Republican candidates. However, the fact that Republican candidates for the state legislature failed to rally these same voters to their own advantage illustrates the extent to which the Arkansas Republican party is still weak at the grassroots. Governor Huckabee's own inability to draw comparable support from these same counties in 2002 was one factor among several that figured in his drop from 60 percent of the gubernatorial vote in 1998 to only 53 percent in 2002.

Another stunning find in the 2004 vote totals is that voter support for Amendment Three—the so-called "Protect Marriage" amendment—was a statewide trend that carried well beyond the usual socially conservative northwestern Republican bastions such as Benton, Baxter, and Boone counties. Nowhere in Arkansas did the amendment receive less than 65 percent of the countywide vote—and northwestern counties such as Boone, Carroll, Franklin, and Johnson could be found at the low end of this spectrum, 10 percent below the statewide norm, while usually Democratic delta counties such as Desha, Nevada, Ouachita, and St. Francis were among those that gave the amendment more than 80 percent of their votes. Thus, state Senator Jim Holt's surprising showing against Senator Blanche Lincoln owed less to his conscious effort to link himself to the amendment than to the coattails of President Bush, whose own voting support in turn correlated significantly, but weakly, with support for Amendment Three—but not nearly as strongly as it correlated with his Arkansas voting base in the preceding presidential election of 2000.

Finally, a potentially disastrous political identity crisis for the Arkansas Republican party looms in these data. Obviously, the statewide strength of voting support for Amendment Three in 2004 suggests that the Republican party could make inroads in traditionally Democratic delta counties by focusing on those specifics of their own socially conservative agenda—such as opposition to gay marriage—that resonate not only in rural Arkansas but apparently with African Americans as well. Doing so in this manner, however, could cost Arkansas Republicans the support of professionals and other better-educated voters in the fast-growing suburban areas of Pulaski, Faulkner, and Saline counties in central Arkansas, and perhaps even some in the boomtowns of northwestern Arkansas. Morris Fiorina, Abrams and Pope's *Culture War?* (2005) compellingly argues that what many Americans in the moderate middle of the political spectrum would prefer regarding divisive social questions such as gay marriage and abortion is for the issue activists at either pole—and that which they are fighting over—to quietly go away. Arkansas political analysts such as the William J. Clinton Foundation's Skip Rutherford have argued for many years that it is precisely the voters in this "moderate middle" who are the key to getting elected in central Arkansas. In so many words, if the state GOP and its candidates for statewide office continue to pursue a "wedge" politics strategy with respect to issues such as gay marriage and abortion, it could prove as difficult thereafter for the party to recruit electable moderates to run for local or legislative office as Republicans as it would be to persuade suburban moderates to vote for Christian conservative candidates.

By mobilizing social conservatives as well as suburban voters thus far since 1990, the Arkansas Republican party has been able to transform itself from a small minority party existing primarily to collect federal patronage into an important, frequently successful force in recent statewide contests (Wekkin 1998, 2003; Blair and Barth 2005). Although this transition has taken place later, and more slowly, in Arkansas than in most Southern states, it has reached a stage sufficient that Republican competitiveness in major statewide races now seems irreversible. However, the Republican Party's ability to extend itself enough at the grassroots to compete for control of the state legislature and, beyond that, the county courthouses, hinges upon the party's ability to avoid, as President Bush did in 2004, a rupture between the party's social conservative and suburban moderate constituencies. The 2006 Republican gubernatorial primary contest between Win Paul Rockefeller and Asa Hutchinson might have been a critical test of whether the Arkansas Republicans are able to expand their base and also their control of the state's political structure, or whether the divisions and difficulties of divided government in Arkansas would continue for another decade. Though this battle has been postponed to some extent, these divisions still exist and may yet surface in future intraparty battles.

REFERENCES

Americans for Democratic Action. 2005. ADA Voting Records. www.adaction.org/votingrecords.htm.

Blair, Diane D., and Jay Barth. 2005. *Arkansas Politics and Government*, 2nd ed. Lincoln NE: University of Nebraska Press.

Blomeley, Seth. 2002. "Governor's Race Gets even More Spirited on Halloween." *Arkansas Democrat-Gazette*, November 1, (front section).

Blomeley, Seth, and Laura Kellams. 2004. "Observers Say Marriage Issue Energized Lincoln's Opponent." *Arkansas Democrat-Gazette* November 4, (Northwest Arkansas section).

Brummett, John. 2002a. "Huckabee vs. Not Huckabee." *The Log Cabin Democrat* (Conway AR), July 23, editorial page.

———. 2002b. "Up Arrows for Pryor, One Huckabee." *The Log Cabin Democrat* (Conway AR), September 24, editorial page.

Dickey, Jay. 2002. jaydickey2002.com/cgi-data/news/files/10.html.

Fiorina, Morris J., Samuel J. Abrams and Jeremy C. Pope. 2005. *Culture War: The Myth of a Polarized America*. New York: Pearson Longman.

Minton, Mark. 2004. "Fast-Growth Counties Vex Democrats." *Arkansas Democrat-Gazette* December 26, (front section).

PoliticalMoneyLine. 2005. Money in Politics Database. www.tray.com/fecinfo.

Robinson, David. 2004. "National Republican Changes Tune on Parks' Use of Campaign Funds." Arkansas News Bureau posting, April 27.

USA Today. 2004. "Kerry Pulls Ads from Arizona, Arkansas, Louisiana and Missouri" (Associated Press story), September 22.

Wekkin, Gary D. 2003. "Arkansas: Electoral Competition and Reapportionment in the 'Land of Opportunity.'" In Charles S. Bullock III and Mark J. Rozell, eds., *The New Politics of the Old South*, 2nd ed. Lanham, MD: Rowman & Littlefield, 195–222.

———. 1998. "Arkansas: Electoral Competition in the 1990s." In Charles S. Bullock III and Mark J. Rozell, eds., *The New Politics of the Old South*. Lanham, MD: Rowman & Littlefield, 185–203.

———. 2003a. "Huckabee Decision Not Surprising." *The Log Cabin Democrat* (Conway AR), September 4, editorial page.

Wickline, Michael R. 2004. "Snyder, Parks Joust over Iraq, Gays, Tax Cuts." *Arkansas Democrat Gazette* October 27, (front section).

———. 2005. "Rockefeller Mass-Mailing Takes Anti-Abortion Stance." *Arkansas Democrat-Gazette* May 7, (front section).

NOTES

1. PoliticalMoneyLine, www.tray.com/fecinfo, March 1, 2005.
2. PoliticalMoneyLine, www.tray.com/fecinfo, March 1, 2005
3. PoliticalMoneyLine, www.tray.com/fecinfo, March 1, 2005
4. Lincoln had received Americans for Democratic Action ratings ranging from "70" to "95" during the years 1998–2002 and could be characterized as moderate-to-liberal. Americans for Democratic Action, www.adaction.org/votingrecords .htm, February 15, 2005.
5. WinRock International has just occupied new offices in Little Rock and maintains agricultural operations in several locations in Pulaski, Conway, and Lonoke counties.

6. Jay Dickey2002, http://jaydickey2002.com/cgi-data/news/files/10.html, December 1, 2002.
7. PoliticalMoneyLine, www.tray.com/fecinfo, March 1, 2005
8. PoliticalMoneyLine, www.tray.com/fecinfo, March 1, 2005
9. PoliticalMoneyLine, www.tray.com/fecinfo, March 1, 2005

10

Oklahoma: Evangelicals and the Secular Realignment

Gary W. Copeland
Rebecca J. Cruise
Ronald Keith Gaddie

The ongoing realignment of the South is in full force in Oklahoma. The Republicans made creeping gains in the state throughout the early 1990s, and followed the general pattern of Republican presidential support and Democratic state government through. The 1994 election initiated a dramatic increase in Republican electoral strength. By 2004 the Republicans controlled both U.S. Senate seats, all but one congressional seat, the state House of Representatives, most statewide constitutional offices and were within two seats of controlling the state senate. No Democrat since 1990 has commanded more than 44 percent for governor or the U.S. Senate. The principal catalyst for political change has been social conservatism and, in particular, the continued mobilizing effort of evangelical Protestants. Democrats remain competitive in certain parts of the state and when economic issues are predominant.

THE EXPATRIATE SOUTHERN STATE

Oklahoma was originally part of the Louisiana Purchase. Most of present-day Oklahoma was set aside from the purchase as Indian territory. During the 1820s the first southerners came to Oklahoma, as the Five Civilized Tribes (the Cherokees, Chickasaws, Choctaws, Creeks, and Seminoles) were forcibly removed from Florida, Georgia, and Alabama to the Indian Territory. Once there, the tribes established five Indian nations that ruled as republics under written constitutions (Morgan, England, and Humphreys 1991). During the Civil War some Indian tribes, most notably the Cherokees, sided with the Confederacy. Many tribes owned slaves, and the potential costs of abolition to the tribes were great. The Oklahoma tribes sent delegates to the Confederate Congress and served in the southern armies.[1]

After the end of the Civil War, the Five Civilized Tribes underwent a reconstruction as harsh as that of the rest of the South. Indian participation in the rebellion gave the federal government sufficient justification to seize the central and west Oklahoma lands from the tribes and to then open the territory to white settlement. In the remaining Indian territories, tribes were forced to free their slaves and to offer the freedmen membership in the tribes. In response to the emancipation of the blacks, the tribes passed segregation laws that created all-black townships and placed limitations on the black freedmen that resembled the Jim Crow laws.

In the 1880s, the Bureau of Indian Affairs declared the tribal reservation system to be an abysmal failure. This evaluation was reached by the Dawes Commission, apparently under some influence from development interests that sought to open the Indian Territory to white settlement. The lands of the Civilized Tribes were broken up, and each tribal member was granted a 160-acre homestead. The territory was partitioned into two territories: Oklahoma Territory, which took in the northern and western parts of the state, and Indian Territory, which covered an area roughly south of a line running from the northeast corner of the state, through Tulsa and Oklahoma City, and on to the Texas border. This partition is reflected in the settlement patterns and subsequent political behavior of the state. White settlers in the Indian Territory were largely expatriate southerners from Texas, Arkansas, and Mississippi. A journey through the southeast corner of the state, commonly referred to as "Little Dixie," reveals that many of the towns and counties take their names directly from Mississippi locales.

So is Oklahoma really southern? Oklahoma stands at the fringe of the South, both in the study of southern politics and in the mind-set of Oklahoma. Oklahoma—then Indian Territory—was not a state at the time of the Civil War, but many of the events and cultural factors that structure

Oklahoma politics are distinctly southern (Price 1957; Ewing 1953). As in many southern states, the GOP has enjoyed a dramatic growth in adherents and has sustained electoral success in contests at all electoral levels. Unlike the Deep South, however, the Republican growth in Oklahoma is a product of the intriguing catalyst of religious, social conservatism. Most southern state studies show that Republican growth can be linked initially to race (Carmines and Stimson 1989; Lamis 1988; Black and Black 1992). Race, though, is not such a divisive issue in Oklahoma. Only 7.5 percent of the state population is black, though Native Americans outnumber blacks, and Hispanics are the fastest-growing minority in the state, leaving Oklahoma with a proportion white population comparable to Alabama. The unique specter of fear of black political and economic empowerment is an historic footnote to Oklahoma's early segregationist history. Tulsa was host to one of the most vicious, deadly race riots in American history eighty-five years ago, and, until the 1960s many small cities and towns were formally segregated by illegal "sundown" laws. Oklahoma did not resist national government efforts to integrate public schools or accommodations. By the 1970s, the wave of integration was viewed with ambivalence, as Oklahoma boomed and culturally diverse Oklahomans—one in four, when asked, will claim Native blood—looked to the sky as oil prices soared. Subsequent to the economic collapse of the oil industry in the 1980s, religion—the growth of the Christian Right—emerged as a major catalyst in the GOP upswing in Oklahoma.

PARTY DEVELOPMENT: WHERE SHOULD
A CONSERVATIVE GO?

The Democratic Party dominated state politics from the first state elections in 1907 until the 1990s. The only exceptions to Democratic hegemony were the two Republicans elected governor in the 1960s and one again in the 1980s, and the brief Republican control of the state legislature from 1920 to 1922. At the presidential level the Democrats faded earlier; Lyndon Johnson is the only Democrat to carry Oklahoma since 1952.

The reputation of Oklahoma politics is conservative. This reputation has not always belied fact. In the early days of statehood the Democratic Party rode to dominance on a progressive platform, following the southern Democratic habit of co-opting the Populists. Soon after statehood a series of economic depressions hit Oklahoma. Many Oklahomans supported socialist candidates, and by 1914 there were numerically more socialists in Oklahoma than in New York State. In fact, the Socialist candidate for governor pulled nearly 20 percent of the vote. This socialist presence cost the Democrats control of the state legislature in 1920, as well as a U.S. Senate seat and three congressional districts. The Democrats regained control of the legislature in 1922, and by the time of the New Deal realignment the GOP was thoroughly devastated. In the late 1950s over half of legislative seats in the state still went to Democrats without contest (Hale and Kean 1996).

The 1950s were a difficult time for the Oklahoma Republican Party. Despite the successive Eisenhower victories in 1952 and 1956, the state political scene was still thoroughly dominated by the Democrats. The 1958 GOP gubernatorial candidate won only 19 percent of the vote and lost every county in the state. While the GOP was politically frustrated, Oklahoma was confronting difficulties with segregation. As we noted earlier, Oklahoma has a relatively small black population. Nonetheless, the state had maintained the Jim Crow laws inherited from the tribes and the territorial government. Unlike the Deep South states, Oklahoma did not get caught up in massive resistance and instead quietly complied with the *Brown* decision.

The 1960s were a better time for the GOP. In 1962 Henry Bellmon was elected the first Republican governor of Oklahoma. As the decade proceeded Republicans won a congressional seat and Goldwater ran ahead of his national average, although Johnson carried the state for President. In 1966 Republican Dewey Bartlett succeeded Bellmon as governor (at that time Oklahoma governors were limited to a single term). Bellmon was subsequently elected to the Senate in 1968, and he was joined in the Senate by Bartlett in 1972.

Below the level of major statewide offices, success by the GOP was at best fleeting. Like many southern states, Oklahoma was forced to reapportion the state legislature and congressional districts to accommodate the one-man, one-vote standards set in *Baker v. Carr* and *Wesberry v. Sanders*. Rural interests had traditionally been overrepresented in the legislature due to guarantees of representation for each county. This malapportionment helped to perpetuate the Democratic domination of both chambers. After reapportionment the Democrats continued to hold substantial majorities, especially in the rural areas, while Republicans were elected almost entirely from the populous metropolitan counties.

As in much of the South the GOP suffered setbacks after Watergate. The governorship and one of the Senate seats were lost to the Democrats, and the GOP lost seats in the legislature. In the 1980s the Republicans embarked on another era of expansion. Republican registration surged and the GOP won more seats in the legislature. Henry Bellmon, retired from the Senate in 1980, returned for another term as governor in 1986. Don Nickles, a thirty-one-year-old Republican businessman from Ponca City who ran with evangelical support, succeeded Bellmon in the Senate in 1980. The GOP held two U.S. House seats from 1986 forward, when James Inhofe was elected to represent the House district surrounding Tulsa (in addition to the Oklahoma City district that had long been controlled by the Republican party). The extent of GOP electoral expansion then stagnated, to be followed by a flood of success in 1994.

A systematic electoral eradication of Democrats started in 1994. Entering the election year the GOP held one Senate seat, two House seats, and no major state office. After the November election, Republicans held both U.S. Senate seats and five of six U.S. House seats and had recaptured the governor's mansion. Moreover, the political force of the evangelical right movement and its influence within the Republican Party, and the state more generally, was undeniable—an influence that persists, if not still growing, today. In 1996 the last Democratic congressional seat was captured by the Republicans, after incumbent Bill Brewster retired and was succeeded by party-switching former incumbent Wes Watkins.

The most direct evidence of changing allegiances in the electorate is in the voter registration figures. Oklahoma uses a partisan registration system with a closed party primary, which allows us to examine the expressed preferences of voter allegiance. With the exception of a brief falloff of support from 1974 to 1978, the Republican proportion of registered voters has increased steadily from less than 20 percent of voters in 1964 to about 35 percent of voters at the start of the new millennium and reaching 38 percent (versus 51 percent Democratic) in 2004 (see figure 10.1). Most of this growth occurred between 1980 and 1990, and the change in partisan balance appears to be related to the falloff in registered Democrats as well as to gains in registered Republicans. Oklahoma has traditionally gained and lost populations with the cycles of sudden economic boom and long, drawn out decline. The most recent of these cycles did not distribute its impact evenly across parties. A general decline of registrants occurred at the depth of the oil bust and lessened the number of Democratic registrants from 1,400,000 to just over 1,100,000, a loss of

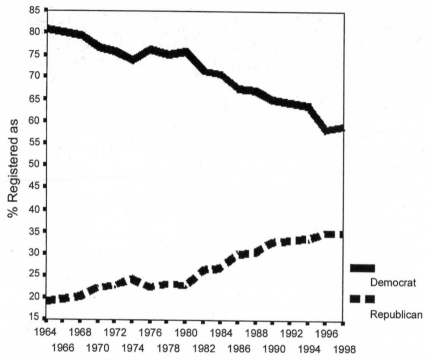

Figure 10.1.   Statewide Party Registration Trend, 1964–2004

300,000 voters. After the oil collapse (1986) the number of GOP registrants hovered around 600,000, before rising to about 822,000 at the start of 2005. The net number of registrants gained by the Republican since 1980 is roughly twice those gained by Democrats, with their number oscillating between 1.1 million and 1.2 million.

The geographic settlement patterns of Oklahoma play a prominent role in explaining the politics of the state. After the Oklahoma Territory was opened to white settlement, the western and northern tier of counties were settled by Midwesterners and plainsmen, especially those steeped in the Jayhawker traditions of Kansas. The southern and eastern counties, especially in Indian Territory, were settled by southerners from Texas, Mississippi, and Arkansas. Democrats dominated politics in the state after co-opting the progressive and socialist movements. The west and north continued as a Republican redoubt.

As the urban centers of Oklahoma grew, the political geography of the state took on the tripartite shape now familiar to Oklahomans. If one draws a line from the northeastern corner of the state to the southwestern corner, it would pass through the urban centers of Tulsa, Oklahoma City, and Lawton. To the north and west of this line and outside of these cities is predominantly Republican and contains about 10 percent of the state population. To the south and east of the line is predominantly Democratic, the "Little Dixie" region that contains about 20 percent of the state. The remaining 70 percent of Oklahomans live in the urban corridor that encompasses the major cities of the state (Morgan, England, and Humphreys, 1991).

The growth of the suburban corridor has not altered the partisan differences that exist between the two major urban counties (Oklahoma and Tulsa) and the rest of the state. Kirkpatrick, Morgan, and Kielhorn (1977) observed that, in the 1960s, the major urban counties voted substantially more Republican than the rest of the state in major statewide elections. As indicated in table 10.1, the average urban/rural difference in gubernatorial elections is 11.9 percentage points. The GOP has won a majority of the urban core counties' vote on six of nine occasions but did not carry the rural vote between 1966 and 1994. The urban vote constituted the margin of victory for the last three Republican governors, none of whom won an outright majority of the vote until Frank Keating was reelected with 57 percent of the vote in 1998. The difference in the rural/urban vote was generally between 10 and 14 points for every election between 1966 and the mid-1990s. A huge gap (18.7 percent) was evident in 1994, but in subsequent elections it declined notably, averaging 7.4 in the last two gubernatorial elections.

The urban/rural split in Oklahoma has become even less pronounced in presidential races. In fact, in 2004 President Bush ran more strongly in out-state regions than in the state's metro areas. Republican presidential candidates have won Oklahoma's electoral votes in every election since 1968, and even in 1964 Goldwater ran six points ahead of his national showing. As in many southern states, Republican presidential candidates run ahead of other Republicans in rural, traditionally Democratic counties. Aistrup (1996) observed that the persistence of Republican success up the ticket in rural localities eventually leads to GOP success downticket in those areas. Southern voters have usually found it far easier to first break with the Democratic Party at the national level, where the policy stands and personal values of the party candidates were often at odds with southern tradition and values. The breaking of the southern/Demo-

Table 10.1.   The Cities and Republican Success
a

Year	State	OKC/Tulsa	Out-State	Difference
Vote for Governor				
1962	55.2	61.2	52.5	+8.7
1966	55.7	65.3	51.0	+14.3
1970	48.1*	57.9	43.3	+14.6
1974	36.1	45.5	31.4	+14.1
1978	47.2	53.9	43.9	+10.0
1982	37.6	47.5	32.6	+14.9
1986	47.5*	54.5	44.0	+10.5
1990	36.2	43.0	32.9	+10.1
1994	46.9*	59.0	40.3	+18.7
1998	57.9	61.9	55.8	+6.1
2002	42.6**	48.2	39.6	+8.6
Vote for President				
1964	44.3	51.3	40.7	+10.6
1968	47.7*	52.9	44.9	+8.0
1972	73.7	76.3	72.2	+4.1
1976	49.9*	58.8	45.1	+13.7
1980	60.5	66.1	57.5	+8.6
1984	68.6	72.3	66.6	+5.7
1988	58.4	64.0	54.6	+9.4
1992	42.6*	48.9	39.1	+9.8
1996	48.2*	54.1	45.1	+9.0
2000	60.3	61.8	59.5	+2.3
2004	65.6	64.3	66.3	−2.0

* GOP plurality win
** GOP plurality loss
Source: Kirkpatrick, Morgan and Kielhorn (1977); Morgan, England and Humphreys (1991). Figures since 1990 computed by authors from data provided by the Oklahoma State Board of Elections.

cratic linkage at the state and local level requires greater effort, especially if the values of Democratic candidates comport to the beliefs and values of the Democratic electorate. When those linkages are broken and the Democratic Party is lost as an avenue of expression for conservatives, the opportunity for GOP growth is greatest (Heard 1952). The great success of President Bush in the non-metropolitan areas in 2004 may open up even more avenues for Republican success in Oklahoma.

The enduring rural-urban split in the 2002 gubernatorial race is explained by conditions that predicate Democratic success elsewhere in the South. The GOP vote effectively split over the entry of a renegade Republican, Tulsa lawyer Gary Richardson, into the contest as an Independent. The Democratic nominee, rural state senator Brad Henry, enjoyed support from the core Democratic constituencies—unions, teachers, and lawyers—and also enjoyed the benefits of an active grassroots effort in the rural counties to oppose a measure banning cock fighting in Oklahoma. While the effort to defeat the cock-fighting measure would fail, the get-out-the-vote effort in rural Oklahoma fused with local Democratic Party organizations to create a strong turnout for the party's nominee. The lackadaisical GOP nominee, Tulsa Congressman Steve Largent, failed to ignite the GOP electoral base, allowing Henry to exploit his rural advantage for a 6,000-vote win. Henry exploited the formula for success of so many other southern governors—taming legalized gambling and enacting a lottery, both to fund education—which helped him with swing voters and further emboldened the Democratic base. Still, Henry pulled only 43.7 percent of the vote, leaving him to seek the seven-percent solution needed to win reelection in 2006.

THE PARTY ORGANIZATIONS

"I don't belong to an organized political party; I am a Democrat."

—Will Rogers

The Democratic and Republican Party organizations in Oklahoma are decidedly different in their degree of organization and unity, and in their relationships with the national parties. The state Democrats resemble the Democratic parties of so many southern states: fractured, teeming with internal conflict, and only loosely linked to the DNC. The Oklahoma Republican Party has been centrally organized since the 1960s, and the state party has sought to follow the "grassroots" development model advanced by former RNC chairman Haley Barbour. More recently the Christian conservatives have firmly established themselves in the party.

For years Oklahoma was what Austin Ranney called a "modified one-party state" (Kirkpatrick, Morgan and Kiehhorn 1977; Hale and Kean 1996), but Republicans nonetheless have demonstrated consistent national-election strength for almost fifty years, even as the Democrats dominated state and local politics. Henry Bellmon, the first Republican governor of Oklahoma, sought to overcome the political anemia of the GOP in the 1950s by actively organizing the party at the county level. Bellmon's "Operation Countdown" emphasized candidate recruitment and voter mobilization. He even ventured into the "Little Dixie" region of the state. Bellmon's grassroots efforts won him the governorship in 1962, as well as the moniker of "father" to the modern Oklahoma GOP. In the 1980s Republicans reinvigorated this strategy, using sophisticated data analysis and polling to target campaigns outside of the GOP strongholds. Grassroots mobilization of Republicans, especially evangelicals, has served to further invigorate the GOP.

For years the state Republican Party was characterized by a bifactionalism between "moneybags" elements from Tulsa (also called country-club Republicans) and "grassroots" elements from the small towns of the western plain and panhandle (Hale and Kean 1996). Bellmon typified the country-club GOP, advocating smaller government and lower taxes; it is widely acknowledged that he has no patience for social-issue conservatives. The emergence of the Christian right as a force in the party has reoriented this factionalism to set traditional Bellmon Republicans against the Christian Right. For the present, though, intraparty disputes have been muted by the success enjoyed by the GOP.

The Oklahoma Democrats are decidedly less organized. Until 1990, the state party did little to organize with the national party. There is minimal paid staff. The Democratic National Committee does not see Oklahoma as a critical state, and consequently national party funds and support are not readily forthcoming. As Hale and Kean put it, "Oklahoma is simply not a priority for the [Democratic] national party" (1996: 303). The most notable exception to this generalization was the rush of interest in Brad Carson's 2004 campaign for the U.S. Senate, when it looked winnable and like control of the U.S. Senate might hinge on the outcome.

The decentralized state Democrats are bereft with internal factional divisions. A mix of urban liberals and unionists, Little Dixie state legislators, and county elected officials composes the principal factions. The struggle between legislators and county officials for control of local projects in part underlies this division, as did the continued efforts of urban liberals and union officials to block a right-to-work law. The large number of local and state legislative Democrats means that there are a variety of ambitious officeholders who are all seeking political advancement, in the wake of a rising Republican tide. Again, quoting Hale and Kean "with so many elected officials . . . seeking the spotlight, it is difficult for any one person to energize or direct the [Democratic] party." By comparison, a series of strong, insightful Republican state chairs such as Tom Cole (now in the U.S. House) have taken advantage of the organizational ground-work laid by Henry Bellmon to develop a set of grassroots organizations and strategies that exploit the division among state Democratic voters. This model of Religious Right mobilization and sophisticated targeting of congressional (and now state legislative) races has paid electoral dividends.

The state Republican Party has exploited its financial model of funding candidates through the statewide coordinated campaign (called the Victory Fund) and by using the state legislative caucus and House and Senate PACs to direct expertise and money to potentially competitive state legislative districts. Democrats, meanwhile, continue to be caught in factional infighting between different constituency groups and, most recently, ousted their state party chairman, Jay Parmley, over his support of Howard Dean as DNC chair (Dean took 8 percent in the 2004 presidential primary in Oklahoma) and replaced him with former state senate candidate, teacher, and grassroots organizer Lisa Pryor.

THE LEGISLATURE

For years Democrats dominated the Oklahoma state legislature. GOP gains in the legislature roughly correspond to the gains by the party among registered voters. The growth of Republicans in the Oklahoma legislature is indicated in table 10.2. In 1962, the last election preceding the court-ordered reapportionment of state legislative seats to comply with one-man, one-vote, the GOP held 24 of 129 House seats (18.5 percent) and 5 of 44 Senate seats (11.3 percent). The reapportionment of seats produced a loss of two seats in the House and a gain of five in the Senate. By 1991 the GOP House caucus had increased to 32 of 101 seats, with a pair of brief setbacks after Watergate and during the 1982 recession.

In 2000 and 2002, Democrats managed to barely hang onto their majority status in the state House of Representatives. But, the question was not one of "if" but rather "when" Republicans would gain the majority. The answer was 2004 and 2004 in a definitive way. Aided by initial imposition of term limits, Republicans achieved a net gain of nine seats and captured 57 of the 101 seats in the House.

Table 10.2.   Party and Race in the Oklahoma Legislature

	Republican %		Black %	
Year	House	Senate	House	Senate
1965	17.2	18.5	2.5	2.0
1975	24.8	18.8	2.9	2.0
1985	31.7	35.4	2.9	4.2
1987	30.7	31.3	2.9	4.2
1989	31.7	22.9	2.9	4.2
1991	31.7	22.9	2.9	4.2
1993	32.7	22.9	2.9	4.2
1995	35.6	27.8	2.9	4.2
1997	35.6	31.3	2.9	4.2
1999	39.6	31.3	2.9	4.2
2001	47.5	37.5	2.9	4.2
2003	47.5	41.7	2.9	4.2
2005	56.4	45.8	2.9	4.2

Note: There were 101 members of the Oklahoma House and 48 members of the Oklahoma Senate as of 2001.
Source: Oklahoma Almanac 1995–1996; National Conference of State Legislatures (2001, 2003, 2005).

Republican success in the state Senate has been more fleeting. Oklahoma state senators serve four-year terms, and those terms are staggered so that only half of the chamber comes up for reelection every two years. From 1964 to 1980, the GOP senate caucus cycled between nine and eleven senators out of forty-eight. GOP representation peaked at seventeen senators in the 1986 elections, but then fell off to eleven seats following the 1990 election. After the 1996 elections the GOP caucus in the Senate stood at fifteen senators. Despite the use of staggered terms, the state senate is more vulnerable to the recent state and national political tides than the house. The peak of GOP senate representation came in the wake of Reagan's successful reelection and the return of Republican Henry Bellmon to the governor's mansion. The subsequent loss of four seats in the 1990 election came in the disastrous twenty-six-point defeat of Republican Bill Price. A rebound in the Republican Senate showing began with the 1994 election and inched forward in 1996. The 2000, 2002 and 2004 elections each brought two more Republicans to the Senate. In fact, several Senate races in 2004 were so tight that it was not until the last votes were counted that it was clear that the Democrats would maintain control of that body.

Republican success in 2004 was a function of the large number of open seats due to the effects of term limits. Oklahoma was the first state to enact term limits, but it has one of the longest terms (twelve years). Incumbents were grandfathered under court interpretation of the legislation, so no one was prevented from seeking reelection until the 2004 campaign. A total of twenty-eight House legislators were forced from office due to term limits. Eighteen of the twenty-eight were Democrats and ten were Republicans. All ten Republican districts elected new Republican legislators; seven formerly Democratic districts brought in Republican officials, with one district retaining Democratic representation by a mere 162 votes. There is little doubt that term limits opened space for Republican gains in the 2004 House elections, as 25 percent of the seats vacated by term limited representatives swung from Democrats to Republicans.

Republicans did not exploit the same opportunism in state Senate races. Of the twelve Senators affected by term limits, eight Democrats and four Republicans, there was only one instance of party turnover. None of the four open Republican seats went to Democratic candidates. The 2006 election, however, might tell a different story as Democrats will face the daunting challenge of defending a two-seat majority with eight Senate seats opened by term limits (plus another opened in 2005) with Republicans losing no senators. Polling of those districts shows that at least five are competitive for Republican.[2] Both parties will try to defend seven seats in the state House.

Despite the traditionally limited level of GOP representation, Republican gains have made an impact on lawmaking in Oklahoma. In the past, Republican governors found themselves largely at the mercy of the Democratic leadership in the legislature; when unified, Democrats had more than sufficient votes to override Republican gubernatorial vetoes. Frank Keating's election as governor in 1994 was accompanied by the first contemporary GOP caucus to exceed one-third of the membership in a chamber. Republicans could finally sustain a gubernatorial veto, which enhanced the limited powers of their governor and increased their capacity to influence legislation. With control of the House, Republicans are more aggressively moving on key elements of their legislative agenda.

As the state legislature became more competitive in terms of parties, it remains a largely white, male institution. There has been little variation over time in black representation in Oklahoma. Currently, there are five black state legislators in Oklahoma: three state house members and two state senators. (Former Member of Congress and Corporation Commissioner J.C. Watts has been the only other prominent African-American officeholder). All black state legislators have been elected from Tulsa and

Oklahoma county districts that are predominantly urban, center-city districts. Additionally, women make up 14 percent of the House and 17 percent of the Senate, which are some of the lowest percentages of female representation in the South or the nation (Wyman 2005).

CONGRESSIONAL REPRESENTATION

The more dramatic change in Oklahoma politics was the partisan turnover of the congressional delegation in the 1990s. Throughout its history the state sent overwhelmingly Democratic delegations to Congress. For a brief period in the 1970s the GOP held both U.S. Senate seats; however, only one majority-GOP House delegation had ever been elected since statehood and that was in 1920. In the 1980s Oklahoma sent three Republicans to Congress: Senator Don Nickles (elected in 1980) and Representatives Mickey Edwards (elected 1976) and James Inhofe (elected 1986), with five Democrats. This alignment continued into the 1990s. Then, after the 1992 election, the partisan balance of the state started to spin precipitously away from the Democrats. In early 1994 Democrat Glenn English resigned his west Oklahoma Sixth District seat. The subsequent special election pitted Republican state representative and rancher Frank Lucas against Democrat Dan Webber, a political aide and protégé of Democratic Senator David L. Boren. This race was one of several such early contests in 1994 that were closely watched as referenda on the presidency of Bill Clinton (Gaddie and Bullock 2000, chapter 6). Republican Lucas defeated Webber, despite the tremendous campaigning and fundraising efforts by Democrats, including David Boren. Bednar and Hertzke (1995a, 1995b) argue that Lucas's success was a product of the political activism of conservative Christians in the Sixth District. Relying heavily on flyers and handbills distributed in evangelical churches, the Christian Coalition mobilized conservative voters to support Lucas's bid. The Christian Coalition used a technique of contrasting the policy stands and beliefs of the candidates in terms of "acceptability" which became a hallmark of subsequent congressional and, gradually, state legislative campaigns. This election provided the first evidence that Conservative Christians could affect elections and of the role they would play in the partisan shift of Oklahoma.

Additional GOP congressional gains followed in the general election of 1994, largely as a consequence of the actions of Senator David L. Boren, the three-term Democratic senator and former governor of Oklahoma. Boren had enjoyed a mercurial political career. Elected to the state legislature while he was still in law school at University of Oklahoma, Boren subsequently was elected governor in 1974 at age thirty-three with 64 percent of the vote, and in 1978 advanced to the U.S. Senate. Boren enjoyed two successful reelections, including a devastating 83 percent win in 1990 in which he carried all but two voting precincts in the state. Despite his electoral security and the respect and seniority accrued during his tenure in the Senate, by 1994 Boren was publicly discussing his dissatisfaction with the Senate and how he was "tired" of the Washington game. He resigned in early 1994 after publicly courting (and then receiving) the presidency of the University of Oklahoma. Boren's departure prompted two congressmen, Dave McCurdy (D-4th) and James Inhofe (R-1st) to give up their seats to seek the open Senate seat. McCurdy's resignation presented an opportunity for another GOP gain in the House, and both the House and the Senate races proved to be heavily influenced by the activities of the Christian Right (Bednar and Hertzke 1995b). This ripple effect, accompanied by the powerful GOP sweep of most statewide constitutional offices in November 1994, revealed the vulnerabilities of the Democrats.

An unexpected opportunity for a GOP gain occurred in the east Oklahoma Second District. Incumbent congressman Mike Synar (D-2nd) survived a bitter primary and runoff in 1992 to gain reelection to an eighth term in office with a 56-41 win. But, in 1994, Synar again faced primary opposition, this time from a lightly regarded 71-year-old retired schoolteacher who was backed by the Christian Coalition. Synar lost his fall bid for party renomination. The GOP nominee, local obstetrician Tom Coburn, was also considered acceptable by the Christian Coalition and won election by four points.

In the two open House seats, a Christian Coalition–backed Republican retained the Tulsa First District vacated by Republican James Inhofe, and Republican evangelical minister and state Corporation Commissioner J.C. Watts won the previously Democratic Fourth District. The defeat of Democrat Dave McCurdy by Republican James Inhofe for the open Senate seat and the election of Republican Frank Keating in a three-cornered gubernatorial contest completed the stunning GOP victory in the major elections of 1994. At the beginning of 1994, five of the eight members of Oklahoma's congressional delegation, and the governor, had been Democrats. By November 8, only one Democrat held major office in Oklahoma:

Representative Bill Brewster (D-3rd), who would soon retire for reasons unrelated to politics. His departure in 1996 created an opportunity for the GOP to complete its sweep of the major elective positions in Oklahoma. Brewster's "Little Dixie" District was historically the most traditionally Democratic part of the state and might have proved a tough nut for the GOP to crack given the popularity of the moderate incumbent. When Brewster retired in 1996, former Democrat turned Independent turned Republican Wes Watkins contested his former seat and reclaimed it with 52 percent of the vote, completing the sweep of the congressional delegation for the Republican Party.

The loss of the Third District to the Republicans was particularly galling for state Democrats. The southeastern corner of Oklahoma—"Little Dixie"—displays the most quintessential (or stereotypical) southern character. Here business is conducted in small towns where nineteenth-century-style courthouses dominate the town square along with monuments to the honored war dead and forgotten founders. This is the most heavily Democratic part of the state; Bill Clinton won the district in 1992 and 1996. With one exception (1908), Little Dixie never elected a Republican to Congress. This is the part of the state where recent Democratic statewide candidates have sought to offset the Republican-voting northern tier of counties and the emergent GOP suburbs around Tulsa and Oklahoma City. *Congressional Quarterly* columnist Phil Duncan observed that "Republicans occasionally travel through [Little Dixie] but they seldom settle there" (in Barone, Ujifusa, and Matthews 1977). The most distinguished political resident of Little Dixie was Carl Albert. Politically active until his late 80s, "Mr. Carl" represented Little Dixie for thirty years after World War II and ascended to become Speaker of the U.S. House of Representatives in 1971. He continued as speaker until his retirement in 1977 (Albert 1990). Now, with former Democrat Watkins in the seat, it was a reasonable to ask: Would the Democratic Party ever again send a representative to Washington?

The answer came fairly quickly. Rep. Tom Coburn, elected in 1994, had served his promised six years and then chose not to seek reelection. His handpicked successor, former aide and car dealer Andy Ewing, lacked Dr. Tom's appeal. A contentious and very expensive race ensued with young Rhodes scholar, Democrat Brad Carson, carrying the seat in 2000.

The decennial census, though, led to the loss of a House seat by the State of Oklahoma in 2002. The decisions by Representatives Watts and Watkins to retire meant that incumbents would not necessarily have to face each other in the ensuing election. The new district boundaries created what should be three very safe Republican districts: generally Tulsa, Oklahoma City and the northwest corner of the state. Incumbent Republicans were returned in each case in those districts. The redistricting also created a seat that would generally be considered a safe Democratic seat by encompassing Democratic elements of Carson's Second District and much of the traditionally democratic Little Dixie. Carson quickly moved to solidify his position in the new parts of his district and easily carried that district in 2002. The Fourth District, running along the southern part of the state, starting with the western part of Little Dixie, is a Republican-leaning district. It is from that district that Watts retired. In 2002 both parties ran spirited primaries. Tom Cole, a long-time Republican operative at both the state and national levels, won the Republican nomination, and Darryl Roberts, a state Senator, former marine and 1996 nominee in the old Third District, won the Democratic nomination. Cole prevailed with 53.8 percent of the votes in an expensive and sometimes-bitter contest that was billed by media observers as one of the most significant, heavyweight political fights in the history of the state.

All incumbents who sought reelection in 2004 won easily. Brad Carson abandoned his safe Second District to jump into the open U.S. Senate race created by the retirement of Senator Don Nickles. Four Democrats and three Republicans sought to take Carson's place. Both primaries were strongly contested, but Wayland Smalley captured the Republican nomination with just short of 52 percent of the votes and Dan Boren captured the Democratic nod with almost 58 percent over a Native American DA, Kalyn Free, who enjoyed support of EMILY's List and the Deaniac organization Democracy for America. Boren was a young (thirty at the time of the campaign) one-term member of the State House, but he benefited from a skilled campaign, a good name (son of a U.S. Senator and governor, grandson of a congressman) and a solid fit with the politics of the district. He carried the seat by a nearly two-to-one margin in the general election.

Senators Nickles and Inhofe consistently enjoyed great electoral success after their initial victories, but Senator Nickles opted not to seek reelection in 2004. A strong set of Republicans lined up for the office: Oklahoma City mayor and Republican Party establishment favorite Kirk Humphreys, iconoclast Corporation Commissioner Bob Anthony, and former U.S. Representative Dr. Tom Coburn. The set of contenders on the Democratic side was not as strong, but the list featured the young and successful Second District member of Congress Brad Carson who easily captured his party's nomination, and the scandal-ridden Democratic insurance commissioner Carroll Fisher (who was in the process of being impeached by the state legislature). On the Republican side the party leadership generally lined up behind Humphreys, but his campaign went downhill almost from the start while Coburn picked up steam as he went along. Coburn's campaign was greatly aided by support from the Washington-based Club for Growth. In the end Humphreys found himself attempting the nearly impossible task of getting to the right of Coburn and just plain failing; the presumptive nominee took just 25 percent of the vote, while upstart former congressman Coburn carried over 60 percent of the vote. Within twenty-four hours of the polls closing there was a great show of Republican unity aimed at putting the primary bitterness behind them and uniting against Carson.

The general election contest featured two candidates who had represented the same congressional district, but whose outcome would be heavily influenced by outsiders. Both the politics of the election and early polling suggested that the seat was a possible pick-up for the Democratic Party. Because, going into the 2004 campaign, it was widely believed that control of the U. S. Senate would turn on one or two outcomes, the race took on substantial national importance. The race was easily the most expensive in the state's history with about $10 million spent in hard money and about $2 million spent in soft money and independent expenditures, including nearly $1 million by the Club for Growth (Gaddie et al. 2005).

Carson gained early momentum as a gun-toting, NRA-backed, conservative Democrat. He also had initial success painting Coburn as an extremist who would not even bring Oklahomans their share of the federal largesse. Coburn promised voters that he would feed at the trough with the rest of the Senate and turn his attack on Carson. Coburn, and his allies, did everything they could to tie Carson to Washington liberals like John Kerry, Hillary Clinton, and Ted Kennedy. Heading into these attacks, the race was a dead heat. But the ads, one of which featured "Dancing Brad" with liberal Democrats pulling his strings and the tag line: "Putting DC Democrats Ahead of Oklahoma Values," proved to be very effective. The ad saturated the state's media markets and those who saw the ad were more favorable to Coburn by about ten points (Gaddie et al. 2005). In the end, Carson could not overcome being saddled with the "sins" of his party, especially in a presidential election year, and Coburn won going away (with 52.8 percent to 41.2 percent).

These most recent rounds of elections demonstrated the continued decline of the division between the politics of the state and national politics. National political organizations entered state party politics in an effort to influence primary elections, and, according to the data collected by the Center for the Study of Electoral Democracy, the national parties and their surrogate organizations targeted the general election in the state as well. The state is generally "red" and, as we will see, getting redder and redder further and further down ticket. It becomes increasingly difficult for state Democratic candidates to avoid the politics of their national party, and, at the same time, it becomes difficult for the Republican Party establishment to avoid the evangelical realignment of their grassroots, which threatens the control of the party organization and message.

THE MODERN OKLAHOMA ELECTORATE

With Democratic registration figures still above 50 percent, a stagnating economy and low prosperity indicators, on paper Oklahoma would appear to be a Democratic state. The state has steadily moved to the Republican Party, if not in voter registration, in actual ideology and votes cast. Oklahoma's conservatism, and subsequent Republican leanings, is in large part a product of the state's firmly ensconced religious right.

The role of Christianity in the state of Oklahoma cannot be overstated. This is a state where prayer only recently was excluded from sporting events, where a gay marriage prohibition amendment was supported by 75 percent of the voters, where 3.2 beer is sold, and where tattoo parlors are illegal. Throughout the state, polling indicates that most Oklahomans describe themselves as evangelical or fundamentalist Christians. Within the electorate in 2004, exit polling placed the proportion of self-identified evangelicals at 44 percent (almost double the national electorate average of 23 percent). Even compared with other Southern, Bible Belt states, Oklahoma appears to be significantly more religiously conservative. The average proportion of the electorate self-identifying as evangelical in the other southern states is 33 percent, and only Arkansas (at 53 percent) showing higher numbers of evangelicals in their electorate (Gaddie et al. 2005). There can be little doubt that Oklahoma is a highly religious state.

A snapshot of the Oklahoma electorate is evidence of just how religious identity is tied to the politics of the state. Exit poll data gathered after the 2004 election (see table 10.3) shows how strongly those who claimed to

Table 10.3.   Dimensions of the Oklahoma Electorate in 2004

	Bush	Kerry
Total Vote	66%	34%
Sex		
Male (48%)	67%	33%
Female (52%)	64%	36%
Partisanship		
Democrats (40%)	32%	68%
Republicans (43%)	96%	4%
Independents (16%)	66%	34%
Age		
18–29 (19%)	62%	38%
30–44 (27%)	69%	31%
45–59 (28%)	65%	35%
60–up (26%)	66%	34%
White Protestant Conservative		
Yes (28%)	90%	10%
No (72%)	55%	45%
Evangelicals		
Yes (44%)	77%	23%
No (56%)	56%	44%
Candidate Qualities		
Strong Leader (22%)	90%	10%
Bring Change (19%)	11%	89%
Clear Views (16%)	84%	14%
Religious (15%)	94%	6%
Honest (10%)	82%	18%
Most Important Issue		
Moral Values (29%)	90%	10%
War on Terror (20%)	89%	11%
Economy (17%)	22%	78%
Iraq (11%)	44%	56%

N = 1,577
Source: CNN Exit polls

be conservative white Protestants and those that defined themselves as evangelical favored the Bush candidacy. Among the white Protestants, 90 percent answered that they had voted for President Bush; of evangelicals, 77 percent backed the president's reelection. Exit poll questions asking respondents to explain their vote choice recorded that their greatest concern for Oklahomans in the presidential election was the issue of morality. Those that viewed morality as the top concern voted overwhelmingly—90 percent—for Bush. Of further interest was a question asking about candidate qualities. While strong leadership was the number one response, 15 percent of those who were asked answered that they felt a candidate's religious affiliation was the most important characteristic; they voted 94 percent in favor of Bush (CNN exit polls).

Religious affiliation is a significant indicator in determining how citizens of the state will vote. In table 10.4 we present a multiple regression estimation of three possible contributors to the structure of the county-level party vote in Oklahoma, in 2004. The dependent variables are the Democrats' share of the two-party vote for President, and U.S. Senate and the "straight-party pull," respectively. The independent variables are the percent registered Republicans in the county; the percent white, Anglo population in the county; and the percent of residents who are members of an evangelical, fundamentalist, or literalist Protestant Christian church (Bullock and Grant 1995; see also Bradley et al. 1992, for data sources). As indicated by the results in table 10.4, fundamentalism, race (Oklahoma is about 78 percent Anglo) and party are highly statistically significant variables in determining Democratic vote share at the county level. To illustrate the impact of concentrations of evangelical Christians, if one holds constant the values of party and race, every additional five percent evangelicals in a county reduced the Democratic vote share by about 1 percent. This is a strong indication that evangelicals not only help elect

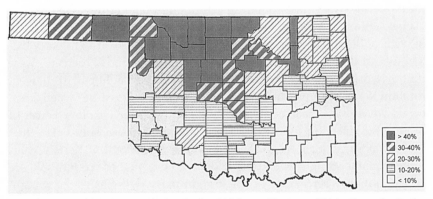

Figure 10.2a.   GOP Representation in the Oklahoma House and Vote Share, by Party Registration, 2004

Table 10.4.   OLS Estimates of the Statewide Democratic Vote in 2004

	President 04	U.S. Senate 04	Straight Party 04
Intercept	83.27	87.38	110.35
% Evangelicals	−0.19	−0.09	−0.15
	(−3.87)**	(−1.97)*	(−3.14)**
% White Population	−0.35	−0.31	−0.40
	(−5.13)**	(−5.35)**	(−6.15)
% GOP Registration	−0.45	−0.51	−0.80
	(−8.35)**	(−10.85)**	(−15.30)**
Adjusted R-Square	0.74	0.84	0.90

N = 77 (counties)
T-statistics in parentheses
* p<.05, one-tailed test
** p<.01, one-tailed test

candidates but also help set the agenda. It also predicts continued difficulties for Democrats in the state, as similar relationships are present in state legislative balloting, though, oddly enough, not in the 2002 gubernatorial vote (Gaddie et al. 2005). The Oklahoma GOP, often utilizing evangelical messages and methods, has been able to mobilize and consolidate support from these quarters. To get elected in the state of Oklahoma, candidates must fill their Sundays and Wednesdays (Bible study night) with stump speeches at local churches. The 2004 elections even had pastors presenting their opinions on the candidates, and churches distributing voter guides outlining candidate virtues to their flock. These effort produced votes—votes for Republican candidates up and down the ticket.

One sign of GOP mobilization was the usage of the straight party pull in favor of Republican candidates.[3] Of the total 656,243 straight party ballots cast in the 2004 presidential election, 358,890, or 54.7 percent, were for the Republican Party. Forty-five percent of the straight party pull went for John Kerry, but this was a reversal from eight years earlier when Democrats were able to take 55 percent of all straight-party ballots. Fewer of those who voted for John Kerry were willing to cast a split ticket than those that voted for George W. Bush. While 59 percent of Kerry's votes came from the straight party pull, and he did best in those counties where he had a higher percentage of the straight party pull, Bush's the straight party pull support came from counties with about two and a half times the population. More voters who vote straight-party vote Republican. But,

Democrats are ever more so dependent on the straight party pull for votes in general, meaning that they are increasingly getting a greater share of their votes from their shrinking partisan base. Those who claim to be evangelical are prone to vote a straight ticket. Referring back to table 10.4, it can be seen that evangelism is significantly related to usage of the straight party ticket. For every seven points increase evangelical in a county, the Democratic share of the pull is lessened by 1 point, controlling for other vote factors (Gaddie et al 2005, 223).

CONCLUSION

The emergence of the Republican Party as the majority party of Oklahoma continues largely unabated. The Republican electorate of the Sooner State resembles the electorate of so many other southern states—white, Anglo, and Protestant, and with a set of issue concerns associated not with the poverty of the pocketbook so much as the poverty of leadership, values, and the soul. This new electorate and its focus presents a very real challenge for state Democrats, who are searching for a viable organizational and issue basis with which to compete for political power.

The challenge for the Democrats is daunting. For decades the Democrats' ability to hold state power was predicated on their status as the majority party and the ability to provide access, goods and services based on majority status. Now, rural Oklahomans, who still provide the foundation for the legislative Democratic Party, find that in the State House they are not the majority Rural Oklahomans are regularly voting for Republicans at the national and congressional level. At some point, if legislative Republicans are willing to take care of the needs and concerns of the dwindling rural Oklahoma electorate, they can compete for votes in these constituencies.

The other challenge, that vexes Democrats the South over, is how to get past the religious impediment with white voters. White evangelicals make up a greater share of the Oklahoma electorate than in virtually any other Southern state, and their vote has become increasingly homogenous. When Democrats have succeeded statewide in Oklahoma since 1994, it has either been in lower-level statewide offices with incumbents or because of rifts in the GOP that fractured the vote, such as in the case of the election of Governor Henry in 2002. When Republicans are united and able to activate their evangelical base, the likelihood of a Republican victory is almost certain, absent the presence of Democratic incumbents.

REFERENCES

Aistrup, Joseph. 1996. *The Southern Strategy Revisited*. Lexington: University Press of Kentucky.

Albert, Carl B. 1990. *Little Giant : The Life and Times of Speaker Carl Albert*. Norman: University of Oklahoma Press.

Barone, Michael, and Grant Ujifusa. 1989, 1991, 1993, 1995. *The Almanac of American Politics*. New York: Barone and Co.

Barone, Michael, Grant Ujifusa, and Donald Matthews. 1977. *The Almanac of American Politics*. New York: MacMillan.

Bednar, Nancy, and Allen D. Hertzke. 1995a. "The Christian Right and the Republican Realignment in Oklahoma." *PS: Political Science and Politics* 28: 11–15.

———. 1995b. "Oklahoma: The Christian Right and the Republican Realignment," in Mark Rozell and Clyde Wilcox, eds., *God at the Grassroots: The Christian Right in the 1994 Elections*. New York: Rowman and Littlefield, 91–108.

Black, Earl, and Merle Black. 1992. *The Vital South: How Presidents are Elected*. Cambridge, MA: Harvard University Press.

Bradley, Martin B., Norman M. Green, Jr., Dale E. Jones, Mac Lynn, and Lou McNeil. 1992. *Churches and Church Membership in the United States 1990*. Atlanta: Glenmary Research Center.

Bullock, Charles S. III. 1988. Regional Realignment: An Officeholding Perspective. *Journal of Politics* 50.

Bullock, Charles S. III, and Loch K. Johnson. 1992. *Runoff Elections in the United States*. Chapel Hill, NC: University of North Carolina Press.

Bullock, Charles S. III, and John Christopher Grant. 1995. "Georgia: The Christian Right and Grass Roots Power," in Mark J. Rozell and Clyde Wilcox, eds., *God at the Grass Roots: The Christian Right in the 1994 Elections*. Lanham, MD: Rowman and Littlefield, 47–65.

Carmines, Edward, and James Stimson. 1989. *Issue Evolution*. Princeton, NJ: Princeton University Press.

Copeland, Gary W. 1994. "The Closing of Political Minds: Noncandidates in the 4th District of Oklahoma," in Thomas A. Kazee, ed., *Who Runs for Congress? Ambition, Context, and Candidate Emergence*. Washington, DC: CQ Press.

Gaddie, Ronald Keith, and Charles S. Bullock III. 2000. *Elections to Open Seats in the U.S. House: Where the Action Is*. Boulder, CO: Rowman and Littlefield.

Ewing, Cortez A. M. 1953. *Uniparty Politics*. Norman, OK: University of Oklahoma Press.

Gaddie, Ronald Keith, Jennifer Christol, Charles Mullin, Katherine Thorne, and Benjamin Wilson. 2005. "Issue Advocacy in the 2004 Oklahoma Senate Election," in David Magelby, Kelly Patterson and Quin Monson, eds., *Soft Money and Issue Advocacy in the 2004 Elections*. Washington, DC: Pew Charitable Trusts.

Gaddie, Ronald Keith. 2004. *A Fish, A Flag, and A "W" Tag*. Invited presentation, Southeastern Oklahoma State University, Durant, OK, December 6.

Hale, Jon F., and Stephen T. Kean. 1996. "Oklahoma," in Andrew M. Appleton and Daniel S. Ward, editors, *State and Party Profiles: A 50-State Guide to Development, Organization, and Resources*. Washington, DC: Congressional Quarterly Books.

Heard, Alexander. 1952. *A Two Party South?* Chapel Hill: University of North Carolina Press.

Hertzke, Allen D., and Ronald Keith Gaddie. 1996. *The Carl Albert Center Poll: 1996 General Election*. Norman: University of Oklahoma.

Kirkpatrick, Samuel A., David R. Morgan and Thomas Kielhorn. 1977. *The Oklahoma Voter*. Norman: University of Oklahoma Press.

Lamis, Alexander. 1988. *The Two-Party South*. New York: Oxford University Press.

Mayhew, David R. 1986. *Placing Parties in American Politics*. Princeton, NJ: Princeton University Press.

Morgan, David R., Robert E. England and George G. Humphreys. 1991. *Oklahoma Politics and Policies*. Lincoln: University of Nebraska Press.

Oklahoma Department of Libraries. 1995. *The Oklahoma Almanac, 1995-1996*. Oklahoma City: Oklahoma Department of Libraries.

Price, H.D. 1957. *The Negro in Southern Politics: A Chapter in Florida History*. New York: NYU Press.

Wyman, Hastings. 2001. *Diversity in Dixie: A Special Report from the Southern Political Report*. Washington, DC: Southern Political Report.

NOTES

1. As early as the 1840s white settlers were anxious for the lands of Oklahoma, and white settlement occurred around the trading posts that would become Tulsa, Sallisaw and Poteau. The federal government attempted to keep white settlers out, but strategic male settlers would often flee their encroaching settlements for Fort Smith, Arkansas, because it was known that the cavalry would not displace women settlers found alone. (Oral history interview with Senator Larry Dickerson, July 16, 1998, conducted by Keith Gaddie.)

2. Confidential interview with Oklahoma pollsters, December 2004.

3. The straight-party pull allows a voter to just check a box at the top of the column of contests and then pick the candidates of the respective party for all contested elections. Until 2002, the straight-party vote had favored Democrats but by decreasing margins. Now the straight-party pull favors Republicans, as voters with top-of-the-ticket Republican preferences are prone to express their down-ticket preferences in partisan (rather than candidate) terms.

11

Florida: Political Change, 1950–2004

Michael J. Scicchitano and Richard K. Scher

I n the last half of the twentieth century, Florida experienced profound changes in its population. These changes largely have been driver by a massive migration of retirees seeking a warmer climate and younger persons seeking employment opportunities. The population of Florida more than tripled between 1960 and 2005. This migration substantially changed the demographic character of the state. The percentage of white residents, for example, has grown steadily since 1900, and the percentage of African Americans has consistently declined. While the rest of the country has gotten younger, Florida's population has aged, and the state now ranks first in the percentage of the population that is sixty-five and older (about 18 percent). In addition, the percentage of the population that is of Hispanic origin has nearly doubled since 1970; the state now has nearly 3 million Hispanic residents, about 17 percent of the total. The change in the demographic characteristics of Florida has not been politically neutral; indeed, because of it the political character of the state has undergone profound changes. This chapter will help us to understand better the nature of the changes to Florida's political system. It will then provide a detailed description of the partisan changes that have occurred in Florida from 1980–2005. Finally, we will examine the impact of demographic changes and party registration on Florida elections for both state and national offices.

THE CHANGING POPULATION OF FLORIDA

If there is one distinguishing feature of the demographic characteristics of Florida, especially in the latter half of the twentieth century, it is growth. In 1900 Florida was one of the least-populated states in the East, but by 2000 it had become the second-most populous state east of the Mississippi and the fourth most populous nationally. In every decade since 1900, Florida's population has grown by about 30 percent. In two of those decades, the growth was more than 50 percent. From 1950 to 1960, the population grew by nearly 80 percent. The population growth, however, has not been uniformly distributed across the state. Before 1950, the state's population center was north Florida, particularly the Jacksonville area. But between 1950 and 1970, population growth was strongest in southern Florida. The central Florida region, with the development of Disney World and other recreational attractions in the Orlando area, has had the highest growth rates since 1970.

The growth in population has largely been fueled by two forces. Like the rest of the nation, Florida has experienced an increase in population from the baby boom generation. The most important reason for the growth rate in Florida, however, has been migration into the state. In the five-year period from 1985 to 1990, for example, nearly 1.5 million people moved into Florida from other states or countries. Between 1990 and 2000 Florida's net in-migration numbered some 1.7 million people.

The tremendous growth that Florida has experienced in the twentieth century, particularly since 1950, has not maintained the demographic characteristics of the state that existed in 1900. Instead, there have been fundamental changes in the demographic patterns in the state. The most significant changes have occurred among three groups. First, the population of Florida has gotten older. Second, the racial composition of the state has changed, and the percentage of African-American residents has declined. Finally, the percentage of Florida residents who are Hispanic has increased. The changes in the age, race, and ethnicity of residents have produced a state that is demographically—and politically—different than it was in 1950.

Changes in Age Patterns

A large number of those migrating to Florida since 1950 have been older people seeking a better climate for their retirement years. The changes in the age of Florida's residents are part of a complex national pattern of aging. Better medical care and nutritional and lifestyle behaviors have permitted people to live longer, while the baby boom produced a surge of younger people that has driven the average age of the population down. Florida did not escape the effects of the baby boom. Still, the state provides an extremely attractive climate for retirees who want to avoid harsh winters in the Northeast and Midwest. Retirees with fixed incomes also find Florida's low taxes and lack of an income tax attractive. As a result of the in-migration of retirees, the age of Florida's population has increased more rapidly than that of other states, and now Florida ranks first in the nation in the number of residents who are sixty-five and older (Smith 1995).

Changes in Race Patterns

At the beginning of the twentieth century, Florida had a large African-American population. In 1900, 44 percent of the state was African American and 56 percent was white. The number of African Americans in the state has increased since 1900. This growth, however, has not equaled the growth of whites. Migrants to Florida have mostly been older whites. As a result of the migration patterns, the relative percentage of African Americans in Florida declined consistently between 1900 and 1980. Since 1980, however, the racial composition of the state has stabilized at approximately 84 to 85 percent white and 14 percent African-American.

Changes in the Hispanic Population

The last major change in the demographic character of Florida is the large increase in the number of Hispanic residents. From 1970 to 1990 the percentage of Hispanic residents nearly doubled, to about 12 percent of the population. Many Hispanic residents, particularly of south Florida, are of Cuban origin. South Florida continues to attract residents from other locations in Latin America as well. The percentage of Hispanics in Florida should continue to grow in the next century; indeed, the increase in the Hispanic population between 1990 and 1995 was 28 percent (Allen 1997).

PARTISAN CHANGES IN FLORIDA

In the years following World War II, the political character of Florida changed from solidly Democratic to one in which the Republican Party, in many regions, became competitive. The transition of this more competitive political environment was fueled by three forces (Scher 1997, 143–

51). The first of these forces was the tremendous in-migration of more conservative, white, middle-class individuals from the North. A second force, related to the first, was the in-migration of large numbers of elderly persons who were also conservative and were more likely to vote for Republican candidates. These new arrivals had a profound effect on Florida politics, especially in the 1980s and 1990s, when the number of new conservative voters became sufficiently large to produce a competitive two-party state. Finally, many traditional Democrats began to question their loyalty to their party, which had become more liberal and "seemed no longer to represent southern interests and concerns" (Scher 1997, 145).

To understand Florida politics, it is important first to examine the changes in party registration in the state in the last two decades. Table 11.1 shows the percentage of the population registered as Democrats, Republicans, and as having no party identification (Independents). This table indicates that while the Democrats were clearly the dominant party in 1980, the political landscape was fundamentally different in 2000. In 1980, nearly two-thirds of registered voters were identified as Democrats. By 2000, less than one-half of registered voters were Democrats. During the 1980s and continuing into the 1990s, increasing numbers of voters registered as Republicans and Independents. The number of Republicans has increased more than one-third, from less than 30 percent of registered voters to about 40 percent. There are far fewer Independents and minor party registrants, but their percentage of registered voters has more than

Table 11.1.   Partisan Identification in Florida 1980–1996

				% Change in Identification		
	Democrat	*Republican*	*Independent*	*Democrat*	*Republican*	*Independent*
1980	65.8	28.8	5.4			
1982	63.0	30.8	6.2	−2.8	+2.0	+0.8
1984	61.0	32.8	6.2	−2.0	+2.0	0
1986	57.1	36.2	6.7	−3.9	+3.4	+0.5
1988	54.0	39.0	7.0	−3.1	+2.8	+0.3
1990	52.2	40.6	7.2	−1.8	+1.6	+0.2
1992	50.1	40.9	9.0	−2.1	+0.3	+1.8
1994	49.5	41.8	8.7	−0.6	+0.9	−.03
1996	46.8	41.5	11.7	−2.7	−0.3	+0.3
1998	44.9	40.1	15.0	−1.9	−1.4	+3.3
2000	43.3	39.2	17.5	−1.6	−.9	+2.5

Source: Florida Statistical Abstract

doubled, from 5.4 percent to nearly 18. By 2004 the combined percentage of Republican and Independent voters was substantially greater than the total percentage of Democrats.

The rates of change in partisanship in Florida largely mirror the growth of the state's population. The right-hand columns of table 11.1 summarize the changes in the percentages of registered voters for the Democrats, Republicans, and Independents over the two-year periods between 1980 and 2004. The middle 1980s were a period of tremendous growth in the state.

The decline in the percentage of Democrats was most dramatic during that period. From 1980 to 1992, Democrats experienced an average loss of 2 percentage points per biennium, with the greatest change in 1986 and 1988, when the combined decrease was 7 percent. The growth in the number of Republicans was greatest in these two years. By the middle of the 1990s, it appears that the decline in Democratic strength had slowed; in 1994, the decrease was only about one-half of a percentage point. In 1996, however, there was another large decline in the relative number of Democrats—nearly 3 percent. The Republicans did not, however, benefit from this decline, since the Republican registration also dropped slightly, but Independents gained by 3 percent. Research indicates that the "motor voter" law contributed significantly to these changes (Mortham 1995). It is evident that partisan registration in Florida is still changing, and it is unclear when it will stabilize.

These data on changes in the registration pattern should not be interpreted as indicating that changes in party registration are uniform across Florida. There are still areas where Democratic or Republican registration is relatively stable. The patterns of these concentrations of party strength in Florida are complex. Democrats are still very strong in some traditional rural and small-town areas and in some inner-city areas where there are concentration of African-American and low-income residents. This pattern of Democratic strength, however, is not found in some of the urban concentrations in the metropolitan Miami-Dade County area, home of large numbers of Cubans who have traditionally voted for Republicans. In general, however, Republicans tend to be concentrated, as in other states, in the more suburban sections of metropolitan areas where voters are largely white and higher income, although some heavily white rural areas are also becoming Republican.

It should also be noted that if one looks at party registration by county, one sees that by the twenty-first century Democrats were becoming increasingly concentrated, if not isolated. By 2004, more than 60 percent of the state's Democrats lived in only ten metropolitan counties; 80 percent lived in just twenty counties. In 2004, Democrat John Kerry received 67 percent of his vote total in the ten most populous urban counties, and a whopping 84 percent in twenty. What this means is that while Democrats can continue to have a major impact on statewide races, and even win some, for Congressional and state legislative races—determined by districts—it will be hard for them to achieve a majority either of the Congressional delegation or in either chamber of the state legislature. There are simply too many Democrats in too few places to expect otherwise.

The changes in party registration are not, of themselves, important. What is important is the impact of party registration changes on state and national elections in Florida. The following sections provide a detailed analysis of the change in election patterns for both national and state executive and legislative offices.

PRESIDENTIAL AND CONGRESSIONAL ELECTIONS

The Presidency

The presidential elections in Florida were the first to demonstrate the emerging strength of the Republican Party. Figure 11.1 provides a summary of the results of presidential contests in Florida. From 1920 to 1948, Floridians generally voted for Democratic presidential candidates. The only exception was the 1928 election, in which the state supported Hoover by a substantial margin over Al Smith, a Catholic from New York. In 1932, however, Floridians abandoned Hoover and voted for Roosevelt by a three-to-one margin. Starting with the Eisenhower election in 1952, a majority of Floridians voted for Republican presidential candidates. Since 1952, Democrats have carried Florida only three times, each time with a southern candidate. In 1964, Lyndon Johnson, in the course of a tremendous national victory, received a majority of only 2.3 percent of the Florida vote. Jimmy Carter, from adjacent Georgia, also won a narrow victory over the incumbent Gerald Ford. Voters abandoned Carter in 1980 and gave a substantial majority to Republican candidate Ronald Reagan.

In 1992 Democrat Bill Clinton ran a close second to the incumbent George Bush, but many potential Bush votes were siphoned off to the Independent candidacy of Ross Perot. Clinton was able, in 1996, to best

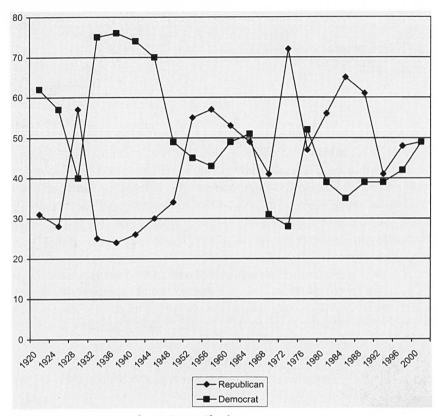

Figure 11.1.   Summary of U. S. Senate Elections

Dole in Florida. In this case, however, Clinton managed to position himself skillfully on several issues of importance to Floridians. Clinton was able to frighten elderly Florida voters with the warning that Dole, as a result of the large budget cut he promised, might be a threat to the health services and other benefits they receive from the federal government, especially social security. Another important issue for Clinton in Florida was immigration. Dole's tough stands against illegal immigration and in favor of cutting benefits for illegal immigrants cost him substantial votes among Hispanics, especially Cuban Americans. Instead of strongly supporting the Republican candidate as they had done in 1992, Hispanics in Florida split their vote almost evenly between Dole and Clinton (Schneider 1996). In 2000, of course, the Florida vote was almost exactly equally divided between Democrat Al Gore and Republican George Bush; the

U.S. Supreme Court decided the race when it stopped vote recounts in *Bush v. Gore*, giving the state to Bush by 537 votes. In 2004, however, John Kerry proved no match for incumbent Bush, losing the state by 461,000 votes.

U.S. Senate Elections

While presidential elections in Florida have resulted in a rapid transition in favor of Republican candidates, the U.S. Senate contests are a more accurate indicator of the gradually changing nature of partisanship in the state. Figure 11.2 provides a summary of the U.S. Senate elections from 1920 to the latest election in 2000. The Democratic Party clearly dominated the U.S. Senate elections to at least the late 1950s. From 1920 until 1962, only one Democratic candidate won by a margin of less than 40 percent of the vote.

That was Park Trammel, an incumbent who faced a strong challenge in 1928, a year in which Republican presidential candidate Herbert Hoover won Florida. Trammel returned in 1934, however, to win an uncontested election. Changes in the nature of U.S. Senate elections began to appear by the late 1950s and early 1960s. During this period, Florida's U.S. Senate seats were held by two strong incumbents, George Smathers and Spessard L. Holland. Holland, a former governor, eventually served four

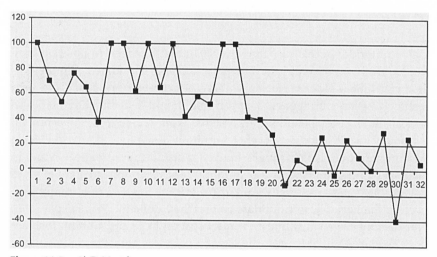

Figure 11.2.   % D Margin

terms, while Smathers served three. Smathers retired in 1968, but would have been reelected had he run for a fourth term. Both Holland's and Smathers's reelection margins for their third terms in 1958 and 1962, respectively, were about 40 percent. While these are solid election victories, they are by less than the typical margin for the previous four decades. Holland won by less than 30 percent in his last reelection campaign in 1963. The dividing line in Florida U.S. Senate election is between the 1964 and 1968 contests. The first Republican senator in at least a half a century was elected in 1968, in an election for the seat Smathers had vacated. From 1968 until 1994, Republicans had tight first-election tries. Dick Stone, a Democrat, and Paula Hawkins, a Republican, won by about 3 percent of the vote in their first (and only) victories. Connie Mack, a Republican, won by less than 1 percent in his first Senate victory in 1988. Once elected, some candidates were able to build support and win more substantial victories. Lawton Chiles's second and third victory margins were each about 25 percent, and Bob Graham, a popular former governor, achieved his second victory by more than 30 percent. None of these reelections, however, was as strong as the Democratic victories from 1920 to 1950. Connie Mack, a Republican incumbent, won his second reelection by more than 40 percent in 1994. However, in a strong Republican year, Mack faced a weak opponent in the relatively inexperienced Hugh Rodham, who had the advantage (or liability) of being the brother of First Lady Hillary Rodham Clinton. In 2000, a well-known state Democrat, Bill Nelson narrowly defeated a discredited Republican, Bill McCollum, who was one of the House floor managers during the Clinton impeachment proceedings; he will face formidable Republican opposition in 2006. In 2004, Republican Mel Martinez defeated former Florida Commissioner of Education and University of South Florida president Betty Castor in a hard-fought, vicious campaign by a mere 83,000 votes out of over 4 million cast. It is clear that the Democratic Party will no longer dominate the U.S. Senate elections in Florida as it did from 1920 until 1950. Instead, both Democratic and Republican candidates will face tough initial election campaigns. Only as incumbents will they be able to build more substantial elections margins.

U.S. House Elections

The U.S. House elections in Florida largely mirror the results that are evident in the Senate elections. Table 11.2 summarizes the results of the U.S.

Table 11.2.   U.S. House of Representative Elections in Florida 1920–2000

	Democratic Seats	Average Democratic Margin (%)	Republican Seats	Average Republican Margin (%)	Republican Seats (%)
1950	6	84.5			
1952	8	58.4			
1954	7	87.3	1	1.5	12.5
1956	7	48.2	1	12.7	12.5
1958	7	82.4	1	17.6	12.5
1960	7	64.6	1	16.8	12.5
1962	10	49.4	2	16.4	16.6
1964	10	73.7	2	21.1	16.6
1966	9	76.4	3	54.5	25
1968	9	38.5	3	74.5	25
1970	9	56.8	3	31.4	25
1972	11	39.1	4	50.4	26.6
1974	10	72.9	5	32.5	33
1976	10	67.2	5	29.0	33
1978	12	55.6	3	53.0	20
1980	11	39.1	4	44.6	26.6
1982	13	48.4	6	28.3	31.6
1984	12	53.5	7	67.6	36.8
1988	10	64.9	9	52.7	47.4
1990	9	36.1	10	58.7	52.6
1992	11	63.3	12	62.8	52.2
1994	8	69.4	15	85.0	65.2
1996	8	70.7	15	70.1	65.2
1998	8	85.7	15	93.0	65.2
2000	8	78.4	15	74.3	65.2

Souce: Congressional Quarterly Guide to U.S. Elections

House elections in Florida from 1950 to 2004. The table presents the year, the number of Democratic and Republican victors, and the average victory margin for Democratic and Republican senators. The last column in the table lists the percentage of House seats held by Republicans.

Democratic candidates dominated Florida House elections from 1920 to 1950. The first Republican was elected only in 1954, when William Cramer won the First Congressional District by a very tight 1.5 percent margin against a one-term incumbent who had narrowly been elected in 1952. Cramer was the only Republican congressman from Florida from 1954 until 1962 and was able to expand his victory margin to about 17 percent. While the election of this single Republican candidate hardly represented an overwhelming change in Florida congressional elections, it was certainly an indication of more substantial changes to come. In the years that followed, the number of Republicans elected to Congress from Florida continued to grow. The size of the Florida congressional delegation has increased to reflect the increase in population, but the percentage of Republican-held seats does not merely parallel the increase in the number of congressional seats. By the 1980s, Republicans held one-third of the seats and by the 1990s they had surged to control more than 60 percent of the Florida delegation. Moreover, the size of the victory margin of Republican candidates has increased to rival that of Democratic candidates.

The number and percentage of total seats, however, do not accurately reflect the growing strength of the Republican Party in Florida. Congressional districts, of course, were drawn by the Democratic officials who still held a majority of the legislature (the districts in 1992 were drawn by a three-judge federal panel after legislators could not agree on a plan). Table 11.2 shows that, interestingly, the number of Republican congressional seats increased after redistricting allocated more seats to rapidly growing areas. Republicans held only one seat in the 1950s, two to three seats in the 1960s, three to five seats in the 1970s, six to nine seats in the 1980s and twelve to fifteen in the 1990s. Both of the House seats which Florida gained as a result of the 2000 census were won by Republicans in 2002 and 2004.

GUBERNATORIAL AND STATE
LEGISLATIVE ELECTIONS

The Gubernatorial Elections

The elections for governor of Florida largely mirror the results for U.S. Senate and House elections. Table 11.3 lists the party of the victorious candidate, as well as the percentage of victory margin for gubernatorial elections in Florida from 1920 to 2002.

Again, we see that Democratic candidates for governor dominated the elections from 1920 until the mid-1950s. The first Republican governor was Claude Kirk, who was elected in 1966. The next Republican, Bob Martinez, was elected in 1986. Both were one-term governors. By 1960, however, the victory margins of Democratic governors were less than 20 percent, substantially smaller than the 56 percent average for the preceding forty years. The margin of victory for subsequent Democratic victors

Table 11.3.　Gubernatorial Races in Florida 1920–1998

	Victor's Party	Victory %
1920	D	60
1924	D	65.6
1928	D	22.0
1932	D	33.2
1936	D	61.8
1940	D	100
1944	D	57.8
1948	D	66.8
1952	D	49.6
1956	D	47.4
1960	D	19.7
1960	D	19.7
1964	D	14.8
1966	R	10.2
1970	D	13.8
1974	D	22.4
1978	D	11.2
1982	D	29.4
1986	R	9.2
1990	D	13.0
1994	D	1.6
1998	R	10.6

Source: Congressional Quarterly Guide to U.S. Elections

was only 15 percent. The gubernatorial elections from 1970 to 1998 were won by three relatively popular Democratic candidates who each served two terms—Rubin Askew, Bob Graham, and former three-term senator Lawton Chiles. Martinez, the sole Republican elected governor after the 1966 Kirk victory, won an open-seat election against a relatively unknown opponent, Steve Pajic, who received the nomination after a divisive Democratic runoff. Pajic was viewed by voters as a liberal, which made defeating Martinez difficult (see Black and Black 1987). Martinez was not able to win reelection against the popular and well-known Chiles. Chiles, after a first term in which he was not viewed as very successful, won an extremely narrow victory against Jeb Bush, son of the former president. Bush was well financed and was able to benefit from running in a year in which the Republican Party was generally successful across the nation. In 1998 Bush won with a margin of 11 points over the Democratic lieutenant-governor, Buddy MacKay. In 2002 Bush handily won reelection against his opponent, 56 percent to 43 percent.

While Democrats largely dominated gubernatorial elections in Florida from 1970 to 1994, this dominance is substantially different from that evident in the 1920–1960 period. The victories from the late 1970s to the present were generally narrow Democratic victories won by capable and popular candidates. It is by no means certain that Democrats will continue to control the governor's office, and it is likely that in the next several elections the office will alternate between parties.

An interesting feature of Florida government is the election of cabinet officers. In most systems of government, the executives appoint, typically with the approval of the legislature, officials to run most cabinet offices. In Florida, the cabinet positions of secretary of state, attorney general, comptroller, treasurer, and commissioners of education and agriculture were elected. But in 2000, constitutional revisions to the cabinet went into effect. The secretary of state and commissioner of education positions were removed from the cabinet; now the governor appoints them. The comptroller and treasurer slots were combined into a chief state fiscal officer. Currently the cabinet consists of the attorney general, commissioner of agriculture, and chief state fiscal officer; the governor continues to sit with this smaller body and makes up the cabinet system.

While many states have multiple elected officials in the executive branch, Florida was unique both in the number and the range of such officials' duties, which were constitutionally and statutorily assigned. As a result, the cabinet served as a collegial governing board for the executive branch (Scher 1994). It is very easy to imagine the difficulty of governing in a system in which the chief executive officers of major departments are not controlled by the governor. It is even more difficult to govern when these individuals are from the opposite party. In 1986, Republican governor Bob Martinez's cabinet offices were all held by Democrats. In 1990, concurrently with the election of Democrat Chiles, two Republicans held cabinet slots, and in 1994 three of the cabinet positions were filled by Republicans. Governor Bush, who won in 1998, has a Republican majority on his cabinet. Currently there are no Democrats in the Florida cabinet. Partisanship is likely to increase in the executive branch, not decrease.

Florida House and Senate Elections

The changing nature of partisanship and elections in Florida is also evident in the races for the state legislature. To understand the changes in Florida state legislative elections, it is important first to examine the partisan registration in House and Senate districts. Table 11.4 presents the

Table 11.4.   Average Party Registration in State House and Senate Districts 1988–2000

	House			Senate		
	Democrat	*Republican*	*Independent*	*Democrat*	*Republican*	*Independent*
1988	27,200	19,595	3,511	81,602	59,010	10,534
1990	26,062	20,395	3,582	78,743	61,212	10,748
1992	27,654	22,274	4,550	82,964	66,824	13,651
1994	27,054	22,892	4,376	81,137	68,676	13,192
1996	31,064	25,575	7,734	93,212	82,727	23,212
1998	30,765	27,438	10,299	92,293	82,314	30,898
2000	31,692	28,585	12,661	95,755	85,756	38,235
% inc.						
'88–00	16.5	45.8	260.6	17.3	45.3	267.0

Source: Florida Department of State general election returns

mean number of Democratic, Republican and Independent party registrations in the Florida House and Senate districts. Data are available only for 1988–2004, but even this short time span clearly demonstrates the changes in partisanship in Florida.

In 1988, the number of registered Republicans was substantially smaller than the number of Democrats. By 2000, however, the number of registered Republicans had increased to approach the number of Democrats. Moreover, by 1996, Independents, and Republicans outnumbered the registered Democrats. The rate of change for each party differs significantly. While the rate of change from 1988 to 2004 is a moderate 30.5 percent for Democrats, it is a much more substantial 65.5 percent for the Republicans. The increase in the number of Independents, though starting from a relatively small number, is a surprising 347.6 percent. While many districts still have a strong Democratic majority, the trend since 1988 is for rapidly increasing number of Republican and especially Independent registrations.

Another perspective on the changing nature of partisanship is provided by table 11.5, on state Senate and House districts. This table lists the number of Florida House and Senate districts in which the Democrats have a majority of the party registrations. In 1988 the Democrats had a majority of those choosing a party in 86 of the 120 House districts (71.6 percent) and 29 of 40 Senate districts (72.5 percent). By 2004, Democrats and Republicans each held a majority in about half of the House and Senate districts. The registration numbers clearly indicate that races for state legislative seats were more competitive in the 1990s.

Table 11.5.   Florida Legislative Districts with Majority Democratic Registration 1988–2000 (in percentages)

	House (120 districts)	Senate (40 districts)
1988	71.7	72.5
1990	65.8	67.5
1992	64.2	67.5
1994	60.8	57.5
1996	55.0	52.5
1998	55.0	52.5
2000	53.3	50.0

Source: Florida Department of State general election returns

In addition to examining the party registration in each district, it is important to examine the party composition of the Florida House and Senate. The percentages of Democratic and Republican membership in the legislature are presented in table 11.6.

This table demonstrates that there has been a significant change in the party composition of the Florida legislature. In 1976, both the House and the Senate were about 75 percent Democratic. Since 1976, there has been a consistent decline in the number of Democratic legislators and a corresponding increase in the number of Republicans. The percentages of the

Table 11.6.   Partisan Makeup of Florida State Legislature 1976–2000 (in percentages)

	House (120 seats)		Senate (40 seats)	
	Democrats	Republicans	Democrats	Republicans
1976	76.6	23.3	72.5	25.0
1978	74.2	25.8	72.5	27.5
1980	67.5	32.5	67.5	32.5
1982	70.0	30.0	80.0	20.0
1984	64.2	35.8	80.0	20.0
1986	62.5	37.5	62.5	37.5
1988	73.3	26.7	57.5	42.5
1990	61.7	38.3	57.5	42.5
1992	54.2	40.8	50.0	50.0
1994	59.2	40.8	47.5	52.5
1996	49.2	50.8	42.5	57.5
1998	42.0	58.0	42.5	57.5
2000	35.8	64.2	37.5	62.5

Source: Florida Department of State general election returns

Democratic and Republican members of the House and Senate are now about equal. In 1996, for the first time since Reconstruction, Republicans took control of the Florida House. As expected, Republican domination of both chambers rose following reapportionment in 2002 and increased in 2004.

RACE AND POLITICS IN FLORIDA

Florida provides an interesting opportunity to examine the impact of federal legislation and court decisions that make it possible for minorities to participate fully in the electoral process. The Voting Rights Act of 1965, extended in 1970, 1975, and 1982, effectively eliminated the roadblocks that states and local governments had erected to minority participation in elections. The 1986 *Thornburg v. Gingles* decision gave a clear indication that states should create minority legislative districts whenever possible. The Florida situation is unique from several perspectives. First, legislative districts for African Americans must be created in a state in which the percentage of blacks has declined throughout the century, apparently stabilizing at about 14 percent. Clearly, crafting legislative districts for African Americans in a declining population is no easy task. The second issue relates to the rapid increase, especially in south Florida, in the size of the Hispanic population. Both African Americans and Hispanics want to maximize their number of districts. Moreover, Hispanics in Florida, in contrast to those in many other states, are conservative and tend to vote Republican. The creation of Hispanic districts, therefore, further increases the number of Republicans in the legislature. The third issue relates in a somewhat different fashion to the population changes that Florida is experiencing. With the declining number of Democratic voters, the creation of districts for African Americans means that many traditional Democratic (African-American) voters will be concentrated in these districts. This will further reduce the number of Democrats and increase Republican strength in adjacent districts.

Finally, it is important to understand that Florida's concentration of three distinct groups—white, African American, and Hispanic—has produced fierce electoral competition. The groups strive to promote candidates who share their race or ethnicity. This competition is particularly keen in the Miami-Dade County area, where all three groups exist in strength. The partisan conflict usually is evident at two levels. The competition between African Americans and whites to promote their Democratic candidates can be evident at the primary level. Hispanics, traditionally Republicans, enter the fray during the general election, when their candidate will oppose the primary winner. In recent years, however, Republicans have also been involved in significant internecine ethnic conflict in local primaries.

One example of racial conflict is the commission races in the city of Miami. M. Athalie Range became the first African-American city commissioner in 1965. She was followed by a succession of African-Americans who occupied her seat. In 1996, however, a Hispanic man won the seat. In fact, the thirteen commission seats in Miami as of 2005 are occupied by seven Hispanics, four African Americans, and two whites; the chair of the commission is Hispanic, but the vice-chair is African American. There is a keen sense of frustration among blacks, who feel that the rise of Hispanic political power symbolizes the "unfulfilled promise" of a better life for African Americans in the Miami metropolitan area (Navarro 1997).

This pattern of race- and ethnic-based electoral conflict may, however, be changing. In the 1996 Miami mayoral (nonpartisan) election, white and Hispanic voters formed a coalition to promote a single candidate. With the increase in the number of younger Hispanic voters who are less conservative, these coalitions may become increasingly common. It is worth noting that Bill Clinton did extremely well among younger Cubans in 1996 (Fiedler 1996). However, Democrat Al Gore did not fare as well among Cubans in 2000, probably as a result of the Elian Gonzalez affair that year. John Kerry however did manage to win Miami-Dade County in 2004 but by a razor-thin 48,000 votes.

To aid in understanding the increase in African-American representation in the Florida legislature, table 11.7 presents the percentage of African-American House and Senate members from 1976 through 2004. It is clear from the table that the number of African-American legislators has increased substantially since 1976. In 1976, there were only a handful of African-American members in the House and none in the Senate. By 2000, the percentage of African-American members in both chambers approached the percentage (approximately 14 percent) of African Americans in the state population. It is also interesting that the change in the number of African-American legislators is largely related to redistricting. Africa-American members of the House jumped from 3.3 percent to 9.2 percent following the redistricting in the 1980s. The percentage of African

Table 11.7. African-American Membership in the Florida Legislature 1976–2000 (in percentages)

	House (120 seats)	Senate (40 seats)
1976	2.5	0
1978	3.3	0
1980	3.3	0
1982	9.2	5.0
1984	9.2	5.0
1986	9.2	5.0
1988	10.0	5.0
1990	11.6	5.0
1992	11.6	12.5
1994	10.0	12.5
1996	11.6	12.5
1998	10.7	12.5
2000	13.3	15.0

Source: Joint Center for Political and Economic Studies; Florida Department of State general election returns

Americans in the Senate jumped from zero to 5 percent. The change following the 1992 redistricting primarily affected the Florida Senate, where African-American membership jumped from 5 to 12.5 percent.

THE 2000 AND 2004 PRESIDENTIAL ELECTIONS

The 2000 presidential election in Florida became a national, even an international, cause célèbre. A statistical tie, the final official results showed that George W. Bush received 537 votes more than Al Gore. However, what is less well known is that official county totals showed that Gore actually won the state by 202 votes on Election Day; it was the 739-vote margin that Bush gained from federal absentee ballots that accounts for the final 527-vote official difference.

While a number of aspects of the 2000 election deserve mention, space limitations will permit just three.

In the first place, the entire presidential election came down to the Sunshine State. Not since 1876 has Florida played such a key role in determining the identity of the next president. Indeed, even late into the twentieth century, Floridians had generally decided early on their presidential preference, to the extent that the presidential contenders largely ceased campaigning there by mid- to late September, as they felt the matter was already resolved for or against them. Beginning in 1992 and then again in 1996, Florida became less predictable, however, and by 2000 it was impossible to foretell the outcome of the election ahead of time (or, for that matter, for a long time after it was over!). It may be, then, that as Republicans and Democrats achieve virtual parity in electoral registration, and Independent voters become still more numerous and thus hold the balance of power, Florida (which will have twenty-seven Electoral College votes in the next election) will be come more central, more valuable, and possibly more unpredictable to presidential contenders.

Second, African-American voters played a key and unprecedented role in making the 2000 presidential election as close as it was in Florida. Not only did black voters turn out in record numbers, but they voted in most counties at above 90 percent for Democrat Al Gore, roughly 5 to 8 percent higher than their usual support for Democratic presidential candidates. Moreover, black voters are still upset because of seemingly nonsystematic but nonetheless troubling evidence of disenfranchisement, discarding of ballots in black precincts and a higher rate of problem ballots in black precincts than in white ones, due in many instances to the heavy reliance on older voting technologies in the black precincts. If black voters continue to show anger and frustration and are willing to come to the polls in upcoming election campaigns, it is entirely likely that their vote might well prove determinative in future elections.

Finally, the 2000 election showed a significant shift in the distribution of Florida voters. Whereas for much of the state's history elections were decided by votes in north Florida and the panhandle, this is no longer the case. Some 73 percent of all the ballots in the 2000 presidential contest were cast in the twenty-six Florida counties lying on or south of I-4 (a major transportation artery running through the geographic middle of the state from Daytona Beach on the east to Tampa Bay on the west); Florida has some sixty-seven counties in all. What this means is that the geopolitical center of gravity of the state has shifted to the central and southern sections of the state. Indeed, with the exception of heavily populated Duval County (Jacksonville) in the northeast, the remainder of the northern tier of the state is almost politically irrelevant as far as statewide elections are concerned. Future presidential candidates, as well as those for U.S. senator, governor, and the remaining cabinet positions, will have to direct their campaigns to the major population centers of the state, leaving voters elsewhere largely out of the campaign loop.

Republicans did much better in the 2004 presidential election than four years earlier. The impact of 9/11, uncertainty about the future, the fear of terrorist attacks, ambiguities about Democrat John Kerry and the very negative campaign that Republicans waged all appear to account for the 460,000 vote margin of victory for the GOP.

However, as they did in other states, Republicans engaged in a new and effective political strategy. They appealed very strongly to the Religious Right/Christian conservatives, who are numerous and powerful in Florida. Both Vice President Cheney and President Bush made trips to carefully identified counties in Florida, even majority Democratic ones, where they found sizeable pockets of evangelical and fundamentalist Protestant voters. These visits proved productive. Turnout in "smaller" rural counties was much higher than normal, and Republican vote totals rose considerably as well. The result was to augment Bush's overwhelming advantage in suburbs and along Interstate 4 in central Florida, dilute the Democratic vote, and propel Mr. Bush to an easy victory in the Sunshine State. Democrats had no comparable strategy to mobilize their voters; unless and until they do, it is likely that Florida will prove to be fertile ground for Republican candidates in future presidential races.

CONCLUSION

The political situation in Florida has been one of the most dynamic of any southern state. The trend toward increasing numbers of Republican and Independent voters means that Democratic candidates are no longer assured of victory. Elections will be increasingly competitive and will be won by the candidates who have the most resources and make the most effective appeals to voters. It is unclear at this time if current trends will continue and Republicans will come to dominate Florida politics. Another scenario is that there will be a partisan balance and elective offices will alternate between parties. It is also likely that the increasing Independent vote will have a decisive influence on the outcome of state and even local elections.

REFERENCES

Allen, Diane Lacey. 1997. "Hispanics in Florida." *Gainesville Sun*, 2 November, 1D.
Black, Earl, and Merle Black. 1987. *Politics and the Society in the South*. Cambridge, MA: Harvard University Press.

Fiedler, Tom. 1996. "Rewriting the Book on Florida," *Miami Herald*, 6 November, 16A.

Mortham, Sandra. 1995. The Impact of the National Voter Registration Act of 1993 on the State of Florida." Tallahassee Florida Secretary of State, November 15. This report can be found on the Internet at election.dos.state.fl.us/reforms/nvra.htm.

Navarro, Mierya. 1997. "As the Population Shifts, Many Florida Blacks Say They Feel 'Left Out.'" *New York Times*, 17 February, 16A, national edition.

Scher, Richard K. 1994. "The Governor and the Cabinet: Executive Policy Making and Policy Management." Chap. 4 in *The Florida Public Policy Management System*, edited by Richard Chackerian. Tallahassee, FL: Askew School of Public Administration and Policy and Florida Center for Public Management.

———. 1997. *Politics in the New South*, 2nd ed. Armonk, NY: M.E. Sharpe.

Schneider, William. 1996. "Immigration Issues Reward Democrats." *National Journal*, 30 November, 2522.

Smith, Stanley K. 1995. "Population Growth and Demographic Change." In *The Economy of Florida*, edited by J.F. Scoggins and Ann Pierce. Gainesville, FL: Bureau of Economic and Business Research.

12

Texas: Lone Star (Wars) State

James W. Lamare
J. L. Polinard
James Wenzel
Robert D. Wrinkle

O nce upon a time, a long time ago, in a galaxy far, far away, there was a place called Texas. The Force was with a group called Democrats. It was rumored that in some states a dark side called Republicans were in power, but most Texans had never seen a Republican, so it was difficult to know whether or not they actually existed. The Force also was with White People. There were, of course, African Americans (they were called "Colored" or "Negro" then, at least in polite company) and Mexican Americans (they were called Latin Americans then), but they had none of the Force. At election time, if an African American or Mexican American attempted to vote as an individual, it was an act of courage rather than citizenship. It was, however, common "to vote" the minority groups, as in "don't forget to vote your Mexicans next week." Indeed, in South Texas so many trucks brought Latino farm workers to the polls that the growers would tie different colored ribbons to the truck beds so that after the workers had marked the correct ballot, they would return to the correct vehicle.

And the Force was only with Men. Although the colorful Miriam "Ma" Ferguson was elected in 1924, she was viewed widely as a stand-in for her ethically challenged husband, who had been booted out of the governor's office in 1917. Women played little role in the politics of this Texas of another era. But that was in a galaxy far away, and long, oh so very long, ago.

We are over a half-century removed from the Texas that native son V. O. Key examined for his classic study of Southern states (Key 1949). No single factor, such as race or oil and gas or conservatism or Key's "modified class politics," can describe the politics in Texas today.

Having said that, one characteristic of Texas politics has not changed in fifty years: The state remains a one-party state. The difference today, of course, is the party. In Key's day, less than a century removed from the Civil War, Texas was solidly Democratic. There were thousands of Texans alive in the 1960s who had never met an actual Republican (or at least one out of the closet). Loyalty to the Democratic Party was so deeply embedded in Texas's political culture that a great many partisans were aptly described as "yellow-dog Democrats," voters who would rather vote for a yellow dog than any Republican.

Today, Texas is Republican—a red state if ever there was one. Including the 2004 elections, no Democrat has won a statewide race since 1994. No Democrat currently holds a statewide office.

Perhaps ironically, the transition from Democrat to Republican is inextricably linked to the state's past, particularly to the roots of its history as a frontier state and to its history of racial politics.

Part of the legacy of Texas's frontier ethic has been the state's basic conservatism. Until the last two decades, electoral competition as well as legislative conflict broke along ideological rather than partisan lines; with few notable exceptions, the only elections that really counted were between conservative and liberal Democrats in the spring primaries. For the most part, conservatives won these battles. Public policy fights in the state legislature similarly were between conservative and liberal legislators, rather than Democrats and Republicans. Even more recently, when Republicans began to contest and win state legislative seats, the conservative Democratic leadership in the statehouse and senate often would appoint GOP conservatives to committee chairs rather than reward the few Democratic liberals.

Texas also is a former state of the Confederacy, and race always has played a role in the state's politics. Historically, blacks in north and east Texas, and Mexican Americans in south and west Texas, have found themselves on the outside looking in when it came to political power. Today, although African Americans and Mexican Americans have won statewide elections and have representation in the state legislature and the congressional delegation, their representation is not proportionate to their percentage of the population. And no African American or Mexican American has held the top three posts in the state: governor, lieutenant governor (which many consider the most powerful political position) and speaker of the House.

We turn now to a detailed examination of the changing politics of party competitiveness, the impact of the 2001 and 2003 redistricting processes, and the politics of race in Texas.

PARTY POLITICS

It is difficult, if not impossible, to separate the politics of contemporary partisanship in Texas from the politics of race. Shortly after Lyndon B. Johnson signed the 1964 Civil Rights Act into law, he predicted he had just ensured the end of the Democratic Party's electoral lock on the South. Certainly race has been a major factor in the Republican upsurge in Texas. As the national Democratic Party became identified as the party representing the interests of African Americans and other racial and ethnic minorities, white Texans increasingly considered the Republican Party as a viable alternative. The subsequent passage of the 1965 Voting Rights Act, which, among other things, sounded the deathknell to race-based literacy tests, further contributed to the Democratic Party's image as the party of minorities, and the 1975 inclusion of Texas as one of the jurisdictions covered by the Voting Rights Act cemented this image and accelerated white flight from the Democrats (Burka 1986).

Ideology also contributed to the emergence of the Republican Party in Texas. The nomination of liberal George McGovern as the Democratic Party's presidential candidate in 1972 increased the perception that the party was controlled by the liberal wing of American politics, and this, too, hastened the exodus of conservative white Texans to the GOP (Dyer and Haynes 1987; Dyer, Leighley, and Vedlitz 1997). Furthermore, the appeal of Ronald Reagan's message during the presidential campaigns of 1980 and 1984, according to the then chairman of the state GOP (George Strake), made "it so easy . . . to court conservatives into the Republican Party" (Robison 2004, 2). During Reagan's stint in the White House some fifty-eight Democratic Texas officeholders switched parties to become Republicans.

Within the electorate, as detailed in figure 12.1, there has been a steady growth of identification with the Republican Party, paralleled by a significant loss of support for the Democrats. In 1964, Democratic identification stood at 65 percent, eight times greater than Republican affiliation (8 percent). By 1974, the gap had narrowed some, but Democratic identifiers still trumped Republicans by about four to one. The divide between the parties had closed dramatically by 1984, with one-third of Texans identifying as Democrats and 28 percent calling themselves Republicans. By 1994, the inevitable occurred: More Texans affiliated with the Republicans than the Democrats. A decade later, this shift became more pronounced: 38 percent Republican and 26 percent Democrat. Texas had completed the transition to a predominantly Republican state.

Demographic patterns also have spurred Republican growth in Texas. Texas is a Sun Belt state with a steady influx of immigrants from other states. Many of these new Texans come from traditionally Republican states, with research suggesting that nearly one-fourth of Texas's Republicans are not native to the state (Dyer, Vedlitz, and Hill 1988, 164). Republican strength lies mainly among younger, higher socioeconomic status (SES), white non-Hispanic Texans, who reside in the more upscale suburbs and satellite communities that encircle the state's largest metropolitan areas. The Democrats draw their support predominately from older, native, lower SES, rural Texans and the state's largest minority groups, a point discussed more fully next (Dye, Gibson and Robison 1997, 767).

In ideological terms, the more things change, the more they stay the

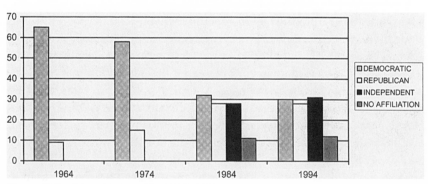

Figure 12.1.   Texas Partnership 1964–2004

Source: Stanley and Windell. 1995. "Gender Politics in Texas Elections," paper presented at the annual meeting of the American Political Science Association; Texas Poll Archives and The Scripps Howard Texas Poll, Fall 2004.

same—at least in Texas. For over a generation, the number of Texans calling themselves liberal, conservative and moderate has remained relatively constant, with the ratio of conservatives to liberals also stable at two to one.

Within the Republican Party there are variant conservative ideological perspectives (such as between the economic conservatives and the social conservatives) and varying degrees of commitment to conservatism. Lately, the Christian Coalition, a group that strongly opposes gay marriage and abortion, has, through a great deal of organizational effort, taken command of the state GOP (Lamare, Polinard, and Wrinkle 2003). Its social conservative message is clear, loud, and appealing.

Given the ideological landscape of Texas, for candidates of both major parties, electoral "victory is gained by trying to convince the electorate that a candidate is more conservative than his opponent" (Champagne and Collis 1984, 142). The difference for the past decade, of course, is the party with which these conservatives now identify.

Voting patterns have paralleled these partisan and ideological trends. Following Reconstruction, no Republican was elected to statewide office until John Tower broke through in 1961 to replace Lyndon Johnson in the United States Senate. Ironically, Tower was elected with the help of liberal Democrats who refused to support Tower's more conservative opponent (Gibson and Robison 1995, 195). Although Texas Republicans would win very few other elections at any level in Texas over the next twenty years, Tower's 1961 election is cited as the beginning of the two-party system in Texas (Davidson 1990, 21).

Throughout the Democratic Party's domination at most levels of Texas politics during the 1960s and 1970s, there were Republican gains, most noticeably Bill Clements' 1978 victory in the governor's race. By the end of the 1970s, the GOP was positioned to compete seriously for elective office.

From 1960 to the mid-1980s the percentage of Texans who identified themselves as Republicans had been steadily, if gradually, increasing (from 8 percent in the early 1960s to 28 percent by the mid-1980s), while the Democrats were on a down elevator, with the Democratic percentage of the population dropping below 38 percent by 1984. In 1980, a Republican occupied the governor's office, a Republican was the state's senior United States senator, and Ronald Reagan, beloved by the conservatives in Texas, had just been elected president. The future was now for the GOP.

Well, not quite. Democrats surprised the Republicans in 1982 by recapturing the governor's mansion, sweeping the statewide offices and maintaining strong majorities in both houses of the state legislature. The 1982 Democratic win can be attributed in part to a ticket that included both liberals and conservatives at the top spots, thereby holding both constituencies in the party, and by the united opposition to the dour Clements. In retrospect, however, this would be the last hurrah for the Democrats in the twentieth century. In the 1984 elections Ronald Reagan easily carried Texas, Phil Gramm became the second Republican from Texas elected to the U.S. Senate, and, perhaps more important, Republicans gained seats in both the state Senate and state House. Republicans also made significant inroads in county elections, winning twice as many seats as they had held prior to the election.

Helped in part by the presence at the top of the ticket, first of Ronald Reagan in 1984 and then favorite son George H. W. Bush in 1988, the GOP upsurge continued throughout the 1980s. Changing party loyalties continued to manifest themselves, both in the sense that some Democrats became Republicans (realignment) and in the sense that some Democrats moved away from the Democratic Party (dealignment) without aligning with the GOP. The net result: By the 1990s party identification was virtually identical between the two parties.

The trend established in the 1980s continued through the 1990s. Although the Republicans would suffer some difficult losses, the most visible being the defeat of GOP gubernatorial candidate Clayton Williams at the hands of Democrat Ann Richards in 1990 (or, more accurately, at the mouth of Williams, whose verbal gaffes in the last weeks of the campaign helped snatch defeat from the jaws of victory), they continued to gain seats in almost every other venue. At the federal level, for example, Texas has supported the Republican candidate for president in every election since 1976. With the election of Kay Bailey Hutchison in 1993, Republicans occupied both of Texas's seats in the U.S. Senate.

At the state level, George W. Bush, son of the former president, defeated incumbent Ann Richards in 1994 to become the second Republican governor of Texas since Reconstruction. The 1994 election also ushered in a Republican sweep of the three seats on the Texas Railroad Commission, which because of its jurisdiction over the oil industry, is perhaps the most important elected administrative agency in the United States. The GOP also gained a majority on the fifteen-person State Board of Education. The state's elected commissioner of agriculture went Republican, while the other elected statewide executives remained Democrats.

However, the handwriting was on the wall. In 1996, Republicans swept every statewide election and, for the first time in 125 years, obtained a majority in the state Senate. The GOP also made a strong showing in races for Texas's House of Representatives, winning 68 of 151 seats that year. By 1998 almost two-thirds of the state's district courts were occupied by Republicans. Nearly 1,100 elected county positions were Republicans. In total, the GOP won more than 1,500 elections at the federal, state, and local level in 1998. Two years later, the Republicans captured control of both houses of the state legislature for the first time since Reconstruction and cemented that control in 2004. Although the GOP leadership still appoints Democrats to some leadership positions in the legislature, the state House and Senate clearly are governed by Republicans. All state-wide offices, including both Texas supreme courts (one for civil, the other for criminal cases), are held by Republicans. Five election cycles have turned since the last time Democrats scratched on a statewide office. Indeed, in the 2000 elections, the Libertarian Party contested more state-wide offices than the Democrats. As these election results indicate, Texas is a one-party Republican state. The only fly in the GOP ointment remained the congressional delegation. Although the GOP had made some gains in the national House seats, following the 2002 congressional elections, Democrats still controlled a majority of the congressional delegation.

But not for long!

THE 2003 REDISTRICTING FIGHT

Like most states, Texas redistricts its state and congressional legislative seats once every ten years, following the U.S. Census. The Census report in 2000 was good to Texas: The state was informed it had picked up two congressional seats, increasing the size of the delegation from thirty to thirty-two.

The Texas effort to redistrict, however, was an exercise in futility. Under the best of circumstances, redistricting is a bitterly fought partisan endeavor. The shape and composition of the district, whether state House, state Senate or congressional districts, quite simply can determine the outcome of the election in that district. Thus, the stakes are high as each representative views redistricting as a question of survival rather than good government.

The 2001 Texas legislature charged with drawing the new lines was not up to the task. Although the Democratic-controlled House and GOP-controlled state Senate worked on their respective redistricting chores, the outcome was dismal. The House passed a redistricting bill that died in the Senate. Still, that was better than the Senate effort. The Texas Senate Redistricting Committee produced a bill that could not muster enough support in the chamber to be sent to the house.

By Texas law, this meant the Legislative Redistricting Board (LRB) would take its turn at bat. The LRB, made up of the lieutenant governor, attorney general, land commissioner, state comptroller and House speaker (the latter was the only Democrat on the LRB), managed to produce redistricting plans for the state House and Senate.

The House plan, however, ran afoul of the Department of Justice, which denied pre-clearance as required by the Voting Rights Act. A three-judge federal court subsequently adopted a plan that would be in place for the 2002 elections.

The senate plan produced by the LRB was pre-cleared by DOJ (although both the Mexican American Legislative Caucus and the Mexican American Legal Defense and Education Fund [MALDEF] challenged the plan unsuccessfully in the courts) and approved by the three-judge federal court.

These would be the redistricting plans that Texans would use for the remainder of the state legislative and state Senate elections through the decade. The 2002 and 2004 elections ratified the assessments of the partisan impact of the new districts: The GOP maintained control of both the state House and Senate.

The Texas Three Step: Ardmore, Albuquerque and Austin

It was a very different matter for congressional districting. The 2001 legislative session was unable to agree on how the thirty-two congressional districts should be drawn; the legislative session finished without new districts in place for the 2002 elections. The LRB's jurisdiction is limited to the state House and Senate seats, so it was not a player in the congressional districting process. That task fell to a three-judge federal district court. The court produced a plan that awarded the two new congressional seats to Republicans and protected the incumbents in the remaining thirty seats.

Despite the overall GOP tenor of the state and the fact that the three-judge court's congressional redistricting map suggested a majority of the thirty-two seats contained GOP majorities, when the dust settled from the 2002 elections, Democrats held seventeen of the thirty-two seats. In part this was due to some congressional districts where the voters chose GOP candidates in the statewide gubernatorial and U.S. Senate races but voted for their Democrat congressional incumbent as a way of protecting their seniority and the goodies that accrue from that seniority. That is, these districts were predominantly Republican in population, but the GOP voters were making a conscious decision to split their ticket when it came to the congressional representative on the ballot.

Enter the U.S. House Republican Leader, Texan Tom DeLay. DeLay saw two benefits in breaking with the tradition of redistricting only once during a ten-year cycle. Redrawing the congressional lines in 2003 would not only produce a GOP congressional delegation from Texas, but, anticipating picking up at least five Republican seats from the redistricting, DeLay would immunize continued GOP control of the U.S. House against any Democratic gains in the 2004 elections.

Democrats cried foul, but the state attorney general declared the state legislature had the authority to redistrict in 2003 and the battle was joined. The Democrats won the early battles by going to the political equivalent of scorched earth. In a conversation one of the authors had, the comment was made that "the Democrats have gone to the mattresses," a reference to the famous line from *The Godfather*. Actually, it was more accurate to say they moved the mattresses. When the state House scheduled floor action on redistricting, over fifty House Democrats fled to Ardmore, Oklahoma, thereby denying the House leadership a quorum. The Democrats stayed in Ardmore until the time ran out for both the regular session and the redistricting bill in early June 2003.

That did not settle the matter. The governor, Republican Rick Perry, called the legislature into special session June 30, 2003, with the express charge of redistricting the thirty-two congressional districts. The session was unsuccessful due to an unusual rule in the Texas state Senate. In effect, to get a bill to the floor of the senate requires a two-thirds vote. The senate was split nineteen to twelve in favor of the GOP, so, if the Democrats could keep at least eleven of their own in the fold, they could prevent any redistricting bill from getting to a floor vote. This worked for the first special session.

The governor then called a second special session. Now it was time for the senate Democrats to hit the road. Taking a cue from their colleagues in the state House, eleven of the twelve senate Democrats took off for

Albuquerque (perhaps a step up from Ardmore in terms of creature comforts). So much for the second special session.

The legislative game, which had been entertaining not only Texans but also the nation (the peripatetic Democrats were the source of numerous one-liners on the late-night television shows), finally ended with a third special session. The lieutenant governor, who presides over the state Senate, tossed the two-thirds rule, and one of the Democrat senators defected. The legislators stayed in Austin. The result was a congressional redistricting bill designed to give the GOP at least twenty-two of the thirty-two seats.

The bill was pre-cleared by the Department of Justice and narrowly (two to one) withstood a challenge before the three-judge panel in the fall of 2003.[1] The 2004 congressional elections were held under the new plan and although the Republicans did not defeat all of the targeted Democrats, they won twenty-one of the thirty-two congressional seats.[2]

THE POLITICS OF RACE

In his classic study, Key suggested race played less of a role in Texas politics than in many other southern states. Instead, Key saw Texas politics as dividing along class lines that closely tracked political ideology (Key 1949, 261). No one familiar with Texas politics, however, would suggest that race and ethnicity are neutral factors in the state's political chemistry.

Paralleling the emergence of the Republican Party in Texas, increased African American and Mexican American political influence largely is a development of the past twenty-five years. This increased influence in large part is a function of two factors: population patterns and the impact of the Voting Rights Act.

Although the percentage of African Americans who make up the overall Texas population has been decreasing for two decades—it now stands at 11.5 percent—the concentration of this population in urban centers enhances its political influence. Over eight out of ten African Americans in Texas live in metropolitan areas; blacks make up at least 25 percent of the population in several of Texas's larger cities, a figure that translates into political power at election time.

The Mexican American population has been growing steadily, and the percentage of the overall Texas population that is Latino (almost all of which is of Mexican origin) likewise has increased accordingly. Mexican

Americans currently constitute 32 percent of the state's population and are by far the largest minority group in Texas.

The increasing urbanization of the black population and the increasing numbers of the Mexican American population have coincided with the utilization of the Voting Rights Act to increase the political power, and representation, of these minority groups. First, the VRA served to register thousands of eligible minority citizens. Then, beginning in the mid-1970s and accelerating through the 1980s, the VRA was used to successfully challenge the at-large voting structures of dozens of city councils and school boards, and the district boundaries of state legislative districts, state senate districts and congressional districts.

The results of these legal challenges were the creation of hundreds of electoral districts designed to enhance minority voting power. A quick glance at the data shows how successful these efforts were. In 1970 there were 29 African Americans serving in elective office in Texas; by 1993 this figure had increased to 472. In 1974 there were 540 Latino elected officials in Texas; twenty years later, there were 2,215.

The electoral success of the racial and ethnic minority candidates has been primarily at the local levels. This is significant, first because these offices have a direct impact on the population, and second, these offices are training grounds for movement to higher offices. In a very real sense, the VRA has produced an invisible revolution at the municipal and school board levels that almost certainly will begin to be manifested at higher offices of the state government in the near future.[3]

As mentioned earlier, partisan commitment in Texas takes a racial and

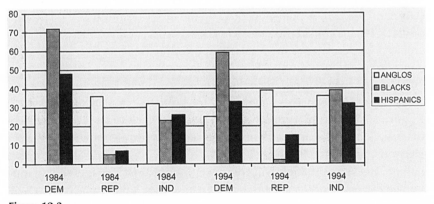

Figure 12.3.

ethnic cast (see figure 12.3). Anglos in Texas have steadily become more Republican over the last two decades. Although most African Americans and Hispanics continue to affiliate with the Democrats, there has been some notable slippage in support. While most of this change has led to a rise in minorities preferring to be called "independents," identification with the GOP has increased some, especially among Hispanics. For example, in 1984 only about 7 percent of Hispanics identified with the GOP (Texas Poll Archives). By 2000, that figure had increased more than three-fold, to 23.5 percent (William C. Velasquez Institute 2000, 5).

Actual voting behavior also reflects these racial and ethnic patterns. In recent elections, Anglos have mostly supported Republican candidates in Texas. Meanwhile African Americans have remained a core component of the Democratic electoral base, usually with 90 percent of this group selecting Democratic candidates (Shannon 2004). Although Hispanics have traditionally cast their ballots for Democratic office seekers, Republican in-roads are discernible. In 2000, for example, George Bush gained nearly one-third of the Hispanic vote in his initial election to the presidency and incumbent Republican U.S. Senator Kay Bailey Hutchison garnered 46 percent of this vote in her reelection (William C. Velasquez Institute 2000, 4). In the 2004 presidential race, George Bush did well in predominately Hispanic South Texas countries, carrying Cameron County and averaging 41 percent in the counties that sit on the Mexican border (Russell 2005, 80).

Moreover, there are signs that a strong streak of conservatism runs through minority populations in Texas. Hispanics are more likely to side with conservatives than liberals on a variety of issues including immigration, welfare, and family responsibility for the actions of their children (Herrick 1996, 23). A poll sponsored by the NAACP found that 40 percent of Black Texans consider themselves conservatives; only 22 percent are liberal and 26 percent are moderates (reported in Tuell 1995, 23). This presents a good opportunity for Republicans.

However, the long-range picture suggests a ray of hope for the Democrats. The Hispanic vote, enhanced by both the impact of the Voting Rights Act and the maturation of the very young Mexican-American population, is expected to increasingly become the pivotal vote in the state's elections. Sometime between 2009 and 2026, demographers estimate that half of Texas's population will comprise "minorities." Most of this change will be the result of the growth of the Latino population (which alone will constitute 38 percent of the state's population by the year 2026). If the

Democrats continue to hold 60 percent plus of that vote and retain their 90 percent preference rating among African Americans, they may be in a position to return to their glory days.

The 2002 state elections may have been a preview of coming attractions. The Democrats hoped for an electoral pot of gold at the end of their "rainbow" ticket. They nominated a Mexican American for governor, an African American for U.S. Senator (a first for both offices) and an Anglo for lieutenant governor. None won, but the Democrats hoped they had cemented their claim to the minority vote in such a way as to pay special dividends down the road.

Both parties must recognize the turnout patterns for ethnic and racial groups in Texas. As indicated in table 12.1, Anglos still constitute most of the pool of voters in Texas. Although Anglos make up a bare majority of the state's population, they are overrepresented among the eligible (62.6 percent), the registered (66.1 percent) and, more to the point, the actual voters (67.9 percent). About 58 percent of Anglos voted in the 2000 presidential contest. African Americans constitute 11.5 percent of the state's population. This proportion is reflected in the number of Texans eligible to vote (10.5 percent), registered (10.7 percent), and voting (11.4 percent) who are African Americans. At 58 percent, the turnout rate of blacks in 2000 equaled that of Anglos.

Although nearly one-third of Texans is Hispanic, only 24.5 percent of the state's eligible voters, 21 percent of its registered voters, and 18.6 percent of its actual voters is Hispanic. Turnout is low. Indeed, in the 2000 presidential race a mere 29 percent of eligible Hispanic voters cast a ballot.

The figures of table 12.1, however, fail to disclose fully the changes that are occurring among Texas voters. The decline in the number of Anglos

Table 12.1. Voting Participation and Ethnicity 2000

Ethnic/Racial Background	Percent of Total Population	Percent Eligible Voters	Percent of Registered Voters	Percent of Actual Voters	Percent Voted
Non-Hispanic White (Anglos)	52.4	62.6	66.1	67.9	57.9
Hispanic	32.0	24.5	21.3	18.6	57.8
African American	11.5	10.5	10.7	11.4	29.5

Sources: Texas Quick Facts, U.S. Census Bureau, and William C. Velasquez Institute (www.wcvi.org)

in Texas recorded over the last decade is mirrored in the decrease of non-Hispanic whites as a portion of the state's eligible, registered, and actual voters. In the early 1990s, for instance, Anglos made up three-fourths of the state's voters; by 2000, that figured had dropped to 68 percent. Over this same period, Hispanics have not only gained as a percentage of Texas's population (from 28 to 32 percent), but also as a percentage of its eligible voters (from 20 to 24.5 percent), its registered voters (from 15 to 21 percent) and its actual voters (from 12 to 18.6 percent). The destiny of political parties in Texas may very well be determined by the way these population and electorate dynamics play out—a point that is fully appreciated by candidates and strategists plotting their future in Texas politics.

CONCLUSION

As Texas moves into the twenty-first century, two parallel political tracks are visible. One is the partisan track, where the Republican Party continues not only to dominate statewide elections, but has cemented its hold on the state through the 2001 and 2003 redistricting processes. Texas arguably has been a one-party GOP state in presidential elections for a generation, and Republicans have won four of the last six gubernatorial elections. Republicans have swept every statewide office in the last four election cycles. Forget Dixie: As far as Texas partisan politics are concerned, old times there have been forgotten.

The second track marks the increasing influence of the minority population in the state, particularly the Mexican-American population. Whereas the first track, the partisan track, favors the Republicans, the second track offers the Democrats virtually their only chance to become competitive in statewide elections.

Demography is destiny. It is only a matter of time, and not very much time at that, until the sociological minority populations are a numerical majority, and these numbers, combined with increased educational and occupational gains, eventually will translate into political power. Both parties know this. Democrats design their strategies to keep the minority voters in the Democrat camp. Republicans increasingly reach out to the Mexican-American vote, recognizing that failure to make inroads into the Democratic lock on the Latino vote will cede the future to the Dems.

The partisan track and the minority track may not be parallel for long.

A clash seems inevitable, and this conflict may inform Texas politics for the next generation.

REFERENCES

Brown, Lyle C., and Jerry Wilkens. 2004. "Redistricting and Electoral Results in Texas in the Twenty-First Century." In *Practicing Texas Politics*, by Lyle C. Brown, Joyce A. Langenegger, Sonia R. Garcia, and Ted Lewis. Boston: Houghton-Mifflin.

Burka, Paul. 1986. "Primary Lesson." *Texas Monthly*, July.

Champagne, Anthony, and Rick Collis. 1984. "Texas." In *The Political Life of the American States*. Edited by Alan Rosenthal and Maureen Moakley. New York: Praeger.

Davidson, Chandler. 1990. *Race and Class in Texas Politics* Princeton, NJ: Princeton University Press.

Dye, Thomas, L. Tucker Gibson Jr., and Clay Robison. 1997. *Politics in America: Texas Edition*. Upper Saddle River, NJ: Prentice-Hall.

Dyer, James, and Don Haynes. 1987. *Social, Economic, and Political Change According to the Texas Poll*. Austin, TX: College of Communication, University of Texas at Austin.

Dyer, James A., Jan E. Leighley, and Arnold Vedlitz. 1997. "Party Identification and Public Opinion in Texas, 1984–1994." In Texas *Politics: A Reader*, edited by Anthony Champagne and Edward J. Harpham. New York: W.W. Norton.

Dyer, James A., Arnold Vedlitz, and David B. Hill. 1988. "New Voters, Switchers, and Political Party Realignment in Texas." *Western Political Quarterly* 41 (March): 164.

Gibson, L. Tucker Jr., and Clay Robison. 1995. *Government and Politics in Texas*. Englewood Cliffs, NJ: Prentice-Hall.

Herrick, Thaddeus. 1996. "Poll Shows Hispanics Conservative." *Houston Chronicle*. February 22.

Key, V. O., Jr. 1949. *Southern Politics in State and Nation*. New York: Vintage.

Lamare, James W., J. L. Polinard, and Robert Wrinkle. 2003. "Texas Religion and Politics in God's Country." In *Marching toward the Millennium: the Christian Right in the States*, edited by John C. Green, Mark J. Rozell, and Clyde Wilcox. Washington DC: Georgetown University Press.

Office of the Secretary of State. 1982. *May Primary Election Analysis*. Austin, TX: Office of the Secretary of State, table 3.

Polinard, J. L., Robert D. Wrinkle, Norman Binder and Thomas Longoria. 1994. *Electoral Structure and Urban Policy*. New York: St. Martins Press.

Robison, Clay. 2004. "Reagan Changed Texas." *Houston Chronicle*. June 13.

Russell, Jan Jarboe. 2005. "Grand Opportunity Party." *Texas Monthly*. March.

Shannon, Kelly. 2004. "Republican Shift Means Changing Definition of Texas Democrat." Associated Press Wire. February 27.

Texas Poll Archives. Scripps Howard Research Center. Abilene, Texas.

Tuell, Sherry Carter. 1995. "Racial Bias Reported in Loans, Jobs' NACCP Poll Hits Texas Problems." *Houston Chronicle*. February 2.

William C. Velasquez Institute. 2000. "2000 Texas Exit Poll of Latino Voters." Los Angeles: William C. Velasquez Institute.

NOTES

Title: With apologies to George Lucas

1. One of the co-authors of this chapter was an expert witness for the plaintiffs in the redistricting case (*Jackson v. Perry*).

2. This is a gift that keeps on giving: The U.S. Supreme Court ordered the three-judge federal court to reconsider its earlier ruling in light of the high court's recent decisions on partisan gerrymandering. In the spring of 2005, the three-judge panel, as expected, declined to alter its earlier decision. For a more detailed analysis of the redistricting, see Brown and Wilkens 2004.

3. For a more detailed analysis of the impact of the VRA, see Polinard et al., *Electoral Structure and Urban Politics: the Effect of the Voting Rights Act on Mexican American Communities*. St. Martins Press: 1994.

13

The Soul of the South: Religion and Southern Politics in the Twenty-first Century

Lyman A. Kellstedt
James L. Guth
John C. Green
Corwin E. Smidt

I n the past half-century, the South has undergone a major transformation, moving from a one-party Democratic bastion toward a solidly
Republican region. Many factors have contributed to this change: the
effects of race, the consequences of economic development and migration,
the nationalization of "moral" issues, and the impact of religion. Religious influences have received considerable attention in the past decade
because of the activities—and foibles—of the Christian Right. However,
the impact of religion extends beyond conservative Protestants and is
closely related to other political transitions in the region. Indeed, the sea
change in the links between religion and politics is critical to the new electoral order that characterizes southern politics in the second term of
George W. Bush. Simply put, the soul of the South is being reincorporated
into the politics of the nation, and the 2004 election is an example of that
trend.

Here we review the political behavior of major religious groups in the

South using survey data, tracing continuity and change from the 1960s to the 2004 election. We find that traditional Protestantism is still an important feature of southern elections, but it operates in a new context. On the one hand, the "white Protestant alliance" that undergirded the Democratic Party of the "solid South" has been reassembled in the Republican Party. And on the other hand, increased religious diversity has helped extend into the South the "coalition of minorities" that has long supported northern Democrats. There are important national consequences to this new electoral order: It allowed both Bill Clinton and George W. Bush to win the White House.

ELECTORAL ORDER AND
SOUTHERN RELIGION

Byron Shafer's (1991:43–45) concept of an "electoral order" is a useful way to discuss the role of religion in southern politics. An electoral order is a stable political relationship between the "social base," "intermediary organizations," and "government institutions." The "social base" is determined by the politically relevant demographic differences among voters, such as race, class or religion; "intermediary organizations" include the formal mobilizers and representatives of such voters, principally political parties, but also informal mobilizers, such as union or church leaders; and "government institutions" are constituted by officials elected by the social base, as mediated by these institutions, such as the President and members of Congress. So, at any one point in time, the electoral order is defined by the support of key social groups for the major parties and their candidates for public office. And changes in social group support can ultimately produce a new order.

According to Shafer (1991:43), religion is one of the fundamental social bases for the electoral order in the United States, and one that is especially important in the South. Indeed, religion was, and still is, central to the region's distinctive culture and politics (Hill 1983). Scholars have noted that the "religious solid South preceded the political solid South" (Weaver 1968:98) and that "the first will apparently outlast the latter" (Reed 1972:57). Thus, it is surprising that students of southern politics have largely neglected religion. For example, Black and Black's two-volume treatise on southern politics (1987, 1992) barely mentions the topic, and John Petrocik's (1987) study of party coalitions in the South ignores it altogether. Of course, V. O. Key's masterful work (1949) was hardly better; its neglect of religion has been replicated in the genre it inspired (e.g., Havard 1972; Lamis 1984). While there are some important exceptions (Baker et al. 1983; Kellstedt 1990; Smidt 1983, 1989; Rozell and Wilcox 1996), religion has yet to become a standard feature in the analysis of southern politics.

The reasons for this neglect are not hard to find. Much of the best work on southern politics has focused on economic questions (Black and Black 1987) and on the critical issue of race (Carmines and Stimson 1989). Just as important, southern religion can be difficult to understand, being both unusually homogeneous and remarkably diverse. First, the South has been dominated by white Protestants; the concentration of pious "Baptists and Methodists" presents a sharp contrast to the religious diversity in the rest of the country (Hill 1966: 31–39). Thus many scholars have assumed that religion did not vary much within the South. But in another sense, southern Protestants are hardly monolithic, exhibiting numerous differences in belief and practice (Harrell 1991): Baptists differ from Methodists, white from black Protestants, and believers from backsliders. And the growth in the southern Catholic population only complicates the matter. This complexity has led many scholars to ignore southern religion on practical grounds.

Recent research on religion offers some conceptual tools with which to simplify this complexity. The first and most basic analytic concept is "religious tradition," constituted by religious communities that share a distinctive worldview. Religious tradition is best measured by grouping those who affiliate with similar denominations, movements, and congregations (Kellstedt et al. 1996a). Scholars typically recognize four major religious traditions in the United States: evangelical, mainline and black Protestants, and Roman Catholics. A fifth group, the non-religious, or secular, population, is analogous to a religious tradition in many respects. The first three traditions have been particularly important in the South, and the last two are increasingly so.

The distinction between historically white evangelical and mainline Protestants is important but often subtle. Evangelicals are more orthodox in belief and practice, stressing "otherworldly" concerns, while mainliners are more modernist in belief and practice, putting greater emphasis on "this worldly" matters (Kellstedt et al. 1996b). By this definition, most white Baptists in the South are evangelicals and most white southern

Methodists are mainliners. Indeed, the two largest American Protestant denominations, the Southern Baptist Convention and the United Methodist Church, dominate the national evangelical and mainline traditions, respectively, and are especially numerous in the South. Another critical distinction is between white and black Protestants. Shaped by centuries of slavery and segregation, black Protestant churches constitute a separate religious tradition (Sernett 1991). Although black Baptists and Methodists share many beliefs and practices with their white counterparts, their religious and political worldviews are quite different. Similar distinctions can be made between the various Protestant traditions and non-Protestants, such as Catholics and seculars.

Another concept useful in making sense of religious complexity is "religious commitment," the extent of an individual's attachment to his or her religion. Religious commitment can be measured in many ways, ranging from the frequency of church attendance to involvement in private devotionalism, but all such indicators help differentiate individuals who take their faith seriously from those with merely nominal attachments (Kellstedt et al. 1996a). Simply put, those with higher levels of commitment are most likely to partake of the distinctive worldview of their religious tradition. Southerners are known for their high religious commitment (Reed 1972), but that commitment is hardly uniform (Stark and Bainbridge 1985).

In combination, these two concepts allow us to identify seven groups that include almost all southern adults: high- and low-commitment white evangelical Protestants, high- and low-commitment white mainline Protestants, black Protestants, Catholics, and seculars (see table 13.1). Given their small numbers in survey data, southern black Protestants and Catholics cannot be reliably divided by levels of religious commitment. Not surprisingly, religious commitment is low among seculars.[1] Although the influence of other demographic factors, such as income and gender, are beyond the scope of this essay, statistical controls for such factors do not substantially change the findings reported (Kellstedt et al. 1996a).

These seven religious groups are related to "southern distinctiveness" in various ways. First, high-commitment evangelicals represent the core of traditional southern Protestantism, with the other three white Protestant groups representing varying departures from it both in belief and practice. Second, the three remaining groups were excluded from traditional southern Protestantism: black Protestants because of the "color line," Catholics and seculars because of what might be called the "papal line" and "theistic line," respectively.

These religious groups were connected to the electoral order in the era of the "solid South." All four white Protestant groups were allied with the Democratic Party. The strength of this alliance produced a powerful faction in the "coalition of minorities" that the Democratic Party assembled nationally, helping elect Democratic presidents and majorities in Congress, from Grover Cleveland to Bill Clinton. High-commitment evangelicals were the core of this "white Protestant alliance," remaining loyal even in the face of regional rebellions, such as the States' Rights agitation in 1948. Indeed, low-commitment white Protestants were most likely to defect to "third party" candidates, whether in the past or more recently (Gilbert et al. 1995; Green 1997).

Mainline Protestants were also less firmly anchored to "Southern Democracy" and most prone to defect to the Republicans, the party of their co-religionists outside the region (as in 1956). Black Protestant, Catholic, and secular voters were largely excluded from this coalition; in response, they sometimes allied themselves with "northern" Democrats in intraparty battles, and sometimes defected to the GOP in general elections. All three groups, however, made up only a small fraction of the southern electorate. Our task is to assess how these patterns have persisted or changed in the last generation, with special attention to the 2004 election.

THE RELIGIOUS COMPOSITION OF THE SOUTH

A good place to begin is with the relative size of the seven religious groups from the 1960s to the present (table 13.1). After all, a social group's size sets the upper bounds on its contribution to the electoral order. One source of continuity is evangelical Protestants, who together accounted for roughly two-fifths of the southern electorate over the period. However, there was a significant shift among evangelicals during the 1990s, with the high-commitment group increasing to one-quarter of the electorate, while their less committed co-religionists fell to less than one-sixth. This shift persisted into the twenty-first century. Mainline white Protestants experienced a relative decline over the period, reflecting national trends, stabilizing at about one-sixth of the southern population after 1990. Thus by 2004 white Protestants had contracted from almost three-

Table 13.1.   Relative Size of Southern Religious Groups 1960s–2004 (in percent)

Protestants	1960s	1970s	1980s	1990s*	2004
Evangelical					
High commitment	18	18	18	25	28
Low commitment	27	26	24	14	8
Mainline					
High commitment	13	7	7	8	10
Low commitment	15	15	10	7	6
Black	15	18	18	18	14
Catholic	6	11	13	13	16
Secular	5	6	7	13	14
Others	2	3	3	3	5

Source: National Elections Studies 1960-1988; National Surveys of Religion and Politics 1992–2004

* Includes 2000

quarters of the southern electorate to just over one-half. But the core of the "white Protestant alliance," high-commitment evangelicals, had actually expanded in relative terms even as the alliance shrank at the periphery. Note also that high-commitment mainline Protestants also increased as a part of that tradition, even as the overall proportion of mainliners in the electorate declined.

The other side of this trend was a steady increase in religious diversity. Prior to the Voting Rights Act of 1965, black Protestants constituted only a tiny part of the electorate, but by 2004 they almost matched the mainline Protestant numbers. Catholics and seculars grew at a faster rate, more than doubling between the 1960s and 2004. Indeed, at present these last two groups together slightly outnumber high-commitment evangelicals on the one hand and greatly exceed all mainline Protestants on the other.

No doubt these changes reflect southern economic development and in-migration, trends which had historically eroded the position of Protestantism at the national level, especially the mainline variety. So, groups once excluded from traditional southern religion expanded as the "white Protestant alliance" changed and contracted. In addition, economic growth and in-migration may have intensified the religious commitment of some white Protestants, contributing to the relative increase in the ranks of high-commitment evangelicals. As we shall see, these changes in the religious composition of the southern electorate are associated with transformations in the electoral order.

RELIGION AND POLITICAL BEHAVIOR

What political changes have occurred among these religious groups? Table 13.2 examines three common measures of political behavior over time: vote choice in presidential and House elections and party identification. To make over-time comparisons easier, the first two measures are restricted to the major party vote and for party identification, partisan leaners are combined with strong and weak partisans, while pure independents are omitted from the table. Each measure reveals very similar patterns, with the presidential vote the most volatile and party identification the least.

By the 1960s, high-commitment evangelicals were already moving away from "Southern Democracy." Partly in reaction to John Kennedy's Catholicism in 1960, but also in response to the 1964 Goldwater and 1968 Nixon campaigns, almost three-fifths cast GOP presidential ballots during this decade. The usual Republican vote expanded to more than two-thirds in the 1970s, remained at this level through the 1980s and 1990s and reached an apex in 2000 and 2004 at approximately four-fifths of the vote. Meanwhile, Democratic support fell to one-fifth of the two-party vote by 2000 and remained at that level in 2004.

A slower but no less dramatic shift occurred in House vote and party identification. Up through the 1980s, high-commitment evangelicals voted overwhelmingly for Democratic congressional candidates and on balance identified with the Democratic Party. In the 1990s, however, they began to vote for GOP congressional candidates and identify with the Grand Old Party. The 2004 election marks the high point of this trend.

The other white Protestant groups show similar patterns. Low-commitment evangelicals voted solidly Democratic for president in the 1960s, and then switched to the GOP in the next decades, but at a lower rate than their high-commitment co-religionists. Partisanship followed the same pattern, albeit at a slower pace, as did House vote (except in 2000, when low-commitment evangelicals split evenly between the parties, before returning to 1992–1996 levels in 2004). Mainline Protestants displayed a variation on this theme. High- and low-commitment mainliners both started the period voting for Republican presidential candidates, a trend that expanded in the 1970s and 1980s, and then stalled a bit in the 1990s, 2000, and 2004. In House voting and partisanship, both mainline groups also moved toward the Republicans. Here the high-commitment

Table 13.2.   Southern Religion and Political Behavior 1960s–1990s

	Presidential Vote (%)											
	1960s		1970s		1980s		1990s		2000		2004	
Protestants	Dem	GOP	Dem	GOP	Dem	GOP	Dem	GOP	Dem	GOP	Dem	GOP
Evangelical												
High comm.	42	58	33	67	31	70	31	69	20	80	21	79
Low comm.	65	35	36	64	39	61	43	57	33	67	36	64
Mainline												
High comm.	45	55	27	73	33	67	35	65	38	62	40	60
Low comm.	41	54	35	65	35	65	44	54	43	57	37	63
Black	91	9	88	12	89	8	86	14	95	5	95	5
Catholic	57	30	40	59	45	55	60	40	52	48	41	59
Secular	58	42	43	57	32	68	45	55	55	45	61	39

	House Vote (%)											
	1960s		1970s		1980s		1990s		2000		2004	
Protestants	Dem	GOP	Dem	GOP	Dem	GOP	Dem	GOP	Dem	GOP	Dem	GOP
Evangelical												
High comm.	74	26	70	30	62	38	36	64	25	75	24	76
Low comm.	81	19	71	29	64	36	40	60	50	50	41	59
Mainline												
High comm.	61	39	61	39	58	42	42	58	42	58	44	56
Low comm.	60	40	61	39	56	44	37	63	38	62	40	60
Black	92	8	93	7	92	8	86	14	82	18	91	9
Catholic	75	26	78	22	64	36	54	46	43	57	50	50
Secular	80	20	65	35	60	40	54	46	68	32	52	48

	Party Identification (%)											
	1960s		1970s		1980s		1990s		2000		2004	
Protestants	Dem	GOP	Dem	GOP	Dem	GOP	Dem	GOP	Dem	GOP	Dem	GOP
Evangelical												
High comm.	71	20	58	30	53	36	32	52	27	63	24	63
Low comm.	71	18	55	26	52	33	40	45	39	52	31	50
Mainline												
High comm.	57	32	48	43	40	51	36	49	41	53	38	46
Low comm.	52	38	49	36	45	44	39	46	30	41	29	55
Black	83	10	80	9	83	10	80	12	93	3	75	3
Catholic	66	20	67	19	54	31	49	39	45	41	43	37
Secular	62	23	55	26	50	35	35	40	52	27	34	29

Source: National Elections Studies 1960–1988; National Surveys of Religion and Politics 1992–2004

group was generally more Republican but not as consistently as were high-commitment evangelicals.

Black Protestants were dramatically different. Over the entire period, they were solidly Democratic at the ballot box and in partisanship. Modest Republican gains in the 1970s, 1980s, and 1990s were erased in the 2000 and 2004 presidential and congressional votes and in partisan affiliation. Although Republicans made inroads among black Protestants in the 2000 congressional vote, this trend was erased in 2004.

Southern Catholics and seculars exhibited more variation. Both were squarely in the Democratic camp in the 1960s, but then voted for GOP presidential candidates in the 1970s and 1980s. Catholics returned to the Democratic column in the 1990s and 2000 but voted strongly for Bush in 2004. However, their Democratic House vote and partisanship declined steadily, so that by 2000 a majority cast ballots for GOP congressional candidates and Catholics reached near parity in party affiliation. Their House vote was split evenly in 2004, while their partisanship revealed a bit of a Democratic bias.

In partial contrast, southern seculars, after voting Democratic for president in the 1960s, supported Republican candidates in the 1970s through the 1990s, but returned to the Democratic fold in the present decade, particularly so in 2004. In House elections seculars remained Democratic over the entire period, increasing their support for congressional Democrats in 2000, but falling back slightly in 2004. The partisan ties of seculars were strongly Democratic throughout the period except for the 1990s, but then returned to Democratic identifications in 2000 and 2004, albeit at a somewhat diminished level in the latter year.

Religious commitment had an independent effect on turnout (Kellstedt et al. 1996a): In each period and for all religious traditions, high commitment was associated with higher levels of voting. Although turnout declined across the board from the 1960s to the 1990s, the downturn was smallest among the high-commitment groups (including high-commitment black Protestants and Catholics). Reflecting their high socio-economic status, mainline Protestants had the strongest turnout, while black Protestants and seculars had the weakest, with evangelicals and Catholics in between. The same pattern appeared in both 2000 and 2004 when turnout increased. Overall, turnout rates in the South trailed the rest of the nation by four percentage points in 2004, and would be reduced by another point if Florida is removed from the regional total (turnout data not shown).

Thus, the transformation of the electoral order in the South had twin religious engines: political change among white Protestants and growing religious diversity. On the first count, high-commitment evangelicals conducted a steady march into the very center of the Republican camp and other white Protestants arrived in the same neighborhood by more circuitous paths. Meanwhile, black Protestants remained solidly Democratic, and although seculars showed some variation, they were also on balance Democratic. The small but growing southern Catholic population bears watching. Their partisanship and House voting remain less Republican than the white Protestant groups, but their vote for Bush in 2004 was close to 60 percent.

RELIGION AND CHANGES IN THE ELECTORAL ORDER

We can illustrate the combined impact of religious influences on the electoral order by looking at major party vote totals at the beginning and end of the period. Accordingly, table 13.3 reports the relative contribution of each religious group to the Democratic and Republican presidential vote coalitions in the 1960s and in 2004. Very similar results were obtained for House vote coalitions and party identification (data not shown). The patterns in table 13.3 starkly reveal the emerging electoral order, with each

Table 13.3. Religion and the Electoral Order Presidential Vote Coalitions

Protestants	1960s Dem	GOP	2004 Dem	GOP	Change Dem	GOP
Evangelical						
High comm.	16	25	16	46	0	+21
Low comm.	24	22	6	8	−18	−14
Mainline						
High comm.	14	18	13	15	−1	−3
Low comm.	11	20	5	6	−6	−14
Black	19	4	27	1	+8	−3
Catholic	8	5	14	15	+6	+10
Secular	6	5	11	6	+5	+1
Others	2	1	9	4	+7	+3
	100	100	101	101		

Source: National Election Studies 1960-1988; National Surveys of Religion and Politics 1992–2004

party's coalition developing a different core religious constituency (Green 2002).

Not surprisingly, the new core of the Republican coalition is the high-commitment evangelical group, reflecting an ironic version of "southern distinctiveness." This group rose from one-quarter of the GOP vote in the 1960s to almost one-half in 2004, a gain of twenty-one percentage points. This gain is due in part to the growth in numbers but also to change in partisan preference and the turnout advantage enjoyed by high-commitment groups. All other Protestants, but especially those with low commitment, declined as a proportion of the GOP vote. Given the increasing GOP tendencies of each group, much of this change results from their reduced size and from turnout differential. Thanks to the GOP surge of high-commitment evangelicals in 2004, white Protestants as a whole provided more than three-quarters of the Republican votes.

The Republicans also made modest gains among Catholics, with their contribution doubling over the time period, but still accounting for only one-seventh of the southern GOP presidential vote. These figures are attributable to both population growth and political change. The GOP lost ground among black Protestants, while holding their own among seculars. "Other" religious groups, mainly Hispanics, also contributed more to the GOP vote in 2004 than in the 1960s, reflecting primarily population growth.

The new core of the Democratic coalition is black Protestants—another ironic version of "southern distinctiveness." In the 1960s, this group accounted for about one-fifth of the Democratic vote, and by 2004, more than one-quarter. This change not only reflects population increases among African Americans but also their enfranchisement since the 1960s. No doubt their electoral impact is reduced by low turnout, especially in 2004, when most of the South was not competitive in the presidential race.

These dramatic gains among black Protestants helped the Democrats replace equally dramatic losses among white Protestants, especially among low-commitment evangelicals and mainliners. Overall, white Protestants fell from almost two-thirds to two-fifths of the Democratic vote over the period. These differences resulted from both population and political change and probably turnout differentials as well. However, it is worth noting that the white Protestants are still critical to the Democratic coalition. Democrats also made modest gains among Catholics and seculars.[2]

RELIGION AND THE NEW ELECTORAL ORDER

Thus, by 2004 the southern electoral order had two new religious centers of gravity: high-commitment evangelicals for the GOP and black Protestants for the Democrats. The major parties divided up the other religious groups in a fashion that contributed to two-party competition and reinforced other changes in southern politics (Kellstedt et al. 1996a). On the one hand, the remaining "southern distinctiveness" increasingly helped the GOP, as traditional southern Protestants became a Republican constituency. On the other, the South has become less "distinctive" to the benefit of the Democrats, as black Protestants, seculars, and other religious groups (Jews, Hispanics) allowed the national Democratic coalition of minorities to extend into Dixie. And although Catholics initially provided a boost for the Democrats, in recent years white Catholics have moved toward the GOP in the South, as in the rest of the nation. These coalition patterns developed throughout the 1990s, achieving the greatest clarity in 2004.

Table 13.4 takes a closer look at the voting behavior of our religious groups since 1990, illustrating these trends in more detail (see Green et al. 1996: chapters 14, 15). The table displays the two-party congressional and presidential vote in chronological order from 1990 to 2004. First, note the steady Republican gains among high-commitment evangelicals, shifting from majority support for Democratic House candidates in 1990 to overwhelming backing of Republicans in 1992 and thereafter. Similarly

Table 13.4.   Religion and Southern Political Behavior: Republican Vote since 1990 (in percentages)

Protestants	1990 Cong	1992 Cong	1992 Pres	1994 Cong	1996 Cong	1996 Pres	1998 Cong	2000 Cong	2000 Pres	2002 Cong	2004 Cong	2004 Pres
Evangelical												
High comm	46	53	62	69	76	76	67	75	80	67	76	79
Low comm	53	52	58	57	69	55	50	50	67	69	59	64
Mainline												
High comm	54	56	68	56	60	62	49	58	62	55	56	60
Low comm	60	60	54	61	66	58	54	62	57	56	60	63
Black	6	7	10	10	9	10	7	18	5	10	9	5
Catholic	44	50	43	43	43	38	50	57	48	44	50	60
Secular	49	54	55	37	37	55	53	32	45	44	48	39

Source: National Surveys of Religion and Politics 1992–2004; National Election Studies, 1990–2002

strong support appears for the GOP presidential tickets, continuing a pattern established in the 1980s. That support peaks in 2000, leveling off thereafter at three-quarters to four-fifths of the group's vote.

These bearers of traditional southern Protestantism were crucial to recent Republican gains in Congress, especially in the decade-long domination of the House of Representatives. Indeed, the importance of the southern evangelical vote is symbolized by the major role played by evangelicals—southern and non-southern—in the House leadership during this period. High-commitment evangelicals also provided a "fire wall" in the Republican presidential defeats in 1992 and 1996. They were central to George W. Bush's capture of the White House in 2000 and his reelection in 2004. Social issues were of particular interest to this theologically conservative group (Kellstedt et al. 1996a), and no doubt the church-based mobilization by Christian Right groups and the Republican Party contributed to their solidification as a strong Republican constituency (Green et al. 1997). Note, however, the slight drop in GOP support among high-commitment evangelicals in off-year House elections since 1996. Despite the Lewinsky scandal and President Clinton's impending impeachment, Democratic congressional candidates fared better in the South in 1998, even among the strongly committed evangelicals, whose support for GOP candidates dropped again in 2002, suggesting that this pattern may be a function of off-year elections.

The other white Protestant groups show patterns similar to the high-commitment evangelicals, but their support for the GOP was often weaker and their path through the 1990s less even. For instance, low-commitment evangelicals often voted less Republican than the high-commitment group, especially in the 1996 presidential election, where their 55 percent for Dole was hardly bigger than their 53 percent for Republican congressional candidates in 1990. Yet their vote for GOP candidates in 2002 slightly exceeded that of their more committed evangelical brethren. The mainline groups tend to be in the Republican camp but give GOP candidates much less support than high-commitment evangelicals do. Note, however, that there is little difference in voting patterns of the two mainline groups.

Mainline Protestants are less influenced by the Christian Right and are attracted to the Republican standard largely for economic reasons—a position consistent, by the way, with the "Protestant ethic" of personal achievement and "free enterprise" (Kellstedt et al. 1996a). Of course, this kind of individualism often conflicts with the moralism of the "old-time religion." This division between "moralists" and "enterprisers" appeared among northern Protestants in the 1920s and has finally emerged in the South. In any event, Republicans have benefited from both groups among southern Protestants, and the challenge is to maintain, strengthen, and refine this new version of the "white Protestant alliance." George W. Bush successfully practiced this kind of politics in 2000 and 2004.

In contrast to whites, black Protestants have remained solidly in the Democratic camp throughout the past fifteen years. Indeed, without this strong backing Democrats would not have remained competitive in the South. Of course, the original source of this support—the struggle for civil rights—was crucial to the erosion of the Democratic allegiance of white Protestants. Certainly the construction of a biracial Democratic coalition was made easier by the exit of many traditionalist whites to the GOP. This expanded black constituency also depends heavily on church-based mobilization, much like high-commitment evangelicals among Republicans (Lincoln and Mamiya 1990). Indeed, "southern Democracy" is now unthinkable without black churches and parachurch groups—an irony of historic proportions.

The growing Catholic and secular populations in the South have also helped the Democrats, but their support is less monolithic and has developed more erratically. Southern Catholics flirted with the Republicans in 1992, but then reverted to their Democratic proclivities, especially in 1996. But in 2004, they voted overwhelmingly for Bush. Southern seculars were even less predictable, backing Bush in 1992 and Dole in 1996, but not the Gingrich-led Republican congressional candidates in 1994 and 1996. Beginning in 2000, however, seculars have given solid voting support to Democrats with issues like abortion and gay marriage being prominent factors. When less "traditional" Catholics and seculars are combined with large minorities of white Protestants and a solid contingent of black Protestants, the Democrats can compete in some parts of the South, as Bill Clinton and Al Gore showed in 1992, 1996, and 2000. Such a "coalition of minorities" is, of course, the stuff of Democratic politics at the national level. Here, too, "northern" politics has invaded the once "solid South."

What about the impact of minor parties on religious voters in the South? With the exception of native sons Strom Thurmond in 1948 and George Wallace in 1968, minor parties have had only a modest impact on the southern vote this century (Green 1997). One reason is that high-commitment religious voters are the least likely to abandon the major parties

(Gilbert et al. 1995). Even the Wallace candidacy depended heavily on southerners with low levels of religious commitment. John Anderson in 1980 and Ross Perot in 1992 and 1996 drew most of their meager southern votes from low-commitment groups, especially seculars. These historic patterns help explain the very poor showing of the 2000 Reform Party nominee, former Republican Patrick Buchanan. Buchanan received virtually no support from high-commitment evangelicals, a group he courted on the basis of abortion and other social issues. He did little better among low-commitment and secular voters, groups less concerned with social issue conservatism. Ralph Nader's Green Party also did poorly in the South, but in 2000 Nader votes might have hurt Gore in closely contested Florida. Third-party candidates had virtually no impact in the South in 2004.

THE SOUTHERN BAPTIST CONVENTION: THE HEART OF THE SOUTH

No consideration of religion as a force in southern electoral politics would be complete without a closer look at the role of the quintessential southern religious institution, the Southern Baptist Convention (SBC). Southern Baptists have for generations been the centerpiece of religion in the South (Reed 1972; Hill 1983; Harrell 1991). Not only is the SBC the nation's largest Protestant denomination, it is especially prominent in its home region.

In table 13.5, we examine the changing role of the SBC in southern politics from 1972 to 2004. The party identification of all southern white Protestants serves as the baseline for the table to which we compare the partisanship of all SBC members, high- and low-commitment members and younger (under forty years of age) high-commitment members. Next, we look at the attitudes of SBC clergy over the period, and finally, we compare SBC to other kinds of southern white Protestants.

Note that SBC members were still the most Democratic white Protestant group during the 1970s but had moved to become the most Republican group by 2004. And this change is greatest among high-commitment Southern Baptists, who were the most Democratic white Protestant cohort during the earlier period, but had moved most dramatically toward the GOP by 2004. In comparison, low-commitment SBC members were considerably less Democratic in the 1970s and considerably less Republican

Table 13.5.   Religion and Party Identification among White Protestants in the South: The Role of the Southern Baptist Convention (in percentages)

	1972–1980		1982–1990		1992–2000		2004		Change Over Time	
	Dem	Rep	Dem	Rep	Dem	Rep	Dem	Rep	Dem	Rep
All Southern white Protestants	**53**	**32**	**48**	**39**	**39**	**50**	**28**	**58**	**−25**	**+26**
Southern Baptist Convention (SBC)	56	27	51	38	43	46	24	65	−32	+38
High-commitment SBC	*63*	*28*	*48*	*44*	*41*	*49*	*23*	*67*	*−40*	*+39*
Low-commitment SBC	*47*	*27*	*54*	*33*	*48*	*39*	*28*	*55*	*−19*	*+28*
Young High-comm. SBC	*48*	*44*	*42*	*47*	*28*	*63*	*21*	*74*	*−27*	*+30*
SBC Pastors	45	27	24	66	16	77	15	81	−30	+54
Other Southern Evangelicals	50	28	51	37	39	52	28	61	−37	+41
Other Southern white Protestants	48	39	41	50	36	55	36	54	−21	+20
Non-SBC Baptists	54	32	48	29	35	48	35	43	−19	+11

Sources: Data from the period 1972–2000 is taken from the National Election Studies Cumulative File. Data for 2004 come from the National Survey of Religion and Politics, University of Akron. Young = under 40. Data for Southern Baptist pastors made available by James L. Guth.

in 2004. The table also shows that the realignment was most pronounced among younger, highly committed Southern Baptists: this cohort was almost evenly divided between the parties in the 1970s but had become three-quarters Republican in 2004.

What role did specifically "religious" mobilization play in this movement? The available data on political change among SBC pastors suggests that elite cue giving played a substantial part (see Guth et al. 1997 on the politics of the SBC clergy). SBC clergy identified as Democrats in the 1970s but moved dramatically in a GOP direction over the next three decades, well ahead of the laity. In 2004, the margin of party identification for the pastors favored the Republicans by five to one. As informal "mobilizers" and prominent cue givers in churches, it appears that the pastors had an important political impact throughout the South. Indeed, the SBC was especially active in the 2004, sponsoring, for example, the "I Vote Values" campaign (www.iVotevalue.com). The effect of such efforts is supported by another piece of evidence: The SBC laity most often in the pews—the highly committed—led the exodus from the Democrats to the Republicans over the period and was especially Republican in 2004.

The last three rows in table 13.5 compare the patterns of SBC members to other white southern Protestants. Other southern evangelicals outside to the SBC, including Pentecostals and nondenominational churches, showed a very similar pattern of change but fell a bit behind the SBC in Republican identification in 2004. Next, non-evangelical white Protestants have also moved in a Republican direction, so that in 2004, a majority identified as Republicans. However, this group went from being 12 percentage points *more* Republican than the SBC in the 1970s to 11 percentage points *less* in 2004. Finally, quite a different pattern occurs among non-SBC Baptists: While they also move toward the GOP over time, the pattern is less even, and by 2004 only about two-fifths were Republicans. In fact, between the 1990s and 2004, Republicans lost ground in this group. This pattern may reflect in part defections from the SBC due to internal theological disputes (Ammerman 1990). Taken as a whole, these data suggest that religion was a critical element in southern political change.

THE SOUL OF THE SOUTH

If nothing else, the preceding analysis confirms the importance of religion as one of the fundamental social bases in the electoral order in the South, and by implication, in the nation. As we have seen, the impact of southern religion on politics is characterized by strong continuities and dramatic changes. The bearers of traditional southern Protestantism, high-commitment evangelicals, are good examples of both: They have maintained their relative size and distinctive outlook in the face of major social changes, and in response, shifted their attachments from the Democrats to the Republicans.

The magnitude of this shift to the GOP is epitomized in that core institution of southern evangelicalism, the Southern Baptist Convention. With the strong encouragement of their pastors, Southern Baptists have moved into the Republican Party at greater rates than other white southern Protestants. This change increases the likelihood that the South has, for the foreseeable future, given its heart to the GOP, "God's Own Party" in the eyes of many white southerners. Other Protestant groups have declined in number but also shifted their political support, so that the "white Protestant alliance" is being recreated in the Republican Party.

The Democratic religious coalition has also been reformed. Like high-commitment evangelicals, black Protestants have displayed both continuity and change: fierce loyalty to the Democrats combined with increased numbers and participation. Catholics and seculars have also grown numerically, helping to bring the Democratic "coalition of minorities" to the South, although the Catholic element has been wooed by the GOP with some success in recent years.

In the second term of George W. Bush, the soul of the South is being reincorporated into the politics of the nation, with religious groups peculiar to the southern experience anchoring both major party coalitions. These changes in the social base of the electoral order have had important repercussions for intermediary political organizations and governmental institutions.

First, these shifts have given both the Republicans and Democrats strong incentives to build sophisticated organizations in a region once bereft of electoral competition. These shifts have also provided incentives for religious-based social movements, from the civil rights movement to the Christian Right, dedicated in large measure to getting religious communities to the polls.

Second, the result of those votes can be seen in traits of elected officials: an increase in Republican officeholders in Congress, state and local offices, and a parallel rise in the number of African Americans and non-Protestants. And for the greatest prize of all, the presidency, the current advantage lies with the Republicans, although the Democrats can be competitive in some areas if they choose their candidates and platforms with care. Indeed, the 2004 election results have prompted many Democrats to reconsider their party's approach to the South. Political changes of this magnitude, if they persist, are bound to produce significant alterations in national policy.

REFERENCES

Ammerman, Nancy T. 1990. *Baptist Battles*. New Brunswick, NJ: Rutgers University Press.

Black, Earl, and Merle Black. 1987. *Politics and Society in the South*. Cambridge, MA: Harvard University Press.

———. 1992. *The Vital South*. Cambridge, MA: Harvard University Press.

Baker, Tod A., Robert P. Steed, and Laurence W. Moreland, eds. 1983. *Religion and Politics in the South*. New York: Praeger.

Carmines, Edward G., and James A. Stimson. 1989. *Issue Evolution: Race and the Transformation of American Politics*. Princeton, NJ: Princeton University Press.

Gilbert, Christopher P., Timothy R. Johnson, and David A. M. Peterson. 1995. "The Religious Roots of Third Party Voting: A Comparison of Anderson, Perot, and Wallace Voters." *Journal for the Scientific Study of Religion* 34:470–84.

Green, John C., James L. Guth, Corwin E. Smidt, and Lyman A. Kellstedt. 1996. *Religion and the Culture Wars.* Lanham, MD: Rowman & Littlefield.

Green, John C. 1997. "The Third Party South," in *The 1996 Presidential Election in the South.* Laurence W. Moreland and Robert P. Steed, eds. New York: Praeger.

———. 2002. "Believers for Bush, Godly for Gore: Religion and the 2000 Election in the South," in *The 2000 Presidential Election in the South: Partisanship and Southern Party Systems in the 21st Century.* Robert P. Steed and Laurence W. Moreland, eds. Westport, CT: Praeger, 11–22.

Green, John C., Corwin E. Smidt, Lyman A. Kellstedt, and James L. Guth. 1997. "Bringing in the Sheaves," in *Sojourners in the Wilderness: The Christian Right in Comparative Perspective.* Corwin E. Smidt and James M. Penning, eds. Lanham, MD: Rowman & Littlefield.

Green, John C., Corwin E. Smidt, James L. Guth, and Lyman A. Kellstedt. 2004. "The American Religious Landscape and the 2004 Presidential Vote: Increased Polarization." www.uakron.edu/bliss/amerlandsccape.php.

Guth, James L., John C. Green, Corwin E. Smidt, Lyman A. Kellstedt, and Margaret Poloma. 1997. *The Bully Pulpit: The Politics of Protestant Clergy.* Lawrence, KS: University Press of Kansas.

Harrell, David Edwin. ed. 1991. *Varieties of Southern Evangelicalism.* Macon, GA: Mercer University Press.

Havard, William C. ed. 1972. *The Changing Politics of the South.* Baton Rouge: Louisiana State University Press.

Hill, Samuel S. 1966. *Southern Churches in Crisis.* New York: Holt, Rinehart, and Winston.

———. 1983. "Introduction," in *Religion and Politics in the South,* Tod A. Baker, Robert P. Steed, and Laurence W. Moreland, eds. New York: Praeger.

Kellstedt, Lyman A. 1990. "Evangelical Religion and Support for the Falwell Policy Positions: An Examination of Regional Variation," in *The Disappearing South.* Robert P. Steed, Laurence W. Moreland, and Tod A. Baker, eds. Tuscaloosa, AL: The University of Alabama Press.

Kellstedt, Lyman A., John C. Green, James L. Guth, and Corwin E. Smidt. 1996a. "Grasping the Essentials: The Social Embodiment of Religion and Political Behavior," in *Religion and the Culture Wars.* John C. Green, James L. Guth, Corwin E. Smidt, and Lyman A. Kellstedt. Lanham, MD: Rowman & Littlefield.

———. 1996b. "The Puzzle of Evangelical Protestantism," in *Religion and the Culture Wars.* John C. Green, James L. Guth, Corwin E. Smidt, and Lyman A. Kellstedt. Lanham, MD: Rowman & Littlefield.

Key, V. O. Jr. 1949. *Southern Politics in State and Nation.* New York: Knopf.

Lamis, Alexander P. 1984. *The Two-Party South.* New York: Oxford University Press.

Lincoln, Eric C., and Lawrence H. Mamiya. 1990. *The Black Church in the African-American Experience.* Durham, NC: Duke University Press.

Petrocik, John R. 1987. "Realignment: New Party Coalitions and the Nationalization of the South." *Journal of Politics* 49:347–75.

Reed, John Shelton. 1972. *The Enduring South.* Lexington, MA: D. C. Heath.

Rozell, Mark J., and Clyde Wilcox. 1996. *Second Coming: The New Christian Right in Virginia Politics*. Baltimore: Johns Hopkins University Press.

Sernett, Milton G. 1991. "Black Religion and the Question of Evangelical Identity," in *The Variety of American Evangelicalism*. Donald W. Dayton and Robert K. Johnston, eds. Knoxville, TN: University of Tennessee Press.

Shafer, Byron E. 1991. "The Notion of an Electoral Order: The Structure of Electoral Politics at the Accession of George Bush," in *The End of Realignment?* Byron E. Shafer, ed. Madison, WI: University of Wisconsin Press.

Smidt, Corwin E. 1983. "'Born Again' Politics: The Political Attitudes and Behavior of Evangelical Christians in the South and Non-South," in *Religion and Politics in the South*, Tod A. Baker, Robert P. Steed, and Laurence W. Moreland, eds. New York: Praeger.

———. 1989. "Change and Stability in the Partisanship of Southern Evangelicals: An Analysis of the 1980 and 1984 Presidential Elections," in *Religion in American Politics*. Charles Dunn, ed. Washington, DC: CQ Press.

Stark, Rodney, and William Bainbridge. 1985. *The Future of Religion*. Berkeley, CA: University of California Press.

Weaver, Richard. 1968. *The Southern Tradition at Bay*. New Rochelle, NY: Arlington House.

NOTES

1. The following analysis is based on the National Elections Studies Cumulative File (1960 to 1988) and the National Surveys of Religion and Politics conducted at the University of Akron in 1992, 1996, 2000, and 2004 (see Kellstedt et al. 1996a and Green et al. 2004 for more details). The sample size varies by decade for the NES data (1,890 in the 1960s; 3,648 in the 1970s; 2,994 in the 1980s); the Akron data sets had sample sizes of 4,001, 4,037, 5,004 and 4,000, respectively. The NES data were made available by the Inter-University Consortium for Political and Social Research; the National Surveys of Religion and Politics were supported by grants from the Pew Charitable Trusts. The authors are solely responsible for the interpretations presented here. Denominational affiliation was coded into religious traditions according to Kellstedt et al. (1996a). Religious commitment was measured by church attendance (high commitment was coded as attending more often than "a few times a year"; low-commitment as attending "a few times a year" or less. Contact the authors for additional details in the coding of religious variables in these data sets. Here, the South is defined as Alabama, Arkansas, Florida, Georgia, Kentucky, Louisiana, Mississippi, North Carolina, Oklahoma, South Carolina, Tennessee, Texas, and Virginia.

2. Traditional distinctions between the Deep and Rim South appear in these data. High-commitment evangelicals and black Protestants appear to be more important to their respective party coalitions in the Deep South, while these groups are less important in the Rim South.

Index

abortion, 21, 233–34
Acuff, Roy, 193
Adams, Ted, 41
African Americans. *See* race
age, 174, 263, 264–65, 266, 269
Aistrup, Joseph, 243
Alabama: civil rights and, 81, 86; competitiveness of elections in, 75–76, 78–84, 88–91; education in, 81, 83–84, 85, 86; election of 1994 in, 82–83; election of 2000 in, 84; election of 2002 in, 10, 85–86; election of 2004 in, 9, 76, 86–87; electorate in, 15, 75–78, 87–88; gambling in, 83–84; governorships in, 10, 25n2, 79, 80–84, 85–86; in House of Representatives, 9, 78, 86; ideology and, 81, 83–84; partisanship in, 15, 78–84, 87–91; party organization in, 87, 89–90; presidency and, 76, 78–80, 84, 86, 89; primary elections in, 93n2; race in, 15, 16, 75, 87–88; in Senate, 15, 86–87; state legislature in, 77, 87; statewide offices in, 84, 86, 87; taxes in, 85–86; Ten Commandments in, 84; voter registration in, 76; voter turnout in, 75–78; Voting Rights Act of 1965 and, 76
Albert, Carl, 252
Alexander, Avery, 131
Alexander, Lamar, 196, 198–99, 202, 205, 207

Allain, Bill, 104
Allen, George, 21, 151, 152–53, 155
Allen, Jim, 25n2
American Conservative Union, 176
Americans for Democratic Action, 235n4
Anderson, Bill, 202
Anderson, Gary, 107
Anderson, John, 315
Anthony, Bob, 253
Arkansas: abortion in, 233–34; competitiveness of elections in, 231–34; election of 1992 in, 3; election of 1996 in, 3; election of 1998 in, 19; election of 2000 in, 4, 221–22; election of 2002 in, 5, 214–16, 222–24, 226–34; election of 2004 in, 4, 6, 217–34; election of 2006 in, 222–26, 234; electorate in, 15, 230–31; gay marriage in, 217–22, 233–34; governorships in, 9, 214–16, 222–26, 233, 234; in House of Representatives, 19, 225, 226–28; ideology and, 217, 224–26, 233–34; partisanship in, 15, 213–14, 230–34; presidency and, 3, 4, 218–24, 231, 233; race and, 15; regional differences in, 217–22, 224–25, 232–33; in Senate, 5, 6, 15, 214–16, 217–24, 231–32, 233; state legislature in, 226–27, 228–30; statewide offices in, 214–26; term limits in, 228–29
Armey, Dick, 22, 23
Arnall, Ellis, 52

321

About the Authors

David Breaux is professor and head of the Department of Political Science and Public Administration at Mississippi State University.

Charles S. Bullock III is Richard B. Russell Professor of Political Science at the University of Georgia.

Gary W. Copeland is professor of political science at the University of Oklahoma.

Patrick R. Cotter is professor of political science at the University of Alabama.

Rebecca Cruise is a Ph.D. student in political science at the University of Oklahoma.

Andrew J. Dowdle is assistant professor of political science at the University of Arkansas.

Ronald Keith Gaddie is professor of political science at the University of Oklahoma.

John C. Green is Distinguished Professor of Political Science and Director of the Bliss Institute at the University of Akron.

Hilary B. Gresham received a master of public policy and administration degree from Mississippi State University (MSU) where she served as a graduate research assistant.

James L. Guth is William R. Kenan, Jr. Professor of Political Science at Furman University.

Lyman Kellstedt is professor of political science (emeritus) at Wheaton College.

James W. Lamare is professor of political science at Florida Atlantic University, Jupiter Campus.

Laurence W. Moreland is a professor of political science at The Citadel.

Michael Nelson is professor of political science at Rhodes College.

Wayne Parent is associate dean of the College of Arts and Sciences and professor of political science at Louisiana State University.

Huey L. Perry is professor of political science and Chancellor's Fellow at Southern University in Baton Rouge, Louisiana.

J. L. Polinard is a professor in the department of political science at University of Texas, Pan American.

Charles Prysby is a professor of political science at the University of North Carolina at Greensboro.

Mark J. Rozell is professor of public policy at George Mason University.

Richard K. Scher is Robin and Jean Gibson Professor of Political Science at the University of Florida.

Michael J. Scicchitano is associate professor of political science at the University of Florida.

Stephen Shaffer is professor of political science at Mississippi State University.

Corwin Smidt is Professor of Political Science at Calvin College.

Robert P. Steed is a professor of political science at The Citadel.

Gary D. Wekkin is professor of political science at the University of Central Arkansas.

James Wenzel is professor of political science at University of Texas, Pan American.

Robert D. Wrinkle is professor of political science, University of Texas, Pan American.